BRITISH COUNTERMARKS ON COPPER AND BRONZE COINS

BRITISH COUNTERMARKS
ON COPPER AND
BRONZE COINS

J. Gavin Scott

SPINK & SON LTD.
LONDON
1975

Designed and Printed by
Robert Stockwell Ltd., London SE1

CONTENTS

For Ann, Andrew, and Martin

INTRODUCTION

My aim here is to throw some light on the hitherto neglected series of copper and bronze coins and tokens countermarked, engraved, or otherwise marked in Britain with the names of traders. Most of these date from the period 1790–1890. It is still possible to obtain such pieces reasonably cheaply, and they form a fascinating field for collecting and study. The fundamental question one always has to ask is why was the coin countermarked, and therein lies the interest; sometimes the purpose is explicit and genuine, while others may be simple cases of vandalism. It is in the vast area between, where the question has to be answered by 'don't know', that I have attempted to draw some conclusions, and where the greatest scope for future research lies.

In this study, I have worked on the basis of the following definitions:

TOKEN: a piece intended to be used as a substitute for coin, either expressing a value, or having a similar countermark to a piece expressing a value. Alternatively, to qualify as a token, the countermark should date from the 18th or 19th century token periods, or from another period of known local shortage where it can be shown that a trader, institution or local authority was responsible for its issue.

SHOP TICKET: a piece not expressing a value, but showing the name and/or town and/or trade of the issuer or, if a name only is shown, giving an indication that a trader is involved – e.g. '& Co.', '& Sons', '&', 'Ltd.', etc. The addition of a date to a surname, with or without a town, and without a trade, is a warning that the piece may be a 'Love Token' (see below) particularly if engraved. Those pieces described in other works as countermarked or engraved on worn halfpennies or on halfpenny-sized copper blanks etc. are included here, but the eligibility of some is open to doubt, as the specimens I have seen often show no trace of the original design.

I am including in this category certain pieces which could be more accurately described as truck tickets or tokens. This is because, with certain pieces, it is not yet possible to say precisely why the counter-marking was done. Let me quote an example from the extensive series of cutlers' countermarks: PAYNE/CUTLER/AYLESBURY (see 3.1 in Table 1 below); if a shop ticket proper, this would have been issued by Payne to a customer, either in change to serve as an advertisement or trader's card – albeit of a rather amateurish nature, or, more likely, as a discount offer against the next transaction. Alternatively, it need not have been given to a customer at all, but to one of Payne's workmen or journeymen who could exchange it at a pub or provision shop where Payne either had some interest, had an account for his workers, or had negotiated a discount on their behalf. A further theory, advanced by Michael Dolley (Bulletin of the Token Corresponding Society, Vol. I, No. 9, 1973) is that these cutlers' countermarks were used as receipts for knives and other implements deposited for resharpening, and were accepted as authority to collect the finished work.

Each theory may be right in individual instances. However, there is unlikely to be one universal solution. The only evidence to hand is the number of pieces of each type in existence, and the probable availability to the trader of the necessary punches. The difficulty in reaching a decision on this subject without more specific local research will be appreciated – hence the inclusion of all such pieces under the general heading of shop tickets.

ADVERTISEMENT TICKET: a similar piece but of more definite use in advertising a particular trader or product and often bearing a slogan. These are usually later in date and of better workmanship than shop tickets.

PAY AND TOOL CHECKS: similar to shop tickets but usually later in date and pierced for storage on spikes etc. before or after issue by pay or stores clerks and/or with a number to identify the individual concerned. Checks merely bearing the name or number of the individual employee are excluded.

UNOFFICIAL ISSUES: produced by workers with access to brand marking tools; these are particularly common in the metal trades throughout the nineteenth century. Some are of good workmanship and it is difficult to distinguish these from pay and tool checks. Most fall into the category that the Australians call 'sports' – the antics of punch-happy workmen. Many seem to originate from Sheffield iron and steel firms. Thus, although all these pieces bear either the name or the brand mark of a firm, they are strictly 'one off' jobs and are included only to show the sort of pieces that exist, and to avoid confusion with shop or advertisement tickets. The species is a common one; each piece is, necessarily, unique.

STORES CHECK: a check used to control stores in military depots, bearing the broad arrow government mark, initial letter of the depot, and, usually, a date.

BIBLIOGRAPHY

It will be seen that the following categories are excluded from this study:

BRITISH COINS AND TOKENS COUNTERMARKED FOR USE IN THE COLONIES

This series is covered by:

ANDREWS, Arthur	'Australasian Tokens and Coins' (Sydney 1921).
CHITTY, Alfred	'Australian surcharged and cast tokens' (Spink's Numismatic Circular, August 1907, cols. 10020–1).
DEACON, J. Hunt	South Australian Numismatic Journal, 1956, p. 3, 16, 20, 31.
DUFFIELD, F. G.	'A trial list of the Countermarked Modern Coins of the World' (Numismatist reprint, 1962).
PARSONS, H. Alexander	'The Colonial Coinages of British Africa' (Spink & Son, London, 1950).
PRIDMORE, F.	'The Coins of the British Commonwealth of Nations to the end of the reign of George VI' (Spink & Son, London).
	Part 1. European Territories (1960).
	Part 2. Asian Territories (excluding India) (1965).
	Part 3. West Indies (1966).
	Part 4. India (in preparation).
	'A curious countermark' (Spink's Numismatic Circular, November 1959, p. 203).
	'The TC countermark' (Spink's Numismatic Circular, June 1960, p. 131–2).
	'Notes on Colonial Coins – countermarked pieces' (Spink's Numismatic Circular, March 1960, p. 54–55).
	'The officially mutilated coinage of British West Africa' (Spink's Numismatic Circular, February 1954, cols 59–64).
	'Notes on Colonial Coins – Trinidad' (Spink's Numismatic Circular, June 1961, p. 141–2, July/August, p. 168–9).
WOOD, Howland	'The Coinage of the West Indies' (American Journal of Numismatics, 1915).

BRITISH COINS AND TOKENS COUNTERMARKED FOR USE IN FOREIGN COUNTRIES
I have in hand a short paper on the French series.

POLITICAL COUNTERMARKS
The Spence pieces are fully described by R. H. Thompson in British Numismatic Journal 1969, p. 154–6 and 1971, p. 138, while these and other similar issues are listed by D. T. Batty in his massive 'Catalogue of the Copper Coinage' (Manchester 1868–95).

IDENTITY DISCS
Not uncommon on British and foreign coins during the First World War.

LOVE TOKENS
These are more appropriately named 'hatch, match or dispatch tokens' – see Mrs. Ella Pierrepoint Barnard in British Numismatic Journal 1918, p. 151–198.

As for the British countermarks, both on copper and on silver, other literature exists as follows:

BATTY, D. T.	Op. cit.
BLISS, Thomas	Sale Catalogue, May 15–19 1916 (Sotheby).
BRUNEL, Christopher	'Framed Coins' (Coins and Medals, March 1974, p. 38–40).
BURZIO, Humberto F.	Diccionario de la Moneda Hispano-americana (Santiago de Chile 1958).
COKAYNE, Francis	Sale Catalogue, July 17 1946 (Glendining).
DAVIS, W. J.	'The Nineteenth Century Token Coinage of Great Britain, Ireland, The Channel Islands and the Isle of Man, to which are added Tokens of Over One Penny Value of Any Period' (London 1904, Second edition B. A. Seaby Ltd., 1969).
DOLLEY, Michael	'Concerning the function of certain incuse countermarks' in Bulletin of the Token Corresponding Society, Vol. 1, No. 9 (1973).
	'A parcel of countermarked early nineteenth-century farthings Irish', (Numismatic Society of Ireland, Occasional Papers, 15–16, 1973).
DUFFIELD, F. G.	Op. cit.
GIBBS, Howard D.	Sale Catalogue, November 19 1960 (Hans Schulman, New York).
HOWARTH, Daniel F.	'Countermarked Coins' (Spink's Numismatic Circular 1897, cols. 2175, 2176, 2376, 2377).
LINGFORD, Herbert M.	Sale Catalogue, October 24–26 1950 (Glendining).
MANVILLE, Harrington E.	'Problems of British Merchants' and Bankers' Countermarked Silver Coins' –
	Part 1. 'Dr. Meili, I presume?' (Spink's Numismatic Circular, November 1967, p. 292).
	Part 2. 'British Countermarks according to W. J. Davis: True or False, (Spink's Numismatic Circular, April 1972, p. 134–6, May 1972, p. 182–6, June 1972, p. 231–2).
	'Silver Tradesmen's Countermarks in Museum Collections' (Spink's Numismatic Circular, December 1973, p. 462 et seq.).
MEILI, Julius	'Das Brasilianische Geldwesen 1645–1822', Part 1 (Zurich 1897), p. 232–43.
	'Englische Stempel auf Spanischen Thalern und auf anderen Aehnlichen Muenzen' (Spink's Numismatic Circular, September 1897, col. 2372–6).
	Sale Catalogue, May 23–26 1910 (Jacques Schulman, Amsterdam).
MURDOCH, John G.	Sale Catalogue, December 12–13 1904 (Sotheby).
NAPIER, D. S.	Sale Catalogue, May 30 1956 (Glendining).
PAGET, H.	Sale Catalogue, June 28 1944 (Glendining).
PRIDMORE, F.	'The Countermark of a crowned V' (Spink's Numismatic Circular, August–September 1954, p. 340–1).
	'A Cornish Advertisement Coin' (Spink's Numismatic Circular, January 1961, p. 6–7). (This countermark, by J. Burton of Falmouth, is known only on brass and copper Japanese coins, and is excluded from the present work as it was not intended for circulation in this country.)
PURVEY, P. Frank	'Coins and Tokens of Scotland', p. 105–14 (B. A. Seaby Ltd., 1972).

QUICK, Richard 'Catalogue (with Illustrations) of the Bowles Collection of Token Coins, Medals, etc.' (Bristol, 1909).

SCOTT, J. Gavin 'French and other European bronze coins countermarked in England for use as advertisement tickets in the late nineteenth century' (Seaby's Coin and Medal Bulletin, December 1970, p. 443–53, March 1973, p. 82–7, and April 1973, p. 124).

'Countermarks on Copper Coins by Cutlers and other tradesmen' in Bulletin of the Token Corresponding Society, Vol. 1, No. 9 (1973).

SEABY, W. A. 'Castlecomer Tokens: An Inquiry' (British Numismatic Journal 1965, p. 139–48).

'Catalogue of Ulster Tokens, Tickets, Vouchers, Checks, Passes etc.' (Ulster Journal of Archaeology 1971, p. 96–106).

SZAUER, Emil Catalogue of Irish Countermarks (Irish Numismatics, 1970, nos. 15–18).

THELLUSSON, A. Sale Catalogue, October 19–20 1931 (Sotheby).

WATERS, Arthur W. 'A list of English Countermarks struck for advertising purposes upon the copper coins circulating in Great Britain' (Spink's Numismatic Circular, May 1898, cols. 2728–9, reprinted October 1955, cols. 423–4, with additional note by author).

WHETMORE, S. A. H. 'Notes on Some Issuers of Countermarked Spanish Dollars' (British Numismatic Journal 1957, p. 620–48).

Sale Catalogue, July 14 1961 (Glendining).

YEATES, F. Willson 'Nineteenth Century Countermarked Tokens – Stirlingshire – Balfron' (Spink's Numismatic Circular, April 1912, col. 13519).

BRITISH COUNTERMARKS
ON COPPER AND BRONZE COINS

HISTORICAL BACKGROUND AND LEGISLATION

Countermarking or engraving of current copper coins by traders and others seems to have started in the early eighteenth century and at first was essentially local and small-scale, and either for advertisement purposes or to remedy local shortages of small change; such shortages seem to have been particularly acute in the earlier part of this period in Ireland – see Szauer op. cit. The practice of engraving or countermarking coins for personal purposes ('hatch, match or dispatch tokens') also developed during this early period, mainly 1700–1850.

There was no legislation against this because governments were chiefly concerned with the gold and silver coinage, and because the practice presented no serious or large-scale problem until the middle of the nineteenth century. For example, the Coinage Offences Act of 1832 (2 Will. IV. c. 34 – passed 23 May) was a consolidation of the coin laws embodying upwards of 40 statutes passed since the reign of Edward 1. Like previous acts it was concerned with the counterfeiting of gold, silver and copper, the possession of moulds or coining tools, and the impairing of gold and silver. It was not concerned with the defacing of current copper coin, which was thus not illegal.

During this early period, particularly 1790–1820, tokens, countermarked on coins, are found in the emerging industrial regions, e.g. the cotton spinning areas of Central Scotland.

Many of the early countermarked shop tickets were issued by cutlers and razor makers, and these seem most common in the period 1820–50. Examples will be found listed in Table 1 below, from Aylesbury, Bath, Bedford, Bicester, Chatham, Chichester, Colchester, Dorchester, Dublin, Gloucester, Hereford, Ipswich, London, Moseley, Oxford, Southampton, Swansea, Tewkesbury and Windsor. Other trades represented from mid-eighteenth century up to the 1840's include apothecaries, attornies, bakers, blacksmiths, button manufacturers, carpenters, cheesemongers, chimney sweeps, clay pipe manufacturers, corn merchants, dentists, fishing tackle makers, furniture brokers, glaziers, grocers, gun makers, hairdressers, hatters, hotel owners, ironmongers, jewellers, maltsters, merchants, mill-bill makers, milliners, needle manufacturers, patent medicine manufacturers, patten makers, pinmakers, portrait painters, rat killers, saddle tree makers, staymakers, tea dealers, tinkers, tobacconists, umbrella manufacturers, venetian blind makers, warehousemen, watchmakers, wherrymen, and wine-merchants. Michael Dolley's theory on the reason for the existence of the cutlers' pieces has already been mentioned in the introduction. Pridmore has described such pieces as 'craftsman's marked' coins, 'produced by the use of the small metal punches carried by most master craftsmen prior to the present machine producing age, e.g. Cutlers, Metal Workers, Carpenters, Cabinet makers, Gunsmiths, Masons etc.' (Spink's Numismatic Circular, June 1956, col. 269). His implication is that these pieces were 'unofficial' issues – see introduction, above. However, although many of the traders I have listed above would have had punches for branding their goods, this would not be true of all, and we must look for other reasons for the existence of these pieces. As suggested in the introduction, many may, in fact, be shop or truck tickets.

In any case, it is important to distinguish here between these early issues and those after about 1850. The early countermarks were not illegal and may well have been produced to meet a local shortage of coin, as well as for advertising or truck purposes. In many cases, several examples of these are known to exist. On the other hand, the later 'punch happy' pieces countermarked by workers in the metal trades were illegal, and were not produced for advertising or to meet a local shortage. It is rare to find more than one example of this type of issue.

The situation gradually changed in the 1830's and 1840's: with the growth in industry, trade and commerce, and in population, mobility and literacy, newspapers and advertising became more wide-spread, although both remained relatively expensive until mid-century; a useful and entertaining account of the development of advertising in this period is E. S. Turner's 'The Shocking History of Advertising' (1952, Penguin edition 1965). The Newspaper Stamp Duty was reduced to one penny per sheet in 1836 (6 & 7 Will. IV c. 76) and abolished in 1855 (18 & 19 Vict. c. 27); the tax of 3s. 6d. per advertisement in newspapers was reduced to 1s. 6d. in 1833 and ended in 1853; and the excise duty on paper was discontinued from 1 October 1861. Advertising posters began to be plastered over every available wall and hoarding in the towns, and on rocks and mountains in the country. The government was gradually made aware that the countermarking of current copper coin was ceasing to be small-scale and local, and was becoming a considerable nuisance. In April 1849, James Anderson, Lord Provost of Glasgow, appealed to the Treasury for a copper recoinage because of the variety of coins in circulation, the number of counterfeits, and because of 'the genuine Copper Coinage being much defaced'. 'The Times' of Wednesday 25 September 1850 included the following letter:

THE COMPLAINT OF A PENNY
TO THE EDITOR OF THE TIMES

Sir,

Bill-sticking and advertising were formerly confined to boards and dead walls. Driven off even these places, as a common nuisance, by the gentle hint, 'Bill-stickers beware', the practice has since intruded itself into higher regions and a company has been established for plastering over and defacing every decent vehicle upon the road or railway. If this can't be cured it must be endured. But, Sir, is it to be endured that the current coin of the realm is to be defaced, without paying for it, by a practice long since driven off dead walls? I am a Penny – 'Dei gratiâ,' &c. was my motto, stamped upon me at my birth, and after the squeeze I got over the lesson I thought my loyalty must be indelible. But, alas! I was mistaken, for it has been obliterated altogether, and round the Royal head I now bear the contemptible advertisement of 'Lloyd's Weekly Newspaper, 3d. post free'. [See 22.28H, 1 in Table 1 below.] Such, Sir, is my present motto, and upon both sides. Permit me to ask, is this sort of mutilation to be extended to my richer relatives – halfcrowns and sovereigns? or am I and my copper tribe of such trumpery consideration that we may be mutilated without redress?

In obedience to your regulations I inclose myself as a guarantee for what I state, and look to you for the publication of my complaint. It is quite against my will, I assure you, that I am thus made to intrude upon your columns. I wish people would confine their vulgar advertisements to you, and pay for them like honest folk, if they are worth it. I come of a good family, and always was what I professed to be till now. But if our genuine badge is to be destroyed, who will be bound to receive us in change? Certain I am that in my present state of degredation I am not honestly worth

ONE PENNY

Parliament Street
Sept. 24

Later in the same year, on 11 December, another complaint appeared:

Sir,

Some months ago a letter appeared in 'The Times' in which a correspondent complained of the penny pieces of the copper coinage being made the medium of advertisement of the works of a publisher. In the instance then brought before the public notice I believe the advertiser contented himself with defacing one side of the coin. Within the last few days, however, several penny pieces of the coinage of 1809 (sic) have passed through my hands with the following words deeply cut on that side bearing the figure of Britannia – 'Lloyd's Weekly Newspaper, 3d., post free'; and on the obverse side, 'Purchase number 1. of Lloyd's last penny publication', [see 22.28J in Table 1 below] as you will see by the enclosed specimen. Surely, the offender should be traced and punished, for, if the practice be allowed with impunity, the abuse will be extended to half-crowns and crown pieces; and besides the insult to the public, the public will have advertisements of patent life pills, ointments &c., thrust upon their eye a dozen times in the course of the day.

Hoping that this may awaken the attention of the proper authorities, I have the honour to be, Sir, your most obedient servant.

T.M.

London

Dec. 10

Edward Lloyd, proprietor and publisher of Lloyd's Weekly Newspaper, does appear to have been the first to countermark his advertisements on copper coins in such quantity as to cause widespread annoyance. For his countermarks, see numbers 22.28A–J in Table 1 below, while a detailed note on Lloyd appears in the section on issuers following Table 1.

Later, in June 1853, the government's attention was more directly drawn to the problem when an anonymous correspondent sent a defaced halfpenny to the Lords of the Treasury. James Wilson, Financial Secretary to the Treasury and MP for Westbury passed this on to the Master of the Mint, Sir John Herschell, as follows:

I am directed by the Lords Commissioners of Her Majesty's Treasury to transmit to you the accompanying halfpenny on which the words 'PURCHASE NUMBER ONE OF LLOYDS LAST PUBLICATION' [see 22.28C, G, J below] and other words are stamped and I am to state that the attention of my Lords has been directed to the mutilation of the Coin of the Country for advertizing purposes which is exhibited on the same being one of a vast number stated to be in circulation.

Their Lordships desire that you will take the necessary steps . . . for effectually putting a stop to the practice. . . .

Herschell quickly confirmed from H. R. Reynolds, the Attorney and Solicitor-General that the 1832 Act was 'altogether silent' on this point, and Reynolds' view, in a letter of 12 July, was that no steps could be taken 'otherwise than by legislation to prevent the practice complained of'. Swift action followed: Wilson introduced a Bill, which was given its first reading on 2 August, its second reading the next day, committee stage and third reading on 5 August, and received the Royal Assent on 20 August. The Act to prevent the defacing of the current coin of the Realm (16 & 17 Vict. c.102) is quoted below:

Whereas a Practice has arisen of defacing the Coin of the Realm by stamping the same for advertising Purposes, and bending the same, and it is expedient to make Provision for preventing the Coin from being so defaced and bent: Be it therefore enacted by the Queen's most Excellent Majesty, by and with the Advice and Consent of the Lords Spiritual and Temporal, and Commons, in this present Parliament assembled, and by the Authority of the same, as follows:

I   If any Person shall deface any of the Queen's current Gold, Silver, or Copper Coin by stamping thereon any Names or Words, whether such Coin shall or shall not be thereby diminished or lightened, or shall use any Machine or Instrument for the Purpose of bending the same, every such Offender shall in England and Ireland be guilty of a Misdemeanour, and in Scotland of a Crime or Offence, and being convicted thereof shall be liable to Fine or Imprisonment, or Fine and Imprisonment, at the Discretion of the Court.

II   No Tender of Payment in Money made in any Gold, Silver or Copper Coin so defaced or stamped as aforesaid shall be allowed to be a legal Tender; and if any Person shall tender, utter, or put off any Coin so defaced, stamped, or bent as aforesaid, he shall, on summary conviction thereof before Two Justices, be liable to forfeit and pay any sum not exceeding Forty Shillings: provided always, that it shall not be lawful for any Person to proceed for any such Penalty as last aforesaid without the Consent (in England or Ireland) of Her Majesty's Attorney General for England or Ireland respectively, or (in Scotland) of the Lord Advocate.

The Act itself produced some queries: a shopkeeper from Chard, in Somerset, wrote to the Lords of the Treasury on 29 August 1853 as follows:

The Act recently passed making the defacing and bending of the Current Coin of the Realm and the passing or uttering thereof punishable offences is of so much importance to the General Shopkeepers and the trading community that they should be placed in possession of some information as to what they are to do with the monies they have now in their possession, an utterance of which the Act I have referred to would make illegal.

May I therefore humbly beg your Lordships to favor me with a reply to this communication stating

What course must be adopted by holders of defaced and bent coins to obtain their value in undefaced and unbent coins

And also if the Act is meant to affect monies bearing any other marks thereon than *words* and *letters*.

This was passed to Herschell, who, in turn, sought Reynolds' views. These, expressed on 19 October, were that '. . . any name or words on any copper coin, although not for advertizing purposes, is within the . . . terms of the 1st Section . . . consequently coin so stamped is within the provisions of the 2nd Section and therefore not current.' Also, because the Act was a penal one, it had to be construed strictly, so 'coin defaced *otherwise* than by stamping *names or words* would not be within the provisions.' Finally 'the Act makes no provision for the reimbursing of persons who happened to be holders of defaced coin at the time of the passing. We are of the opinion that such persons have no claim, in *point of law,* against anyone.'

Here it would not be inopportune to mention various references in recent works to the voting of money to replace the coin defaced by Lloyd. Examples of these are 'The Mad Old Ads' by Dick Sutphen (London, 1968) p. 12, E. S. Turner, op. cit., p. 76 (Penguin edition), Forbes Leslie in 'Coins and Medals', December 1968, p. 955 and Philip J. Leighton in 'Coin Monthly', August 1971, p. 17–18. All of these seem to have derived their information directly or indirectly from Henry Sampson's 'History of Advertising' (London, 1874), p. 31–32. I quote below the relevant extract:

'Among other forms of advertising, that on the copper coinage must not be forgotten. The extensive defacement of the pence and halfpence of the realm in the interests of a well-known weekly paper ultimately led to the interference of Parliament, and may fairly be regarded as the cause, or at all events as one of the principal causes, of the sum of £10,000 being voted in July 1855 for the replacement of the old, worn, battered and mixed coppers by our present bronze coinage.'

In fact the only vote in July 1855 concerning coinage was in Supply Committee of 31 July of £52,500 to defray the expenditure of the Mint and for medal services – the latter accounting for £36,000. What Sampson was referring to was the vote of £10,000 in August 1859 (reduced from £50,000 because it was not found to be necessary to supply presses to the contractors) in connection with the preliminary expenses of the changeover from copper coinage to bronze. The Chancellor of the Exchequer, W. E. Gladstone, in making a statement, referred to the fact that, following an examination in London, Birmingham and other large towns, a great deal of the copper coinage was found to be in a very bad condition. He mentioned the age of the coinage – more than one fifth was 'of dates between 1797 and 1805 (sic)', the variation in weight between the heavy but worn out older coins and the minority of lighter more recent Victorian issues, and the number of counterfeit and foreign coins in circulation. Another part was 'injured, battered and inscribed, according to the fancy of individuals' such as he had stated – he had mentioned that he had 'a specimen of one of Her Majesty's pennies, and there appeared round the edges: 'Lloyd's Weekly Newspaper, post free' (see 22.28C, G, J below), and on the other side some equally interesting announcement.' One third of the copper coinage needed renewal – for all these reasons – and because of cheapness of production, the profits to be made by the Mint, the improved durability and hardness of the coinage, and the ease of handling leading to increased demand, it was proposed to replace the entire copper coinage with bronze, as had been done so successfully in France. It would not be fair to regard the coin defaced by Lloyd as being more than merely one of a number of factors contributing to the timing and extent of this recoinage, and it is to be hoped that these remarks now put the matter in proper perspective; there was certainly no vote of public money specifically to replace Lloyd's countermarked coins – that there would not be had already been prophesied by the Attorney and Solicitor-General's view of 19 October 1853 – see above.

LOOPHOLES

In the short term, at least, the 1853 Act seems to have been successful. To take account of the new bronze coinage, acts relating to copper coins were made applicable to those of mixed metal by the Coinage Act of 1859 (22 & 23 Vict. c.30). The provisions of the 1853 Act stayed on the statute book, being incorporated in the Coinage Offences Act of 1861, which, in turn, was largely included in the Coinage Offences Act of 1936.

1 Foreign Bronze Coins

However it was not long before loopholes were found. One was that it was not illegal to deface foreign bronze coins. From the late 1860's these began to circulate freely as pennies and halfpennies, especially in London and the South of England, and traders were not slow to realise the advertising possibilities. At the rate of exchange then operating, it was possible to import penny-size 10 centime pieces at 252 to the £, thus yielding a profit of a shilling per £, and satisfying the public demand for small change. This was encouraged in that importing these pieces was not illegal.

These bronze pieces were mainly French, but coins also came from Italy, Luxembourg and Spain. They were never, of course, legal tender as coins in this country, but were very commonly accepted. Several firms countermarked them as advertisement tickets. The 'Pears' Soap' countermark on French coins is the commonest, but probably not the earliest of these. (See 22.218 in Table 2 below.) By the late '70's and early '80's, up to 10 per cent of the copper coin circulating in London was said to be foreign. A question in the Commons on 31 May 1886 went further: the Member for Tower Hamlets, Whitechapel, asked the Chancellor of the Exchequer if he was aware that foreign copper made up a fifth of the copper coins circulating in the East End of London.

At first the government was sceptical that there was any problem – see Commons questions, 20 November 1884, 22 May 1885 – but by 1886 had changed its tune. On June 11, in the debate on the Customs Bill, Sir William Harcourt, asked by an Edinburgh member why legislation to prohibit the import of foreign bronze was necessary, stated that these coins were imported in very large quantities indeed, and great injury was done to the working classes in having coin passed to them which anyone could legally refuse. The result was the Customs Amendment Act, passed 25 June 1886, of which Section 2 provided for a proclamation prohibiting the importation of foreign coin.

After a fall of government, the proclamation, prohibiting the import into the United Kingdom of all foreign coins other than gold or silver, duly came on 25 March 1887. The immediate outcome was an immense outcry from press and public: the proclamation was assumed by the people to prohibit the circulation of foreign bronze coins, not merely their import, although, as stated above, they never had been legal tender in England. The 'Times' conducted a lively correspondence on the subject, with frequent outspoken editorial comment. The government succumbed to the pressure, and announced on 14 April that these coins would be received for exchange in cash or stamps at any Post Office, at the rate of 13 to the shilling, minimum quantity a shilling's worth, from the following Monday, 18 April, for six weeks until 31 May. This was to alleviate hardship to the poor inadvertently caused by the proclamation. The minimum amount was reduced to six-pennyworth on 15 April by Treasury Minute – the 'Times' had pressed for this in its issue of the same day. A Post Office Circular of 16 April was worded accordingly, and instructions given to Postmasters not to reissue the coins but to send them to local Head Post Offices, or to the Metropolitan Office. The public were informed by the press, and by notices in local Post Offices.

On 13 June the Chancellor announced that withdrawal of these coins from circulation was practically complete, and that there had been no special demand for British bronze in consequence, either in the Metropolitan district or the provinces. He issued a further warning: a notice by the Commissioners of Customs dated 27 June warned the public that foreign bronze coins were not legal tender, and their import was prohibited. 23,000 copies were sent for exhibition at Post Offices, particularly in seaport towns.

The final balance-sheet of the withdrawal operation may be summarised as follows:

	Note	£ s. d.
Paid to Postmaster-General for coin	(1)	22,577 15 7
Expenses of withdrawal	(2)	767 10 3
		23,345 5 10
Amount of sale of coin	(3)	16,869 1 0
Net loss		6,476 4 10

NOTES

(1) By far the greater part withdrawn from London and seaport towns in the south and south east. Collected via Post Offices at rate of 1s for 130c and conveyed to the Royal Mint.

(2) Including Post Office expenses of £169 5s 1d incurred in receipt at Receiver and Accountant General's Office and conveyance of coin to the Mint. Also Mint expenses, freight, brokerage, insurance etc. Sorting and examination were carried out by staff of the Mint Operative Department in the gold melting-house in December 1887 and January 1888 before the coins were finally disposed of.

(3) Sold to Allard of Paris, following an offer to the Mint by the firm. In total there were just over 55 tons of coin, face value 567,000 French francs (£22,500 at 25.20 francs to the £). This consisted of:

(i) Just over 50 tons of undamaged coins, mainly French, some Italian, face value approx. 515,455 francs, sold 'at a price somewhat below the nominal value'. (Face value £20,455 at 25.20 francs to the £.) (Assuming, say, 2 10 centime pieces to each 5 centimes, this would represent 4,123,640 10c pieces, 2,061,820 5c pieces.)

(ii) 5 tons of defaced and miscellaneous coins (presumably countermarked pieces, and coins of countries other than France and Italy), face value approx. 51,545 francs, sold at a lower rate, but well above scrap metal price. (Face value £2,045 at 25.20 francs to the £.) (Assuming, say, 2 10 centime pieces to each 5 centimes, this would represent 412,360 10c pieces, 206,180 5c pieces.)

Source: Royal Mint reports 1886, 1887, 1889; Post Office Records 1887.

For details of European bronze coins countermarked in England in the 1880's see Table 2 below. The subject is discussed in more detail in my article in Seaby's Coin and Medal Bulletin, December 1970 p. 443–53, March 1973, p. 82–7, and April 1973, p. 124.

2 Demonetized Copper Coin

Another ploy lay in the fact that the old copper coin ceased to be legal tender after the introduction of the bronze coinage and thus could be legally defaced as it was not the 'Queen's current Copper Coin'. People were encouraged to return coppers to the Mint by a premium of 2 per cent on their face value until 31

December 1869. Copper coin was then demonetized in the United Kingdom but was accepted by the Mint at face value, though without premium, until 30 July 1873. In the colonies, demonetization of British copper was deferred until 31 December 1877. By this time £580,000 in copper coins had been withdrawn in this country and £44,000 from overseas – i.e. less than half the copper issued from 1787 (sic) of which £656,376 remained unaccounted for. (See Sir John Craig, 'The Mint', 1953, p. 325.) This may be a reason for a number of the unofficial countermarks on copper coins by workers in the metal trades, as well as some shop and advertisement tickets (e.g. 22.66 in Table 1 below). It also accounts for the large number of countermarks on worn British copper found in Australia.

Quite apart from the legal question, demonetization always provided a stimulus to countermarking in that a supply of coin was available that people would not accept in normal trade. There are several examples of this well before the 1853 Act: by an Order in Council dated 30 January 1814, the Mint accepted 'Tower' halfpence issued 1719–75 at their face value in quantities of not less than 280 lbs. – i.e. about £32. This continued until a proclamation on 17 December 1817 declared an end as from 31 December the same year. In all only a little over £56,000 was withdrawn, including counterfeits, compared with a total Mint issue of £230,000. Thus a number of individuals and small traders had useless coin on their hands. This helps to explain the issue of countermarks such as 22.10, 22.56 and 22.64 in Table 1 below.

The demonetization of copper tokens by the Act of 27 July 1817 (57 Geo. III c.46) provided a similar incentive (see 22.36 in Table 1 below), as did the proclamation of 12 July 1826 demonetizing certain Irish copper pieces (see 22.57 in Table 1 below).

3 Paper Labels

Yet another loophole was the affixing to English copper and bronze coins of adhesive paper labels bearing advertisements. The earliest example known to me, again involving a newspaper – the 'Penny Newsman' (see 22.44 below) dates from 1860–4 and is on the reverse of an 1806/7 penny. The practice became more common in the 1880's – a period of intensive competition among advertisers.

The Master of the Mint, C. W. Fremantle, was often asked, between 1880 and 1884, whether this practice was legal. Warned by the Attorney General on the inadvisability of expressing an opinion, Fremantle merely referred enquirers to the 1861 Coinage Offences Act. Enquiries came from Margate (April 1880 and August 1881), Andover (July 1881), Ipswich (December 1881), Uxbridge (January 1882), Guildford (October 1882), Bristol and London (December 1883) and Bath (April 1884). From these letters, preserved in the Mint records, it appears that the practice was fairly widespread, although, inevitably, few of these paper labels have survived. On the legality of the practice, the Attorney General wrote to Fremantle on 28 October 1882 in connection with a Guildford bookseller's complaint about a Salvation Army 'War Cry' sticker on a shilling (see 22.67 below):

> I return Mr. Lasham's letter and his 'defaced shilling'! in a registered envelope as I receive it. I think he wastes a good deal of valuable indignation on the 'War Cry' advertisement, which being merely an adhesive bit of paper may be removed by moistening it with the end of the tongue.
>
> Of course the Advertiser has no legal right to stick a bit of paper on a shilling, which, as it can be, removed as I have suggested, does not appear to me to be 'a stamping' within 24 & 25 Vict. c. 99 [1861 Act] rendering the sticker liable to a year's hard labour.

Paper labels appear mainly on British copper and bronze coins, and those known to have existed are recorded in Table 1 below. One example on a French bronze coin is also known (22.207) and is included in Table 2.

This was really the end of large-scale advertising on current coin. Small-scale, local and illegal countermarking, both for advertisement purposes and as 'hatch, match or dispatch tokens' has continued into the present century. Some of the former are included in the lists that follow, as are some of the large number of unofficial issues with names or marks of traders struck on coins by workers with access to brand-marking punches.

4 Aluminium Rings

If advertising *on* coins had virtually finished, the idea of placing an advertising slogan *around* a coin without defacing it was a new variation on an old theme; during the last 70 years, certain firms have adopted the practice of encircling small coins with an aluminium ring or collar. The examples I have seen have been United States cents or British farthings surrounded by an aluminium collar, diameter 32–38 mm, with, usually, on one side 'KEEP ME AND YOU WILL NEVER BE (or GO) BROKE' within a horseshoe, and on the other an advertising slogan. This was a clever means of evading the coinage offences acts by ensuring that the coin itself was not defaced, and seems to have been used in this country c. 1900–55, mainly in the late 1930's. Unlike earlier advertising on coins, this method suffered from the disadvantage that the coin could, of course, no longer circulate. Examples are listed in Table 3 below. Many were supplied, complete with the farthing inserts, by J. R. Gaunt & Son Ltd., the Birmingham and London makers.

5 Cardboard Discs

The value of coins for advertising is shown by an advertisement in the 'Daily Telegraph' on 2 January 1862 for Windsor's Advertising Medallions (quoted by R. N. P. Hawkins in Seaby's Coin and Medal Bulletin, July 1968, p. 250). These were penny-like cardboard discs incorporating advertisements. The practice persisted into the 1920's.

As explained above some coins countermarked for use as truck tickets have been included in this study. A short note on the truck system is therefore appropriate here.

The supply of currency, particularly small change, was not enough to meet the demand of the innumerable industrial concerns being formed all over the country in the early nineteenth century. Thus many firms had their own shops, either on the premises or nearby, where truck tokens or tickets, forced into existence by the shortage of coin, could be exchanged for goods. A more cogent reason for the existence of these shops was that many employers realised that the high nominal wages they needed to offer to attract labour could be offset by charging high prices and/or selling low quality goods to their workers. However it is true that, with the new spinning mills set up in remote areas near the sources of water power, and collieries and ironworks started in open country, there were no shops in the neighbourhood; add to this the cost of bringing in a large supply of weekly cash over poor roads, and a truck shop was a virtual necessity. The credit system went hand in hand with truck: a House of Commons Select Committee on Manufactures reported in 1833 that half of all goods bought by the labouring people of Stockport for domestic purposes was on credit – at prices 10–20 per cent dearer than for cash payments (see Questions 10566–71). The truck system was also widespread in rural areas, particularly in Scotland and Ireland.

Much of the early legislation against the truck system had been concerned with hand-loom weaving, hand-made nail making, framework knitting, and other domestic industries – see G. W. Hilton, 'The Truck System' (1960), p. 10. In 1817 specific Acts were passed to cater for the cutlery and coal mining industries. In October 1831 an Act was passed repealing the 18 earlier Acts concerned with the payment of wages other than in current coin (1 & 2 Will. IV c. 36). These Acts dated from Edward IV to George III. At the same time a new consolidation Act appeared on the statute book 'to prohibit the Payment, in certain Trades, of Wages in Goods, or otherwise than in the Current Coin of the Realm' (1 & 2 Will. IV c. 37). The main provisions were that contracts for hire should be made in current coin and make no stipulation about how and where wages, which should be paid in current coin, should be spent. The Act applied only to workers employed in the iron and steel, mining, quarrying, brick making, metal manufacturing and pottery and glass industries. Penalties for non-compliance were up to £10 for a first offence, £20 for a second and £100 for a third. Ireland was not covered. The Act was not effective, as was shown by a select committee appointed to examine its operation in April 1842; it is quite clear that the truck system – either in the form of payment in goods or insistence on the expenditure of money wages at the truck or 'tommy' shop was still widespread in these industries. After an unsuccessful Bill in 1853, a Royal Commission on the Truck System in 1871 showed a similar position, although, in fact, there was by now less of a problem. More effective legislation came belatedly with 'An Act to amend and extend the law relating to truck' (50 & 51 Vic. c. 48) passed in September 1887. This covered all workmen as defined in Section 10 of the Employers and Workmen Act 1875 – i.e. all manual labourers except those in agriculture and domestic employment. It applied to Ireland as well, and provided for enforcement by the Factories and Mines inspectorate.

The truck system died out with the increase in weekly payment of wages and improved credit facilities in the late nineteenth century, though the legislation may have helped. It continued until the 1870's and 1880's, particularly in Ireland; elsewhere it probably reached a peak in the 1840's – see Hilton, op. cit., p. 145. Some truck shops were replaced by consumer cooperatives, and there is quite a series of bread tickets, cooperative society checks and canteen vouchers from the end of the century onwards.

THE LISTS

The lists below cover all countermarked and engraved coins etc. falling into the categories defined in the introduction to this work that I have come across so far. They are listed by counties, which are in alphabetical order for, successively, England, Wales, Scotland and Ireland. There follows a section on pieces I have not been able to attribute even tentatively to a particular area. The numbering system adopted allows for expansion when additional pieces come to light. Following each list are some notes, in the same order, on individual issuers, where such information is available.

It is probable that some of the very large series of countermarked coins bearing only names or initials (no town or trade) were, in fact, used as token, shop tickets, or pay/tool checks. A number of these are listed by Batty and Szauer, while others have appeared from time to time in Spink's Numismatic Circular and Seaby's Coin and Medal Bulletin. The countermarking of worn British coin, foreign coins, and underweight counterfeits in this way could well have been the traders' means of ensuring their acceptance at full rate during a period of local shortage of small change. In the absence of any proof of this or definite attribution to particular traders, these are excluded from the present study. There is considerable scope, however, for more research in this field, and for the more exact attribution of some of the pieces I have listed. I shall be very pleased to hear from readers who can add to my lists or notes in any way. To assist future research, appendices will be found at the end of this work listing other *counter-marked* names and initials known to me, but not included with the main tables as it is not yet possible to attribute them definitely to traders. Engraved names and initials have not been listed – the majority of such items are 'hatch, match or dispatch' tokens or vandalised pieces.

I have included foreign coins and British silver coins in Table 1 where it is reasonable to assume that the countermark also occurs on British copper and bronze coins or tokens.

The content of the various tables is as follows:

TABLE 1   List of countermarks etc. on British copper and bronze coins.
TABLE 2   List of countermarks etc. on European bronze coins.
TABLE 3   List of aluminium advertisement rings applied to British bronze coins.
APPENDIX 1   Alphabetical list of unattributed names countermarked on British copper and bronze coins.
APPENDIX 2   Alphabetical list of unattributed initials countermarked on British copper and bronze coins.

A comprehensive alphabetical index of countermarks etc. included in Tables 1, 2 and 3 will be found after the notes following Table 3.

It is difficult to be precise in describing the size of lettering on specimens from so many sources. In general, 'small' should be assumed to mean letters 2 mm high or less and 'large' 4 mm or more.

An asterisk preceding a listing indicates that the type is illustrated in the plates.

A NOTE ON RARITY, CONDITION AND VALUES

With the exception of the Lloyd's Weekly Newspaper and Pears' Soap countermarks, these pieces were not issued in large quantities (250,000 or more). One index of relative scarcity is the number of sources recorded for any one item in the lists below.

Unattributed names or initials (Appendices 1 and 2) are the most inexpensive of these pieces obtainable today. Once firmly attributed to particular traders, however, their value is likely to be significantly increased.

At the other end of the scale, paper labels on coins are scarce, and I know of few in private hands. Some of the early nineteenth century shop tickets and tokens are also scarce.

It is difficult to generalise about condition: usually countermarked British copper coins are found in poor to fair condition, with the countermarks themselves F to VF; for the later series of European bronze pieces, the coins are usually F to VF, the countermarks VF to EF.

Another factor that can add to the value of a piece is the coin on which the countermark occurs – if it is of a type other than the normal for the item in question.

An approximate, but, I hope, realistic, guide to relative values as at December 1974 is shown below for a few selected examples. Valuations are for the commonest varieties of each type.

No.	TYPE	COUNTERMARK / LEGEND	CONDITION OF COUNTERMARK	VALUATION (£)
	UNATTRIBUTED			
APPENDIX 2	INITIALS ON BRONZE	FK	VF	0.25
,,	INITIALS ON COPPER	NC	VF	0.50
APPENDIX 1	NAME ON BRONZE	MCCONNELL	VF	0.50
,,	NAME ON COPPER	F. BENNETT	VF	0.75
123.360	'UNOFFICIAL' TRADER'S MARK etc ON BRONZE	(Crown) / T.W.	VF	1.00
123.50	'UNOFFICIAL' TRADER'S MARK etc ON COPPER	(Crown) / CH	VF	1.50
122.80	'UNOFFICIAL' TRADER'S NAME ON BRONZE	EASTERN / CUTLERY / COMPᵧ etc	VF	1.50
122.70	'UNOFFICIAL' TRADER'S NAME ON COPPER	DEAKON & CO / PATENT	VF	1.75
	ATTRIBUTED			
40.37	'UNOFFICIAL' TRADER'S MARK etc ON COPPER	SPUR	VF	1.75
98.7	'UNOFFICIAL' TRADER'S NAME ON BRONZE	W. KAVANAGH / & SON / DUBLIN	VF	1.50
40.24	'UNOFFICIAL' TRADER'S NAME ON COPPER	B. HUNTSMAN	VF	2.00
22.218A	COMMON ADVERTISEMENT TICKET	PEARS' / SOAP.	EF	1.50
22.304		.HOOPER STRUVE'S. MINERAL WATERS	EF	1.50
22.28 1		–LLOYD'S WEEKLY NEWSPAPER 3D POST FREE	VF	1.50
22.202		BORWICK'S / BAKING / POWDER	EF	2.50
22.40A	OTHER ADVERTISEMENT TICKETS	–TRY NEVILLS. PATENT LENTILS FOR SOUP	VF	3.50
22.205		CLAPHAM OBSERVER	EF	3.50
22.44		PENNY NEWSMAN etc	VF	10.00
28.4A	SHOP TICKETS	ROBINSON / CUTLER / OXFORD	VF	2.50
22.10		T. COULSELL / Nᴼ 29 / QUEEN Sᵀ / BOROUGH / LONDON etc	VF	5.00
22.12A		DAVIS / WINE & BRANDY / MERCHANT etc	VF	5.00
22.36	PAY OR TOOL CHECKS	* MILDWATER / 2	VF	2.00
40.2	TOKENS	BRADFORD / WORKHOUSE	VF	3.00
77.2		DEANSTON COTTON MILL	VF	10.00
77.3		DUN. MᶜLAREN MERCHᵀ LOCHEARN	VF	25.00
64.1		DUMBARTON HALFPENNY / G + L	VF	50.00

ACKNOWLEDGEMENTS

I am indebted to the museums and private collectors who have described or loaned coins to me. Their names will be found in the source reference column of the various tables. In particular I should like to mention here the following, who have contributed material for the plates: Director, City Museum & Art Gallery, Birmingham; Director, Ulster Museum, Belfast; Christopher Brunel, Dr. G. H. L. Bullmore, A. G. Davies, P. R. Davies, C. Hanson, R. N. P. Hawkins, J. L. Short, A. Watson, and Jean M. White.

The London dealers A. H. Baldwin & Sons Ltd., B. A. Seaby Ltd. and Spink & Son Ltd. have been most helpful and patient in showing me material of interest.

To the staff of libraries and museums all over the country who have assisted my research I am very grateful.

I should also like to acknowledge the authors of the other literature on this series as listed in the bibliography.

TABLE 1: COUNTERMARKS ETC. ON BRITISH COPPER AND BRONZE COINS

KEY   Column A   Countermarked (c), engraved (E), or with printed paper affixed (P).
Column B   Incuse (I) or relief (R).
Column C   Obverse (O) or reverse (R).
Column D   Purpose: token (T), shop ticket (S), advertisement ticket (A), pay or tool check (P), unofficial (U).
SCMB   Seaby's Coin & Medal Bulletin.
SNC   Spink's Numismatic Circular
†   Not known or illegible.

NUMBER	LEGEND	A	B	C	D	COIN TYPE	SOURCE REFERENCE	APPROX. DATE
ENGLAND								
I	**BEDFORDSHIRE**							
* 1.1A	ABBEY/BEDFORD (curved)/CUTLER (curved) Medium (1st line) and small (2nd & 3rd lines) letters with serifs	C	I	O	S	Irish Penny 1805 Penny 1806	J. G. Scott J. G. Scott	1830–9
B	ABBEY (curved)/GUNMAKER (curved) BEDFORD (curved) Small letters with serifs (see also 17.1)	C	†	†	S	Penny 1797	SNC Nov./Dec. 1920.col. 527 no. 88089	1830–9
		C	I	R	S	Penny 1797	C. Brunel	
1.2	Richard/Partridge CRANFIELD	E E	I I	R O	S	Halfpenny William III	D. G. Vorley	Before 1797
2	**BERKSHIRE**							
2.1	MOODY/READING Small letters with serifs	C	I	O	S	Middlesex Halfpenny Token (D & H 454)	J. G. Scott	1825–50
2.2	G.W.R. LOCO. & CARR. DEPT. WINDSOR Small plain letters forming a circle. Large 4 in centre. 4 in centre	C	I	O	P	'Copper coin' (31mm)	SCMB Oct. 1972 TP652	
		C	I	R				
2.3	PRIDIE/WINDSOR/CUTLER/ENGRAVER Small letters with serifs	C	I	O	S	Halfpenny 1806/7	D. G. Vorley	1835–53
3	**BUCKINGHAMSHIRE**							
* 3.1	PAYNE/CUTLER/AYLESBURY Small letters with serifs	C	I	R	S	Penny 1797	County Museum, Aylesbury J. G. Scott R. N. P. Hawkins D. G. Vorley	1816–30
		C	I	O	S	Halfpenny 1806	D. G. Vorley	
3.2	IOHN/TALBOT/ETON/1817 Large crude letters with serifs	C	I	R	S, P or U	Penny 1797	D. G. Vorley	1817
* 3.3	W. COVINGTON Medium letters with serifs [attributed to Stony Stratford]	C	I	O	S	Penny 1806	J. G. Scott	Before 1830
4	**CAMBRIDGESHIRE**							
5	**CHESHIRE**							
5.1	DENTIST/CHESTER/X Small (1st and 2nd lines) and medium (3rd line) letters with serifs	C	I	O	S	Penny 1862	Ulster Museum	
* 5.2	DAVENPORT Small letters with serifs	C	I	O	S or U	Penny 1797	J. G. Scott	
6	**CORNWALL**							
* 6.1A	TREGEL/LAS Very small letters with serifs	C	I	O	S	Penny 1831 Penny 1834 Halfpenny 1831	J. G. Scott J. G. Scott C. Brunel	1830's
B	(T)REGELLAS Small letters with serifs	C	I	R	S	Penny 1797	C. Brunel	

NUMBER	LEGEND	A	B	C	D	COIN TYPE	SOURCE REFERENCE	APPROX. DATE
7	CUMBERLAND							
8	DERBYSHIRE							
* 8.1A	BOLSOVER Small letters with serifs	C	I	O	S or U	Halfpenny 1799	C. Brunel	
B	(Fleur de lis on side) TOME/BOLS/OVER (Fleur de lis on side) TOME (twice) Small letters with serifs	C C	I I	O R	S or U	Farthing †	Charles Dobie	
8.2	(crowned tower?)/HB in rectangle (twice) BUXTON in horse-shoe shaped punch	C	R	†	S or U	Halfpenny †	P. R. Davies	
8.3	JAMES/LOVETT/MALSTER/IN DERBY in script	E	I	†	S	Halfpenny †	SCMB Jan. 1971 TP475 D. G. Vorley	Before 1787
8.4	Thos/Rawfor/Derby	E	I	O	S	Halfpenny †	D. G. Vorley	
9	DEVONSHIRE							
* 9.1	GB/T. CORNS BEAR TOWN Large letters with serifs	C C	I I	R O	S	Penny 1797	J. G. Scott	
9.2	I. GOVER/CREDITON Medium letters with serifs	C	I	O & R	S	Penny 1797	D. G. Vorley	1830–50
9.3	GRAHAM/ROYAL CLARENCE HOTEL/EXETER Very small letters with serifs, with rays below. Rays forming a sun	C C	I I	R O	A	Penny 1860	Spink: stock May 1971	1860–6
9.4	+AMOS+ – POTTER – HAIR-DRESSER – EXON * – 1789 Small letters with serifs	E	I	EDGE	S	Halfpenny 1772 Edge 'buffed' to 3mm thick	J. G. Scott	1789
9.5	I. CLARKE/HONITON Small letters with serifs (also large O obv.)	C	I	O&R	S	Twopence 1797	J. G. Scott	1823–44
9.6	J. TAPPER/TOPSHAM (twice) Small letters with serifs	C	I	R	S	Penny 1806/7	D. G. Vorley	1840's
10	DORSET							
*10.1	GEALL/DORCHESTER/CUTLER Very small (1st & 2nd lines) and small (3rd line) letters with serifs	C	I	O	S	Penny 1797	J. G. Scott	1824–44
10.2	(rose)/RA in rectangular indent/IP/POOLE Small (1st line) and large (2nd & 3rd lines) letters with serifs	C	I & R	R	S	Halfpenny 1746	D. G. Vorley	
10.3	W.B./BEST within a garter etc. A female seated; ONE SHILLING etc. [Poole]	C C	R R	† †	T	Walsall Church Penny	Davis 27	1812
11	DURHAM							
*11.1	THOMAS (curved)/DURHAM Large letters with serifs	C	I	O&R	S	Penny 1797	J. G. Scott	1856
11.2	MAKERS TO/HER MAJESTY /(Royal Arms)/ PHILADELPHIA/DM Small letters with serifs	C	I	O	U	Penny 1807	A. G. Davies	1865–77

For key to column headings, please refer to page 19.

NUMBER	LEGEND	A	B	C	D	COIN TYPE	SOURCE REFERENCE	APPROX. DATE
11.3	Sᵒ SHIELDS above a shield with a ship in full sail	C	R	†	T	Halfpenny Charles II	SNC Oct. 1933 col. 352 no. 27664	18th century
		C	R	†	T	Halfpenny †	Batty 170	
		C	R	†	T	Halfpenny †	British Museum	
		C	R	†	T	Halfpenny George III	Davis 30	
		C	R	†	T	France: Sou †	H. D. Gibbs Sale 1960 lot 136	
12 12.1	ESSEX GREEN CULVER ST (curved)/COLCHESTER Very small letters with serifs	C	I	O&R	S	Halfpenny 1799	J. G. Scott	1840–54
12 2	PHILIPPS. CHEMIST (curved)/.PLAISTOW ESSEX. (curved) in an oval collar within oval indent Small plain letters (1st line) and small letters with serifs (2nd line)	C	R	O	S	Penny 1806/7	C. Brunel	1850–75
13 13.1	GLOUCESTERSHIRE For Clothing at First Cost (curved)/ THE DON/45,/WINE St./BRISTOL/ ΩΩ in black ink on white gummed paper	P	–	†	A	†	Royal Mint records	1883
*13.2	J. GREE(N)/BRISTOL Small letters with serifs	C	I	O	S	Halfpenny 1807	F. Banks	1830–51
*13.3	B. HALL/GLAZIER. &/GLASS. BENDER/ BRISTOL Medium (1st & 4th lines) and small (2nd & 3rd lines) letters with serifs	C	I	O	S	Penny 1797	P. R. Davies SCMB Jan. 1971 TP468	1820–35
13.4	EDWARDS/CHELTENHAM Small letters with serifs	C	I	O	S	Halfpenny 1806/7	D. G. Vorley	1840's
13.5	W. LANE/GLOSTER/(pipe with curved stem, inverted) (heart on side) Small letters with serifs	C	I	R	S	Penny 1797	D. G Vorley	1820–51
13.6	HAYWARD/TEWKSBURY/HAYWARD HAYWARD/TEWKSBURY Small letters with serifs	C C	I I	O R	S	Penny 1797	D. G. Vorley	1830–45
14 14.1	HAMPSHIRE (unknown Andover trader)	P	–	†	A	†	Royal Mint records	1881
14.2A	(arrow) Po/NOV/1827 in a circular depression	C	R	O	STORES CHECK	Irish Halfpenny 1805	R. N. P. Hawkins	1827
B	(arrow) PO/MAY/1860 in a circular depression [attributed to Portsmouth Dockyard]	C	†	†	STORES CHECK	Penny 1860–94	A. G. Stone	1860
14.3	CLARK/CUTLER/BRIDGE STREET/ SOUTHAMPTON Small letters with serifs	C	I	O	S	Penny 1806	D. G. Vorley	1827–37
*14.4	PEGLER/WORKING/JEWELLER/ SILVERSMITH/GUN–MAKER/SOUTHAMPTON PEGLER/CUTLERY/SOUTHAMPTON Small letters with serifs	C C	I I	R O	S	Penny 1797	J. G. Scott	1815–34

For key to column headings, please refer to page 19.

NUMBER	LEGEND	A	B	C	D	COIN TYPE	SOURCE REFERENCE	APPROX. DATE
15 *15.1A	HEREFORDSHIRE CASWALL/HEREFORD/CUTLER Small plain letters (1st line) Small (2nd line) and medium (3rd line) letters with serifs CASWALL/HEREFORD Very small letters with serifs	C	I	O	S	Halfpenny 1806/7	R. N. P. Hawkins	1811–35
B	CASWELL/CUTLER/BUTCHERS ROW/ HEREFORD Medium plain letters	C	I	R	S	Penny 1797	Hereford City Museum	
15.2	CROOSE/HEREFORD, and CROOSE to left CROOSE/CROOSE/HEREFORD Medium letters with serifs	C C	I I	O R	S	Twopence 1797	Hereford City Museum	1822–30
*15.3	TOWNSEND/HEREFORD/CUTLER Small letters with serifs	C	I	R	S	Penny 1797	J. G. Scott D. G. Vorley	1835–53
15.4	CASWALL/LEOMINSTER Very small letters with serifs	C	I	R	S	Penny 1797	Birmingham Museum	1820's
15.5	WINES (curved)/& Spirits/Wholefale/ & Retail/By/WATLING (curved)/ LEOMINSTER (curved)	C	I	O	S	Counterfeit Halfpenny George III	D. G. Vorley	1794–1811
16 16.1	HERTFORDSHIRE (Cross Fleury)	C C	I I	O&R O&R	S or P S or P	Halfpenny 1771 Halfpenny 1775	British Museum Ditto	1781–1803
		C	I	R	S or P	Farthing William III	Ditto	
	[attributed to Hoddesdon Brewery]	C	I	R	S or P	Farthing 177?	Ditto	
17 *17.1	HUNTINGDONSHIRE ABBEY/GUN MAKER (curved)/ST. IVES Medium (1st line) and small (2nd & 3rd lines) letters with serifs (see also 1.1 A & B)	C	I	O	S	Penny 1797	J. G. Scott D. G. Vorley	1830–1
18 18.1	KENT BARNES WINE & BRANDY MERCHANT CANTERBURY	C	†	†	S	Stafford Penny Token	Bliss Sale 1916 Lot 824	1840's
18.2	COLE CHATHAM	C	I	†	S	Penny 1797	SCMB Jan. 1971 TP459	1825–45
18.3A	(Arrow) C/NOV/1812 in a circular depression	C	R	R	STORES CHECK	Halfpenny 1806	J. G. Scott	1812
* B	(Arrow) C/JUN/1813 in a circular depression	C C	R R	O R	STORES CHECK CHECK	Halfpenny 1799 Halfpenny 1806	C. Brunel J. G. Scott	1813 1813
C	(Arrow) C/AUG/1813 in a circular depression	C	R	†	STORES CHECK	Farthing †	Batty 2151	1813
D	(Arrow) C/SEP/1814 in a circular depression	C	R	O	STORES CHECK	Halfpenny 1806	Duffield 1523	1814
E	(Arrow) C/APR/1818 in a circular depression	C	R	†	STORES CHECK	Halfpenny 1807	A. G. Stone	1818
	[Attributed to Royal Dockyard, Chatham]							
18.4	BUNYAR/MAIDSTONE Small letters with serifs	C	I	O&R	S	Penny 1806/7	D. G. Vorley	1825–50

For key to column headings, please refer to page 19.

NUMBER	LEGEND	A	B	C	D	COIN TYPE	SOURCE REFERENCE	APPROX. DATE
18.5	DARBYSHIRE'S (curved)/HAVANA/ Cigar Warehouses/3 Paradise S^t.&/ 3 Forthill, MARGATE/A good Havana Cigar/ a well known brand/4 for 1^s	P	–	†	A	Penny †	Royal Mint records	1880
18.6	John/Hooper 7 Oaks/Kent In script	E E	I I	O R	S	Twopence 1797	D. G. Vorley	1824–47
*18.7	(large crown)/W. HUNT Large letters with serifs (tobacco pipe) [Attributed to Sheerness]	C C	I I	R O	S	Halfpenny 1799	R. N. P. Hawkins	1845–55
18.8A	S (Arrow)/JAN/1841 in a circular depression	C	R	†	STORES CHECK	Halfpenny † Halfpenny 1841	H. D. Gibbs sale 1960. Lot 158 Edwin C. Leslie	1841
B	S (Arrow)/JUN/1845 in a circular depression [Attributed to Sheerness Dockyard]	C	R	R	STORES CHECK	Penny 1806/7	J. G. Scott	1845
19 *19.1	LANCASHIRE CARK/COTTON/WORKS/1787 Medium letters with serifs in a ribbed circle	C	R	O	T	Halfpenny 1775	Birmingham Museum Davis 31	1787
19.2	(Hand holding tricorne hat)/THO FLETCHER/Liverpool/MAKER Reversed for sealing	E	I	†	S	Halfpenny † edge hammered into a collar	D. G. Vorley	1766 or earlier
19.3	CHURCH (curved)/LR/HOUSE/24/TAVERN (curved) Medium letters with serifs [Lower House]	C	I	†	S	Penny-size disc	C. Brunel	
19.4	JOSEPH DAWSON STAYMAKER MANCHESTER	E	I	†	S	Halfpenny †	SCMB June 1969 TP257	1772–88
19.5	WR/(small crown)/DOBSONS PATENT [Manchester]	C	I	†	S or U	Halfpenny 1806	Batty 4055A	1834–8
19.6	FG/MANCHESTER Large (1st line) and small (2nd line) letters with serifs	C	I	R	S or U	Penny 1806/7	C. Brunel	
19.7	MANCHESTE(R) Large letters with serifs Large G (twice) and 18	C E	I I	2XO 1XR R	P or U	Penny token 1812 (Davis not local 43)	J. G. Scott	
19.8	(rose) MARY. HAMPSON. & SON in a circle, in centre */MAN/CHES/TER/* Large letters with serifs	C	R	†	T	Halfpenny George II Halfpenny George III Halfpenny †	Cokayne sale 1946 Lot 107 Davis 32 SCMB Sept. 1970 Cmk 32	1811–12
19 9	(sprig)/(quatrefoil)IO(?)MIL(NE)/Attorney/ MANCHESTER/(ornamentation)	E	I	O	S	Halfpenny †	D. G. Vorley	1808–20
19.10	WARBURTON/SURGEON/85/PORTLAND/ STREET/MANCHESTER In a circular indent	C	R	†	S	Penny †	H. D. Gibbs sale 1960. Lot 142	1820–5
19.11	PENDLETON Very small letters with serifs	C	I	R	S or U	Halfpenny 1806/7	J. G. Scott	

For key to column headings, please refer to page 19.

NUMBER	LEGEND	A	B	C	D	COIN TYPE	SOURCE REFERENCE	APPROX. DATE
20	**LEICESTERSHIRE**							
20.1	LATEMAN	C	I	†	S	Halfpenny †	SNC Jan./Feb.	
	SILEBY in an oblong indent	C	R	†			1921 col. 82 No. 89466	
21	**LINCOLNSHIRE**							
*21.1	A. PACEY/ALFORD Large letters with serifs	C	I	O&R	S	Penny 1797	J. G. Scott	1841–9
*21.2	W. TUPLING/1852/GRIMSBY Medium letters with serifs Variety: (i) W. RICHARDSON Small letters with serifs in addition on reverse, also incuse	C	I	O	S	Penny 1797	British Museum C. Brunel D. G. Vorley	1852
*21.3	J. BLINKHORN/HOLBEACH Small letters with serifs in indent BLINKHORN small letters with serifs	C C	R I	O R	S	Penny 1797	J. G. Scott	1835
21.4	TATE/& LILL/LOUTH in a rectangle, twice Small letters with serifs	C	R	O	T or S	Halfpenny 1806 Octagonal lead blank	Davis 2. Szauer 51 Birmingham Museum Spink: stock April 1972	1806–40
21.5	J. HENSON TIDD GOTE Large letters with serifs	C C	I I	R O	S	Penny 1797	Dr G. H. L. Bullmore	1842–56
22	**LONDON**							
*22.1	Robᵗ Andⁿ London (cross fleury) Edinburgh Invernefs in circle round floral device	E	I	R	S	Halfpenny William III	J. G. Scott	1800–12
22.2	(Crown)/GR/BARRON PATENT	C	I	O	S, P or U	Twopence 1797	SCMB Jan. 1971 TP452	1830–50
22.3	BARTLEET & SONS LONDON & BIRMINGHAM (Elephant?)	C	†	†	S	Penny George III	SCMB June 1969 TP262	1835–45
22.4	W. BENNETT HACKNEY	C	†	†	S	'Spanish coin 1788'	SCMB Jan. 1971 TP454	1805–33
*22.5A	BLUNT/OPERATOR FOR THE/TEETH AND BLEEDER/GREAT WINDMILL/STREET NEAR BREWER/STREET GOLDEN/SQUARE In crude script (Also known with arrows on reverse)	E	I	†	S	Halfpenny †	J. G. Scott British Museum Seaby stock – April 1971 Batty 805	1785– 1809
B	As above but last four lines GREAT WINDMILL/STREET NEAR THE/HAY MARKET/ LONDON	E	I	†	S	Halfpenny †	W. Whelan stock Sept. 1972	
*22.6	X BOND X (curved)/LONDON (curved) Small letters with serifs in oval indent ✶✛✶ in centre	C	R	O	T or S	Halfpenny 1799	Birmingham Museum	Before 1840
22.7	John/BRADSHAW/TICKET *PORTER*/ Custom House/17 (Crown) 65	E	I	R	S	Halfpenny George II (pierced 12 o'c)	D. G. Vorley	1765
22.8	Burch/Waterman/at Pauls/Wharf (Arms: crossed oars, rampant dolphins each side of shield, man rowing below. 'BY COMMAND OF OUR SUPERIOR' in a garter)	E E	I I	† †	S	Halfpenny †	D. G. Vorley	

For key to column headings, please refer to page 19.

NUMBER	LEGEND	A	B	C	D	COIN TYPE	SOURCE REFERENCE	APPROX. DATE
22.9	(A lion couchant)/CLARK in a rectangular indent (A royal crown)/LON/DON in a rectangular indent Small letters with serifs	C	R	O	T or S	Halfpenny 1770–5	Davis 36 Birmingham Museum	1800–18
*22.10	.RULES & UMBS MADE & REPD WHOLE &c BY in circle round T. COULSELL (curved)/No 29/ QUEEN ST./BOROUGH/LONDON (curved) Very small letters with serifs in circular indent	C	R	R	T or S	Halfpenny George II Halfpenny 1752 Halfpenny † Halfpenny George II Halfpenny †	British Museum Spink: stock May 1971 R. N. P. Hawkins J. G. Scott (3) D. G. Vorley	1799–1814
*22.11	CRYPTO Large plain letters	C	I	O&R	U	Penny 1863	C. Brunel	1884–1912
*22.12A	DAVIS (curved)/WINE & BRANDY (curved)/MERCHANT/46/HOUNDSDITCH/ LONDON (curved) Very small letters with serifs in circular indent Variety: i) 43 on obverse and reverse in addition, incuse	C	R	R	T or S	Penny 1806 Halfpenny 1806 Penny 1806/7	Seaby: stock Feb. 1971 SNC Nov. 1905 No. 21949 Seaby: stock Feb. 1971 J. G. Scott (2) Birmingham Museum	1810–22
B	Ditto but without first D in 5th line HOUNSDITCH (curved)	C	R	R	T or S	Penny 1806 Halfpenny 1806	Batty 237, Davis 35 Davis 37 Bliss Sale Lot 782 C. Brunel SNC Nov. 1905 No. 21950 D. G. Vorley	1810–22
22.13	(Crown)/DAVIS/LONDON Small letters with serifs	C	I	O&R	S	Penny 1797	J. G. Scott	1845–53
*22.14A	S. DRABBLE/I HIGH ST/MARY LE BONE/ CUTLER Small letters with serifs	C	I	R	S	Penny 1797	C. Brunel J. G. Scott D. G. Vorley Dr. G. H. L. Bullmore. SCMB Jan. 1971 TP462 Waters 7 A. G. Davies Batty 869 J. G. Scott	1835–53
		C	I	†	S	Penny 1806		
		C	I	R	S	Halfpenny 1807		
		C	I	O	S	Halfpenny George III		
		C	I	R	S	Irish Halfpenny 1823		
* B	DRABBLE/I HIGH STREET/MARYLEBONE/ CUTLER Small letters with serifs	C	I	R	S	Penny 1797	J. G. Scott	
22.15	THO. EDWARDS WATCHMAKER 1755 (Pot of flowers)	E E	I I	O R	S	Halfpenny †	SCMB Jan. 1971 TP463	1755
22.16	FIRMIN & CO. (curved)/LONDON (curved) Small letters with serifs forming a circle (ornate crown)/AS in script	C E	R I	R O	S or U	Penny 1797	British Museum	1800–11

For key to column headings, please refer to page 19.

NUMBER	LEGEND	A	B	C	D	COIN TYPE	SOURCE REFERENCE	APPROX. DATE
22.17	ㅈ (twice) Large letter with serifs 18 (ewer) 26 in shaped indent Medium figures with serifs [Founders Company]	C C	I R	R R	U	Halfpenny 1806/7	D. G. Vorley	1826–78
22.18	I. GREAVES/LONDON Medium letters with serifs	C	I	R	S or U	Penny 1797	A. G. Davies	1812–33
22.19	JOHN PARKER HALL (curved)/LONDON (curved) Small plain letters	C	I	R	S, A or U	Penny 1862	D. G. Vorley	
22.20	A. Hamilton/Fenchurch/Street/106 ½ a crown/Reward	E E	I I	O R	S	Halfpenny †	Barnard BNJ 1918 No. 196	1783–7
22.21	HATCHETTS HOTEL PICCADILLY	C	I	†	S	Halfpenny George III	Batty 949	1837–53
22.22	HAYES/DENTIST/MAYS/BUILDINGS Small letters with serifs	C	I	O	A	Halfpenny 1807	D. G. Vorley	1834–46
22.23	HEMS & SON LONDON	C	I	†	S	Halfpenny George III	Batty 951	1836–53
*22.24A	HUNDLEY/LONDON Large (1st line), and medium (2nd line) letters with serifs	C	I	O	S or U	Penny 1797	A. G. Davies	1806–28
B	HUNDLEY Small letters with serifs	C	I	O	S or U	Halfpenny George II	C. Brunel	1806–28
22.25	H&C in rectangle twice, CHING in oval twice, HUX(LEY), 6B Small letters with serifs H&C in rectangle, B twice Small letters with serifs [Huxley & Ching]	C C	I I	O R	U	Halfpenny 1861	J. G. Scott	1860's
22.26	JOHNSON/101/GREAT TITCHFIELD ST. Small letters with serifs	C	I	O&R	S	Penny 1825	Ulster Museum	1842–53
*22.27	.KILBURN. in serrated indent Large letters with serifs	C	R	O	T or S	Penny 1797	J. G. Scott	
22.28 * * * * *	[Edward Lloyd's Newspapers] There are five main varieties of Lloyd's countermarks: 1 .READ.LLOYD'S.PENNY.SUNDAY.TIMES In a circle in thick medium plain letters just within inner rim of coin 2 LLOYD'S WEEKLY NEWSPAPER THREE PENCE POST FREE —·— In a circle in thin medium plain letters just within inner rim of coin 3 LLOYD'S WEEKLY NEWSPAPER THREE PENCE in outer circle/POST/FREE in 2 curved lines in inner circle Medium plain letters 4 – LLOYD'S WEEKLY NEWSPAPER 3^D POST FREE In a circle in thin medium plain letters 5 PURCHASE NUMBER ONE OF (medium plain letters) LLOYD'S (medium letters with serifs) LAST– (medium plain letters) in outer circle/NEW PENNY/PUBLICATION in 2 curved lines in inner circle, medium plain letters							

For key to column headings, please refer to page 19.

NUMBER		LEGEND	A	B	C	D	COIN TYPE	SOURCE REFERENCE	APPROX. DATE
		These are referred to below as cmks. I–5 and are found in 10 different obv./rev. or rev./obv. pairings as follows: 1/, 2/4, 2/5, 3/, 3/3, 3/4, 3/5, 4/, 4/4, 4/5 There are also some sub-varieties listed under the appropriate main type							
*	A	Cmk 1/	C	I	O	A	Penny 1797	J. G. Scott (4) A. G. Davies Seaby: Stock March 1973(2)	1846–7
		Varieties:							
		(i) with addition of T. COOKE across centre, medium letters with serifs	C	I	O	A	Penny 1797	Spink: Stock May 1971	
		(ii) with addition of 5362 and 1847 around ⋈	C	I	O	A	Penny 1797	Spink: Stock May 1971	
		(iii) with addition of large 1P in field	C	I	O&R	A	Penny 1797	R. N. P. Hawkins	
		(iv) with addition of W. H. TAYLOR across centre [reverse 'similar but without W. H. TAYLOR and in different style'; it is not clear exactly what this means]	C	I	O	A	Penny 1797	P. Withers list Nov. 1971	
		(v) with addition of W. F. SADLER Medium letters with serifs	C	I	R	A	Penny 1797	J. G. Scott	
*	B	Cmk 2/Cmk 4	C	I	O&R	A	Penny 1797	Birmingham Museum	1850
			C	I	R&O	A	Penny 1797	J. G. Scott (3) British Museum	1850
	C	Cmk 2/Cmk 5	C	I	O&R	A	Penny 1797	J. G. Scott (4)	1850
			C	I	R&O	A	Penny 1797	C. Brunel	
	D	Cmk 3/	C	I	R	A	Halfpenny George IV	J. G. Scott	1850
	E	Cmk 3/Cmk 3	C	I	O&R	A	Halfpenny 1806/7 Irish Halfpenny 1805 Canada Halfpenny token 1837 (Charlton 19a)	J. G. Scott (4) C. Brunel J. G. Scott J. G. Scott	1850
	F	Cmk 3/Cmk 4	C	I	O&R	A	Halfpenny 1806/7	J. G. Scott	1850
*	G	Cmk 3/Cmk 5	C	I	O&R	A	Halfpenny 1799	R. N. P. Hawkins	1850
			C	I	R&O	A	Halfpenny 1799	Batty 4390A J. G. Scott (2)	
			C	I	O&R	A	Halfpenny 1806/7	Batty 4394 J. G. Scott (2)	
			C	I	R&O	A	Halfpenny 1806/7	Batty 4393 J. G. Scott (7)	
			C	I	O&R	A	Irish Halfpenny 1805	R. N. P. Hawkins J. G. Scott	
			C	I	R&O	A	Irish Halfpenny 1805	Batty 4391A J. G. Scott (2)	
			C	I	R&O	A	Penny 1797	British Museum	
			C	I	R&O	A	Penny 1797 (also has no. 22.33B on obv.)	J. G. Scott	
			C	I	R&O	A	Penny 1806/7	R. N. P. Hawkins	
		Varieties:							
		(i) NEW omitted	C	I	R&O	A	Halfpenny 1806	Batty 4394D	
		(ii) POST omitted	C	I	O&R	A	Halfpenny 1806	Batty 4392A	
		(iii) (Sun) incuse added to both sides 10 mm diameter. 16 rays	C	I	R&O	A	Halfpenny 1806	J. G. Scott	

For key to column headings, please refer to page 19.

NUMBER	LEGEND	A	B	C	D	COIN TYPE	SOURCE REFERENCE	APPROX. DATE
H	Cmk 4/	C	I	R	A	Halfpenny 1826	C. Brunel	1850
		C	I	R	A	Halfpenny 1827	Batty 4394A	
		C	I	R	A	Penny 1826	J. G. Scott	
		C	I	R	A	Irish Penny 1822–4	R. N. P. Hawkins	
		C	I	R	A	Dublin Penny token 1816 (Davis 10)	D. G. Vorley	
* I	Cmk 4/Cmk 4	C	I	O&R	A	Halfpenny 1799	Batty 4394B J. G. Scott (2)	1850
		C	I	O&R	A	Halfpenny 1806/7	Batty 4394C J. G. Scott P. R. Davies	
		C	I	O&R	A	Irish Halfpenny 1805	British Museum A. G. Davies	
		C	I	O&R	A	Penny 1797	J. G. Scott (3) C. Brunel P. R. Davies R. N. P. Hawkins	
		C	I	O&R	A	Penny 1806/7	J. G. Scott (5)	
		C	I	O&R	A	Irish Penny 1805	C. Hanson	
		C	I	O&R	A	Dublin Penny token 1814 (Davis 22–24)	A. G. Davies	
	Varieties: (i) Large serif'd BW additional in field	C	I	O	A	Penny 1797	British Museum	
	(ii) Large serif'd R·P additional in field	C	I	O	A	Penny 1797	J. G. Scott	
* J	Cmk 4/Cmk 5	C	I	R&O	A	Halfpenny 1799	J. G. Scott	1850
		C	I	O&R	A	Penny 1797	J. G. Scott (2)	
		C	I	O&R	A	Penny 1806/7	J. G. Scott (5) A. G. Davies	
		C	I	R&O	A	Penny 1806/7	J. G. Scott	
		C	I	O&R	A	Irish Penny 1805	C. Hanson	
		C	I	R&O	A	Irish Penny 1805	J. G. Scott	
	Variety: (i) ⚹ additional on reverse [see A(ii)]	C	I	O&R	A	Penny 1797	Birmingham Museum	
*22.29	LLOYD & CO (curved)/TEA IMPORTERS/ 141/ALDERSGATE Sᵀ/LONDON (curved) Small letters with serifs in a circle	C	I	O	S	Penny 1797	J. G. Scott (2) R. N. P. Hawkins National Museum of Wales D. G. Vorley (cf. also Batty 1002F)	1833–41
22.30	LONDON Medium letters with serifs	C	I	†	S or U	Penny 1797	D. G. Vorley	
*22.31	LONDON/LONDON Very small letters with serifs	C	I	R	S or U	Penny 1797	J. G. Scott	1840's
22.32	(large crown) LONDON Also engraved with an elephant	C	†	†	U	Halfpenny †	H. D. Gibbs Sale 1960. Lot 157	
22.33A	LOOKER/42 LEADENHALL Sᵀ. Small letters with serifs	C	I	O	S	Penny 1797 (silvered) Penny 1797	J. G. Scott D. G. Vorley	1838–56
B	LOOKER/42 LEADENHALL STREET Slightly smaller letters with serifs	C	I	O	S	Penny 1797 (see 22.28G)	J. G. Scott	1838–50
22.34	W. LUND/24 FLEET STREET Small letters with serifs	C	I	R	S	Halfpenny 1807	British Museum	1833–44
*22.35	W. MASON'S/PATENT/LONDON Medium letters with serifs	C	I	R	S or U	France: Décime An 5–9A	J. G. Scott	1825–32

For key to column headings, please refer to page 19.

NUMBER	LEGEND	A	B	C	D	COIN TYPE	SOURCE REFERENCE	APPROX. DATE
*22.36	*MILDWATER in circle/2 in centre Large letters with serifs	C	I	O&R	P	Coventry Halfpenny 1792 (D & H 231–7)	J. G. Scott	1856–77
22.37	Fs. MONCRIEFFE LONDON. 1777.	E	I	R	?	Halfpenny George III	Batty 1052A	1777
22.38	TRY A. MORRALL'S NEEDLES 'Horseshoe shaped punch'	C	I	†	A	Halfpenny 1807	Waters 5	1850–3
22.39	H. W/MORTIMER (curved) in sunken oval (twice) Small letters with serifs	C	R	†	U	Halfpenny †	Birmingham Museum	1780–1812
*22.40A	.TRY NEVILLS.PATENT LENTILS FOR SOUP Small letters with serifs in circle (28.5mm)	C	I	O	A	Penny 1797	J. G. Scott British Museum Ulster Museum	before 1853
	Variety: G.C in rectangular indent twice in field	C C	I R	R O	A A	Penny 1797 Penny 1797	D. G. Vorley Spink: Stock May 1971	
B	Similar – but no stops between words, and smaller circle (26.5mm)	C	I	O	A	Penny 1797	J. G. Scott	before 1853
22.41	NOAKES (curved)/&/HOLBOROW/LONDON (curved) Small plain letters in 9mm circle, twice, (double struck) and 20	C	I	O	P or U	Canada cent 1913	J. G. Scott	1920's
22.42	(An Oak Tree)	C	I	O	U	Halfpenny 1806	Batty 5254	
22.43	W. PAYS/HOTEL Medium letters with serifs	C	I	O&R	S	Halfpenny 1799	J. G. Scott	1842–4
*22.44	HAVE YOU ANYTHING TO SELL (curved)/IF SO/ADVERTISE/IN THE/PENNY/NEWSMAN/THE/BEST PAPER EXTANT (curved) in black ink on white gummed paper	P	–	R	A	Penny 1806/7	J. G. Scott	1860–4
22.45	40 PERCY ST./TOTTENHAM/COURT ROAD/LONDON Small letters with serifs	C	I	†	S or U	Halfpenny †	D. G. Vorley	1823–33
22.46	(a lion couchant gardant fondling a dog) EXETER CHANGE LONDON PIDCOCK (a beaver eating a root) THE BEAVER 1801	C C	R R	O R	T	Halfpenny 1799	Batty 1154D cf Davis 38	1801
22.47	JAR (monogram) in script, in centre, surrounded by MILLINER MANTUA MAKER Large letters with serifs No 5 VILLARS (curved)/YORK/BUILDINGS/London/1787/STREET (curved)	E E	I I	† †	S	Halfpenny †	D. G. Vorley	1787
22.48	RICHARDS/WOOD & Co/LONDO(N) Medium (1st & 2nd line) and large (3rd line) letters with serifs	C	I	O&R	S, P or U	Penny 1797 (4.5mm hole, 12 o'c)	J. G. Scott	1828–43
22.49	ROBINSON/AVERY ROW/LOWER/GROSVENOR ST./CUTLER/LONDON Small letters with serifs	C	I	O	S	Penny 1797	D. G. Vorley	1824–8
*22.50	.USE.ROGERS.FAMILY.LOTION. (curved)/& LUMBAGO/FOR.CHILBLAINS (curved) Large plain letters	C C	I I	O R	A A	Penny 1797 Penny 1797	J. G. Scott D. G. Vorley C. Brunel cf Chitty SNC Aug. 1907 col 10021 No. 81	1825–56

For key to column headings, please refer to page 19.

NUMBER	LEGEND	A	B	C	D	COIN TYPE	SOURCE REFERENCE	APPROX. DATE
22.51	↓ D/(DE)C/182. in circular indent Large letters with serifs [Attributed to Royal Dockyard, Deptford]	C	R	R	STORES CHECK	Halfpenny 1807	J. G. Scott	1820's
22.52	PEWTERER (inverted)/E.RUSE 1st line in medium plain letters 2nd line in large letters with serifs	C	I	R	S or A	Jersey Penny 1877	D. G. Vorley	1885–91
*22.53	R. SAVAGE (curved)/CHEESEMONGER/ 28 WHITE CHAPEL Large (1st line) and small (remainder) letters with serifs	C	I	O	S	Penny 1797	Dr. G. H. L. Bullmore C. Brunel	1834–8
22.54	W. SMEETON 17 TOTTENHAM S$^{T.}$ 1822	E	I	O	?	Halfpenny 1806	Batty 1234	1822
22.55A	Spence/operator/for Teeth/Grays Inn/ Lane (The hand of the dentist holding up for the inspection of a patient, whose head is shown, a recently extracted molar. The dentist has a lace ruffle at his wrist.)	E E	I I	O R	S	Halfpenny †	Barnard BNJ 1918 No. 200	
B	1722/Spence/Operator/of Teeth 172./Grays/Inn/Lane	E E	I I	O R	S	Farthing † Halfpenny †	British Museum D. G. Vorley	1722
*22.56	SPRING (six times) and LONDON (twice) Small letters with serifs	C	I	O	S or U	Halfpenny 1739	J. G. Scott	1830's
22.57A	J. STANTON/METAL TUBE/WIRE/&/ TIN PLATE/WAREHOUSE/73 SHOE LANE Medium (1st line) and small (remainder) letters with serifs	C	I	R	S	Irish Halfpenny 1805	British Museum	1827–53
* B	J. STANTON/METAL/&/TUBE/WAREHOUSE/ 73 SHOE LANE Small letters with serifs	C	I	R	S	Irish Halfpenny 1805	J. G. Scott	1827–53
* C	J. STANTON/WIRE/&/TUBE/WAREHOUSE/ 73 SHOE LANE Small letters with serifs	C	I	R	S	Irish Halfpenny 1805	J. G. Scott	1827–53
D	J. STANTON/WIRE/&/TIN PLATE/WAREHOUSE/ 73 SHOE LANE Small letters with serifs	C	I	R	S	Irish Halfpenny 1805 (pierced 12 o'c)	D. G. Vorley	1827–53
E	J. STANTON/TUBE/&/METAL/WAREHOUSE/ 73 SHOE LANE Small letters with serifs	C	I	R	S	Irish Halfpenny 1805 (one pierced 8 o'c)	D. G. Vorley (2)	1827–53
22.58	SWALLOW LONDON within rectangle	C	†	†	S	Farthing 1807	SNC Jan. 1968 p. 22 T.72	1807–26
22.59	(Swan with two necks) covering whole of design	C	I	O	T or S	Sheffield Penny token 1812 (Davis 137)	J. G. Scott	
22.60	S.S Large letters with serifs in centre of square formed by LONDON (4 times) Small letters with serifs	C	I	O&R	S or U	Penny 1807	J. G. Scott	
22.61	IOHN TATE & SON. LONDON. Large letters with serifs in a circle, with a woolsack within an inner circle	C	R	†	T or S	Halfpenny George III	Davis 39 Birmingham Museum	1789– 1811

For key to column headings, please refer to page 19.

NUMBER	LEGEND	A	B	C	D	COIN TYPE	SOURCE REFERENCE	APPROX. DATE
22.62A	THOMAS /104.BLACKMAN/STREET.BORO/ CUTLER Small letters with serifs	C	I	R	S	Penny 1797	Spink: Stock May 1971 Seaby: Stock Feb. 1971	1813–8
	RAZOR/MANUFACTURY Small letters with serifs	C	I	O				
* B	THOMAS/104.BLACKMAN/STREET.BORO/ CUTLER Small letters with serifs	C	I	R	S	Penny 1797	J. G. Scott (3) Jean M. White	1813–8
	RAZOR/MAKER/MANUFACTURY/BORO. ROAD Small letters with serifs	C	I	O				
C	JOHN/THOMAS/CUTLER/104.BLACKMAN/ STREET.BORO Small letters with serifs	C	I	R	S	Penny 1797	D. G. Vorley	1813–8
	RAZOR/MAKER Small letters with serifs	C	I	O				
D	JOHN/THOMAS/CUTLER/104.BLACKMAN/ STREET.BORO Small letters with serifs	C	I	R	S	Penny 1797	D. G. Vorley	1813–8
	MANUFACTURY/FACING/NEWINGTON/ CAUSEWAY Small letters with serifs around bust	C	I	O				
22.63	(large crown)/GR/TOWER (curved) Large letters with serifs	C	I	O	U	Halfpenny 1806/7	C. Brunel	1807–30
*22.64	UNDERWOOD Very small letters with serifs	C	I	R	S or U	Halfpenny William III	J. G. Scott	1812–42
22.65	VERINDER Small letters with serifs	C	I	2XO 4XR	U	Penny 1797	C. Brunel	1823–51
22.66	WADDEN'S (curved)/HAIR DYE/2/6/ GOSWELL Rᴰ (curved) Medium plain letters	C	I	O & R	A	Penny 1806/7	D. G. Vorley	1884–6
22.67	(WAR CRY) (Wording uncertain)	P	–	O & R	A	Shilling †	Royal Mint Records	1882
22.68	WARNER'S/LONDON/BEST MALLEABLE ZINC (curved) 'From a large punch, the same size as the coin'	C	I	†	A	Penny 1861	Waters 8	1861–79
22.69	LONDON in rectangular indent/ WG/ (inverted eagle) (?) within shaped indent Medium (1st line) and large (2nd line) letters with serifs	C C C	R I R	O	S	Halfpenny 1752	J. G. Scott	
22.70	C. WHITEHOUSE/CORN METERS/OFFICE/61 Gᵀ TOWER/STREET (London shield)	E E	I I	O R	S or P	Halfpenny † (pierced 12 o'c)	D. G. Vorley	
22.71	T. WILLIAMS/14 SMITHFIELD Small letters with serifs	C	I	O	S	Penny 1797	D. G. Vorley	1834–53
22.72A	W/APR/93 Large letters with serifs in 16mm circular indent	C	R	†	STORES CHECK	Counterfeit Farthing †	Dr. G. H. L. Bullmore	1793
* B	↓ W/AUG/99 Similar	C	R	O	STORES CHECK	Halfpenny George II	Dr. G. H. L. Bullmore	1799
C	↓ W/JUL/1809 Similar [Attributed to Woolwich Dockyard or Arsenal]	C	R	O	STORES CHECK	Halfpenny George II	Dr. G. H. L. Bullmore	1809

For key to column headings, please refer to page 19.

NUMBER	LEGEND	A	B	C	D	COIN TYPE	SOURCE REFERENCE	APPROX. DATE
23	MIDDLESEX							
23.1	HENRY A. PITKIN (curved)/FOR/ Shoes & Useful/ULSTERS/AND/Jackets/ 51 HIGH STREET, UXBRIDGE (curved) Black print on pink paper	P	–	†	A	†	Royal Mint Records	1882
24	NORFOLK							
*24.1	EDWARD SPRIN (curved)/around G/ ALL in centre Very large letters with serifs	C	I	R	S	Halfpenny 1807	Dr. G. H. L. Bullmore	1845
	ACLE Very large letters with serifs	C	I	O				
*24.2	LYNN Medium plain letters [Kings Lynn]	C	I	2XO IXR	S or U	Penny 1797	C. Brunel	
24.3	R. GILLHAM/NORWICH Large letters with serifs	C	I	R	S	Norwich Twopence Token (Davis 17)	County Museum, Aylesbury	1830–45
*24.4	GRIFFIN [attributed to Norwich] Medium letters with serifs	C	I	R	S	Norwich Halfpenny 1793 (D & H 46 etc.)	Batty 1777	
		C	I	R	S	Norwich Halfpenny (D & H 16)	J. G. Scott	
		C	I	R	S	Norwich Halfpenny 1811 (Davis 21)	C. Brunel	
		C	I	O	S	Counterfeit Halfpenny 1775	Batty 4231D	
		C	I	R	S	Halfpenny William III	J. G. Scott	
24.5	I. PARKERSON Large letters with serifs [Attributed to Norwich]	C	I	R	S	Norwich Twopence Token (Davis 17)	C. Brunel J. G. Scott	before 1822
25	NORTHAMPTONSHIRE							
25.1	BROOKSHAW OUNDLE	C	I	O	S	Halfpenny 1771	Batty 1786A	
25.2	G NEALE/R. READ/GILSBRO Medium letters with serifs	C	I	R	S	Penny 1797	D. G. Vorley	before 1849
	TA Large letters with serifs	C	I	O				
25.3	RICKMAN/PETERBORO' Very small letters: 1st line with serifs, 2nd line plain	C	I	2XO	S	Halfpenny 1862	British Museum	1874–1906
*25.4	↑/M.S.D/WEEDON Large (2nd line) and medium (3rd line) letters with serifs [Military Stores Depot]	C	I	†	STORES CHECK	Penny size blank (34mm)	J. G. Scott	
26	NORTHUMBERLAND							
*26.1A	ALNWICK Medium letters with serifs	C	I	R	S or U	Halfpenny 1806	J. G. Scott	
B	ALNWICK Large letters with serifs	C	I	R	S or U	Penny 1797	C. Brunel	
26.2	.IOHN BELL. (curved)/BOOKSELLER.QUAY (curved) forming a circle round shield with 3 castles Medium letters with serifs, reversed for sealing [Newcastle upon Tyne]	E	I	†	S	Halfpenny †	D. G. Vorley	1811

For key to column headings, please refer to page 19.

NUMBER	LEGEND	A	B	C	D	COIN TYPE	SOURCE REFERENCE	APPROX. DATE
26.3	JOHN ELLIOTT (curved)/1814/ TOBACCONIST/QUAY-SIDE (curved)/ NEWCASTLE (curved) 'indented and inverted'	C	I	O		Halfpenny George II	Batty 1823 (cf Davis 34)	1814
					T or S			
	SWEET, LOVELY, TENDER VIRTUOUS WOMAN	E	I	R				
26.4	IOHN/LEIGHTON/N. CASTLE	E	I	O	S	Halfpenny †	Barnard BNJ 1918 No. 224	
	NICHOLAS/TEMPERLEY	E	I	R				
26.5	.YELLOLEY'S POTTERY. (curved)/OUSEBURN (curved) in a dotted circle (22.5mm) around an inner dotted circle (13mm) with value 5/- Small letters with serifs	C	R	†	T	Halfpenny blank (25mm)	Cokayne Sale 1946 Lot 118 J. G. Scott	1801
27	**NOTTINGHAMSHIRE**							
27.1	I. CHEETHAM NOTTINGHAM 1790	C	I	R	S?	Anglesey Mines Halfpenny 1788	Batty 3005	1790
28	**OXFORDSHIRE**							
*28.1A	CARTHEW/CUTLER/BISTER Small (1st & 3rd lines) and very small (2nd line) letters with serifs [Bicester]	C	I	O	S	Penny 1797	A. G. Davies	1824–44
* B	CARTHEW Small letters with serifs	C	I	†	S	Halfpenny †	J. G. Scott	1824–44
*28.2	GREAT TUE (curved)/SG (script)/OXON (curved) [Great Tew]	E	I	R	S	Halfpenny William III	J. G. Scott	
28.3	THOˢ BUCKLAND/CHIMNEY SWEEPER/ OXFORD Small letters with serifs	C	I	'o'	S	Twopence 1797 cut in half and hollowed out, leaving reverse	J. G. Scott	1840's
*28.4A	ROBINSON (curved)/CUTLER/OXFORD Small letters with serifs	C	I	O	S	Halfpenny 1799	J. G. Scott	
		C	I	O	S	Halfpenny 1806	J. D. Stott J. G. Scott	1825–50
		C	I	O	S	Halfpenny 1807	Dr. G. H. L. Bullmore J. G. Scott	
		C	I	O	S	Irish Halfpenny 1805	British Museum	
		C	I	O	S	Penny 1797	C. Brunel P. Withers	
		C	I	O	S	Penny 1806/7	Jean M. White	
		C	I	O	S	Penny 1806	J. G. Scott	
		C	I	O	S	Penny 1807	J. G. Scott	
* B	ROBINSON (curved)/CUTLER/RAZOR/ MAKER/OXFORD 1st, 2nd & 5th lines small letters with serifs. 3rd & 4th lines medium letters with serifs	C	I	O	S	Penny 1797	Spink: stock May 1971 Waters 6 J. G. Scott C. Brunel	
* C	(Crown)/ROBINSON/OXFORD/CUTLER Medium letters with serifs	C	I	O	S	Halfpenny 1799	J. G. Scott	
		C	I	†	S	†	Batty 1854A	
		C	I	O	S	Irish Halfpenny 1805	Spink: Stock May 1971	
		C	I	O	S	Halfpenny 1806/7	C. Brunel D. G. Vorley	
		C	I	O	S	Penny 1797	Ashmolean Museum J. G. Scott	
		C	I	O	S	Penny 1806/7	D. G. Vorley	
	Variety (i) As above but VR between (crown) and ROBINSON	C	I	O	S	Penny 1797	D. G. Vorley	

For key to column headings, please refer to page 19.

NUMBER	LEGEND	A	B	C	D	COIN TYPE	SOURCE REFERENCE	APPROX. DATE
D	(Crown)/ROBINSON Small letters with serifs	C	I	O	S	Penny 1797	Spink: Stock May 1971	
E	(Crown)/ROBINSON/CUTLER (at right angles)/OXFORD (at right angles) Medium letters with serifs	C	I	O	S	Halfpenny 1806/7	Dr. G. H. L. Bullmore	
		C	I	O	S	Halfpenny 1807	J. G. Scott (2) Ashmolean Museum	
	Variety (i) As above, but with, in addition, to right (Crown)/VR	C	I	O	S	Penny 1797	Spink: Stock May 1971	
* F	ROBINSON/CUTLER (at right angles)/OXFORD (at right angles) Small letters with serifs	C	I	O	S	Halfpenny 1806	J. G. Scott	
		C	I	†	S	Halfpenny 1806	Batty 1854	
		C	I	O	S	Halfpenny 1806/7	C. Brunel	
						Halfpenny 1807	J. G. Scott	
		C	I	O	S	Penny 1797	P. R. Davies	
		C	I	O	S	Penny 1806	D. G. Vorley	
	Variety (i) Large serif'd inverted F in field to right	C	I	O	S	Penny 1797	Spink: Stock May 1971	
* G	ROBINSON/CUTLER/OXFORD 1st line small letters with serifs 2nd & 3rd lines medium letters with serifs	C	I	O	S	Penny 1797 Penny 1806	J. G. Scott J. G. Scott	
29	RUTLAND							
30 *30.1	SHROPSHIRE (head of old man, bearded, with ruff, facing) above, within scroll OLD THO PARR (curved) Medium letters with serifs 2 countermarks in 'tête-bêche' form [Attributed to Alberbury]	C	R	R	S	William III Halfpenny	J. G. Scott	
30.2	. . . . . . RNS CUTTY. P. . . (Southern's Cutty Pipe) in inverted letters within a sunken line (for sealing?) [Attributed to Broseley]	C	R	†	S or U	George III Irish Halfpenny	Batty 1855A	1828–35
*30.3	WINES & SPIRITS (curved)/BY/BOWYER/LUDLOW (curved)	C	I	†	A	Halfpenny †	Batty 1868 Spink: Stock May 1971 J. G. Scott D. G. Vorley	1856–63
30.4A	WINES (curved)/& Spirits by/HARDING/LUDLOW (curved)	C	I	†	A	Halfpenny †	Batty 1869 Spink: Stock May 1971 A. G. Davies D. G. Vorley	1830's
B	WINES AND SPIRITS WHOLESALE & RETAIL BY HARDING LUDLOW	C	I	†	A	Halfpenny †	Montague Guest 1279	
30.5A	WINES/& SPIRITS/V BY MASSEY/LUDLOW T X W45 Large and medium letters with serifs	C C	I I	O R	A	Halfpenny †	Batty 1870	1828–56
B	As obv. last but without V	C	I	O&R	A	Halfpenny †	Batty 1870A	
* C	As obv. last within dotted border	C	I	†	A	Halfpenny †	Batty 1870B A. G. Davies J. G. Scott D. G. Vorley	

For key to column headings, please refer to page 19.

NUMBER	LEGEND	A	B	C	D	COIN TYPE	SOURCE REFERENCE	APPROX. DATE
*30.6	WINES &/SPIRITS/BY I. THOMAS/LATE FARRERS/*LUDLOW* Large and medium letters with serifs	C	I	O&R	A	Halfpenny †	SNC Nov./Dec. 1920. Col. 527 No. 88108	1856–9
		C	I	†	A	Halfpenny †	Ashmolean Museum	
						Halfpenny † (William III?)	J. G. Scott	
						Halfpenny †	D. G. Vorley	
31 31.1A	SOMERSET (TC Monogram?)/Hooper's Arms/Bath/13 Italic lower case letters, with serifs	E	I	R	S	Penny 1806/7	Victoria Art Gallery, Bath	
B	6ᴰ Identical, except that 14 replaces 13	E	I	O		,,	,,	
*31.2A	BATH/CUTLER/THOMAS/Nᵒ 3/COCK (at 45 degrees)/LANE (at right angles) 1st and 2nd lines in small letters with serifs 3rd line very small plain letters 4th line medium letters with serifs remainder, medium plain letters	C	I	R	S	Halfpenny 1773	Dr. G. H. L. Bullmore SCMB Jan. 1971 TP487	1791–3
		C	I	†	S	Halfpenny †	D. G. Vorley	
B	THOMAS/RAZOR MILL/OR Nᵒ 3/COCK LANE/BATH/CUTLER 1st, 5th and 6th lines small letters with serifs 2nd, 3rd and 4th lines medium letters with serifs	C	I	R	S	Halfpenny George II	D. G. Vorley	
31.3	(Unknown Bath trader)	P	–	O	A	Bronze Halfpenny	Royal Mint Records	1884
31.4	A. LOCK DRAPER.&.GROCER.CURRY RIV(EL)L. [or RIVA.L.] forming a circle Small letters with serifs	C	I	O	S	Penny 1797	C. Brunel	1845–58
31.5	HAMBRI Large letters with serifs	C	I	R		Penny 1847	J. G. Scott	
	DGE Large letters with serifs	C	I	O	S or U			
*31.6	TAUNTON in rectangular indent, twice Very small letters with serifs	C	R	R	S or U	Halfpenny 1807	J. G. Scott	
32 32.1	STAFFORDSHIRE JOB/WILKES/DARLASTON/1813	C	†	†	T	Birmingham Workhouse Penny	H. D. Gibbs Sale 1960 Lot 164	1813
*32.2	H WRIGHT/FAZELEY in serrated oval Medium and small letters with serifs	C	I	O	T or S	Counterfeit Halfpenny GEORGUIS II	J. G. Scott	
						Counterfeit Halfpenny 1775	J. G. Scott	
32.3	S. WOODWARD/LICHFIELD/1796 In script	E	I	R	S?	George II Halfpenny	Dr. G. H. L. Bullmore	1796
32.4	ELWEL/FORGE/WEDNESBU(RY) (curved) Medium letters with serifs	C	I	O	S or U	Penny 1806/7	J. G. Scott	1830–50
33 33.1	SUFFOLK BURY W. HOUSE [Attributed to Bury St. Edmunds]	C	I	O&R	T	'Old copper farthings'	Davis 42	
						'Small Dutch coin'	Batty 119	

For key to column headings, please refer to page 19.

NUMBER	LEGEND	A	B	C	D	COIN TYPE	SOURCE REFERENCE	APPROX. DATE
*33.2	B. PARKER (incuse)/(crown) above PARKER at right angles all in indent in relief/ BURY in oval indent in relief Small letters with serifs	C	I&R	O	S	Halfpenny 1806	J. G. Scott	1824–55
*33.3	R. MARJORAM/HADLEIGH in oblong indent Small letters with serifs	C	R	2XR	S	Penny 1797	R. N. P. Hawkins	1830's
33.4	'Try our STANDARD B.B. TEA. 2/- per lb. (curved)/BENNETT/& BROOKES/THE/ Popular Grocers /35, Tavern St/IPSWICH Black print on yellow paper	P	–	†	A	Bronze pennies	Royal Mint records	1881
*33.5	W. SMITH/IPSWICH/CUTLER 1st & 2nd lines in small letters with serifs 3rd line medium letters with serifs	C	I	O	S	Penny 1797	R. N. P. Hawkins	1830–50
34 *34.1	SURREY SQUIRE Medium letters with serifs (C)HARLWOOD Small letters with serifs	C C	I I	O R	S	Halfpenny 1771	J. G. Scott	
*34.2	ROBINSON/FARNHAM Small letters with serifs	C	I	O	S	Halfpenny 1753	J. G. Scott	1822–32
*34.3	(Large crown)/I. C/GUILDFORD Very large (2nd line) and small (3rd line) letters with serifs	C	I	R	S or U	Penny 1797	C. Brunel	1832–46
35 *35.1	SUSSEX W. SHAW/39 OLD STEINE [Brighton] Small letters with serifs	C	I	O	S or A	Penny 1797	C. Brunel	1843–53
35.2	BROADHURST	C	†	†	S or U	Penny 1797	H. D. Gibbs Sale 1960 lot 143	
35.3A	R. BARKER/CUTLER/CHICHESTER	C	I	R	S	Penny 1797	Brighton Museum	1826–39
B	BARKER/CUTLER/CHICHESTER Small letters with serifs	C	I	†	S	Halfpenny †	D. G. Vorley	
35.4	R. BLAKE/CHICHESTER	C	I	R	S	Penny 1797	Brighton Museum	before 1823
*35.5A	JAˢ_ BUDDEN/CHICHESTER Medium letters with serifs	C	I	O	S	Penny 1797	A. G. Davies	1823–51
B	JAˢ_ BUDDEN/CHICHESTER STINTON/HANWORTH	C C	I I	R O	S	Penny 1797	Brighton Museum	1823–51
35.6	TISANOLD/RYE Small plain letters	C	I	R	?	Penny 1907	Seaby: Stock Feb. 1971	
35.7	WALDRO(N) (curved)/(lion rampant)/ GREEN (curved) Large letters with serifs	C	I	O	S	Halfpenny 1799	D. G. Vorley	
36 36.1	WARWICKSHIRE (crown)/VR/ATKIN & SONS (curved)/ BARFORD Sᵀ/BIRMᴹ Large (2nd line) and medium (remainder) letters with serifs	C	I	O	S or U	Twopence 1797	A. G. Davies	1839–47
36.2	Wᴹ BOWN (curved)/308/SUMMER LANE (curved) Small letters with serifs (1st line) and small plain letters (3rd line) [Birmingham]	C	I	O	A or U	Penny 1861	D. G. Vorley	1875–90

For key to column headings, please refer to page 19.

NUMBER	LEGEND	A	B	C	D	COIN TYPE	SOURCE REFERENCE	APPROX. DATE
*36.3	(large ornate crown)/V.R/ B.S.A & M. C⁰/ 1874 Medium (2nd line) and small (3rd line) letters with serifs [Attributed to Birmingham Small Arms & Metal Co. Ltd]	C	I	O&R	P or U	Penny 1866	A. G. Davies	1873–96
36.4	Henry/Wilkins/Pinmaker/Cov^y When this you see remember me	E E	I I	O R	S	Halfpenny †	D. G. Vorley	
36.5	SIMMONS (curved)/WATCH MAKER/ WARWICK (curved) Small letters with serifs	C	I	O	S	Halfpenny 1846	J. G. Scott	1846–53
37	WESTMORLAND							
38 38.1	WILTSHIRE SARUM (twice) Very small letters with serifs	C	I	O	S or U	Penny 1797	J. G. Scott	
39 *39.1	WORCESTERSHIRE Wines (curved)/and Spirit/ Wholefale &/Retail by/Maffey/ KIDDERMINSTER (curved)	C	I	†	A	Halfpenny †	Batty 2781, 2781a British Museum Spink: Stock May 1971 J. G. Scott P. R. Davies D. G. Vorley	
*39.2	J. M. TODD/MOSELEY Small letters with serifs FORGET ME NOT (curved) above flower in oval indent Small letters with serifs	C C	I R	R O	S or A	Penny 1797	C. Brunel	1850–4
39.3	JOSHUA BRIDGES WHERRYMAN MARQUIS OF GRANBY QUAY WORCESTER	C	I	†	S	Penny 1797	SCMB Jan. 1971 TP455	1820
39.4	HIGGINS/FISHING TACK/MAKER/GREEN MAN/ WORCESTER Medium letters with serifs	C	I	†	S	Halfpenny †	Seaby: Stock Feb. 1971 Spink: Stock May 1971 Birmingham Museum	1790– 1820
		C	I	R	S	Halfpenny George II	D. G. Vorley	
40	YORKSHIRE							
40.1	THO MOORE (curved)/RAT/1800 (curved) KILLER (curved)/BEVERLEY (curved) Large letters with serifs	C C	I I	R O	S	Penny 1797	Charles Dobie	1800
40.2	BRADFORD/WORKHOUSE Small letters with serifs in 2 curved indents	C	R	O	T	Birmingham and South Wales Penny	Batty 630	1813
		C	R	O	T	Birmingham Penny 1812 (Davis 65–73)	Batty 551	
		C	R	R	T	Birmingham Penny 1812 (Davis 65–73)	Batty 632 J. G. Scott	
		C	R	R	T	Birmingham Penny 1812 (Davis 74–77)	Batty 631 J. G. Scott (2) cf Davis 50 Duffield 266	

For key to column headings, please refer to page 19.

NUMBER	LEGEND	A	B	C	D	COIN TYPE	SOURCE REFERENCE	APPROX. DATE
*	Varieties: (i) incuse circle 10.5mm diam. between countermarks	C	R & I	R	T	Ditto Davis 74–77	J. G. Scott	
	(ii) J. ORD between Bradford and Workhouse. Medium letters with serifs	C	R & I	R	T	Ditto Davis 65–77	J. G. Scott	
	(iii) BRADFORD stamp missing	C	R	R	T	Ditto Davis 75	C. Brunel	
*40.3A	KEIGHLEY Small letters with serifs in rectangular indent	C	R	O	T	Birmingham Penny 1812 (Davis 65–73)	Batty 645	1818
	KEIGHLEY/KEIGHLEY (curved) Small letters with serifs, 1st line in rectangular indent, 2nd line incuse	C	R & I	R		Birmingham Penny 1812 (Davis 74–77)	Dr. G. H. L. Bullmore Batty 644 J. G. Scott Davis 51	
B	As 40.3A, with GR countermarked in addition to or in place of relief	C	R	O	T	Birmingham & Neath Penny	Batty 649	
	KEIGHLEY on reverse	C	I	R		Birmingham & South Wales Penny	Batty 648 Davis 52	
* C	As 40.3B but countermarked JM	C	R	O	T	Birmingham & South Wales Penny	J. G. Scott	
		C	I	R		Birmingham Penny 1812 (Davis 74–77)	Batty 646	
						Birmingham & Neath Penny	Batty 650 Davis 53	
D	As 40.3B but countermarked WW	C	R	O	T	Walthamstow Penny	Batty 647 Davis 54	
		C	I	R		Bilston Penny (Davis 33–36)	SCMB July 1972 p. 296	
E	KEIGHLEY (curved) Medium letters with serifs	C	I	R	T	Hull Lead Works Penny 1812	Spink Stock: August 1971	
*40.4	T. REXTON (or T. R. EXTON)/K:H Large plain letters within rectangular indent. Lower corners cut away [Attributed to Kingston-upon-Hull]	C	R	†	S	Penny 1797	F. Banks	
40.5	0/1881 ◦/(PH)OENIX/4 lb ½ oz [Attributed to Rotherham]	₊C C	I I	O R	U	Halfpenny 1750	J. G. Scott	
40.6	HILL/HAT MAKER/SCARBRO Large letters with serifs, reversed for sealing	C	I	O	S	Sweden 2 Or. 1760	Dr. G. H. L. Bulmore	
40.7	W. HARGREAVES SETTLE	E	I	†	S?	Barnsley Penny token	SCMB June 1969 TP200	
*40.8	£.s.d. within a diamond [Attributed to Edgar Allen & Co., Sheffield]	C	I	O	P or U	Halfpenny 1861	J. G. Scott	after 1870
40.9	BEST'S (Crown) twice Large letters with serifs [Attributed to Sheffield]	C	I	R	U	Penny 1797	Seaby: Stock Feb. 1971	
40.10	JAMES BINGHAM/UNIVERSALLY APPROVED/CONGRUENT RAZOR/NEWCHURCH ST SHEFFIELD in 4-sided indent with curved ends Very small letters with serifs	C	I	O	S or U	Penny 1797	D. G. Vorley	1833–41

For key to column headings, please refer to page 19.

NUMBER	LEGEND	A	B	C	D	COIN TYPE	SOURCE REFERENCE	APPROX. DATE
40.11	BRAMALL Very small letters with serifs	C	I	O	S or U	Halfpenny 1799	J. G. Scott	1840–60
40.12	W BRISCOE & SON TOLEDO STEEL H CUTLER OLD ENGLISH STEEL	C C	I I	O R	S or U	Halfpenny 1806	Batty 3976A	1840's
40.13	(dagger)/(maltese cross)/ΓYAS/BROO(M)/HEAD QUIT to left ELAM to right Medium letters with serifs except Broomhead (small)	C	I	O	U	Halfpenny William III	J. G. Scott	
40.14	L. CADMAN four times, BEN GALL	C	I	†	S or U	Halfpenny 1744	Duffield 1518	1787
40.15	J&R CARR CAST STEEL 51 (Two Dogs pointing, under one STANCH)	C	I	†	P or U	Halfpenny 1861	Batty 4021D	1861–77
*40.16	C CONGREVE/SHEAR STEEL (twice)/SANDERSON/SHEAR STEEL JAMES FOX/SHEAR STEEL/(2 stars)/RHH HH RH/V (Crown) R/SHEAR STEEL Small letters with serifs except RHH HH RH (medium)	C C	I I	R O	U	Penny 1797	C. Brunel	1830–45
*40.17	1772 Small figures with serifs [Attributed to Jonathan Dungworth, Sheffield]	C	I	R	U	Halfpenny 1729 (pierced)	J. G. Scott	1787–97
40.18	T. ELLIN & Cº (curved)/SHEAR STEEL/(anchor) Small letters with serifs	C	I	R	S or U	Penny 1797	Ulster Museum	1825–53
40.19	J. FENTON/& SONS/SHEFFIELD Very small letters with serifs	C	I	4XO	U	Halfpenny 1862(?)	C. Brunel	1875–1900
40.20	A. FIELD/SHEFFIELD Small plain letters	C	I	O	S or U	Farthing 1853	C. P. C. Parish	1870's
40.21	GROVES/SHEFFIELD Small letters with serifs	C	I	O	S or U	France: Liard 1773 W	Sheffield Museum	before 1830
40.22	W. HALL/W. HALL/CAST STEEL/W. HALL Medium (1st & 4th lines) and small (2nd & 3rd lines) letters with serifs	C	I	O	S or U	Penny 1797	D. G. Vorley	1840's
*40.23A	W. I. HORN & Cº (curved)/SHEFFIELD Medium letters with serifs, in semi-circular serrated indent	C	R	R	U	Penny 1806/7	J. G. Scott	1833–75
B	W. I. HORN & Cº /CAST STEEL Small letters with serifs	C	I	O	U	Halfpenny 186?	J. G. Scott	186?–75
40.24	B. HUNTSMAN in a rectangle	C	R	O	U	Halfpenny 1739	Batty 4299B	
40.25	T. MANNING & Cº SHEFFIELD	C	I	O	U	Penny 1862	Batty 2939G	1862–77
*40.26	(open crown on its side) PEKIN Small plain letters [Attributed to Marsden & Beeten]	C	I	O	U	Penny 1862	J. G. Scott	1893–1931
40.27	MOILLIET & GEM (curved)/(three crowns)/WARRANTED (curved) Small letters with serifs	C	I	O	S or U	Halfpenny 1806/7	D. G. Vorley	1852–6

For key to column headings, please refer to page 19.

NUMBER	LEGEND	A	B	C	D	COIN TYPE	SOURCE REFERENCE	APPROX. DATE
40.28	(Scales)/WILLIAM MORTO(N)/SHEFFIELD (BOS)COMBE SPA in a scroll round HOTEL in an oval Small letters with serifs	C C	I I	R O	U	Penny 1874 H	D. G. Vorley	1875–90
40.29	NEWBOULD & C⁰ NEWBOULD	C	I	†	U	Halfpenny 1720	Batty 4478A	
40.30	PEACE BROS/ SHEFFIELD Small letters with serifs To left, at right angles, 2 lis with a diamond above	C	I	R	U	Halfpenny 1799	Spink: Stock May 1971	1850's
*40.31	S. PEACE & CO/T Medium (1st line) and large (2nd line) letters with serifs CAST.STEEL/S.PEACE & CO (inverted)/ CAST.STEEL Small (1st & 3rd lines) and medium (2nd line) letters with serifs	C C	I I	O R	U	Halfpenny 1851	J. G. Scott	
40.32	EPHO(D) Medium letters with serifs [Attributed to Abraham Revel]	C	I	O&R	U	Halfpenny †	J. G. Scott	1787
40.33	SANDERSON SANDERSON & KIRK SANDERSON SANDERSON & KIRK	C C	I I	O R	S or U	Sheffield Penny 1815 (Davis 134–5)	Batty 671	1815–20
40.34	SMITH & HAWKSLEY'S /CELEBRATED RAZOR/ SHEFFIELD/HOLY (inverted) R (Crown) S/L/WARRANTED/(crown)/V Small letters with serifs	C C	I I	O R	S or U	Penny 1806/7	D. G. Vorley	1845–60
40.35	(Maltese cross) ROBERT. SORBY SHEFFIELD EDMUNDSON DUBLIN	C C	I I	O R	S or U	Halfpenny 1806	Batty 2939B	1830's
40.36	SPENCER CAST STEEL	C	I	R	S or U	Halfpenny 1807	Batty 4838A	1830 s
40.37	SPUR (three times)	C	I	O	U	Counterfeit Halfpenny 1775	Batty 4838B	
40.38	STU . . . . 74 SHEFFIELD	C	I	†	P or U	Farthing 1806	Batty 2939A	
40.39	THOMPSON CAST STEEL CAST STEEL	C C	I I	R O	S or U	Farthing 1837	Batty 2572	
*40.40	T. TILLOTSON/COLUMBIA PLACE/SHEFFIELD Small letters with serifs	C	I	O&R	S or U	Penny 1797	A. G. Davies	1849–59
40.41	MERIT SHEFFIELD TWIGG BROˢ & C⁰ BROOM HALL WORKS TWIGG BROˢ & C⁰ BROOM HALL WORKS LEVISON & SHERMAN FENTON & MARSDENS SHEFFIELD	C C	I I	O R	S or U	Halfpenny 1806	Batty 2939	1840's
40.42	W. A. TYZACK & Co/(ST)ELLA WORKS Very small plain letters 66 Medium figures	C C	I I	R O	P or U	Halfpenny 1861	J. G. Scott	1875–1900
40.43	(Portuguese cross)/LISBON [Attributed to Thomas Warburton]	C	I	O	U	Halfpenny 1773	Batty 5102A	1774–1829
40.44	WARD & PAYNE (curved)/ W (crossed hammers over anvil) P/ SHEFFIELD T. TURNER/& CO./SHEFFIELD Very small letters with serifs	C C	I I	2XR O	U	Penny 1862	D. G. Vorley	1875–1900

For key to column headings, please refer to page 19.

NUMBER	LEGEND	A	B	C	D	COIN TYPE	SOURCE REFERENCE	APPROX. DATE
40.45	H. WRAGG SHEFFIELD	C	I	R	S or U	Halfpenny 1807	Batty 2939H	1840's
40.46	W. YATES (5 times) CAST STEEL (several times)	C	I	O	U	Penny 1797	Ashmolean Museum	1856–84
	W. YATES (twice) ⅍—	C	I	R				
40.47	Dringhouses/York. Small Old English letters in an oval indent	C	R	O	S	Penny 1797	C. P. C. Parish	before 1850
40.48	HARRISON. SPRING STEEL YORK CITY (Three Crowns)	C C	I I	O R	S or U	Early Irish Halfpenny George III	Batty 2973D	
40.49	PRINCE YORK	C	I	O	S	Penny 1797	Duffield 1484	1805–17

WALES & MON-MOUTH

NUMBER	LEGEND	A	B	C	D	COIN TYPE	SOURCE REFERENCE	APPROX. DATE
41	ANGLESEY							
42	BRECKNOCK							
43	CAERNARVON							
44	CARDIGAN							
45	CARMARTHEN							
46	DENBIGH							
47	FLINT							
48	GLAMORGAN							
*48.1	JOYCE/CUTLER Small letters with serifs [Swansea]	C	I	O&R	S	France: 12 deniers 1792 N	J. G. Scott Batty 4317B	1840's
48.2	J. LOCK GROCER SWANSEA	C	I	†	S	Penny 1797	SCMB June 1969 TP261	1860–79
49	MERIONETH							
50	MONMOUTH							
*50.1	Wines/and Spirits/Wholesale/and Retail by/Mafsey/Abergavenny (curved) within dotted border	C	I	†	A	Halfpenny †	J. G. Scott	1811
51	MONTGOMERY							
52	PEMBROKE							
53	RADNOR							

SCOTLAND

NUMBER	LEGEND	A	B	C	D	COIN TYPE	SOURCE REFERENCE	APPROX. DATE
54	ABERDEEN							
54.1	W. ANDREW/KEMNAY	C	I	†	P or S	'A Russian coin' (Penny-size)	SNC Nov./Dec. 1920 col. 527 no. 88091	1853–93
55	ANGUS							
55.1	A. BUTCHART in a circle	C	†	†	T	Bodle, Charles II	SNC Apr. 1933 p. 131	1860–1
56	ARGYLL							

For key to column headings, please refer to page 19.

NUMBER	LEGEND	A	B	C	D	COIN TYPE	SOURCE REFERENCE	APPROX. DATE
57	AYR							
*57.1	J & T YOUNG (curved)/AYR/N<u>o</u> 69 Medium letters with serifs	C	I	O&R	P or S	Penny 1866	J. G. Scott	1866–88
57.2	CATRINE COTTON. WORKS. in circle Small letters with serifs 4/9 in circle in centre	C	R	†	T	Irish Halfpenny 1805	Cokayne Sale 1946 Lot 122	1795–1805
58	BANFF							
59	BERWICK							
60	BUTE							
60.1A	PAYABLE AT ROTHSAY MILLS + in a circle Small letters with serifs	C	R	†	T	Halfpenny George III	Davis 65 Duffield 1535	1813–26
		C	R	†	T	Halfpenny 1774	Batty 3248A	
		C	R	†	T	Counterfeit Halfpenny 1775	Batty 3248B	
		C	R	O	T	Halfpenny 1772	Dr. G. H. L. Bullmore	
		C	R	†	T	Irish Halfpenny George III †	SCMB Aug. 1958 NT65A	
		C	R	O	T	Penny, George III	Duffield 292	
		C	R	†	T	Halfpenny Token John Wilkinson	Bliss Sale Cat. Lot 796	
		C	R	O	T	Glasgow Halfpenny 1791	Batty 3248 J. G. Scott	
		C	R	O	T	Anglesey Halfpenny 1793	H. D. Gibbs Sale 1960 Lot 303	
		C	R	†	T	Anglesey Halfpenny	Thellusson Sale Lot 386	
		C	R	†	T	Edinburgh Halfpenny †	SCMB Aug. 1958 NT65	
B	PAYABLE AT ROTHSAY COTTON MILLS in a circle, in the centre a woolsack	C	R	†	T	Halfpenny George III	Davis 66 Birmingham Museum	
61	CAITHNESS							
62	CLACKMANNAN							
62.1A	ALLOA COLLIERY	C	†	†	T	19th century token Halfpenny	Duffield 319	
B	+PAYABLE AT ALLOA COLLIERY In a circle Small letters with serifs	C	R	†	T	Halfpenny, George II and George III	Davis 70 Duffield 1533 Birmingham Museum	
63	DUMFRIES							
63.1	LOCHMABEN	C	I	†	T	Penny 1806	SCMB Jan. 1971 TP379 Dumfries Museum	
64	DUNBARTON							
64.1	DUMBARTON HALFPENNY in a circle around G + L	C	R	†	T	Halfpenny blank	Cokayne Sale 1946 Lot 135	
65	EAST LOTHIAN							
66	FIFE							
67	INVERNESS							
68	KINCARDINE							
69	KINROSS							

For key to column headings, please refer to page 19.

NUMBER	LEGEND	A	B	C	D	COIN TYPE	SOURCE REFERENCE	APPROX. DATE
70	KIRKUDBRIGHT							
71	LANARK							
71.1	DC Large letters [Attributed to David Cummings, Glasgow]	C	I	†	T	Halfpenny †	Cokayne Sale 1946 Lot 207	c.1810
71.2	LANARK. COTTON. MILLS. (curved) Small letters with serifs In the centre a shield of arms under thistle sprigs Monogram TCD (script) above	C	R	†	T	Bodle, William III Brass farthing size flan	Davis 88 Cokayne Sale 1946 Lot 167 National Museum of Antiquities, Edinburgh David McFarlan	
72	MIDLOTHIAN							
*72.1	J. S in a rectangular indent with corners cut away struck over CRAMOND in a rectangular indent Large (J. S) and medium (CRAMOND) letters with serifs. Also 24 incuse	C	R	†	S, P or U	Penny 1806/7	J. G. Scott	1864
*72.2	.WILKISON. (curved)/EDINBURGH (curved) Small letters with serifs In the centre a thistle	C	R	†	T, S or U	Halfpenny †	Davis (88a) Birmingham Museum	1820's
72.3	Jo Yetts/EDIN^B	E	I	†	S or P	Halfpenny †	City Museum, St. Albans	1775-1835
*72.4	LEITH MILLS Medium letters with serifs (crown)/LEITH MILLS Medium letters with serifs	C C	I I	O R	S or U	Penny 1806/7	C. Brunel	
73	MORAY							
73.1	ELGIN Large letters with serifs	C	I	O	S or U	Irish Halfpenny 1805	J. G. Scott	
74	NAIRN							
75	ORKNEY							
76	PEEBLES							
77	PERTH							
77.1A	ADELPHI COTTON WORK in a circle Large letters with serifs In the centre a woolsack Four/Shillings/and/Six Pence/1786	C C	R R	O R	T	Halfpenny George III	Davis 90 Batty 3942 Cokayne Sale 1946 Lot 171	1786
B	Similar to 77.1A Shilling/and/Six Pence/1/6	C C	R R	O R	T	Halfpenny 1774	Cokayne Sale 1946 Lot 172	1786
C	Similar to obv. 77.1A Righthand knot over the R in WORK	C	R	O	T	Halfpenny George III Irish Halfpenny 1769 Counterfeit Halfpenny George III	Davis 91 Batty 3941 J. G. Scott Batty 3941A Bliss Sale Cat. Lot 809	1785-94

For key to column headings, please refer to page 19.

NUMBER	LEGEND	A	B	C	D	COIN TYPE	SOURCE REFERENCE	APPROX. DATE
D	ADELPHI ✳ COTTON WORK ✳ In a circle. Righthand knot over the O in WORK	C	R	O	T	Halfpenny †	Davis 92 Batty 3943	1785–94
		C	R	†	T	Halfpenny George III	Bliss Sale Cat. Lot 809 Cokayne Sale 1946 Lot 173	
E	A . . . COTTON WORKS round woolsack	C	†	†	T	Farthing George III	SNC Apr. 1933 p. 131	
*77.2	DEANSTON COTTON MILL in a circle Large letters with serifs	C	R	O	T	Halfpenny Charles II Bawbee Charles II Halfpenny George II Halfpenny George III Counterfeit Halfpenny George III Penny 1797 Dundee Halfpenny W. Crooms Manchester Halfpenny	Batty 3452 Davis 94 SCMB May 1949 p.248 Davis 94 Bliss Sale Cat. Lot 811 Duffield 270 SNC Nov. 1905 No. 21968 SCMB Mar. 1965 p.119	after 1794
		C	R	R	T	Irish Halfpenny George II	J. G. Scott	
*77.3	DUN. MᶜLAREN MERCHᵀ·. LOCHEARN. In a circle. Large letters with serifs	C	R	R	T	Coventry Halfpenny 1793 (Pro Bono Publico type) Dundee Halfpenny 1797 D & H 18–20 Halfpenny George II or III	Davis 95 J. G. Scott Cokayne Sale 1946 Lot 176	
77.4	PERTH Small letters with serifs	C	I	1XO 2XR	S or U	Dublin Penny Token 1816 (Davis 10)	J. G. Scott	
78	**RENFREW**							
78.1	J. MᶜLEAN (curved)/Cott: St. Paisley (curved) in oval around 5/3 in centre	C	R	O	T	Penny 1797	Cokayne Sale 1946 Lot 196	1812–13
78.2	JOHN MORRIS/.PAISLEY. Small letters with serifs in a circle 5/3 in centre within a cable circle	C	R	†	T	Penny George III	Purvey ST86A	1812
78.3	ROBᵀ CRIGHTON. (curved)/Pᵀ GLASGOW Medium letters with serifs forming a circle	C	I	†	T	Halfpenny George III	Cokayne Sale 1946 Lot 146	
78.4	.RENFREW. Vᵀ SOCIETY in a circle Medium letters with serifs	C	R	O	T	Halfpenny George II	H. D. Gibbs Sale 1960 Lot 275	before 1828
79	**ROSS & CROMARTY**							
80	**ROXBURGH**							
81	**SELKIRK**							
82	**SHETLAND**							

For key to column headings, please refer to page 19.

NUMBER	LEGEND	A	B	C	D	COIN TYPE	SOURCE REFERENCE	APPROX. DATE
83	STIRLING							
83.1	BALFRON FRUIT forming a circle	C	R	O	T	Middlesex Halfpenny 1795 (D & H 292–3) Glasgow token	Duffield 1534 Duffield 1534	
83.2	BALFRON: VICT: SOCIETY in a circle	C	R	†	T	Halfpenny George III	Duffield 263	
		C	R	O	T	Halfpenny 1772	Cokayne Sale 1946 Lot 138	
83.3	ZUILL BALFRON in a circle	C	R	O	T	Cronebane Halfpenny 1796	Cokayne Sale 1946 Lot 139	
83.4	BALLINDALLOCH COTTON WORK In a circle, in the centre, a woolsack Large letters with serifs	C	R	†	T	Halfpenny George III	Davis 72	
83.5	PAYABLE AT CULCREUCH MILL∗ In a circle, in the centre, incuse THOˢ/WHYTE Small letters with serifs	C	R	†	T	Halfpenny George II (Young head)	SCMB June 1971 p. 233	
		C	R	†	T	Liverpool Halfpenny	SNC Nov. 1905 No. 21971	
		C	R	R	T	Middlesex Halfpenny 1793 (D & H 1033 etc.)	Batty 4482 (cf. Davis 116)	
		C	R	†	T	Middlesex Halfpenny (D & H 1042)	SCMB June 1971 p. 233	
		C	R	R	T	Lancaster Halfpenny (D & H 9 etc.)	Birmingham Museum	
83.6	P. (Payable) BY. ROBERT MᶜNEE FINTRY ∗ in a circle Medium letters with serifs	C	R	†	T	Glasgow 18th century token Halfpenny	Davis 119 Birmingham Museum	
84	SUTHERLAND							
85	WEST LOTHIAN							
86	WIGTOWN							
86.1	CARTY Medium letters with serifs	C	I	†	T or S	Farthing †	Szauer 44 b	
IRELAND IRELAND – NORTHERN								
87	ANTRIM							
88	ARMAGH							
∗88.1	Cᴼ ARMAGH Small letters with serifs	C	I	O	T?	Penny 1797	J. G. Scott Ulster Museum (Szauer 83) C. Brunel	after 1822
88.2 A	IOHN. OVEREND. PORTADOWN ∗ P ∗ III. 1736. I PROMISE TO. PAY. THE BEARER. THREE. PENCE.	C	†	O	T	Halfpenny George II	SNC June 1906 Col. 9138	
		C	†	R		Halfpenny George III	Duffield 284	
B	As 88.2A but rev. I PROMISE TO PAY THREE PENCE	C	†	R	T	Halfpenny 1770–5	Szauer 34	

For key to column headings, please refer to page 19.

NUMBER	LEGEND	A	B	C	D	COIN TYPE	SOURCE REFERENCE	APPROX. DATE
89 89.1	DOWN YOUTH AND BEAUTY (a peacock, left) 2 P behind I/PROMISE/TO PAY THE/BEARER TWO/ PENCE ALLEX/McCLURE/BELLYLONA/ GHAN/1735	C C	R R	O R	T 	Glasgow Halfpenny 1791 (D & H 5d)	Ulster Museum Davis 18 Szauer 35	
89.2A	PAYABLE AT M^{RS} SOMERVILLS. DOWN in a circle Medium letters with serifs	C C C C	† R R †	† O&R O †	T T T T	Halfpenny George III Halfpenny George II or III Macclesfield Halfpenny (Charles Roe) Middlesex Halfpenny	Davis 120 Cokayne Sale 1946 Lot 202 Cokayne Sale 1946 Lot 203 SCMB Dec. 1964	
B	(E. or T.) SOMERVILL DOWN	C	†	†	T	Halfpenny †	SNC April 1933 p. 131 (Szauer 40)	
C	I. SOMERVILL. DOWN in a circle	C	R	R	T	Halfpenny 1771	W. A. Seaby DN:V19	
90 90.1	FERMANAGH INNISKILLING (curved)/(a castle with gateway)/VI·D all in circle Small (1st line) and medium (3rd line) letters with serifs	C	I	R	T, U or Stores Check	Halfpenny 1806	Cokayne Sale 1946 Lot 203 (Szauer 38)	
91 *91.1A	LONDONDERRY D. ALLEN/IMPLEMENT/MAKER/ MONEYMORE 1st line medium letters with serifs 2nd line large plain letters 3rd line large letters with serifs 4th line medium plain letters	C	I	O	S	Penny 1797	Ulster Museum (Szauer 84)	1858–68
91.1B	As 91.1A but D. ALLEN/MONEYMORE/ IMPLEMENT/MAKER	C	I	R	S	Penny 1797	Ulster Museum (Szauer 84)	1858–68
92 *92.1	TYRONE DOUGHERTY added later: A. HAUGHTON & (curved) Large plain letters FINTONA added later: A. HAUGHTON & (curved) Large plain letters	C C	I I	R O	S	Penny 1874	Dr. G. H. L. Bullmore	1892–4
IRELAND – SOUTHERN								
93 93.1	CARLOW TIERNEY (curved)/(star)/APOTHECARY/ (star and four branches)/BAGENALSTOWN (curved) Reversed for sealing Large (1st line) and medium (3rd & 5th lines) letters with serifs	E	I	R	S	Irish Penny 1805	J. G. Scott	1830–50
94 94.1	CAVAN (CAVA)N MURRAY CAVAN	C C	I I	O R	S	Penny 1806	Ulster Museum (Szauer 85)	1824–38 or c. 1846
95	CLARE							

For key to column headings, please refer to page 19.

NUMBER	LEGEND	A	B	C	D	COIN TYPE	SOURCE REFERENCE	APPROX. DATE
96	CORK							
*96.1A	J. J. BUCKLEY/CORK Small plain letters	C	I	O	S	Penny 1860–94 Penny 1904	J. G. Scott M. Scammell	1904–11
* B	J. J. BUCKLEY Small plain letters	C	I	O	S	Penny 1869	J. G. Scott	1904–11
C	J J./CORK Small plain letters	C	I	O	S	Penny 1860–94 (1877?)	J. G. Scott	1904–11
97	DONEGAL							
98	DUBLIN							
*98.1A	BIGGER/BOLTON ST/CUTLER/DUBLIN Small letters with serifs	C	I	R	S	Penny 1797	J. G. Scott Batty 900 Szauer 52	1836–8
* B	JAˢ. IRELAND/BELFAST/BIGGER/36 BOLTON STR(EET)/CUTLER/DUBLIN (G·S on rev.)	C	I	O	S	Penny 1797	Ulster Museum	
* C	BIGGER/DUBLIN Small letters with serifs	C	I	O	S	Penny 1797	J. G. Scott Batty 901 Szauer 53 Szauer 54	
		C	I	†	S	Token Penny 19th cent. (Davis 50/150)		
*98.2	CHRISTIAN/COLE: ALLEY Medium letters with serifs	C	I	O	S	Irish Halfpenny 1682 Irish Halfpenny 1775–82 Counterfeit Irish Halfpenny 1783	D. G. Vorley Szauer 61 J. G. Scott	1795–1806
98.3	R. DELAHOYD Medium letters with serifs	C	I	R	S or U	Irish Halfpenny 1783	Szauer 64	1784–1804
*98.4	(open crown on its side) DUBLIN Very small letters with serifs	C	I	15XO 15XR	S or U	Twopence 1797	British Museum	
		C	I	R	S or U	Penny 1806	J. G. Scott	
98.5	GEALE (curved)/&/MACBRIDE/17/WESTMORLAND/STREET/DUBLIN (curved) FASHIONABLE (curved)/(ornamentation)/FURNISHING/(ornamentation)/IRONMONGERS (curved) Small letters with serifs	C	I	O		Halfpenny †	D. G. Vorley	1806–16
		C	I	R	A			
*98.6	M. GRIFFIN (curved) Large letters with serifs	C	I	O	S	Irish Halfpenny 1782	Szauer 70	1824
		C	I	R	S	Dublin Halfpenny 1792 (D & H 362)	C. Brunel	
*98.7	W. KAVANAGH (curved)/& SON/DUBLIN (curved) Small plain letters	C	I	R	S or U	Penny 1861	J. G. Scott	1890–1900
*98.8	75/Summer Hill./E. KEOGH'S/Gentlemen's First-Class/Hairdressing Saloon./Razors/Carefully/Ground and/Set. Black print on white label, 29mm	P	–	R	A	Penny 1895–1901	J. G. Scott	1901–10
98.9	MᶜMAHON/CUTLER/28 PILL LANE Small and (3rd line) very small letters with serifs	C	I	O	S	Penny 1797	D. G. Vorley	1846–8

For key to column headings, please refer to page 19.

NUMBER	LEGEND	A	B	C	D	COIN TYPE	SOURCE REFERENCE	APPROX. DATE
*98.10	OSBORNE/DUBLIN Very small letters with serifs	C	I	O	S	Penny 1797	J. G. Scott	1839–60
98.11	VICKERS SS	C C	I I	O R	S or U	Irish Farthing 1760	Szauer 160	1824
99 99.1	GALWAY MENLOUGH CASTLE 6D	C	I	†	S	Dublin: Camac Halfpenny Token	Batty 3890 Davis & Waters 31 Szauer 37	1819
100	KERRY							
101	KILDARE							
102	KILKENNY							
103	LEITRIM							
104	LEIX (QUEEN'S)							
105	LIMERICK							
106	LONGFORD							
107	LOUTH							
108 *108.1	MAYO MALVERNBURY/HOLLYMOUNT Small letters with serifs	C	I	O	S	Penny 1876H	J. G. Scott	
109 109.1	MEATH I. MITCHELL. H(ill of). DOWN In a circle	C	R	†	T	Dundee Halfpenny Halfpenny 1806	H. D. Gibbs Sale 1960 Lot 154 Davis 135 Szauer 36 Cokayne Sale 1946 Lot 203	
109.2	TRIM Small letters with serifs	C	I	O&R	S or U	Penny 1884	British Museum	
110	MONAGHAN							
111 111.1	OFFALY (KING'S) B. EGAN. BIRR Medium letters with serifs	C	I	O&R	S	Twopence 1797	Szauer 225	1830–54
112	ROSCOMMON							
113	SLIGO							
114	TIPPERARY							
115	WATERFORD							
116 116.1	WESTMEATH ATHLONE Small letters with serifs	C	I	O	S or U	Halfpenny 1863	J. G. Scott	
*116.2	J^N GEOGHEGAN (curved)/KILBEGGAN Medium plain letters (crude work) B Large letter with serifs	C C	I I	O R	S	Penny 1862	J. G. Scott	1875–1900
117	WEXFORD							
118	WICKLOW							

For key to column headings, please refer to page 19.

NUMBER	LEGEND	A	B	C	D	COIN TYPE	SOURCE REFERENCE	APPROX. DATE
CHANNEL ISLANDS & ISLE OF MAN								
119	GUERNSEY AND DEPENDENCIES							
120	JERSEY							
120.1	SULLIVAN (curved)/W. MOLLET/ W. MOLLET Small (1st line) and medium (remainder) letters with serifs	C	I	R	S	Jersey 1/26 shilling 1841	Seaby: Stock Feb. 1971	1875– 1900
121	ISLE OF MAN							
UNAT- TRIBUTED								
122	NAMES							
122.5	9/(tiger)/W. ADAMS/7 Medium letters with serifs	C	I	O	S, P or U	Penny 1797	Birmingham Museum	
	INGALL Medium letters with serifs	C	I	R				
122.10A	(crown)/E/S. BAGSHAW	C	I	†	S, P or U	Halfpenny George II Halfpenny George III	SNC Dec. 1908 Col. 11079–80 Duffield 340	
B	(crown)/I/S. BAGSHAW	C	I	†	S, P or U	†	SNC Dec. 1908 Col. 11079–80	
122.12	F.BALL/WAS/ESTABLISHED/FEBY 7TH/1766 F. BALL/WAS BORN/JANY 30TH/1740	E E	I I	O R	S or U	Halfpenny †	D. G. Vorley	1766
122.15	C. BAXTER/1s Large letters with serifs	C	I	†	S	Thin penny-size flan pierced centre	C. Brunel	
122.20	(cock) G. BEDFORD	C	I	R	S, P or U	Leith Halfpenny 1796	Batty 3441	
*122.25	BEST (double struck) Large letters with serifs B (incuse) (lion standing to right) in relief within indent	C C	I I&R	O R	U	Penny 1797	C. Brunel	
122.28	S. BOWKER Medium letters with serifs	C C	I I	O R	S S	Halfpenny 1750–55 Halfpenny George III	Ulster Museum Batty 3976	
122.29	BRADLEY/CAST/STEEL in a rectangle Medium letters with serifs *HILL* (curved)/BRIDGWATER (curved) forming a circle around rectangle Slightly larger letters with serifs	C	I	O&R	S or U	Penny 1797	D. G. Vorley	
122.30	.BRIGDEN J. B in crown-above-rectangle-shaped serrated indent JB (4 times) Large letters with serifs	C C C	I R I	R O O	S or U	Penny 1797	J. G. Scott	
*122.32	W. H. BROADFOOT Small plain letters	C	I	R	S or U	France: 2 Sols 1791–3 God protects the Just Medalet by Kettle	J. G. Scott C. Brunel	

For key to column headings, please refer to page 19.

NUMBER	LEGEND	A	B	C	D	COIN TYPE	SOURCE REFERENCE	APPROX. DATE
122.33	BROTHERS & C⁰ Small letters with serifs	C	I	O	U	Penny 1826	J. G. Scott	
	COMPANY/CAST STEEL/(Keyhole?) Medium letters with serifs	C	I	R				
122.35	M. BRYAN. M.B.	C	I	R	S, P or U	Lancaster Halfpenny 1792 (D & H 21–28)	Batty 500	
122.40	CAMPBELL/& C⁰ Medium letters with serifs Also, at right angles BARKER/WILLIAMS Large letters Similarly	C	I	O				
					P or U	Penny 1862 (pierced 12 o'c)	A. G. Davies	
	CAMPBELL/& C⁰ and BARKER	C	I	R				
122.42A	CAST STEEL Three times forming a triangle	C	I	†	U	Isle of Man Penny 1798	Duffield 1498	
B	CAST/STEEL Small letters with serifs	C	I	O	U	Penny 1797	A. G. Davies	
122.45	CITY/PRISON Small plain letters	C	I	2XR	P or U	Penny 1884	Charles Dobie	
122.50	F & T CLARK	C	I	O&R	S	Halfpenny 1806	Batty 4004	
*122.55	T (diamond) in semi-circle/JOSEPH/ CLARK in rectangle Very small letters with serifs	C	I	R	S or U	Halfpenny 1806/7	P. R. Davies	
122.58	THE (curved)/CONCINNUM (curved) Small letters with serifs	C	I	O	A or U	Halfpenny 1862–92	D. G. Vorley	
122.60	(Crown) COTTON M BRIDGE	C	I	R	S, P or U	Penny 1797	Montague Guest 1413	
122.65	CRYPTOCONCHOIDSYPHONOSTOMATA round CHARLES/COLLETTE/1875 in a circle	E	I	R	S or U	Penny 1860–94	D. G. Vorley	1875
122.68	(crown)/W. DAVIS in a shaped indent Medium letters with serifs	C	R	O	S or U	Penny 1797	D. G. Vorley	
122.70	DEAKON & CO/PATENT	C	I	†	S, P or U	Penny 1797	H. D. Gibbs Sale 1960 Lot 165	
122.72	D (3 times) Large letter with serifs DE/MILT (twice), WALKER (twice), GIBSON, PS, D (twice) Small letters with serifs	C	I	R	U	Twopence 1797	J. G. Scott	
122.74	J. DOLLARD/ID/(sailing ship) Medium (1st line) and large (2nd line) letters with serifs	C	I	O	S	Irish Halfpenny 1775	Szauer 67	
		C	I	†	S	Irish Halfpenny 1781	Szauer 68	
122.75	DRIVE Small letters with serifs	C	I	O	U	Halfpenny 1771	J. G. Scott	
*122.76	DUNG/FORD (twice), WOOD/WARD WOOD/WARD (three times) Very small letters with serifs	C C	I I	O R	U	Penny 1797	J. G. Scott	

For key to column headings, please refer to page 19.

NUMBER	LEGEND	A	B	C	D	COIN TYPE	SOURCE REFERENCE	APPROX. DATE
122.78	(Crown) DURHAM	C	I	†	S, P or U	†	SNC Dec. 1908 Col. 11079–80	
*122.80	(triangle)/EASTERN/CUTLERY/COMP^Y and 4 dots Very small plain letters CAST/STEEL Very small letters with serifs	C C	I I	O 2XR	A or U	Penny 1861	J. G. Scott	
122.81	GIVES INSTROCTIONS IN DRAWING (curved)/ ON RESENABLE (curved)/S. Eddy (Old English letters)/TERMES/PORTRAIT PANINTER (curved) reversed for sealing	E	I	O	S	Penny 1797	D. G. Vorley	
122.83	J. FITZ–P Large letters with serifs	C	I	O	S	Irish Halfpenny 1776 Irish Halfpenny 1782	Szauer 72 Szauer 71	
*122.85	B.FLETCHER/WARRANTED/CAST STEEL Small letters with serifs 20 Large figures	C C	I I	O R	P	Penny 1863	J. G. Scott	
122.88	FORREST Large letters with serifs	C	I	O	S	Penny 1797	British Museum J. G. Scott	
122.90	C. GEE & SON	C	I	R	S	Halfpenny 1799	Batty 4098E	
122.95	S. GIBSON INVENTOR	C	I	O	S or U	Walthamstow Halfpenny 1811 (Davis 17–26)	Batty 217	
122.100	V. GILPIN (1st I over H)/ ..DGES MILLS/H.T 5/H.T/GILPIN MILLS	C C	I I	O R	U	Penny 1797	Ashmolean Museum	
122.103	HAMPSTEAD R^D Small letters with serifs	C	I	R	S or U	Halfpenny 1807	J. G. Scott	
*122.105	HANDCUT Medium plain letters	C	I	O	U	Halfpenny 1885	J. G. Scott	
122.107	(Crown)/HILDICK Large letters with serifs	C	I	IXO 2XR	S or U	Halfpenny 1806/7	C. Brunel	
122.108	T. HOBSON Small letters with serifs	C C	I I	R O	T or S T or S	Brighton Halfpenny (D & H 3a) Brighton Halfpenny (D & H 3a)	J. G. Scott J. G. Scott Batty 2150	
122.110	(Standing angel, left) IN HOC to left, SIGNO above, VINCES to right Small letters with serifs in rectangular indent	C	R	O	S or U	Halfpenny George II	A. G. Davies	
122.120	T. KELLY Medium letters with serifs	C C	I I	O †	S S	Irish Halfpenny 1775–82 (2 examples) Irish Halfpenny 1781	Szauer 77 Szauer 78	

For key to column headings, please refer to page 19.

NUMBER	LEGEND	A	B	C	D	COIN TYPE	SOURCE REFERENCE	APPROX. DATE
*122.125	A. LEE (3 times), PATENT (curved, twice) Small letters with serifs PATENT (curved) Medium letters with serifs (crown)/GR Small letters with serifs PATENT (curved) Small letters with serifs, blundered	C C	I I	R O	 U	Halfpenny 1807	J. G. Scott	
122.127	Lip/Salve (reversed for sealing)	E	I	R	S or U	Halfpenny George II	D. G. Vorley	
122.132	(Crown)/R MINIFIE Large letters with serifs	C	I	IXO 2XR	S or U	Anglesey Halfpenny 1788 (D & H 273)	J. G. Scott	
122.135	(Fox running) J. MITCHELL	C	I	†	S or U	Penny 1797	SCMB Jan. 1971 TP476	
122.150	THE OLYMPIC BRACE	C	I	†	U	Penny 1861	A. Watson	
122.152	OSBORN Small letters with serifs	C	I	O	T or S	Halfcrown 1688 Twopence 1797	J. G. Scott J. G. Scott	
122.155	W. PAR[KER or KES] (curved)/Swan Large letters with serifs	C	I	O&R	S	Irish Halfpenny 1769	R. N. P. Hawkins	
122.158	PATEN(T)/& AXLE/1246 Very large letters with serifs	C	I	O	U	Penny 1797	D. G. Vorley	
122.160A	PATENT (curved) Very small letters with serifs	C	I	O&R	U	Dublin Penny 1815 (Davis 52) Overstruck on Davis 22–24	C. Brunel	
B	PATENT Medium plain letters	C	I	O	U	Penny 186?	A. G. Davies	
122.162	H. PERRY Medium letters with serifs	C	I	O	S	English Halfpenny token, 18th century Irish Halfpenny 1775–82	Szauer 81 Szauer 82	
122.165	POTTS & Cº	C	I	O&R	S	Halfpenny 1806	Batty 4573	
122.170	Qᴿᴺ LOAF Large and medium letters with serifs	C	I	O	S	Penny 1797	National Museum of Wales	
122.171	RACKHAM'S (?) (curved)/IMPROVED/ PATENT (curved)/(large crown) Medium (1st & 3rd lines) and small (2nd line) letters with serifs	C	I	O	S or U	Halfpenny 1807	D. G. Vorley	
122.173	RAVANAGE (?)/FOUNDRY Medium letters with serifs	C	I	O&R	S or U	Penny 1862	D. G. Vorley	
*122.175	T. RICHARDS, (a hand pointing left) below, all in serrated semi-circular indent/H.B (incuse) below Large letters with serifs	C	R&I	O	S or U	Penny 1797	A. G. Davies	
*122.180	ROSS & Cº (curved, twice) Large letters with serifs	C	I	O&R	S	Penny 1797	R. N. P. Hawkins	

For key to column headings, please refer to page 19.

NUMBER	LEGEND	A	B	C	D	COIN TYPE	SOURCE REFERENCE	APPROX. DATE
*122.185	(goat)/J. RUSSELL Medium letters with serifs	C C	I I	† O	S or U S or U	Halfpenny George III Irish Halfpenny 1783	SNC July/Aug. 1922 Col. 367 J. G. Scott	
122.186	SALT in serrated rectangular indent Large letters with serifs	C	R	O	DOCK OR LOAD TICKET	Penny 1806	D. G. Vorley	
122.187	James/Shipdem/1742 A/Tinker	E E	I I	O R	S	Halfpenny †	D. G. Vorley	1742
122.188	SINGER/& CO Medium letters with serifs (R is formed by O struck over top half of K)	C	I	O	P or U	Penny 1862	J. G. Scott	
122.190	V(crown) R/SMITH BROTHERS/ REFINED STEEL Small letters with serifs	C	I	O&R	U	Penny 1863	D. G. Vorley	
122.192	SPRING (five times) and STEEL Small letters with serifs	C	I	O&R	U	South Wales Farthing 1793 (Pro Bono Publico)	Seaby: stock Feb. 1971	
122.195	2 STONE	C	I	O	DOCK OR LOAD TICKET	Penny 1797	Batty 1083	
*122.200	H. STREET (4 times) Large letters with serifs	C	I	O	S	Halfpenny 1799 (pierced)	F. Banks	
122.202	P/SUN Very large (1st line) Medium (2nd line) letters with serifs G T Medium letters with serifs 4 Very large, between	C C E	I I I	† † †	S or P	Halfpenny †	J. G. Scott	
122.203A	V. TAGART Medium letters with serifs	C	I	R	S	Irish Halfpenny 1782	Szauer 227	
B	As A on rev., but with J. TERNAN on obv. Medium letters with serifs	C	I	O&R	S	Irish Halfpenny 1775–82	Szauer 228	
122.205	I. TAYLOR & SON./I TAYLOR & SON D$\underline{O}$ PATENT. I. TAYLOR & SON PATENT.	C C	I I	O R	S or U	Halfpenny 1806	Batty 4879	
122.210	TULLY MARYPORT STREET	C	I	†	S	Halfpenny 1806	Batty 4906	
122.225	P: WARD (curved) BICH: O: W: A: GALAS: in a circular line round IS Large crude letters with serifs	C C	I I	R O	S or P	Penny 1826	J. G. Scott	
122.230	WARRANTED	C	I	O	U	Birmingham Workhouse Threepence 1813	C. Brunel	
122.235	WARRANTED/CAST STEEL Small plain letters	C C	I I	O 4 X O	U U	Penny 1866 Penny 1863	British Museum D. G. Vorley	

For key to column headings, please refer to page 19.

NUMBER	LEGEND	A	B	C	D	COIN TYPE	SOURCE REFERENCE	APPROX. DATE
*122.237	WARRANTED (curved)/(Crown)/PATENT Small letters with serifs UPON AN (curved)/IMPROVED (curved) PATENT (curved) PRINCIPLE (curved, twice) Small letters with serifs	C C	I I	O R	U	Warwickshire Penny Davis 104-5	C. Brunel	
122.238	Oˢ WATSON around (man standing holding a gun in right hand) in ribbed circular indent	C	R	O	S	Halfpenny George II	D. G. Vorley	
122.240	JOHN WILK/APPLEBECK/1884 1st line large letters with serifs 2nd line large plain letters	C	I	R	S, P, or U	Penny 186?	British Museum	
122.245	J. Wᴹ SON Medium letters with serifs	C	I	O	T or S	Early Irish Halfpenny George III	Szauer 229	
122.250	⌐Nᴼ⌐ ⟨Y⟩ ⌐ATE⌐ 6 (incuse) Small letters with serifs	C	R&I	R	U	Penny 1797	C. Brunel	
123	INITIALS AND/OR BRAND/ TRADE MARKS							
123.10	A (Crown)	C	I	O&R	U	Penny 1862	Numismatist June 1954 p. 604-5	
123.15	A (Fleur de lis) 1	C	I	†	T or U	Irish Halfpenny 1683	Szauer 119	
*123.20	A (Fleur de lis) L Large letters with serifs	C C C C	I I I I	† O † O	T or S T or S T or S T or S	Halfpenny George II Irish Halfpenny 1782 18th Cent. Eng. Token Halfpenny Munster Halfpenny 1795 (Mule D & H 1a/15–16	Szauer 90 J. G. Scott Szauer 89 J. G. Scott	
*123.30	(Crown)/B Large letter with serifs	C	I	R	U	Halfpenny 1806	J. G. Scott	
123.35	(Crown)/BC	C	I	†	U	†	SNC Dec. 1908 Col. 11079–80	
123.36	B·E·W·Co Large plain letters	C	I	R	S or U	Penny 1871	J. G. Scott	
*123.37	(Corkscrew)/B/H Medium letters with serifs	C	I	R	U	Dublin Halfpenny 1792 (D & H 91–122)	J. G. Scott	
123.40A	(Crown) in a depression	C	R	†	U	Halfpenny George III	Duffield 1531	
* B	(Ornate royal crown)	C	I	O&R	U	Halfpenny 1806	J. G. Scott	
C	(Large ornate crown)	C	I	O	U	Irish Halfpenny 1805	C. Brunel	
D	(Large ornate crown) – flatter	C	I	O	U	Penny 1806/7 (pierced 12 o'c)	Baldwin: Stock April 1972	
E	(Large plain crown)	C	I	O	U	Halfpenny 1729	C. Brunel	

For key to column headings, please refer to page 19.

NUMBER	LEGEND	A	B	C	D	COIN TYPE	SOURCE REFERENCE	APPROX. DATE
F	(Small open crown)	C	I	R	U	Hawkhurst (Kent) Halfpenny 1794 (D & H 50)	C. Brunel	
* G	(Small neat crown) within cable circle (10mm)	C	R	O&R	U	Guernsey 4 Doubles 1830	J. G. Scott	
H	(Crown)	C	I	O	U	Penny 1862	British Museum	
I	(Large crown)	C	I	1X0 2XR	U	Penny 1797	A. G. Davies	
*123.50	(Crown)/CH Large letters with serifs	C	I	2XR	U	Penny 1806	J. G. Scott	
*123.55	D (lis in circular indent) H	C	I&R	O	T or U	Halfpenny 1694(?)	J. G. Scott	
*123.57	DM Small letters with serifs	C	I	O	T or S	Irish Halfpenny George II Halfpenny George III 177?	J. G. Scott J. G. Scott	
		C	I	†	T or S	Halfpenny †	J. G. Scott	
123.60	(Winged dog seated) within a circular indent	C	I	O	S or U	Halfpenny George II(?)	J. G. Scott	
123.65	DW within a sunken crown	C	R	O	U	Halfpenny 1770–5	Batty 4066 b	
123.68	(Elephant) facing left	C	I	O&R	S or U	Penny 1797	J. G. Scott	
123.75	(Crown)/ES Large letters with serifs	C	I	O	U	Halfpenny 1773	A. G. Davies	
123.76	(Crown) E.S.	C	†	†	U	Halfpenny George II	Cokayne Sale 1946 Lot 96	
123.78	(Maltese Cross) in shaped indent/EW (incuse) Medium letters with serifs	C	R&I	O&R	S or U	Halfpenny 1745	J. G. Scott	
*123.80	(Sunken crown)/F. within square indent	C	I&R	O	S or U	Halfpenny Charles II	J. G. Scott	
123.85	(Crown)/F.B Large letters with serifs	C	I	O	U	Halfpenny 1806/7	Dr. G. H. L. Bullmore	
123.87	(Fleur de lis)/(crescent)/9	C	I	R	U	Anglesey Halfpenny (1791)	J. G. Scott	
123.88	(Fleur de lis), with (crescent) above	C	I	R	U	God Preserve London/Elephant Halfpenny	Seaby – client's enquiry July 1973	
123.90	(Crown)/G	C	I	R	U	Irish Halfpenny 1774–83	Dealer's stock: Oct. 1971	
123.92	(Open crown on side) GAN Medium letters with serifs	C	I	O&R	U	Birmingham Halfpenny 1793 (D & H 50)	A. G. Davies	
123.94	★G★/E+ Sca/1793 Very small letters in 8-sided indent	C	R	O	S	Bath Farthing 1670 (W6) Halfpenny 1773	J. G. Scott J. G. Scott	1793
*123.96	G & P Very large letters with serifs	C	I	O	S or U	Penny 1806/7	J. G. Scott	

For key to column headings, please refer to page 19.

NUMBER	LEGEND	A	B	C	D	COIN TYPE	SOURCE REFERENCE	APPROX. DATE
123.98	(Crown)/G.R./(broad arrow) (Crown)/(2 sceptres in saltire)	C	I	O	U	Washington Penny	SNC Nov./Dec. 1920 Col. 527. no. 88092	
123.100	(Crown)/G.R.	C	I	O&R	U	Twopence 1797	Bliss Sale Cat. Lot 1000	
		C	†	†	U	†	Cokayne Sale 1946 Lot 96	
123.105	(Crown)/G.R	C	I	O&R	U	Penny 1874 H	J. G. Scott	
123.108	(Griffin passant) J.D D also incuse obv.	C	R&I	O&R	S or U	Penny 1797	C. Brunel	
123.110	(Griffin's head left) in shaped indent	C	R	O&R	S or U	Edinburgh Halfpenny 1791 (D & H 50)	C. Brunel	
*123.112	(Plume)/GS Large letters with serifs (Rev. engr. Horton/Flee)	C	I	†	U	Halfpenny †	J. G. Scott	
123.115	H (Maltese Cross) D Large (1st letter), very large (2nd letter) letters with serifs	C	I	R	S or U	Halfpenny 1855	J. G. Scott	
123.119	(Crown)/I Large letter with serifs	C	I	O	U	Penny 1797	Dealer's Stock March 1971	
123.120	(Crown)/I Small letter with serifs	C	I	O	U	Penny 1862	Seaby: Stock April 1972	
123.122	(Crown)/IB all in rectangle with cut corners Very large letters with serifs	C	I	O&R	U	Penny 1797	A. G. Davies	
123.123	(Crown)/ID Small letters with serifs	C	I	O	U	Farthing 1746	J. G. Scott	
123.125	(Crown)/II Large letters with serifs	C	I	O&R	U	Twopence 1797	Seaby: Stock Feb. 1971	
123.128	I.S Large letters with serifs	C	I	O&R	T or S	Halfpenny 1774 Halfpenny 1775	J. G. Scott J. G. Scott	
*123.130	(Crown)/IS Small letters with serifs	C	I	O&R	U	Halfpenny 1773	J. G. Scott	
123.132	(Crown)/I.S.	C	†	O&R	U	Farthing 1799	Bliss Sale Cat. Lot 1020	
*123.135	(Crown)/ISR (curved) all within circle Large plain letters	C	I	O	U	Penny 18(7)7	J. G. Scott	
123.136	I/S (crown) R/3 all within circle Medium letters with serifs	C	I	O&R	P or U	Penny 1862	J. G. Scott	
123.140	(Crown)/IW Large letters with serifs	C	I	R	U	Manchester Halfpenny 1793 (D & H 135e)	A. G. Davies	
123.142	(Crown)/I.Y Medium letters with serifs	C	I	†	U	Halfpenny †	J. G. Scott	
*123.144	JB Large letters with serifs	C	I	O	T or S	Halfpenny 1723 (over medium FW) Halfpenny 1770–5	J. G. Scott J. G. Scott	

For key to column headings, please refer to page 19.

NUMBER	LEGEND	A	B	C	D	COIN TYPE	SOURCE REFERENCE	APPROX. DATE
123.145	(Crown)/JB Large letters with serifs	C	I	O	U	Halfpenny 1806	Seaby: Stock April 1972	
123.146	JB/1811. in ribbed circular indent Large (6mm) letters with serifs and small figures [A few of the countermarked 1806 English and Irish Farthings have additional secondary countermarks – see note]	C	R	R	T or S	Irish Farthing 1744	Dolley op. cit.	1811 or later
		C	R	R	T or S	Penny 1797	J. G. Scott	
		C	R	R	T or S	Farthing 1806(2)	Dolley op. cit.	
		C	R	O	T or S	Irish Farthing 1806(91)	Dolley op. cit.	
		C	R	R	T or S	Irish Farthing 1806(97)	Dolley op. cit.	
		C	R	†	T or S	Irish Farthing 1806(18)	Dolley op. cit.	
		C	R	R	T or S	Irish Farthing 1806	A. G. Davies	
123.150	(Crown)/JC	C	I	O	U	Counterfeit Halfpenny 1775	Batty 4306	
*123.155	J.C.C/PATENT/5535 1st line small letters with serifs 2nd line small plain letters	C	I	O	U	Penny 1867	J. G. Scott	
*123.160	JDV in ornamental oval indent Medium letters with serifs	C	R	†	S	Token Halfpenny(?) Halfpenny †	J. G. Scott Baldwin: Stock April 1972	
123.165	J.F.R and a horse shoe	C	I	†	U	Penny 1860	Batty 4263A	
*123.170	J::H/I⁸ Large letters with serifs	C	I	†	S	Halfpenny †	J. G. Scott	
*123.175	(Bucket) surrounded by beaded border/ J–K all within crown-above-rectangle- shaped serrated indent Large letters with serifs	C	R	R	S	Halfpenny 1799	J. G. Scott	
*123.180	2D/J:R Large letters with serifs	C	I	†	S	Halfpenny †	J. G. Scott	
*123.182	(Crown)/J.S Large letters with serifs	C	I	R	U	Penny 1797	J. G. Scott	
123.183	J★T Large letters with serifs	C	I	†	T or S	Irish Halfpenny 1775	Szauer 99 (2 examples)	
		C	I	R	T or S	Halfpenny 1775	Szauer 100	
		C	I	O	T or S	Irish Halfpenny 1782	Szauer 101	
123.185	(A figure of Justice holding scales)	C	R	†	S or U	English 18th Century Token	Duffield 1537	
123.188	JW & C⁰ (reversed) Large letters with serifs	C	I	O	U	Siam: 2 Atts 1887–1905	C. Brunel	
123.190	JW/JW DJ (?) J.T./JR/AMJ within shaped indents Very small letters with serifs (except 2nd JW, plain)	C	R	O	U	Farthing 1875	J. G. Scott	
123.195	(Crown)/K all within shaped indent Medium letter with serifs	C	R	O	U	Counterfeit Halfpenny 1771	C. E. Blunt	
123.200	(Crown)/L Large letter with serifs	C	I	O	U	Penny 1797	C. Brunel	

For key to column headings, please refer to page 19.

NUMBER	LEGEND	A	B	C	D	COIN TYPE	SOURCE REFERENCE	APPROX. DATE
123.205	(Crown)/LN Small letters with serifs	C	I	O	U	Halfpenny George I	A. G. Davies	
123.208	(Man in moon) 18mm tall, nose to left, eye in relief	C	I	2xO IxR	U	Penny 1855	R. N. P. Hawkins	
*123.210	M Medium letter with serifs	C	I	O	T or S	South Wales Farthing 1793 (D & H 27a) Warwickshire Shilling 1799 (Atkins 4) Cambridgeshire Farthing 1795 (D & H 36) Farthing 1806	C. Brunel Seaby: Stock January 1973 Seaby: Stock April 1972 J. G. Scott A. G. Davies	
123.211	MB in rectangular indent Large plain letters	C	R	R	T or S	Halfpenny 1799	C. Brunel	
123.212	M.G Large letters with serifs	C	I	†	T or S	English Token Halfpenny 18th Century	Szauer 104	
		C	I	O	T or S	Dublin Halfpenny Token (D & H 29 etc.)	Szauer 105	
*123.215	M.I (script) in rectangular indent	C	R	†	T or S	Irish Halfpenny 1723	H. D. Gibbs Sale Nov. 1960 Lot 277	
		C	R	R	T or S	Claudius Romanus /Pax. Pla. Cid. Evasion Halfpenny 1775	J. G. Scott	
		C	R	R	T or S	Halfpenny †	SNC Nov./Dec. 1920 Col. 527 88106	
123.225	(open crown)/(mushroom-like device)	C	I	R	U	Halfpenny William III	J. G. Scott	
123.230	(Crown)/N Large plain letter	C	I	†	S or U	Halfpenny George II	SNC Apr. 1897 Col. 2175/6	
		C	I	O	S or U	Halfpenny 1770–5	VG 1019	
		C	I	O	S or U	Penny 1807	VG 1018	
123.232	(Crown)/NB Medium letters with serifs	C	I	O&R	U	Penny 1797	J. G. Scott	
123.238	OK SS	C C	I I	R O	T or S	Irish Farthing George II	Szauer 142, 143	
123.240A	O.W/WARRANTED/DEC. 1790/32.G. in an oval Large (1st & 3rd lines) and medium (2nd line) letters with serifs	C	R	R	S or U	Warwickshire Halfpenny 1790 (D & H 387)	British Museum SNC June 1929 Col. 249	
		C	R	†	S or U	Anglesey Penny †	A. G. Stone	
		C	R	R	S or U	Cronebane Halfpenny	Batty 3864A	
B	O.W/WARRANTED/DEC. 1790/28 Large (1st line) and medium (2nd & 3rd lines) letters with serifs	C	R	O	S or U	Cronebane Halfpenny 1789 Token Halfpenny 1790	Batty 3864 J. G. Scott Michael O'Hara 1967	
		C	R	O&R	S or U	Liverpool Halfpenny 1791 (D & H 61–78)	J. G. Scott	

For key to column headings, please refer to page 19.

NUMBER	LEGEND	A	B	C	D	COIN TYPE	SOURCE REFERENCE	APPROX. DATE
123.245	(Owl-like device)	C	R	R	T or S	Ireland: Camac(?) Halfpenny 1794	Szauer 231	
		C	R	O	T or S	Barbadoes: Penny 1788	Szauer 232	
123.250	(Crown)/P	C	I	O	U	Halfpenny 1799	Batty 4495 SNC Dec. 1908 Col. 11079/80	
						Counterfeit Halfpenny George II	Numismatist June 1956 p. 658 no. 134	
123.255	(Large crown)/P	C	I	O	S or U	Penny 1797	SNC Dec. 1908 Col. 11079/80	
	(Large crown)/WH Large letters with serifs	C	I	R		Halfpenny 1799	Duffield 339	
*123.270A	(Tobacco pipe with triangular bowl and straight stem)	C	I	O	U	Penny 1797	J. G. Scott	
B	(3 tobacco pipes with straight stems)	C	I	O&R	U	Penny 1797	British Museum	
C	(2 tobacco pipes with curved stems)	C	I	O	U	Farthing 1839	Seaby: Stock April 1972	
* D	(2 short tobacco pipes, crossed)	C	I	†	U	Halfpenny †	J. G. Scott	
		C	I	O	U	Penny 1862	Seaby: Stock Oct. 1971	
* E	(Short pipe crossed by line) I.B Large letters with serifs	C	I	O	U	Penny 1797	J. G. Scott	
		C	I	R				
F	(Short pipe crossed by line)	C	I	O	U	Penny 1891	Seaby: Stock April 1972	
* G	(Pipe) to right, I to left	C	I	O	U	Penny 1797	J. G. Scott (2)	
H	(Large pipe with curved stem) (anchor on reverse)	C	I	O	U	Penny 1797	Birmingham Museum	
I	(Small pipe with curved stem)	C	I	R	U	Farthing 1674	Birmingham Museum	
J	(Short pipe with tall bowl)	C	I	O	U	Penny 1797	Birmingham Museum	
K	(Long pipe with tall bowl)	C	I	O	U	Dublin Halfpenny 1820 (Davis 68)	J. G. Scott	
L	(2 long tobacco pipes with slightly curved stems, crossed)	C	I	R	S or U	Halfpenny 1806/7	J. G. Scott	
M	Similar to L above	C	I	O	S or U	Penny 1862	J. G. Scott	
N	(Pipe)	C	I	O&R	S or U	Halfpenny †	SNC Nov./Dec. 1920 Col. 527 No. 88103	
O	Similar to L but with 2 additional pipes	C	I	O&R	S or U	Penny 1797	C. Brunel	
P	Similar to L above	C	I	O	U	Isle of Man Penny 1839	J. G. Scott	
*123.275	(A plume of 3 feathers) in shaped indent	C	R	O	S or U	Irish Halfpenny 1805	J. G. Scott	

For key to column headings, please refer to page 19.

NUMBER	LEGEND	A	B	C	D	COIN TYPE	SOURCE REFERENCE	APPROX. DATE
*123.280	(A Railway Locomotive)	C	I	O&R	S, P or U	Penny George IV	J. G. Scott	
		C	I	R	S, P or U	Irish Halfpenny 1823	Batty 4389 b	
123.285	R. Cⁱ Large letters with serifs	C	I	R	S or U	Penny 1797	D. G. Vorley	
*123.290	Rᴰ 459419 Very small letters and figures	C	I	R	U	Halfpenny 1860–94	J. G. Scott	
123.291	R & G Medium letters with serifs	C	I	O&R	S or U	Halfpenny †	D. G. Vorley	
*123.293	R (Fleur de lis) N Large letters with serifs	C	I	O	T or S	Halfpenny George II	J. G. Scott	
123.295	(Royal Arms) in shaped indent	C	R	R	U	Twopence 1797	J. G. Scott	
123.297	R.S./& Co. in star	C	†	†	S or U	Irish Halfpenny †	Szauer 124	
123.300	(Crown)/RW	C	†	†	U	"Ireland – token"	Duffield 1551	
123.305	RY Medium letters with serifs	C	I	R	T or S	Halfpenny 1806	City Museum, St. Albans, C. Brunel J. G. Scott	
						Penny 1807	J. G. Scott	
						Halfpenny 1826	J. G. Scott	
123.310	(Crown)/S	C	†	†	U	Penny 1797	SNC Dec. 1908 Col. 11079/80 Duffield 337	
		C	I	O	U	Penny 1806	C. Brunel	
		C	I	†	U	Halfpenny †	SNC Apr. 1897 Col. 2175	
123.313	(Shamrock)	C	I	O	U	Halfpenny George II	J. G. Scott	
*123.315	(Crown)/SD	C	I	O&R	U	Penny 1797	Token Corres. Soc. Bulletin Dec. 1971 p.44	
*123.320	S*D/2*6	C	I	R	S	Anglesey Penny (1788) (D & H 186)	Token Corres. Soc. Bulletin Dec. 1971 p. 44	
123.325	*S*/3.6/* all in beaded circle	C	R	†	S	Halfpenny †	Duffield 1529	
*123.326	3 6 Small figures	C	I	O	S	Walsall Penny 1811 (Davis 107–113)	J. G. Scott	
123.330	S.D/13 6 G (Crown) R/THIRTEEN & SIX PENCE	C C	† †	O R	WEIGHT	Halfpenny 1773	Duffield 1519	
*123.332	(Open crown)/SS (closed crown)/SS (closed crown)/SS Medium letters with serifs	C C	I I	O R	U	Halfpenny 1745	J. G. Scott	

For key to column headings, please refer to page 19.

NUMBER	LEGEND	A	B	C	D	COIN TYPE	SOURCE REFERENCE	APPROX. DATE
123.333	SS Large letters with serifs [See also Szauer 44A, 144, 157, 161, 238 listed in Appendix 2, and 98.11, 123.238 above]	C	I	†	T or S	Halfpenny 1693	Szauer 139	
		C	I	†	T or S	St. Patrick Halfpenny	Szauer 140	
		C	I	O	T or S	Irish Halfpenny 1766	Szauer 112	
		C	I	†	T or S	Halfpenny Token †	Szauer 134	
		C	I	†	T or S	Farthing †	Szauer 137	
		C	I	†	T or S	Irish Farthing George II	Szauer 152	
		C	I	†	T or S	Imitation Irish Farthing George II	Szauer 150	
		C	I	†	T or S	Farthing George III	Szauer 145	
		C	I	O	T or S	France: Liard Louis XIV (1655–8)	J. G. Scott cf. Szauer 136	
		C	I	†	T or S	Russia: Denga 1753	Szauer 141	
*123.334	(A large shield of Swiss type quarterly argent in the first quarter a dagger or tall fleur de lis)	C	I	O	S or U	Penny 1797	J. G. Scott	
*123.336	(Stag trottant, left)	C	I	†	S or U	Halfpenny (?) 28.5mm	J. G. Scott	
*123.338	(Swan, to right) (twice)	C	I	O	U	Penny 1863	J. G. Scott	
123.342	(Crown)/TB Large letters with serifs	C	I	R	U	Halfpenny 1799	A. G. Davies	
123.345	(Crown)/TE	C	I	R	U	Halfpenny 1806	Szauer 113	
123.353	(Crown)/TS Small neat letters with serifs	C	I	R	U	Warwickshire Halfpenny 1788 (D & H 383)	C. Brunel	
123.354	(Crown)/TS	C	I	O&R	U	Irish Halfpenny 1805	Batty 5145	
123.355	(Crown)/T.S	C	I	†	U	†	SNC Dec. 1908 Col. 11079/80	
123.360	(Crown)/T.W.	C	I	†	U	Halfpenny 1862	SNC Jan./Feb. 1921 Col. 82	
123.380	(Crown)/V in an oval four times As above once, (Crown)/P in an oval three times	C	R	O	U	Twopence 1797	SNC Aug./Sep. 1954 Col. 339	
		C	R	R	U			
123.385	(Crown)/V	C	I	O	U	Halfpenny 1861	SNC Mar. 1894 Col. 601	
123.390	(Crown)/V (harp) R/249 Large letters with serifs	C	I	R	P or U	Penny 1863	Szauer 243	
123.392	(Crown)/VR/T Medium letters with serifs	C	I	O&R	S or U	France: 5C An 8 w	J. G. Scott	
123.395	(A lion) W (a male head) each in a small depression	C	R	†	U	Halfpenny 1738	Duffield 1517	
123.397	(Small open crown)/W Small letter with serifs	C	I	O&R	U	Halfpenny 1739	J. G. Scott	
123.398	(Crown)/W (and heart-shaped piercing)	C	†	†	U	Halfpenny George II	Bliss Sale 1916 Lot 1018	
123.400	(Crown)/WB Large letters with serifs	C	I	O	U	Halfpenny 1770–5	J. G. Scott	

For key to column headings, please refer to page 19.

NUMBER	LEGEND	A	B	C	D	COIN TYPE	SOURCE REFERENCE	APPROX. DATE
123.403	(Crown)/wc	C	I	O	U	Penny 1797	H. D. Gibbs Sale 1960 Lot 456	
123.405	(A horse rampant in oblong depression)/ wc in oblong depression	C	R	†	S or U	Halfpenny 1722	Duffield 1515	
123.408	wf (script) in a small rectangular indent	C	R	O	S or U	Twopence 1797	J. G. Scott	
123.410	(Wheatsheaf and sickle)	C	I	O	S or U	Halfpenny George III	Batty 5021	
123.412	W.H.J Large plain letters 6D	C C	I I	O R	S	Bronze Halfpenny(?)	J. G. Scott	
123.414	WII Large letters with serifs	C C	I I	O †	T or S T or S	Halfpenny George 1 Halfpenny †	J. G. Scott J. G. Scott	
*123.415	W & J S.S Large letters with serifs	C	I	1XO 2XR	S, P or U	Penny 1797 8mm centre hole	C. Brunel	
123.417	WM/1 Large (1st line) and very large (2nd line) letters with serifs	C	I	R	T or S	Middlesex Halfpenny 1795 (D & H 985a)	J. G. Scott	
123.419	W & T.E Large letters with serifs	C	I	O&R	S, P or U	Penny 1862	D. G. Vorley	
123.420	(Crown)/ww Large letters with serifs	C	I	O	U	Penny 1806	Seaby: Stock April 1972	
123.430	(Crown)/x Medium plain letter	C	I	R	U	Twopence 1797	J. G. Scott	

For key to column headings, please refer to page 19.

NOTES ON THE ISSUERS OF PIECES
LISTED IN TABLE 1

The sources consulted to compile these notes and those on pieces listed in Tables 2 and 3 include the following:

Directories – where available. Unfortunately directory coverage outside London is scanty, particularly before 1850. In some cases it has proved possible to provide supplementary information from Rate Books, Poll Books, Indexes to Wills etc.

Various specialist standard works listing craftsmen's names and marks. Those most frequently consulted are:

C. H. Baillie: 'Watchmakers and Clockmakers of the World' (London 1929).

Frederick Bradbury: 'History of Old Sheffield Plate' (Sheffield 1968).

A. Merwyn Carey: 'English, Irish, and Scottish Firearms Makers' (London 1967).

Howard Herschel Cotterell: 'Old Pewter – its makers and marks' (London 1929).

Ian Glendenning: 'British Pistols and Guns 1640–1840' (London 1951).

Geoffrey A. Godden, F.R.S.A.: 'Encyclopaedia of British Pottery and Porcelain Marks' (London 1964).

Griffith's 'Guide to the Iron Trade of Great Britain' (London 1873).

Dudley S. Hawtrey Gyngell: 'Armourers' Marks' (London 1959).

Sir Charles James Jackson, F.S.A.: 'English Goldsmiths and their Marks' (London 1921).

White's 'Hardware Trade Marks', 1st edition (Sheffield 1892).

J. H. Whitham & D. Vickers: 'Register of Trademarks of the Cutlers Company of Sheffield' (Sheffield 1919).

Bennet Woodcroft: 'Alphabetical Index of Patentees of Inventions, March 2 1617–October 1 1852' (London 1854).

ENGLAND

1 Bedfordshire
Bedford

1.1 ABBEY
Pigot & Co's National Commercial Directory for 1830–1 has an entry for Edw. Abbey, gun-maker and cutler, Angel Street. The 1839 entry is for Robert Abbey, gunmaker and cutler, St. Peter's Green.

Probably related was William Abbey, gunsmith and cutler, of High Street, Newport Pagnell (1830); the 1823–4 directory describes him as a cutler, at North Street, Newport Pagnell. See also St. Ives (Huntingdonshire).

Cranfield

1.2 PARTRIDGE
There is no record of the Partridge family in the Cranfield parish registers, published up to 1812, nor any entry for the death of a Richard Partridge in the burials 1825–35. Land Tax assessments show a Joseph Partridge holding large estates in Cranfield 1797–1832. The Bedfordshire County Record Office has maps showing the estate of Joseph Ashby Partridge Esq. before enclosure (1807: x206/1) and after enclosure (1840: x206/2), while the Post Office Directory for 1847 describes Joseph Ashby Partridge as Lord of the Manor.

There are also references to a Partridge family in Woburn until the early eighteenth century, and in Tilsworth, where a Richard Partridge, farmer, aged 21, was married to Eliz. Scroggs, aged 20, of Houghton Regis on 23 May 1778. He was buried 30 November 1819. He had a son named Richard, but no connection with Cranfield can be found, and it is probable that this piece was issued by a relative of Joseph Ashby Partridge before 1797.

2 Berkshire
Reading

2.1 MOODY
There are several entries for Moody in the Reading directories as follows:
1826 Charles Moody, butcher, 84 Chatham Street.
1830 Robert Moody, register office for servants, 115 London Street.
Charles Moody, brewer, 106 Castle Street.
1842, 1844 Ann Moody, fruiterer and greengrocer, 166 Friar Street.
1854 Mary Moody, straw bonnet maker, 2 Hope Place.
Voters Lists show Charles Moody, malster, Eton Place, and Robert R. Moody, poulterer, London Street (1826) and Robert Richmond Moody, greengrocer, Friar Street (1837).

It is not possible to say whether one of the above traders was responsible for this countermark, or whether it might have been issued by another trader, perhaps a cutler, at a time not covered by the directories. The piece probably dates c. 1825–50.

Windsor

2.2 G.W.R. LOCO(MOTIVE) AND CARR(IAGE) DEPT.
The Great Western Railway branch line from Slough to Windsor was opened on 8 October 1849. It is difficult to date this paycheck, which could have been issued any time from the opening of the line to nationalisation on 1 January 1948. Such discs are unusual on copper – it cannot be shown conclusively that a coin has been used. The piece may well date from the early 1900's.

2.3 PRIDIE
George Pridie is listed in Robson's 1838 Directory as a silver engraver and repairer, and beer

retailer, at William Street, Peascod Street, but does not appear in Pigot's 1830 Directory. Pigot's 1844 and Slater's 1851 Directories list George Pridie, cutler, at 78 Peascod Street. By 1864 Charles Green, cutler, was at 64 Peascod Street. The countermark probably dates from c. 1835–53.

3 Buckinghamshire
Aylesbury
3.1 PAYNE
William Payne, cutler, Market Place, appears in the "Universal British Directory" (1793), the Poll of Electors for 1804, and the Sketch Plan of Aylesbury Householders, 1809. Charles Payne, cutler, is listed in Underhill's Biennial directory for 1816–17, and his address is shown as Temple Street in Pigot's 1830 Directory. He does not appear in the Poll of Electors for 1831 or 1839, or in Kelly's 1842 Directory.

Eton
3.2 TALBOT
Talbot is not listed in Pigot's 1823–4 or 1830 Directories, or Robson's 1838 issue, and may not have been a trader.

Stony Stratford
3.3 COVINGTON
This attribution can only be tentative. The name is not common – no likely W. Covington has been traced in nineteenth century London directories. It is possible that the issuer was William Covington, listed by Baillie as a watchmaker in Stony Stratford (1785) and referred to as an executor of Thomas Kingston, shopkeeper, of Little Brickhill, in a deed of 1802. He is listed in the "Universal British Directory" (1798). John Covington, watch and clock maker was active in 1811, 1816–17 and 1824, latterly at Eastside.

5 Cheshire
Chester
5.1 X DENTIST
To countermark a penny of 1862 was illegal, hence the 'x' in the interests of anonymity. The piece probably served as some sort of receipt or discount check. There are 6 dentists listed in the 1880 directory, and 8 in 1896, mostly in Abbey Street, Whitefriars and Watergate Street.

5.2 DAVENPORT
In the absence of an initial, this has been assumed to be a place-name not a surname, but this attribution must remain extremely tentative. Other possibilities are R. Davenport, the Birmingham gunmaker (1800–12) – see Glendenning, or S. and E. Davenport, the London Wholesale Goldsmith and Hardwaremen, of 15 Lime Street (1806/18/27/28/36, E. Davenport only 1837/8). Another might be J. Davenport, the London pewterer (3 Dean Street and 15 Gt. Smith Street 1827/28, 15 Gt. Smith Street only 1836/42). 'DAVENPORT', impressed, was an early mark of the well-known Longport firm of potters, active

1794–1887. John Davenport (1765–1848) built his Unicorn Bank Pottery in 1794.

6 Cornwall
Truro
6.1 TREGELLAS
There is a hamlet of Tregelles (sic) near St. Kew, but this instance is assumed to be the surname, which is not uncommon in Cornwall (5 in 1970 telephone directory). The countermark is tentatively attributed to John Tabois Tregellas, General Merchant, Quay, Truro, who appears in the 1844 and 1847 directories, born in 1792, Purser of Cornish Mines, and author of many stories in the local dialect. He died in 1863. His son, Walter Hawken Tregellas was born 10 July 1831, and his father may have countermarked coins of that year in celebration of the event. Walter, a writer on Cornish and other subjects, died in 1894. Another possibility is Mary Tregellas or Tregelles, Ironmonger of Boscawen Street, Truro, who also appears in the 1844 and 1847 directories. Tregellas is also a family name in St. Agnes, near Truro; Thomas Tregellas ran a public house there, the Smith's Arms, for many years, and died in 1862 aged 71.

8 Derbyshire
8.1 BOLSOVER
In the absence of an initial this has been assumed to be a place name. The main industry in Bolsover in the early nineteenth century was buckle-making. The Universal British Directory (1798) lists one bucklemaker, James Rhodes, who was also a gunsmith, and it is possible that he issued piece no. 8.1A. However, the possibility that Bolsover is a brand mark cannot be overlooked: Gales and Martin's Sheffield Directory for 1787 shows that 'BOLSOVER' was the mark of Joseph Mitchell & Co., edge tool maker, Shudehill. Tome has not been traced as a surname or brand mark.

Buxton
8.2 H.B
Attribution of this piece must remain extremely tentative. A possible issuer is Henry Brown, King's Head, Market Place (1857), although it is equally likely that this is an unofficial countermark from Birmingham or Sheffield.

Derby
8.3 LOVETT
There is no entry for James Lovett in those directories available for years between 1784 and 1828/9. However a James Lovett of Derby was buried at St. Werburgh's Church on 17 October 1787.

8.4 RAWFOR
No trader of this name is listed in the following directories: 1784 (Bailey's), 1791 (Universal British), 1805–7 (Holden's), 1818, 1822, 1835 (Pigot's). These span the likely period of issue, but, in view of the sparseness of directory cover it should not be concluded that Rawfor was not a trader.

9 Devonshire

Bear Town

9.1 CORNS

Bear Town is an alternative spelling of Bere Town or Beer Town, better known as Bere Ferrers, near Plymouth. Corns is an unusual name in Devon, and no trace has been found in the directories.

Crediton

9.2 GOVER

Directories show the following entries:

1822–3, 1823–4 (Pigot's) Gover, Saml. and John, turners and chairmakers.

1830 (Pigot's) Gover, Jas., tinplate worker and patten maker, West town.
Gover, Jane, milliner, dress and straw-hat maker, West town.
Gover, Samuel, patten maker, West town.

1838 (Robson's) Gover, James, patten, clog and bellows maker, High Street.
Gover, James, tinplate worker.
Gover, John, London Inn, High Street.

1844 (Pigot's) Gover, James, patten maker, High Street.
Gover, Jane, milliner, dress and straw-hat maker, High Street.
Gover, Samuel, patten maker, High Street.

1850 (White's) Gover, Jas., brush and bellows maker.
Gover, John, brush and bellows maker.

1852 (Slater's) Gover, James and Samuel, ironmongers, High Street.
Gover, James and John, patten makers, High Street.
Gover, John, London Tavern, High Street.

1856 (Kelly's) Gover, James, ironmonger and tinplate worker, High Street.
Gover, James, patten, clog and brush maker, High Street.
Gover, Samuel, ironmonger and tinplate worker, High Street.
Gover, Eliza (Mrs.), London Inn, High Street.

1857 (Billing's) Gover, James, ironmonger.
Gover, James, patten, clog and bellows maker.
Gover, John, pattern (sic), clog and brush maker.

The countermark probably dates from before the 1853 Act, most likely c. 1830–50, and was almost certainly issued by James Gover.

Exeter

9.3 GRAHAM

The Royal Clarence Hotel dates from 1770, and from at least 1838 was owned by Sarah Street. Robert Dymond in 'Old Inns and taverns of Exeter' (Transactions of the Devonshire Association, 1880) says of the Clarence: 'Mrs. Street finally let the hotel to a Mr. Graham but it was soon afterwards sold by her executors to Mr. Birkett...' The Exeter Journal shows J. Graham at the Clarence from 1860 to 1866. By 1879 J. Headon Stanbury had replaced W. Birkett as proprietor. This is one of the earliest countermarks on the bronze series, and, being after the 1853 Act, was an illegal issue.

9.4 POTTER

The issuer of this early and unusual piece is listed in Trewman's 1807 Directory as Amos Potter, peruke-maker, Fore-street. He is not listed in Bailey's 1784 Directory or Pigot's 1824 edition.

Honiton

9.5 CLARKE

A possible issuer might be Joseph Lott Clarke, saddler and harness maker, listed in Pigot's 1823–4 Directory. He does not appear in the 1830 issue. Another possibility is Joseph Clarke, boot and shoemaker, and beer retailer, High Street, who appears in Robson's Directory c. 1839 and Pigot's 1844 Directory, but not in White's 1850 Directory.

Topsham

9.6 TAPPER

J. Tapper appears in directories as follows:

1830 (Pigot's) No entry.

1838 (Robson's) J. Tapper, shoeing smith, Fore Street.

1850 (White's), 1852 (Slater's), 1856 (Kelly's) John Tapper, blacksmith, High Street.

Billing's 1857 Directory shows Wm. Tapper, blacksmith at Topsham.

The countermark probably dates from the 1840's.

10 Dorset

Dorchester

10.1 GEALL

Pigot's 1824 Directory lists Wm. Geale, working cutler and truss maker, High Street. He does not appear in 1816–17 or 1830, but the 1844 issue shows William Geall, cutler, High West Street. By 1855 Miss Jane Geall, dressmaker is shown at High West Street.

Poole

10.2 RA

No trader with these initials is listed in Pigot's 1824, 1830 or 1844 Directories. It is possible that the additional countermark I.P represents the initials of someone with the surname Poole and that this is not a Dorset piece at all. For the present the matter must remain unresolved.

10.3 BEST

William B. Best was a draper in Poole in 1812. The dies for the silver tokens were made, and the tokens themselves struck, by Kempson and Son of Birmingham. This piece must be a freak or trial produced by one of Kempson's workers. See Arthur W. Waters' 'Notes on the silver tokens of the Nineteenth Century' (1957) p. 3. William Best, linen draper, High Street, is listed in Pigot's 1823–4 Directory, but not in subsequent issues.

11 Durham

Durham

11.1 THOMAS

Joseph Thomas, 55 Claypath, is listed under 'Shopkeepers' in Whellan's 1856 Directory. The name is not common in this area and does not appear at all in the directories for 1827, 1828, 1834, 1849, 1851, 1858, 1873, 1877 or 1890. The only other nineteenth century entry that has been traced is for Mrs. Thomas, Queen Street (1866).

11.2 PHILADELPHIA
This village, famed chiefly for coalmining and earthenware, is 1½ miles north of Houghton le Spring. The countermark is presumably the result of unofficial use of a brand marking punch by an employee of a local firm, possibly the Britannia Iron Works c. 1865–77.

11.3 SOUTH SHIELDS
The origin of these scarce pieces is obscure. In 1750 South Shields was little more than a village, with salt works established in the late fifteenth century and glassworks 200 years later. The chemical industry developed in the eighteenth century, and, with increasing industrialisation presumably came the need for tokens to supplement the scanty supply of regal coinage. Equally, these pieces could be truck tickets.

12 Essex
Colchester

12.1 GREEN
John Green, cutler, is listed in directories at 10 High Street (1845), St. John Street (1848) and 2 North Hill (1851). He does not appear in the issues for 1839 or 1855. It is probable that Green had premises in Culver Street for a time during the period 1840–54, and that he issued this countermark.

Plaistow

12.2 PHILIPPS
Philipps does not appear in Pigot's Directories for 1826, 1832 or 1839, in White's Directory for 1848, or in the Post Office Directories for 1845, 1851, 1855, 1862, 1866, 1870, 1874, 1878 or 1882. Samuel Catton, at first (1826) described as a grocer, but by 1845 as a grocer and druggist, was for many years the only chemist listed under Plaistow. Initially in Broadway, he had moved to Park by 1862. Charles Phillips (sic), grocer and cheesemonger, is listed in the 1866 and 1870 directories at North Woolwich Road, Canning Town – included in Plaistow. It is just possible that, like Catton, he combined the trades of chemist and grocer, and therefore issued this countermark. Another possibility is that Philipps was active at a time not covered by directories, perhaps preceding or following the firm of Charles Tothill & Co., manufacturing chemists, shown at Plaistow Works in the 1855 directory.

13 Gloucestershire
Bristol

13.1 DON
'The Don' traded as a tailor at 45 Wine Street in the 1880's. An example of his paper labels was sent to the Mint on 17 December 1883 by a trader at 42 Wine Street, who wished to know if the practice was legal as, if so, he intended to get some labels printed. By the early 1900's, The Don had a shop at 74 Queen's Road, Clifton. Directory entries are as follows:
1885 Don Association of Woollen Manufacturers (Thomas Edward Donne and William H. Forsyth, managers) 45 Wine Street, John Parks and Sons, linen drapers, 46 Wine Street.
1890, 1895 The Don (Association of Woollen Manufacturers) 45 and 46 Wine Street. W. H. Forsyth, agent.

13.2 GREEN
The final letter of the surname is not clear, looking like a mis-struck K, N or X. Clearly N is the most likely. The probable issuer was Joseph Green, working cutler, 68 Redcliff Street (1830), (29) Back Street (1844, 1849, 1851).

13.3 HALL
The entries in the Bristol directories are as follows: 1795 Benjamin Hall, glazier, Barrs Street, 1799/1800 glazier and glass-bender, same address; 1810 glazier, glassmaker, bender, painter on glass and burner, and compound metal fan-light manufacturer, 2 Barrs Street; 1820 glazier, stainer in glass, and glass-bender. Coach lamp manufacturer and fan-light maker. Similar entries continue up to and including 1835. For 1836–8 there are two entries: A. Hall, glazier, 2 Barrs Street and Benjamin Hall, glass-bender and stainer, 2 Barrs Street. By 1839 the firm had become Hall and Pedder of 2 Barrs Street. The countermark probably dates from the period c. 1820–35.

Cheltenham

13.4 EDWARDS
The most likely issuer of this countermark was James Edwards, boot and shoemaker, who appears in directories as follows:
1830 (Pigot's) 269 High Street.
1851 (Slater's) 11 Market Arcade.
1856 (Post Office) 11 Arcade, High Street.
1858 (Slater's) 11 Market Arcade.
1863 (Post Office) James Thomas Edwards, shoemaker, 305 High Street.
Another possibility might be William Edwards, silversmith, watch and clock maker and jeweller, 370 High Street. The countermark probably dates from the 1840's.

Gloucester

13.5 LANE
William Lane, cutler and toy dealer, is listed in R. Gell & T. Bradshaw's 1820 Directory and Pigot's 1822 Directory at Westgate Street. In 1830 he is shown as a cutler in Bell Lane, and in 1844 and 1851 in London Road. He does not appear in the 1856 Post Office Directory.

Tewkesbury

13.6 HAYWARD
George Hayward, cutler, appears in directories as follows:

1820 (R. Gell & T. Bradshaw's). No entry.
1830 (Pigot's) George Hayward, cutler, High Street.
1844 (Pigot's) George Hayward, cutler, High Street.
1856 (Post Office) Geo. Hayward, ironmonger & cutler, High Street.
1858 (Slater's) George Hayward, cutler, 123 High Street.
1863 (Post Office) Hayward & Son, ironmongers & cutlers, High Street.
1922 (Morris') Hayward & Sons, ironmongers, 125 & 126 High Street.
The countermark probably dates from c. 1830–45.

14 Hampshire

14.1 ANDOVER

On 28 July 1881, Samuel Shaw and Son, family grocers, tea dealers and provision merchants of High Street, Andover, wrote to the Mint asking if paper advertisement labels on coins were legal, quoting a local example whose circulation was stated to be 'very large in this town on copper coin'. He would obviously have liked to adopt this form of cheap advertising, but was referred by the Mint to the 1861 Act. The trader who used the labels is not named in the Mint Records, but examples may still exist locally.

Portsmouth

14.2 (PORTSMOUTH DOCKYARD)

These countermarks are similar in style to those tentatively attributed to the dockyards at Chatham, Sheerness and Deptford, and to the Woolwich Arsenal or Dockyard pieces – see below. It is possible that they served as stores checks at Portsmouth Dockyard. The dockyard, situated in Portsea, included large naval stores, described as follows in Pigot's 1824 Directory: 'The Gun Wharf is an establishment which rivals the celebrated arsenal of Venice; in it are kept in store immense quantities of guns, carriages etc. and every species of ammunition, both for naval and military service.' In 1830, William Pennell was storekeeper at Portsea Dockyard.

Southampton

14.3 CLARK

Directories show the following entries:
1830 (Pigot's) James Clark, working cutler, Bridge Street.
1839 (Fletcher & Son's) Mrs. Clark, working cutler, 36 High Street.
1844 (Pigot's) Adam Clark, cutler, 36 High Street.
1849 (Forbes & Knibb's), 1851 (Slater's) Adam Clark, cutler, 2 West Street.
Clark is not listed in Pigot's 1824 Directory and the countermark probably dates from c. 1827–37.

14.4 PEGLER

Daniel Pegler, son of a Blandford Forum jeweller and clockmaker, established his watchmaker's business in Southampton in 1794. The 1803 directory shows Peggler (sic), watchmaker, 138 High Street. The 1811 entry shows him at 53 High Street, and Nathanial Pegler (proprietor from 1815), jeweller and gunmaker at 151 High Street. Daniel Pegler, watchmaker, continues to appear at 115 East Street (1823–4), and 115 (sic) High Street (1830). Nathaniel was succeeded as proprietor by George Pegler in 1834, but still appears in the 1836 directory as a silversmith and jeweller at 151 High Street. In 1843, George is shown as a silversmith and jeweller at the same address while in 1845 he is described as a goldsmith, jeweller and silversmith, watch and clockmaker. An advertisement in this edition of the directory announces that 'chronometers and watches of every description are repaired on the premises by first-rate London workmen'. Alfred Pegler inherited the business in 1849, and in the 1851 directory is described as 'goldsmith, silversmith and jeweller, watch and clock manufacturer and engraver'. He also inserted the following advertisement: 'Alfred Pegler has one uniform price, and, as that price is the lowest the articles can possibly be rendered at, he neither allows discount or gives credit. A connection embracing the greatest portion of the South of England is the best proof that can be offered of the success of the system adopted in accordance with the spirit of the times – of small profits, no credit, and consequently no chance of loss.' The enterprising Alfred Pegler also exchanged foreign coins. His son Alfred took over the business and ran it until his death in 1921. The firm became Pegler and Wyatt in 1925, and Parkhouse and Wyatt in 1940 (W. L. Parkhouse & Son were established in 1893). The premises and records were destroyed in the blitz of 30 November 1940, but the firm of Parkhouse and Wyatt are still in business at 96 Above Bar. For further information on the Peglers see 'Since 1794 . . . the Story of Parkhouse and Wyatt' by Gordon Sewell (1969). I assume the countermark to date from the period 1815–34.

15 Herefordshire
Hereford

15.1 CASWALL, CASWELL

Samuel Caswell (sic), cutler, is listed in the 1811 and 1816–17 directories at St. Owen Street, and in those for 1822–3, 1830, and 1835 at Hightown, Hereford. He does not appear in the issues for 1793 or 1840. In the 1834 Voters' list, under the Parish of St. Peters, is an entry for no. 2889, Samuel Caswell, Butchers Row, Freehold House, Maylords Lane. Butchers Row was in Hightown.

15.2 CROOSE

George Croose, ironmonger, Hightown is listed in Pigot's 1822–3, and 1830 Directories, but not in those for 1816–17 or 1835. The County Record Office has Bill Headings of 1824 and 1830 with 'George Croose, ironmonger, 9 Hightown. For this information, I am indebted to John Parry.

15.3 TOWNSEND

William Townsend, cutler, appears in the directories for 1835, 1844, 1851 and 1859 at Eign

Street, but not in the 1830 issue. By 1868, Eliza and Martha Townsend, cutlers, were at 79 Eign Street. The countermark probably dates from before the 1853 Act.

Leominster
15.4 CASWALL
S. Caswell (sic), cutler, Drapers Lane, is listed in Pigot's Directory for 1822–3, but not in directories for 1791–8, 1811, 1816–17, 1830, 1835, 1844 or 1851, or in voters' lists for 1835 or 1849. It is possible that the issuer was connected with Caswall of Hereford (see 15.1 above). The piece probably dates from the 1820's.

15.5 WATLING
Robert Watling, wine and brandy merchant, is listed in the Universal British Directory for 1794 and in Holden's 1811 Directory. He does not appear in Bailey's 1784 or Pigot's 1822 Directories. This shop ticket forms part of a series by wine and spirit merchants that seems to have been used along the Welsh Marches – see also Ludlow, Kidderminster and Abergavenny below.

16 Hertfordshire
Hoddesdon
16.1 HODDESDON BREWERY
This business started about 1700 – see Tregelles' 'History of Hoddesdon' (1908). At first it was in the possession of the Plomer family, of whom William Plomer died in 1728. In a perambulation of parish boundaries in 1736 it is described as 'Mr. Plomer's brewhouse'. On the death of the last Plomer, Robert, in 1742, Rene Briand took over the business. He seems to have had a partner – N. Darren. Briand died in 1781 and was succeeded by a Mr. Whittingstall of Hitchin. Following Whittingstall's sudden death in 1803, Messrs. Christie and Cathrow bought the business from his executors, rapidly extending it by the purchase of numerous houses and additions to the brewery premises. They started the Hertford Bank in 1807, transferring it to S. Adams & Co. in 1814. William Christie (1744–1811) was the first of the family to settle in Hoddesdon. His nephew Peter (1791–1865) was apprenticed to the firm, and in 1842 the business was sold to Peter Christie (died 1865), Robert Hunt (retired 1852) and John Back (retired 1865). Christie's son, Charles Peter (1829–98) took over as sole owner in 1865 until his death, when the business became a limited liability company largely controlled by his sons. In this period the entries in the local directories describe the firm as brewers, maltsters and wine and spirit merchants. In March 1928 the business was absorbed by the Cannon Brewery Co. of London, who later came under the control of Taylor, Walker & Co. At this time much of the building was pulled down, including the tall chimney on the main block. The 1929–30 directories have entries for Christie and Lucas, wine, spirit and beer merchants, wholesale and retail, 94 High Street. It is interesting to note that the old 'Thatched House', immortalised by Isaac Walton, stood on the site of the brewery offices adjoining the brewery in the High Street.

Mr. H. C. Andrews, the prominent East Hertfordshire antiquarian, presented three of the countermarked pieces to the British Museum in 1929, the fourth being given by W. Trevithick in 1926. Mr. Andrews gave a talk in which the countermark was discussed just before the first world war, according to Mr. E. Paddick, the curator of the Hoddesdon Museum.

However, it is not clear to which period the countermark belongs. There is no evidence that the cross fleury was ever the brewery's trade or brand mark – in fact, from about 1870, a picture of Hoddesdon Clock House (built in 1835) was used as a trade mark. Hoddesdon Museum has no examples of the countermarked coins and Mr. Paddick knows of none in private collections although the brewery was the biggest local employer of labour for many years.

These factors and the date of the coins combine to indicate that the countermark is early, probably before the Christie and Cathrow era (1803). The pieces probably served as some form of pay check or barrel tally or receipt.

17 Huntingdonshire
St. Ives
17.1 ABBEY
There is no entry for this trader in the directories for 1792, 1811, 1823–4, 1839, 1840 or 1850. The countermark is similar to that used by Abbey of Bedford (see above) about 1830–9 – presumably the same man, or a relative.

18 Kent
Canterbury
18.1 BARNES
Thomas Richard Barnes, grocer, 12 Palace Street, appears in the Post Office Directory for 1845, but not in Pigot's 1839 Directory. The entry is for Thomas Richard Barnes and Sons in the 1874 and 1878 directories, but the firm is not listed in the 1890 issue. The countermark probably dates from the 1840's.

Chatham
18.2 COLE
This countermark was probably issued by Samuel Cole, a Chatham cutler listed in local directories as follows:
1824 Cole and Corrie, cutlers, Military Road.
1826–7 Cole & Co., cutlers and ironmongers, Military Road.
1832–3 Samuel Cole, brazier and tinplate worker, Military Road.
1845 Samuel Cole, ironmonger and cutler, 18 Military Road.
1851 Mrs. Ann Cole, ironmonger, Military Road.
The countermark probably dates from the period 1825–45.

18.3 (ROYAL DOCKYARD)

This countermark is similar in style to the Woolwich Arsenal or Dockyard checks (see 22.72 below) and has been tentatively attributed to the Royal Dockyard, Chatham. By 1900 the Dockyard covered 500 acres and contained a ropery, machine shops and foundries. These pieces were presumably used in the stores. Holden's 1811 Directory shows W. S. Cooper, storekeeper, Chatham Yard. In 1832, Wm. P. Smith was storekeeper and Thomas Irving, store receiver at the Royal Dockyard.

Duffield 1523 appears in the text as heart and G, but is illustrated as broad arrow and C, thus conforming with the other pieces listed in Table 1.

Maidstone

18.4 BUNYAR

Directory entries are as follows:

1823–4 (Pigot's) John Bunyar, corn factor, merchant, and dealer, and coal dealer, Moat Road.

1826–7 (Pigot's) as above, but address shown as 108 Stone Street.

1832–4 (Pigot's) as above, also shown as dealer in oil cake.

Edward Bunyar, shopkeeper, and dealer in groceries & sundries, Market Street.

1839 (Pigot's) John Bunyar, coal and corn merchant, Stone Street.

Thomas Bunyard (sic.), shopkeeper &c., 38 Camden Street.

1845 (Post Office) Bunyar & Son, millers & corn dealers, Stone Street.

Edward Bunyar, ginger beer manufacturer, Union Street.

Thomas Bunyard, coal dealer, Camden Street.

1847 (Bagshaw's) Bunyar & Son, coal and corn merchant, Stone Street.

Thomas Bunyar, coal merchant, Camden Street.

1888 (Melville & Co's) John Bunyar, miller, Stone Street.

Thomas C. Bunyar, shopkeeper, Astley Street.

The countermarked piece was probably issued by John Bunyar c. 1825–50.

Margate

18.5 DARBYSHIRE

William Darbyshire, Tobacconist, Paradise Street, appears in the Post Office Directory for 1878. In April 1880, the Mint were asked for a legal opinion on one of his paper advertisement labels affixed to a penny, but the enquiring solicitor was merely referred to the 1861 Act. On 17 August 1881, Mr. Charles Arkoll, of Maidstone, wrote to the Mint forwarding three copper coins with labels affixed 'received in change at the shop in Margate, not noticing the labels till afterwards'. Very probably these were also Darbyshire's labels.

Sevenoaks

18.6 HOOPER

John Hooper, furniture broker, is listed in Pigot's Directories for 1824 and 1829. He is shown as a furniture dealer in the High Street in Bagshaw's 1847 Directory.

Sheerness

18.7 HUNT

The shape of the clay pipe impressed on the coin shows it to date from the first half of the nineteenth century, a time when W. Hunt of Sheerness was a notable maker. Directories show the following entries:

1840 Henry Hunt, Jnr., Mile Town, tobacco pipe maker.

1847 William Hunt, High Street, tobacco pipe maker.

1852 William Hunt, High Street, Mile Town, tobacco pipe maker.

1862 William Henry Hunt, 144 High Street, Mile Town, tobacco pipe maker.

1874 William Henry Hunt, 2 Ebenezer Place and 250½ High Street (Mile Town), tobacco pipe maker and coffee rooms.

1878 William Henry Hunt, 3 Invicta Terrace and High Street, picture frame and tobacco pipe maker.

1890 William Henry Hunt, 17 High Street, fancy repository.

Henry Hunt, 216 High Street, shopkeeper.

Alfred Hunt, 9 Queen's Terrace, tobacco pipe maker.

1895 Alfred Hunt – as in 1890 directory.

The countermark presumably dates from the period c. 1845–55.

18.8 (SHEERNESS DOCKYARD)

This countermark is similar in style to the Woolwich Arsenal or Dockyard checks (see 22.72 below), and has been tentatively attributed to Sheerness Dockyard. Started in 1814, the Dockyard covered 60 acres by 1900 and contained 3 basins and 5 docks. These, like the Chatham Dockyard pieces, were probably used in the naval stores.

19 Lancashire

Cark

19.1 CARK COTTON WORKS

Cark Cotton Mill was opened about 1782 by James Stockdale and others, including, probably, William Hall. Stockdale had been associated with Boulton and Watt in mining in Cornwall and Wales, and with John Wilkinson, the ironmaster. By 1756 he was the chief worker of haematite ore in Furness, sending the iron to Watt in Greenock. One of Watt's first steam engines was constructed by Wilkinson and installed in the mill – see Dr. W. H. Chaloner's article 'The Stockdale Family . . . and the Cotton Mills at Cark-in-Cartmel c. 1782–1800' in 'Transactions of the Cumberland and Westmorland Antiquarian and Archaeological Society', New Series, lxiv 1964.

Directories have entries for Edward Hall, miller (1824), miller and maltster (1834). By 1855 John Hall and 1861 John A. Hall are shown at Cark. By 1885, and continuing to 1895, Edward Hall, besides being a miller, was merchanting corn and flour. Presumably the Halls then leased the premises, owned by David Hall in 1907 – the 1901 and 1905 entries are for Dickenson Bros., millers and maltsters. The mill was gutted by fire in the late 1930's.

Liverpool

19.2 FLETCHER

Thomas Fletcher & Son, hat makers, of Castle Street, are listed in Gore's 1766 Directory.

John Fletcher, hat maker also of Castle Street, and presumably the son, appears in Gore's 1767, 1769 and 1773 Directories. In the 1774 issue he is shown as a hatter and laceman at 4 Castle Street and in 1790 at 108 Dale Street. He does not appear in the 1796 directory, but there is an entry for William Fletcher, hatter, at 8 Golding's Court, Shaw's Brow. William Fletcher, hatter and victualler, Prescot Lane, Low Hill, is listed in the 1803 directory.

The engraved piece presumably dates from 1766 or earlier.

Lower House (near Burnley)

19.3 CHURCH TAVERN

This public house has not been traced in local directories. An alternative reading of this countermark – Lower House Tavern, Church (Accrington) – does not help as directories throw no light on this hostelry either. There was a Lower House Inn in Derker Street, Oldham c. 1864–73. The eligibility of this piece is open to doubt, as a coin may not have been used.

Manchester

19.4 DAWSON

Joseph Dawson, reedmaker, appears in the 1772 and 1773 directories at Acker's Gate, in 1781 and 1784 at Exchange Street and in 1788 at St. James Square. No directories are available for 1774–80, 1782–87, 1789–93 and there is no entry for Dawson in the 1794 issue. The 1804 directory has an entry for Joseph Dawson, iron founder, 96 Great Ancoats Street.

19.5 DOBSON

It has been assumed that the issuer of this countermark was granted a patent in the reign of William IV. Benjamin Dobson was the holder of patent no. 6552, dated 6 February 1834, for machinery for roving and spinning cotton and other fibrous materials. This, and the fact that the piece is listed by Batty (a Manchester man) indicate a Manchester provenance. Pigot's 1838 Directory lists Benjamin Dobson, cotton spinner and manufacturer of muslins &c., 18 Bridgwater Place, Manchester; works, Waterloo Mill, Chorley. By 1843, the entry is for the executors of Benjamin Dobson, cotton spinners and machine makers at the same address.

19.6 F.G

Assuming this to be a shop ticket, in which case other specimens ought to exist, possible issuers are as follows:

Francis Gardner, shopkeeper, at various addresses in Back Piccadilly (c. 1813–32).

Felix Grimes, warehouseman, 394 Oldham Road (1824–5).

Frederick Gardner, warehouseman, 8 Somerset Street (1828) (and hat manufacturer, 225 Great Ancoats Street).

Frederick Green & Co., Rainbow Coffee House and Hotel, and Wine and Spirit merchants, 2 Spring Gardens (c. 1838–50).

However, it could, of course, be an unofficial issue, in which case there are many other possibilities:

Francis Grant, bespoke boot and shoemaker, Downing Street (1819–20).

Francis Goddard, smith, 3 Charlotte Street (1829), Pritchard Street (1830).

Francis Gallipher, shoemaker, 54 Loom Street (1832).

Frederick Goos, machine maker, 2 Juno Street (1836) and jacquard machine maker, 28 William Street, Prussia Street (1840).

Frederick Godill, smith, 11 Broster Street (1848).

Frederick Goss, boilermaker, Gorton (1850).

Fitz Gibbon, shoemaker, Spear Street (1850).

Frederick Greenwood, toolmaker, 7 Lower Albion Street (1843).

Francis Gornell, blacksmith, 9 Heath Street, Pendleton (1843).

19.7 G.G

If the two engraved G's were intended to be associated with the 'MANCHESTER' countermark, possible issuers might be G. Giles, whitesmith, 7 Birtles Square, Salford, or G. Grimshaw, typemaker, 27 Bark Street, listed in Underhill's Biennial Directory for 1816–7. However this attribution is extremely tentative.

19.8 HAMPSON

Holden's Triennial Directory 1805–7 has an entry for Thomas Hampson, dimity &c. manufacturer, Shepherd's Court. The only other entries I have traced are for Mary Hampson, widow, Harding's buildings, Salford (1821/2) and Mary Hampson fustian cutter, 4 Back Thomas Street (1824–5). Directories have also been checked for the years 1772–3/81/88, 1804/08–9/13/15/17/19–20. The countermark has been assumed to date from c. 1811–12, the peak period of nineteenth century copper token production.

19.9 MIL . .

It is assumed that this piece was issued by John Milne, who appears in directories as follows:

1808–9 John Milne, attorney, house 59 King Street.

1811 John Milne, attorney, office 2 Hatter's Lane, house Gorton.

1813 as 1811 but house at Rusholme Lane.

1815 John Milne, solicitor, 2 Hatter's Lane, King Street.

1818–20 John Milne, attorney and coroner, 2 Hatter's Lane.

1821–2 John Milne, coroner and solicitor, 2 Hatter's Lane, house 1 Bloomsbury, Rusholme Lane.

1824–5 John Milne, coroner and solicitor, 15 Back King Street.

1828 John Milne, coroner, 41 Back King Street, house Chorlton Cottage, Bloomsbury, Chorlton Row.

1832 John Milne, coroner, 38 Back King Street, house 18 Bloomsbury, Chorlton Row.

The engraved coin probably dates from c. 1808–20.

19.10 WARBURTON
John Warburton, surgeon and druggist, was at 85 Portland Street from 1820 until at least 1825. By 1828 he had moved to 98 Portland Street, and in 1832 to number 28. In 1838 the business is in the name of Mary Warburton, presumably daughter or widow of John.

19.11 PENDLETON
In the absence of initials or trade this counter-mark has been assumed to represent the Man-chester suburb of Pendleton. It could, of course, be a surname – e.g. Richard Pendleton, the London watchmaker active c. 1780–1808.

20 Leicestershire
Sileby
20.1 LATEMAN
No trace of a trader named Lateman has been found in directories for 1822–3, 1828–9, 1835–6, 1841, 1846, 1849 or 1861, either under Sileby or the nearby settlement of Mountsorrel. In 1841 Sileby had 1473 inhabitants, many of whom were framework knitters, so it is possible that this countermarked coin served as some form of check or ticket in connection with that industry. Alterna-tively it is possible that Sileby represents a sur-name rather than the place name.

21 Lincolnshire
Alford
21.1 PACEY
The 1828–9 and 1835 directories have entries for Robert Pacey, ironmonger and brazier, Market Place. This is followed, presumably after his death, by entries in 1841, 1842 and 1849 for Mrs. Ann Pacey, ironmonger, tinplate worker and brazier at the same address.

Grimsby
21.2 TUPLING
William Tupling, of Loft Street, Peppercorn appears in the 1826 and 1828 directories as a boot and shoemaker, and in 1835 and 1842 as a boot and shoe merchant. The inclusion of a date (1852) in the countermark could mean that this is of the 'hatch, match or dispatch' variety (see above), especially as no entry for Tupling has been found in directories available for years subsequent to 1842. However, three specimens are known, and 1852 may be a redemption date. No link with W. Richardson has been found.

Holbeach
21.3 BLINKHORN
James Blinkhorn, Whitesmith, appears in the 1835 directory, but not in those for the years 1826, 1828/9 or 1842.

Louth
21.4 TATE AND LILL
Davis attributed this countermark in error to Louth, Ireland. Carey says (p. 95) that Tate and Lill, general gunsmiths, had a shop in Louth, Lincolnshire, about 1800. Holden's 1811 Direc-tory shows Bryan Tate, gunsmith, but no Lill. Pigot's 1819–20 and 1835–6 Directories show Bryan Tate, gunmaker, ironmonger and white-smith, Butcher Market, and Michael Lill, gunmaker and whitesmith, Upgate. Lill was making percussion pocket pistols about 1840. By 1841 Bryan and Richard Tate, gunmakers, are listed in Corn Market. The countermark dates from c. 1806–40, but may not be a token; the existence of the mark on a piece of lead indicates a trial piece for either a token or a shop ticket.

Tidd Gote
21.5 HENSON
John Henson, blacksmith, appears in the direc-tories for 1842, 1853 and 1856. The 1849 directory has an entry for W. Henson, blacksmith.

22 London
22.1 ANDERSON
Robert Anderson appears in the London direc-tories as follows:

1800 Robert Stewart Anderson (Anderson & Co., merchants), 37 Broad Street.

1810 Robert Anderson, merchant, 17 Old Pay Office, Broad Street.

1812 R. Anderson & Co., copper merchants, same address.

Entries for Robert Anderson & Co., merchants, occur during the same period in the Edinburgh directories, the address being given as 30 St. Andrews Square.

In the 1770's, a Robert Anderson was Master of St. John's Lodge of Freemasons in Inverness, but there is no record of his profession.

22.2 BARRON
From Samuel Timmins' 'Birmingham and the Midland Hardware District' (1866) we learn that 'Mr. Robert Barron, of London, a mechanic of considerable ingenuity, obtained for himself, in the year 1774, the right of constructing locks in which the security was effected by fixed wards, with the addition of lifting tumblers or levers. This invention was at once received with favour, and is still in great demand, being both useful and secure.' Woodcroft (op. cit.) gives the date of Barron's patent (no. 1200) as 31 October 1778. Directories show the following entries:

1772 Rob. Barron, brazier and ironmonger, Strand.

1794 Rob. Barron, Patent Locksmith, 66 Barbican. Barron & Son, Ironmongers, 475 Strand.

1798–1818 Francis Barron & Son, ironmongers and braziers, 476 Strand.

1827–8 Francis Barron & Son, ironmongers, 479 Strand.

1832 Barron & Son, ironmongers, 1 and 2 Charing Cross.

1836 F. W. Barron & Son, ironmongers and smiths, 436 West Strand.

1839–40 Francis Barron & Son, ironmongers and locksmiths, 436 West Strand.

1842–57 Barron & Son, ironmongers to Her Majesty, smiths and locksmiths, 436 West Strand.

By 1864 the firm had become Barron, Son & Wilson, and had additional premises at 7 King William Street. By 1870 they were known as Barron & Wilson, and the 1879 directory shows them also as gas and water engineers, with additional premises at 8 King William Street. Having vacated 436 West Strand, their address in 1885 is 7, 8 and 9 King William Street and Strand Works, 7 Rose Street, Soho, W, while by 1888 these premises are occupied by Wilson & Son, ironmongers.

The countermark, presumably the firm's brandmark as applied to their locks, is assumed to date from the 1830's or 1840's.

22.3 BARTLEET

Thomas Bartleet appears in the Birmingham directories for 1800 and 1805–7 as a manufacturer of gilt and plated buttons, thimbles, sleeve links and children's clasps, and as bell founders and casters in general at 39 Great Charles Street. By 1828, then Bartleet & Sons, the address is given as 126 Great Charles Street where the firm remains until 1858. From 1860 to 1877 directories show the firm at 22 Newhall Street. In the 1830's Bartleets opened premises in London, the earliest directory entry being in 1834 at 1 Maiden Lane, Wood Street. Entries continue as follows:

1835 Thos. Bartleet, buttonmakers and general dealers, 18 Noble Street.

1836–7 Thos. Bartleet & Sons, buttonmakers and hardwaremen, 118 Noble Street (sic).

1838–45 Address shown as 18 and 19 Noble Street.

1848 Same address, but described as buttonmakers, Manchester and woollen warehousemen.

1851 Address shown as Falcon Hall, Silver Street, Wood Street.

1855–64 Address shown as 17 Silver Street.

1870 Described as 'manufacturers of buttons, thimbles, pins, needles, fish-hooks and other articles, Manchester and woollen warehousemen, wholesale dealers in cutlery, combs and general hardware and all goods suited to the East India and other markets, and importers of French and German goods' at 13 Little Britain, Aldersgate Street, E.C.

1879–85 Address shown as 46 Commercial Street, E., and described, in addition to the above, as importers of 'a large variety of goods for fancy shops and bazaars'.

1888–91 Charles Bartleet & Sons, needle manufacturers, 42A Noble Street, E.C.

By 1900, entries have ceased.

The countermark probably dates from the period c. 1835–1845. The 'elephant' trade mark has not been traced.

22.4 BENNETT

William Bennett, carpenter, of Well Street, Hackney, appears in Holden's Triennial Directories 1805–7, 1808–11 and 1811–14, and Pigot's London Directories 1824, 1826–7 and 1832–3.

22.5 BLUNT

Stephen Blunt, dentist, of 29 Gt. Windmill Street, appears in Holden's Triennial Directory 1805–7. There are also entries for him at the same address in the Westminster Rate Books from 1785 to 1809.

In Lickey Coins' List for October 1973, no. 6396 is described '1797 Bluns (sic.) operator of teeth, Great Windmill St. . . . on worn halfpenny.' This may be an additional variety, or the inaccurate description of an existing one. The inclusion of a date is interesting, though it is not clear whether this is contemporary with the rest of the piece.

22.6 BOND

Bond is, of course, a common name in the London directories, and it is not possible at this stage to give a firm attribution for this countermark. However it does seem quite likely that it could have been issued by one of the many and related gunmakers named Bond in the late eighteenth and nineteenth centuries, though I have not yet found a gunmaker's mark corresponding exactly to the countermark. Directories show the following entries:

1791/4 Bond, Edward, gunmaker, 59 Lombard Street.

1798–1806 Bond, P., gunmaker, 59 Lombard Street and 45 Cornhill.

1805–7/10 Bond, Phillip, gunmaker, 45 Cornhill.

1805–20 Bond, William, gunmaker, 59 Lombard Street.

1827–45 Bond, William, gunmaker and sword-cutler, 59 Lombard Street.

1817–19 Bond, E. J., gunmaker and sword-cutler, 45 Cornhill.

1820–34 Bond, E. and J., gunmakers and sword-cutler to the Hon. East India Company, 45 Cornhill.

1835–45 Bond, Edward and William, gunmakers and archery warehouse, 45 Cornhill.

1846–55 as above, but at 45 Cornhill and at Hooper Square, Goodman's Fields.

1857 Bond, Edward and William, gunmakers and sword-cutlers to the Hon. Board of Ordnance and the Hon. East India Co., 142 Leadenhall Street and Hooper Square, Leman Street, Goodman's Fields.

1872–9 Bond, Edward and William, gunmakers, 4 Northumberland Alley, Fenchurch Street, E.C.

1864–70 Bond, Edward Philip, gunmaker, Hooper Square, Goodman's Fields.
For further information see Carey, p. 10.
Other possibilities could be

1794–1828 Bond, Thomas, fishing tackle and needle-maker, 37 Crooked Lane, Cannon Street.

1832–51 Bond, Thomas, fishing-rod, hook and tacklemaker, 62 Cannon Street.

1817–18 Bond, John, mast and blockmaker, Fore Street, Limehouse.

1827–28 as above, address 22 Fore Street.

1836–38 Bond, Thomas, same address.

1842 Bond, Thos. Durley, same address.

1857 Bond, John, same address.

On balance I favour one of the gunmaking Bonds, probably before 1840.

22.7 BRADSHAW
This engraved piece was issued by John Bradshaw, a Ticket Porter at the Custom House, Lower Thames Street, in 1765.

22.8 BURCH
Burch, Waterman, Paul's Wharf, has not been traced in the London directories. The piece probably dates from before 1830.

22.9 CLARK
Clark is a very common name in the directories; there are, for example, 40 entries in the 1806 issue. It is thus difficult to attribute this countermark, although a strong probability is the early nineteenth century Fleet Street firm of cutlers and silversmiths who have the following entries in the directories:

1791–8 Clark, Ebenezer, hardwareman and silversmith, near St. Dunstan's Church, Fleet Street.

1800–12 Clark, E. and J., variously described as hardwaremen and silversmiths or cutlers and silversmiths, St. Dunstans, Fleet Street.

1817–18 Clark, E., cutler and silversmith, Fleet Street.

1819–23 Clark and Weatherley, cutlers, silversmiths, and manufacturers of tea urns and japanned-wares, Fleet Street.

1824–32 As above at 186 Fleet Street.

The Davis text has this as Clarke, but Plate J, no. 3 clearly shows Clark.

The countermark was probably issued within the period 1800–18.

Another possibility is the Clark mentioned by Carey (p. 17) who had a Royal Government contract for flintlock muskets, and a shop in High Holborn (1785–1840). The 1806 directory shows Wattell Clark, gunmaker, at 43 High Holborn. The countermark is certainly similar in style to other gunmakers' marks.

22.10 COULSELL
Thomas Coulsell, manufacturer of rules in box and ivory, was at 29 Queen Street, Southwark between 1799 and 1814. In style and date this countermark, not recorded by Davis, belongs to the nineteenth century token series. Other directory entries for Coulsell and family are:

1815–28 Coulsell, Thomas, rule manufacturer, 41 Union Street, Southwark.

1829–39 address shown as 153 Union Street.

1839 Coulsell, Eliz., 41 Union Street, Borough.

1815–57 Coulsell, William, mathematical instrument maker, 9 Castle Street, Borough.

1870–2 Coulsell, William, rulemaker, 156 Salmons Lane, Limehouse, E.

I have, so far, only seen this countermark on the reverse of George II halfpennies. The Order in Council of 30 January 1814 providing for the demonetization and withdrawal of Tower halfpence may have stimulated the issue of these countermarks in the same year.

22.11 CRYPTO
'Crypto' was the trademark of the Crypto Cycle Co. Ltd. of London in 1892 (White's 'Hardware Trade Marks', no. 278). This firm appears in directories as follows:

1884 Crypto Cycle Co., licensees and manufacturers of the patent Crypto-dynamic gearing for tricycles and bicycles, 3 Queen Victoria Street, E.C.

1885–88 As above at 73A Chiswell Street, E.C.

1889–90 Crypto Cycle Co. Ltd., manufacturers of bicycles and tricycles, Crypto-dynamic gearing, Crypto cyclometer and general engineers, 64 City Road, E.C. (late of 73 Chiswell Street).

1893 As above with additional address 47 Farringdon Road.

1894–1904 Crypto Works Co. Ltd., bicycle manufacturers, 29 Clerkenwell Road, E.C.

1905–6 Crypto Car and Cycle Co., 14 Mortimer Street, W.

1907/10/12 as above, with cycle works also at 15 Berners Mews, W.

1915–33 Crypto Car and Cycle Co., motor valve manufacturers, 14 Mortimer Street.

The countermark is probably unofficial, dating from c. 1884–1912.

22.12 DAVIS
Davis, writing in 1904, says: 'These countermarked pieces were issued in the silver token period by Davis of the Falstaff Inn. There is a public house of that sign in Houndsditch at the present time.' The following entries appear in the directories:

1808 Davis, Samuel, wine and brandy merchant, 45 and 46 Houndsditch.

1810 Davis, Sam. & Co., wine and brandy merchants, 46 Houndsditch.

1811–12 Davis, S. & Wm., wine and spirit merchants, 45 and 46 Houndsditch.

1817–22 Davis, Samuel, wine and spirit merchant, 46 Houndsditch.

The countermark presumably dates from about 1810 – i.e. when the firm was at 46 Houndsditch only, described as wine and brandy merchants.

22.13 DAVIS
It is assumed that this countermark was issued by J. Davis, cutler and razor maker, who appears in the London directories as follows:

1833–5 Davis, J., razor maker, 5 Church Row, Aldgate.

1836–8 Davis, J., manufacturing cutler, 88 High Street, Aldgate.

1842–4 Davis, John, razor maker and cutler, 20 Aldgate High Street.

1845–7 as above but address shown as 69 Leadenhall Street.

1851–3 Davis, John, cutler and inventor of the norman razor and maker of the unrivalled razor strop, 69 Leadenhall Street and 39 Threadneedle Street.

1854 Davis, John, 39 Threadneedle Street.

1856 Davis, John & Son, manufacturing cutlers, 69 Leadenhall Street.

1857–63 Davis, John and William, as above.

1864–79 Davis, John Charles, as above.

1880–1 Davis, John Charles, 62 Leadenhall Street.

The countermark probably dates from the period 1845–53.

22.14 DRABBLE

Waters' 1898 article has E. Drabble, but this must be a misprint. (The only E. Drabble, cutler, I know of was at Eyre Street, Sheffield in 1805–7). The London directories show the following entries for Drabble and his family:

1834 Samuel Drabble, cutler, 35 Marylebone Lane.

1835–80 Samuel Drabble, cutler, 1 High Street, Marylebone.

1881 Samuel Drabble, working cutler, 109 Wardour Street, Soho.

1882–1908 Mrs. Mary Drabble, cutler, 109 Wardour Street, Soho.

1882–4 Henry John Drabble, cutler, Bridle Lane, Golden Square, W.

1893–4 Samuel Drabble, cutler, 106 Marylebone Lane.

The countermark presumably dates from the period between 1835 and the passing of the 1853 Act. It is certainly earlier than 1870, when recorded by Batty. The premises were destroyed by enemy action in the Second World War.

22.15 EDWARDS

The only Thomas Edwards active in 1755 and listed by Baillie is a London watchmaker who was apprenticed in 1749 and a member of the Clockmakers' Company until 1766. His address is not given and he does not appear in the directories for 1740, 1757 or 1760.

22.16 FIRMIN

It is probable that this countermark was issued by Firmin's, the well-known London button manufacturers, who used the style 'Firmin and Company' c. 1800–11 — see Sally C. Luscomb 'The Collector's Encyclopaedia of Buttons' (New York 1967), p. 74. Directories show the following entries:

1763 Samuel Firmin, metal buttonmaker to His Majesty, Strand, opposite the New Church.

1806 Firmin & Westall, buttonmakers, 153 Strand.

1812 Firmin & Langdale, button sellers, 153 Strand.

1818–23 Firman & Langdon (sic) same address and Clare Court (1823).

1823–4 Firmin & Sons, buttonmakers, 153 Strand and 10 Clare Court, Drury Lane.

1827 Firmin & Sons, buttonmakers, 153 Strand; Robert Firmin, buttonmaker, Clare Court, Drury Lane.

1828–32 P. & R. Firmin, buttonmakers, 153 Strand.

1836–7 P., R. & S. Firmin, as above.

1838 Samuel Firmin & Sons, as above; Firmin & King, buttonmakers and sword-cutlers, 13 Conduit Street, Regent Street.

1839 Firmin & Sons, 153 Strand and White Horse Yard, Drury Lane; Philip & Samuel Firmin, 13 Conduit Street; Samuel Firmin, buttonmaker, 20 Stanhope Street, Clare Market.

1842 Philip & Samuel Firmin, buttonmakers and sword-cutlers, 13 Conduit Street, Bond Street, and 153 Strand.

1857 Firmin & Sons, wholesale army and navy button, military and naval ornament manufacturers to the Queen and Royal Family and wholesale trimming warehousemen, 153 Strand, 13 Conduit Street, Bond Street, 12 White Horse Yard, Drury Lane and 20 Stanhope Street, Clare Market.

1870–2 Address shown as 153, 154, 155 Strand, W.C.; manufactories, 12 White Horse Yard, Drury Lane, W.C., 13 Conduit Street, W. and 2 Dawson Street, Dublin.

1879–1900 Firmin & Sons Ltd., as above, also die sinkers and medallists, helmet, chaco, caps and accoutrement makers.

1930 As above, address shown as 8 Cork Street, Bond Street, W.1. Factory: Birmingham.

1970 Firmin & Sons Ltd., button, badge, accoutrement and metal smallware manufacturers, embroiderers etc., 81 Ford Road, E.3.

22.17 FOUNDER'S COMPANY

The Founder's Company was established about 1300 and granted a charter in 1614. It had sole rights of examining and marking all brazen weights. The mark of a ewer with a curving spout projecting to the left was struck on every weight tested by the Company after 1590. During the 18th century it became common practice for coin weights to be tested at Founders Hall and marked with the ewer mark. The mark of a ewer between 18 and 26 was introduced when the Weights and Measures Act of 1824 became effective in 1826. It was used for stamping avoirdupois and troy weights of brass and bronze manufactured within three miles of the City of London until the Company's rights were extinguished by the Weights and Measures Act of 1878. $\overline{A}$ is an archaic form of A standing for avoirdupois. For this information I am indebted to Mr. Ronald Stocks, Chief Inspector of Weights and Measures at Dover. The countermarked coin is clearly a trial or unofficial piece dating from 1826–78. The directories for 1842 and 1846 show John Gray, junior clerk, Founders Hall, Founders Hall Court, 47 Lothbury.

22.18 GREAVES

It is not possible to be certain about the issuer of this countermark, but a strong probability is James Greaves, saddle tree maker of 6 Hollen Street, Soho (c. 1812–20), 7 Hollen Street (1822) and 26 Berwick Street (1823–33). From 1835 to c. 1840 Abraham Greaves was at 26 Berwick Street, followed c. 1844–51 by James Greaves, saddle tree maker at 31 Crown Street. The countermark probably dates from c. 1812–33.

22.19 HALL

John Parker Hall has not been traced in the commercial section of the London directories for 1870, 1875, 1880, 1885, 1890, 1895 or 1900.

22.20 HAMILTON

Andrew Hamilton, merchant, was at 29 Lawrence Lane (1777), 5 Jefferies Square (1782), 106 Fenchurch Street (1783–7), 95 Fenchurch Street (1788) and 2 Little Tower Hill (1791). R. T. Hamilton, upholsterer, was at 126 Fenchurch Street (1820–36) and 127 Houndsditch (1837). The engraved coin dates from 1783–7.

22.21 HATCHETT'S HOTEL

Bradshaw's 'Railway Manual, Shareholders' Guide and Directory' for 1869 includes the following advertisement: 'Hatchett's Hotel, Piccadilly and Dover Street. Established 100 years. Good beds, good living, cleanliness, and comfort, combined with moderate charges. Porter up all night. Warm baths. Servants charged if desired. Celebrated for the sale of choice wines.' Hatchett's Restaurant still (1973) exists, and a potted history displayed outside states that it was established in 1702. However, directory entries start much later, as follows:

1811 Hatchett, Hatchett's Hotel, Piccadilly.
1825 Hatchett & Co., wine merchants, Hatchett's Hotel, 67 Piccadilly.
1827–8 Hatchett & Beare, wine and brandy merchants, 67 Piccadilly.
1837–42 Thomas Thomas, wine merchant, Hatchett's Hotel, 67 Piccadilly.
1845 Hatchett's Hotel and New White Horse Cellar (Thomas Thomas), 67 Piccadilly.
1848–51 Address shown as 67 and 68 Piccadilly.
1855 Hatchett's Hotel and Tavern and New White Horse Cellar (Thos. Thomas, Baily Thomas Farmer Esq.).
1861–79 As above but Joseph C. Bowles replaces Thos. Thomas.
1885 As above but Hatchett's Hotel Co. Limited, Walter Tyler, Secretary.
1888 Hatchett's Hotel and Tavern and New White Horse Cellars, Ruggero Pratti, proprietor, 67 and 68 Piccadilly.
1891 White Horse Cellars Restaurant, 67A Piccadilly.
1900 Hatchett's Restaurant, 67A Piccadilly.
1922 Hatchett's Ltd., Restaurant, 72 Aldermanbury, E.C.2.; Hatchett's White Horse Cellars Ltd., Restaurant, 67A Piccadilly.
1930–61 Shown at 67A Piccadilly and 1 Dover Street.
1968 Hatchett's Restaurant, 67 Piccadilly.
1970–1 Address shown as 67A Piccadilly.

The countermark probably dates from before the 1853 Act, and certainly from before 1870, when it was recorded by Batty, but it is difficult to be more precise.

22.22 HAYES

Relevant directory entries are as follows:
1823 George Canton, surgeon and apothecary, 5 Great Mays Buildings.
1834–5 J. Hayes, dentist and cupper, 5 Great Mays Buildings.
1838 H. Hayes, as above.
1842–6 Henry Hayes, dentist, 5 Mays Buildings and 12 Bedford Court, Covent Garden.
1848 Edmund Home, gasfitter, 5 Great Mays Buildings.

Thus, while the countermark undoubtedly dates from the period 1834–46, it is not clear whether J. Hayes or H. Hayes was the issuer.

22.23 HEMS

This countermark is assumed to have been issued by the Whitechapel firm of cutlers, shown in the directories as follows:
1808–12 Hems, William, cutler, 40 Whitechapel.
1816 Hems, Wm. & Son, cutlers, 39 Whitechapel.
1817–19 Hems, William, cutler, 39 Whitechapel.
1820–4 Hems & Son, cutlers, 39 Whitechapel.
1825–8 Hems & Sons, cutlers, 39 and 135 Whitechapel.
1832–3 as above, but shown at 39 and 142 Whitechapel.
1836–7 Hems & Son, as above.
1838 Hems, Wm. & Son, cutlers, 39 and 142 Whitechapel High Street.
1839 Hems & Son, manufacturing cutlers, 39 High Street, Whitechapel.
1842–5 Hems, Wm. & Son, cutlers and ironmongers, 39 and 142 Whitechapel.
1848–67 as above at 39 Whitechapel High Street, and 23 Aldgate.

The countermark probably dates from the period 1836–53.

The only other possible issuers are John Hems & Son, cheesemongers, 234 Shoreditch (1818–19), or William & Benjamin Hems, cutlers and ironmongers, 49 Blackman Street, Borough (1837–8).

22.24 HUNDLEY

C. Hundley was a saw maker of Red Lion Market, White Cross Street, and appears in the London directories between 1806 and 1828. A less likely, though possible, issuer was Francis Hundley, engraver and printer, of 64 St. Martins Lane, c. 1836–51.

22.25 HUXLEY & CHING

The following entries appear in the London directories:
1842–57 Huxley & Heriot, wholesale ironmongers, gas apparatus and stove makers, manufacturers in brass and iron, 16, 28 and 29 Castle Street, Long Acre.

1858–9 Huxley & Ching, wholesale ironmongers, gas engineers and stove makers, as above.

1860–94 Ching, Comyn & Co. (late Huxley & Ching), wholesale ironmongers, gas engineers and stove makers, manufacturers in brass and iron, and cabinet brass founders, 28 and 29 Castle Street, W.C., 24 Little St. Andrews St., W.C.; workshops 3 Little White Lion Street.

1903–34 Ching, Comyn & Co. Ltd., as above, but no mention of Huxley and Ching.

1935 Ching Properties Ltd., 54 Castle Street.

The countermark, which is unofficial, probably dates from the 1860's, the 1861 halfpenny being countermarked *after* the takeover by Ching Comyn & Co., some old brand-marking punches being used.

22.26 JOHNSON

The following entries appear in the London directories:

1840 Joshua Fox, saw maker, 101 Great Titchfield Street.

1842 John Johnson, saw and tool maker, same address (Street section); Joseph Johnson, saw and tool maker, 101A Great Titchfield Street (commercial section).

1843–68 Joseph Johnson, saw, tool and busk maker, 101 Great Titchfield Street.

1869–72 Joseph Johnson, saw maker, 69 Great Titchfield Street.

1873–85 Joseph Johnson, saw maker, 105 Great Titchfield Street.

1886–92 Joseph Johnson, saw maker, 39 Upper Marylebone Street.

1893–5 Joseph Johnson, saw maker, 2 Brunswick Mews, Bryanston Square.

The countermark probably dates from before the 1853 Act. See also Appendix 1.

22.27 KILBURN

This is assumed to be the place-name, in the absence of initials or any indication of trade.

22.28 LLOYD, EDWARD

Edward Lloyd was to this series of countermarks what Thomas J. Barratt of Pears' Soap was to the later series of countermarked European bronze coins. Like Barratt he was by far the most prolific, but not the earliest, issuer. Barratt's advertisements, and the general circulation of European bronze with and without countermarks, resulted in legislation to prohibit the importation of such coins (1886) and facilitate their withdrawal through the Post Offices (1887) – see Seaby's Coin and Medal Bulletin, December 1970 and March 1973. Lloyd's advertisements resulted in the 1853 Act prohibiting the defacing of coin of the realm, and, with a number of other factors, contributed to the changeover from copper coinage to bronze in 1860 – see above.

Lloyd was born in Thornton Heath, Surrey, on 16 February 1815. In 1833 he compiled 'Lloyd's Stenography', and between 1836 and 1856 published upwards of 200 'Penny Bloods' – romantic and horror stories – issued from, successively, premises at 44 Wych Street, Strand,

62 Broad Street, Bloomsbury, 44 Holywell Street, Strand and 31 Curtain Road, Shoreditch.

From 1841 to 1843 he was established as a printer and publisher at 231 Shoreditch High Street, with additional premises at 12 and 13 Salisbury Square, and Crown Court, Fleet Street, by 1844–6. Between 1848 and 1922, his newspaper offices were at 12 Salisbury Square.

In September 1842, Lloyd produced an illustrated penny paper. This had eight small pages and contained two serial stories – but no news; because of this it was unstamped. On 27 November 1842 appeared the first of seven issues of 'Lloyd's Illustrated London Newspaper', also with eight pages, of three columns each, with some small woodcuts, and priced at twopence. It was designed to compete with the sixpenny 'Illustrated London News', and led to a dispute with the Stamp Office, for, although unstamped, it contained news. From 15 January 1843 the paper reappeared as 'Lloyd's Weekly London Newspaper', at first with eight pages of five columns and no illustrations at twopence halfpenny (stamped) and later, from 24 September 1843, with twelve pages at threepence. This was cheaper than any stamped newspaper that had preceded it. The first editor was a Mr. Ball, the original 'Censorius' of the 'Weekly Dispatch', followed in 1844 by William Carpenter (1797–1874), the zealous political reformer. The paper prospered, aided by its low price and the formation of the Electric Telegraph Company in 1846. Some time between issues 301 (27 August 1848) and 321 (14 January 1849) it was retitled 'Lloyd's Weekly Newspaper'. The majority of the countermarks must therefore date from the period between late 1848 and 25 September 1850 when a letter of complaint appeared in 'The Times' – see above.

The slightly less common countermark advertising Lloyd's Penny Sunday Times was a little earlier – probably 1846–7; it will be noted that one variety (22.28 Aii) is countermarked additionally '1847'. The 'Penny Sunday Times and People's Police Gazette' first appeared on 12 September 1841 and continued until 3 January 1847. It was a penny weekly of four large pages, adorned with rough illustrations, giving narratives of the sensational crimes of the day, and was followed in 1843 by other publications in the same vein. It was this sort of paper that was being advertised in the slogan 'Read Number 1 of Lloyd's last new penny publication' that appears along with many of the Lloyd's Weekly Newspaper countermarks. A new paper, 'Lloyd's Weekly Miscellany (and Penny Sunday Times)' appeared in 1850–1, perhaps indicating that the two-slogan countermarks date from 1850.

It is fairly clear that the initiative for countermarking advertisements on coins came from Lloyd himself rather than his editors. He took particular personal interest in promoting the sale of his paper by posters and advertisements, and sent a free copy each week to every toll-gate keeper who could be persuaded to put up a bill by the roadside. He paid half the wages of his men in countermarked coin so that it should be well distributed. No information is available on the number of coins so countermarked, but it must have run into several thousands. Despite the calling-in of the old copper coinage (see above) the pieces are still fairly common. Some scarce examples are known countermarked on Irish and Canadian tokens (see 22.28 E, 22.28 I).

When Douglas Jerrold became editor of Lloyd's Weekly Newspaper on 18 April 1852, average circulation was 70,000. In 1853 this increased to 90,000, helped by the abolition of the Advertisement Tax (18d. per advertisement) in the same year. It was still running at this level when Thomas Catling joined the paper on 18 April 1854 – he became news editor in 1866 and editor in 1884. Other restraints on the press disappeared: the Newspaper Stamp Act of 1855 abolished the newspaper stamp (reduced to a penny in 1836), and the price of Lloyd's Weekly Newspaper was reduced from threepence to twopence, circulation increasing to 107,000. On 1 October 1861, the duty on paper was abolished – Lloyd had anticipated this in September by reducing the price to one penny. The circulation was then 170,000, increasing to 350,000 by 1863, 500,000 in 1867 and one million in 1896.

The paper was retitled 'Lloyd's Weekly News' on 30 November 1902, 'Lloyd's Sunday News' 2 June 1918, 'The Sunday News' 7 October 1923, and 'Sunday News' 16 March 1930. After 9 August 1931 it was incorporated in the 'Sunday Graphic'.

In 1876 Lloyd bought the 'Daily Chronicle and Clerkenwell News' for £30,000 and, after spending £150,000 (on, among other things, some brass, farthing size, advertisement tickets – e.g. Batty 386) established it as a London daily paper.

He was one of the first to introduce Hoe's American printing presses into England. He established a large paper-making factory at Sittingbourne, growing and importing esparto grass from Algeria, where he leased 100,000 acres. He died, very wealthy, on 8 April 1890 at 17 Delahay Street, Westminster, and was buried at Highgate cemetery. He left a widow and a large family.

Bibliography:

'Dictionary of National Biography', Vol. xxxiii (London 1893).
H. R. Fox Bourne, 'English Newspapers', Volume 2 (1887).
Blanchard Jerrold, 'Life of Douglas Jerrold', 2nd ed. (1869).
Thomas Catling, 'My Life's Pilgrimage' (London 1911).
John Medcraft, 'Bibliography of the Penny Bloods of Edward Lloyd' (Dundee 1945).

22.29 LLOYD, THOMAS

Lloyd appears in the London directories as follows:

1805–12 Thomas Lloyd, grocer and tea dealer, 156 Aldersgate Street.
1816 Thomas Lloyd, grocer, 141 Aldersgate Street and 7 Bridge Street, Lambeth.
1817–32 Thomas Lloyd, grocer and tea dealer, 141 Aldersgate Street.
1836–39 Thos. Lloyd & Co. as above.
1842–48 Thos. Lloyd & Co., grocers and tea dealers, 141 Aldersgate Street and 4 Plumber's Row, City Road.
1851 Thos. Lloyd & Co., merchants, 9 Austinfriars.

By 1857 Wm. Ladd & Co., grocers and tea dealers were at 141 Aldersgate Street. Lloyd also issued a brass halfpenny-size advertisement ticket – see Batty 1002F. It is assumed from the above that the countermark dates from the period c. 1833–c. 1841.

22.30 LONDON

It is assumed that this countermark represents the place name rather than a surname, but it is not possible to identify the issuer. This is probably an example of unofficial use of one of a series of brand-marking punches.

22.31 LONDON

The countermark is assumed to represent the trader's surname and the place-name.

The most likely issuer was Edward London, gunmaker, shown in the directories at 50 London Wall (1826–7) and 51 London Wall (1828–72). Carey (p. 61) says William London made screw cannon barrel flintlock pistols (1825–40) and Edward London made percussion duelling pistols with silver mountings, also percussion sporting guns (1840–72). The coin is very worn, and the countermark could be as late as the 1840's.

Another possibility, less likely in view of the worn state of the coin, is John London, Furnishing ironmonger, 4 Bishopsgate without (1800–23).

22.32 (CROWN) LONDON

Assumed to be the brand mark of a London firm, possibly a gunmaker.

22.33 LOOKER

Henry William Looker, manufacturing cutler, is listed in the London directories at 42 Leadenhall Street, 1838–56. In 1857, John Garland & Son, wine merchants, appear at the same address.

One variety of this countermark (22.33B) must date from before 1850, as a specimen in my own collection on a penny of 1797 has a Lloyd's Weekly Newspaper countermark struck *over* it. (22.28 G on rev. and obv.)

22.34 LUND

Lund's were established in Cornhill in 1796, and are still in existence – but can throw no light on the countermark. Directory entries are as follows:

1805–12 Thomas Lund, 57 Cornhill, variously described as pen and quill warehouse, pen, quill, sponge, filtering stones &c., cutler.
1817–26 Thomas Lund, cutler and manufacturer of portable writing desks, importer of filtering stones &c., warehouses 56 and 57 Cornhill.
1827–32 William Anderson, cutler and razor-maker, 24 Fleet Street.

1836–44 Wm. Lund (late Anderson), manufacturer of dressing-cases, fine cutlery, and real drilled-eyed needles, 24 Fleet Street.
1843–45 Thomas Lund, cutler and writing desk maker, 56 and 57 Cornhill.
1845 Wm. Lund, cutler, dressing case maker and ivory turner, 23 and 24 Fleet Street, City.
1846–58 Wm. Lund, cutler and dressing case maker, 56 and 57 Cornhill, 23 and 24 Fleet Street.
1870–72 William Lund, cutler, desk, dressing case and pocket book maker and ivory turner, also patentee and manufacturer of Lund's double patent everpointed pencil in wood and ivory; Lund's London lever for drawing corks; Lund's London rack corkscrew with patent spring ends; Lund's gravitating decanting machines; Lund's London letter clips and sliding tubes for binding papers and periodicals; and Lund's portable double lever letter-copying press and Lund's patent durable double fold umbrellas, 23, 24, 25 Fleet Street, E.C., 56 and 57 Cornhill, E.C.
1879–80 William Lund & Son as above – also making Lund's incisor for opening tins of provisions.
1885–1900 Address shown as 56 and 57 Cornhill E.C. and 25 Fleet Street.
1910 William Lund & Son, cutlery manufacturers, goldsmiths, silversmiths, jewellers, watch and clockmakers, ivory and tortoise-shell workers, dressing bag and case makers, purses, fancy leather goods etc., 56 and 57 Cornhill, E.C.
1922 Address shown as 63 and 64 New Broad Street, E.C.2., 7 Whittington Avenue, E.C.3., Leadenhall Buildings, E.C.3.
1930 92 Old Broad Street, E.C.2 – established 1796 (late of Cornhill).
1949–53 54 Old Broad Street.
1970–71 As above and at 1 Bishopsgate Churchyard, E.C.2.
The countermark apparently dates from the period c. 1833–44.

22.35 MASON
William Mason appears in the London directories as follows:
1823 Coach-spring maker, 22 Castle Street East, Oxford Street.
1826–7 Patent axle-tree maker, 22 Castle Street East, Oxford Market.
1828 As above but address shown as 6 Margaret Street, Cavendish Square.
1832 As above but with additional address 22 Castle Street East, Oxford Market.
1837–8 Coachmaker, 75 Kingsland Road.
Mason's 'improvements on axle-trees' are listed in an advertisement in Pigot's 'London & New Provincial Directory' for 1826–7:
'1st. There are four long Reservoirs in the Centre of the Box, which contain a greater quantity of Oil (than usual) that is always circulating round the Arm, which will prevent the Wheel ever sticking fast, and runs with considerable more ease.
2nd. The Fixtures are such as to prevent the possibility of the Wheel coming off.

3rd. To let out the Wheel when travelling on bad roads with perfect safety.'
His patents are mainly concerned with axle-trees but cover other fields as well:

Number	Date	Concerning
5188	18 June 1825	Axle-trees.
5451	15 January 1827	Construction of axle-trees and boxes for carriages or mail coaches.
5986	24 August 1830	Construction of axle-trees and the boxes applicable thereto.
6151	10 August 1831	Construction of wheeled-carriages.
6872	7 August 1835	Making firearms and artillery.
6873	7 August 1835	Manufacture of steam engines, cylinders, pistons, bearings, pumps and cocks
6895	24 September 1835	Wheels, boxes and axle-trees of carriages for carrying persons and goods on common roads and on railways.

I only know of this countermark on a French décime, but it may well exist on British coins. It is assumed to date from c. 1825–32.

22.36 MILDWATER
Mildwater seems to be a London surname: a search of current telephone directories produced seven entries in London and the neighbouring parts of Hertfordshire, Middlesex, Kent and Surrey, but none in Birmingham, Coventry, Liverpool, Manchester, Glasgow, Sheffield, Newcastle or Nottingham. Only one Mildwater appears in the London directories during the nineteenth century:
1856–7 Joseph Mildwater, builder, 5 Werrington Street, Somers Town.
1859 As above, builder and decorator, 8 Werrington Street, N.W.
1870–77 As above, 122 Gloucester Road, N.W.
The countermarked piece presumably served as a pay or tool check: others, with different numbers, may well exist. On a demonetized Coventry halfpenny such an issue would not have been illegal.

22.37 MONCRIEFFE
It has not proved possible to trace Francis Moncrieffe in the London directories. Burke does not list a Francis in the two well-known Moncreiff, Moncrieff or Moncrieffe families of the period. The only entry for this surname at this time is for Lady Elizabeth Moncrieffe, 14 Baker Street, Portman Sq. (1805–7). The piece may have been issued by a visitor to London, or by a resident rather than a trader, and probably belongs to the 'hatch, match or dispatch' category.

22.38 MORRALL

Abel Morrall, needlemaker, is shown in the London directories from 1850:

1850 134 Upper Thames Street (Thos. Linnell, agent).

1853 Inventor of the grooveless needle and all other improvements in sewing needles and the machinery for making the same, warehouse 40 Gresham Street, manufactory, Studley, Warwick.

1855-7 40 Gresham Street.

1870-2 Sole inventor and patentee of the grooveless and egg-eyed needles, pins, thimbles etc., 4 Gresham Street, E.C.

1879-92 22 Gresham Street.

1900-10 Abel Morrall Ltd., needlemakers, 20 Gresham Street, E.C.

1922-30 Manufacturers of needles, pins (glass heads), hat pins, safety pins and smallwares, showrooms, 10 King Edward Street, E.C.1, mills, Redditch.

By 1949 the firm had ceased to have a London office. In 1967 they were still at Clive Works, Redditch.

I have seen no reference to this countermark since Waters' article of 1898.

It is not possible to be precise about the date of issue – this could be either c. 1850-3 (before the 1853 Act) or c. 1870-80 (after the demonetisation of copper coin).

22.39 MORTIMER

H. W. Mortimer, gunmaker by Royal Warrant, was at 89 Fleet Street c. 1780-1812. He made flintlock pistols and blunderbusses for the guards of Royal Mail coaches.

22.40 NEVILL

Alfred Nevill had varied business interests, as will be seen from the following directory entries:

1845-6 Alfred H. Nevill, corn chandler, 17 Chichester Place, Grays Inn Road.

1848-51 As above but 16A Chichester Place.

1851 Mrs. Eliza Nevill, grocer, 6 Chichester Place.

1853 Alfred H. Nevill & Co., lentil maker, 16A Chichester Place, Grays Inn Road, and 12 Liverpool Street, King's Cross.

1855-7 Alfred Hooper Nevill & Co., arabica food and patent lentil manufacturers, 17 Laurie Terrace, St. George's Road, Westminster Road; and steam millers, Valentine Place, Blackfriars Road.

1864 Millers, Valentine Place, Blackfriars Road, S.

1870 Charcoal grinders, drug mills, Ewer Street, S.E.

1872 A. H. Nevill & Co., coal dust grinders and manufacturers of charcoal or founders' blacking, drug mills, Ewer Street, Southwark, S.E.; Alfred Hooper Nevill, turkish baths, 35 and 36 Railway Approach, London Bridge, S.E.

1888 James Forder & Henry Nevill, turkish bath proprietors, 7 and 8 Railway Approach, London Bridge, S.E., 44 Whitechapel High Street, 7 Commercial Road East, Northumberland Avenue, Charing Cross and Northumberland Passage, Craven Street, Strand.

1953 Nevill's Turkish Baths, Bishopsgate Church-yard, E.C.2 and 7 Railway Approach, London Bridge, S.E.1.

The countermark is very similar in style to that for 'Lloyd's Penny Sunday Times' (see above), and probably dates from the early 1850's.

22.41 NOAKES & HOLBOROW

Noakes & Holborow, engineers, brassfounders and finishers, high class steam and water fittings, valves, cocks, lubricators and motor accessories are listed in the London directories at 16 and 17 Devonshire Square, E.C. and 9A White Horse Lane, E. (1907-15) and at 14 and 14A Old Bethnal Green Road, E.2 (1916-57). It is assumed that the countermark dates from the 1920's.

22.42 (AN OAK TREE)

This is probably a brand or trade mark, and could have been issued by the London firm of Henry Bond, though it is not, of course, possible to confirm this. Bond had this entry in the 1879 and 1880 directories:

'Original marking-ink maker, prepared by William Christian, successor to the husband of the late Mrs. E. C. Bond. Established 1815. The proprietor of this most valuable marking-ink has removed the business to 44 Bevenden Street, East Road, City Road N., where all orders should be addressed, or to any of the agents. Trade mark, an oak tree. No other person can manufacture H. Bond's Marking Ink. Wholesale agents, C. & E. Layton, 150 Fleet Street, Barclay & Sons, 95 Farringdon Street, Butler & Crispe, 4 Cheapside, and J. Sanger & Son, 150 Oxford Street, W.'

Other Bonds made marking-ink in the late nineteenth century: Mrs. Elizabeth Richmond Bond – trademark, a unicorn, and John Bond – 'Crystal Palace' brand.

22.43 PAY

Although no town is indicated, this countermark has been tentatively attributed to William Pay, of the 'Goat' public house, 9 Queen Street, Gainsford Street, S.E., listed in the Post Office directories for 1842 and 1844.

By 1857 only nos. 2, 6, 20 Queen Street (Horselydown) were occupied. Pay is not a common name in the London directories.

22.44 PENNY NEWSMAN

The 'Penny Newsman' was issued from 28 January 1860 to 10 July 1864, continuing as the 'Newsman' from 17 July 1864 to 12 February 1865.

The 1862 directory shows the offices of the 'Penny Newsman' and 'Sunday Morning Mail & Telegraph' at 135 Salisbury Court, Fleet Street, E.C. – George J. Ransom, publisher. In 1864 James Meldrum published the 'Penny Newsman' at 12 York Street, Covent Garden, W.C.

This is the earliest example known to me of a paper label affixed to a coin for advertising purposes.

22.45 PERCY STREET

Johnstone's 1817 Directory lists no number 40 in Percy Street. The following directory entries for 40 Percy Street have been found:

1823 (Robson's) William Sandbach, furnishing ironmonger.

1823–4 (Pigot's) William Sandbach, French horn bugle and trumpet maker.

1828 (Robson's) Wm. Sandback (sic), French horn and trumpet maker.

1833 (Robson's) Albion Wyatt (late Sandbach & Wyatt), French horn, trumpet and bugle manufacturer.

1834 (Robson's) William Johnson, writing desk maker.

In 1835 and 1836 William and George Wright, tailors, are shown at unnumbered premises between 39 and 41 Percy Street, while A. and A. V. Wyatt, musical instrument makers, are listed at 16 North Street, Lambeth.

Directories for 1838, 1842 and 1844 show a gap between numbers 38 and 41 Percy Street.

It is probable that this piece was used by William Sandbach or Albion Wyatt as a shop ticket between 1823 and 1833, employing the punch used to mark their instruments. It may have been given out as a repair receipt.

22.46 PIDCOCK

There are advertisements for Pidcock's Royal Menagerie from at least 1791, when the price of admission was one shilling. Gilbert Pidcock appears in the directories for 1802, 1806 and 1808 as an importer of foreign animals at Exeter Change, and seems to have built up a very fine and varied collection – see Christopher Brunel's article in Spink's Numismatic Circular, December 1965, p. 256. By 1808, the cost of admission had risen to 2s. 6d. Davis says Pidcock died in February 1810, aged 67. The exhibition was subsequently taken over by various people in turn, but had to move when Exeter Change was taken down for street improvements in 1829 – at first to the King's Mews, Charing Cross, then to the Surrey Zoological Gardens, near Kennington Road. Pidcock, of course, issued many non-countermarked tokens – see Dalton & Hamer, 414–58, Davis 49–60, 69–73.

22.47 J·A·R

It has not proved possible to identify this trader. York Buildings was rated locally for one owner and the tenants cannot be traced, also no entry has been found in the directories for a milliner with these initials. However, Bailey's 1784 Directory shows Thomas Ripley, corn chandler, Villiers Street, York Buildings, and it is possible that J.A.R was his wife or a relative.

22.48 RICHARDS, WOOD & CO.

The following entries appear in the London directories:

1826–7 Richards Brothers, wholesale ironmongers, 21 Martins Lane, Cannon Street.

1828–32 Richards, Wood & Co., export iron-mongers and edge tool manufacturers, 21 Martins Lane, Thames Street.

1833–5 Richards, Wood & Co., export iron-mongers, 117 Bishopsgate Street within.

1838 Richards, Wood & Co., export ironmongers and iron merchants, 117 Bishopsgate Street within and 4 West Parade, Birmingham.

1840–3 Richards, Wood & Co., export iron-mongers and iron merchants, 117 and 118 Bishopsgate Street within and at Birmingham.

1844–5 Thomas S. Richards & Co., export iron-mongers, iron merchants, manufacturers of colonial machines etc., same address.

The countermark therefore dates from c. 1828–43.

22.49 ROBINSON

Jonathan Robinson is listed under Avery Row in the Brook Street Ward rate books for 1824–8, with total rates of £1 15s. od. (1824–5), £2 (1826), £2 6s. od. (1827), and £2 9s. od. (1828). Despite these apparent additions and improvements to his property, he only seems to have occupied it during 1824. This short span of activity probably accounts for the fact that he does not appear in the London directories. It is interesting to note that no cutlers are listed in Avery Row in the nineteenth century directories.

22.50 ROGERS

Chitty says (Spink's Numismatic Circular, 1907) that this was an English countermark which found its way to Australia along with the Lloyd's pieces. This being so, it is likely that it originated from London, but it has not been possible to prove this. There are three London chemists who might have issued the countermark during the period:

1825–9 Arnold Rogers, chemist and druggist, 93 Cheapside.

1840–3 David Rogers, pharmaceutical chemist, Kingsland Green.

1851–6 William Wilcox Rogers, chemist and druggist, 3 Eldon Place, Low Street, Islington.

22.51 (ROYAL DOCKYARD, DEPTFORD)

This countermark is similar in style to the Chatham Dockyard, Sheerness Dockyard and Woolwich Arsenal or Dockyard checks, and was probably used in the stores. Established by Henry VIII, the old naval dockyard at Deptford was filled up in 1869. In 1798 the Dockyard store-keeper was Ralph Paine (Universal British Directory), who received a salary of £200 and a £10 stationery allowance. Holden's 1811 Directory shows John Hodgskin, storekeeper, Deptford yard.

22.52 RUSE

Edward Ruse, pewterer, is listed in directories at 64 Russell Street, Whitechapel, E., from 1885 to 1891. Frederick John Ruse, pewterer, general bar fitter, brass finisher and gas fitter also appears in the 1885 and 1886 directories, at 189 Jamaica Road, Bermondsey. By 1891 he had moved to 2A Stork's Road, Bermondsey, and by 1922 to 1 Keeton's Road, Bermondsey.

22.53 SAVAGE

Edward Savage, wholesale cheesemonger, was at 28 Whitechapel in 1817. From 1818 to 1830, directory entries are for E. Savage & Son at the same address, while in 1831–3 and 1836–7 they are for C. & R. P. Savage. In 1834, Richard Savage, cheesemonger, is shown, in 1835 Richard Savage, provision and potato warehouse, and in 1838, Richard P. Savage, wholesale cheesemonger, at 28 Whitechapel High Street.

The countermark presumably dates from 1834–8.

22.54 SMEETON

G. Smeeton, printer, 17 St. Martin's Lane (1820–2) is the only trader of that name in the London directories of the period. It is possible that W. Smeeton was a resident, rather than a trader, or a visitor to London, and that this piece properly belongs to the 'hatch, match or dispatch' category.

22.55 SPENCE

Dated 1722, this is the earliest engraved trader's coin known to me. Spence is not listed in the 1740 directory, but there are some dentists of that name in the next century, perhaps descendents: G. Spence, dentist to His Majesty, 21 Old Bond Street (1806), David Spence, dentist, 1 Arlington Street, Piccadilly (1837–9), 28 Down Street, Piccadilly (1842).

22.56 SPRING

Spring is not a common name in the London directories. The most likely issuer was James Spring, painter and glazier, 83 Great Portland Street (1805, 1808), who, in 1811 is also described as a painter on stained glass. In 1817 and 1820 the entry is for Spring and Son, painters and glaziers. Subsequent entries are:

1825 Spring & Son, plumbers, Gt. Portland St.
1830 William Spring, house decorator, 82 Gt. Portland Street.
1835, 1837 Spring & Son, plumbers, painters and glaziers, 83 Gt. Portland Street.
1840 William Spring, plumber, 48 Gt. Portland Street.

The countermark probably dates from the 1830's. For another glazier's countermark see 13.3 above.

22.57 STANTON

The directories for 1818–21 show Robert Stanton, pewterer and surgical syringe manufacturer, at 37 Blackman Street, Borough. Cotterell says that James Stanton, a pewterer of Shoe Lane, active c. 1819, died on 3 November 1835. The 1821 directory gives two entries, presumably for James' son: John Stanton, telescope manufacturer and tube-drawer, 73 Shoe Lane, and wire and tin-plate warehouse at the same address. Subsequent entries are as follows:

1827 John Stanton, telescope manufacturer and tube drawer, 73 Shoe Lane.

1839–42 John Stanton, telescope manufacturer and tube drawer, metal, tube, wire, file, tin and tinplate warehouse &c., 73 Shoe Lane.

1857–85 Stanton Brothers, manufacturers of drawn tube for telescopes, pumps, garden and surgical syringes, musical instruments, roller moulds &c., wire drawers, metal, steel, tube, wire, file, tin and tinplate warehouse, 73 Shoe Lane, Holborn, E.C.

The firm continues at the same address in directories between 1892 and 1960, having in addition a zinc warehouse in 1892, making copper tubes for motor cars by 1910, and being known as Stanton Bros. (Metals) Ltd. by 1960. In 1966 they were at 49 St. Johns Square, E.C.1 as non ferrous metal stockists, aluminium and duralumin, brass and copper sheets, rods and strips, and metal merchants.

It is difficult to date the countermark, except to say that it was almost certainly before the 1853 Act. It is interesting to note that all known examples are found on the 1805 Irish halfpenny, which, since the proclamation of 12 July 1826, had ceased to be legally current coin in the United Kingdom. However it is clear from approaches to the Mint in the 1840's that Irish halfpence continued to circulate, although they were generally refused.

22.58 SWALLOW

James Swallow, hatter, was at 169 Piccadilly in 1806, and at 2 St. James' Street, c. 1812–26. From c. 1827–32 Swallow and Hance were at the same address. The countermark probably dates from 1807–26.

22.59 (SWAN WITH TWO NECKS)

The 'Swan with Two Necks' was an old coaching inn in Lad Lane, and the booking-office and headquarters of the coaches leaving London for the north. The Vintners' Company marked their swans on the Thames with two nicks on the upper mandible, which may be the origin of the 'Two Necks'. Lad Lane was in Cheapside between Milk Street and Wood Street and was swept away, in 1845, for the enlargement of Cateaton Street, which was then renamed Gresham Street. The inn, rebuilt c. 1668, and demolished c. 1859 was the subject of an early nineteenth century token halfpenny – see Davis 64. It is not clear whether this countermarked piece served as some form of token, hotel ticket, or barrel check in connection with the inn, or whether the 'Swan with Two Necks' device was adopted by some other trader as a brand mark. Other inns of this name were at Whetstone, Middlesex (1809–11) and 6 Great Carter Lane (1820's–1890's), while the 'Swan and Two Necks', Tothill Street, existed from the 1740's until 1827 – see Bryant Lillywhite, 'London Signs', London, 1972, p. 543.

22.60 S.S

It is not possible to attribute this countermark positively. It could have been issued by Samuel Smith, gun and pistol maker, 6 Newcastle Street, Whitechapel, c. 1839–43, but the possibilities here are legion.

22.61 TATE

The following entries appear in the directories:

1772–7 John Tate, warehouseman, 26 Bucklersbury.

1789–1808 John Tate & Son, warehousemen, 26 Bucklersbury.

1811 John Tate & Son, warehousemen, 11 Crescent, Minories.

1810–12 George Tate, merchant, 11 Crescent, Minories.

1817–29 George Tate, merchant, 33 Dowgate Hill.

1819–20 M. Tate & Co., merchants, 26 Bucklesbury.

1821 M. Tate & Co., merchants, Batson's Coffee House, Cornhill.

1822–9 William Tate & Co., warehousemen & merchants, 8 Old Jewry.

It is not possible to date the countermark more precisely than 1789–1811.

22.62 THOMAS

The following entries appear in the London directories for John Thomas, cutler:

1806 (Post Office) John Thomas, cutlery manufactory, Borough Road, Southwark.

1807, 1809 (Post Office) John Thomas, cutlery manufactory, 12 Newington Causeway.

1811, 1812 (Post Office) John Thomas, working cutler, 19 Newington Causeway.

He is not listed in Post Office Directories 1812–22, Underhill's 'Biennial Directory' 1816–17, or Johnstone's 'London Commercial Guide and Street Directory' 1817–18. In Robson's 'New London Directory' for 1819 is an entry for John Thomas, cutler, at 425 Oxford Street, and similar entries appear in other directories until 1836. From at least 1830 he is described as a working cutler. In 1837 the entry is for Jno. Keans, cutler, at the same address. Johnstone's 1817 Directory shows a gap between 422 and 426 Oxford Street, and T. & T. Chamberlain, brush manufacturer, at 19 Newington Causeway. Blackman Street is shown as 390½ yards long with 150 houses. 104 was on the west side between Mint Street and Lant Street, and was occupied by Geo. Scrogg, tobacco & snuff manufacturer.

Scrogg is listed in directories as follows:

1799 (Holden's) George and R. Scrogg, tobacconist, 104 Blackman Street.

1800 (Kent's) George Scrogg, as above.

1801 (Post Office) G. & R. Scrogg, as above.

1802–12 (Post Office) G. Scrogg, as above.

1813–14 (Post Office) Geo. Scrogg, 101 (sic) Blackman Street.

1815–27 (Post Office) Geo. Scrogg, 104 Blackman Street.

1828–34 (Robson's) Geo. Scrogg, 87 Blackman Street.

John Holland is shown at 87 Blackman Street in Robson's 1835 Directory. Geo. Scroggs (sic) is shown at 104 Blackman Street in Poor Rate returns for the parish of St. George the Martyr, Southwark, for 1796, 1800, 1821 and 1824. Samuel Tunnicliff, wine merchant, is shown at 104 Blackman Street in Robson's 1828 Directory.

From at least 1830 (Robson's Directory), 104 Blackman Street was a public house – the 'George and Dragon', with licensees Bush (1831–2), John West (1833–42), and James Woodnut (1844–5). The Post Office Directories for 1846 and 1847 show no number 104, with Robin Hood Court intersecting between numbers 103 and 105.

The pub was renamed (having been rebuilt?), and appears as the 'St. George' from 1848, with licensees Morris Frost (1848), Thomas King (1849–50), Archibald Reid (1851), Miss Emma Shaw (1852), Jno. Hembrey (1853–8), Richard Carpenter (1863), James Halford (1864), Thomas Jordan (1866), Jonathan Stott (1867), Alfred Honeywood (1873), Thomas Borrodell (1878) and Robert Draper (1879). By 1885 it had again been renamed – the 'St. George's Tavern', with Edwin Brady, licensee. From 1891, Blackman Street disappears, being renumbered as the southern extension of Borough High Street, the 'St. George's Tavern' becoming number 204. The 1897 Post Office Directory shows the pub renamed the 'Hole in the Wall', still with Edwin Brady as licensee.

It will be noted that two varieties of this countermark read 'John Thomas' (22.62 C, D); all show the address as '104 Blackman Street, Boro', one variety showing the 'manufactury' at 'Boro. Road' (22.62B), another 'facing Newington Causeway' (22.62D).

Borough Road joined the southern end at Blackman Street, where it ran into Newington Causeway, at the west side. It is likely that Thomas retained his workshop in Borough Road, as shown in the 1806 Post Office Directory, but had a retail outlet at 104 Blackman Street, probably after leaving Newington Causeway c. 1812 and before moving to Oxford Street c. 1819, assuming the same trader is involved. The countermark probably dates from this period, which is earlier than most other cutlers' countermarks. Some measure of support for this theory is afforded by the directory entries for 1813 and 1814 (see above), and the Records of Commissioners of Land Tax for Southwark, which show that Geo. Scroggs (sic), who occupied premises owned by J. & T. Batt, increased the number of rentals (from 30 to 40) between 1813 and 1815, possibly indicating that he sublet his tenancy, or a part of it. This continued after Thomas left – Robson's 1823 Directory also shows Thos. Abell, livery stable keeper, at 104 Blackman Street (shown as horse dealer &c. Yorkshire Grey, Blackman Street, in Holden's 'Triennial Directory' 1802–4). Land Tax records also show that Abell owned property in Blackman Street.

22.63 TOWER

This is assumed to be the unofficial use of an official punch by a workman at the Royal Armouries, Tower of London. In 1699, the Master of Ordnance ordered the word 'Tower' to be stamped or engraved on all arms ordered or stored there – see Carey, op. cit., p. 97. All arms produced by private firearms makers and proved or viewed by the London, or, after 1813, the Birmingham Proof Houses, were so marked on delivery to the Tower to show they had become government property. The countermark must date from the period between 1806/7 – the date of the coin, and 1830, the end of the reign of George IV. There is also the possibility that the piece was used as a stores check.

22.64 UNDERWOOD

This countermark is tentatively attributed to one of the London cutlers of this name, who appear in the directories as follows:

H. T. Underwood, corner of Russell Court and Drury Lane (1812).

Yeeling Underwood, 8 Great Turnstile, Holborn (1812–32).

George Underwood, 8 Great Turnstile, Holborn (1836–42).

Henry Underwood, 56 Haymarket, and 74 Drury Lane (1823).

R. Underwood, 56 Haymarket (1836).

Henry Underwood, 56 Haymarket (1839).

Henry and Thomas Underwood, 56 Haymarket (1842), 55 and 56 Haymarket (1851).

Miss Mary Underwood, 8 Burlington Arcade (1839–42).

The piece probably dates from c. 1812–42.

22.65 VERINDER

H. Verinder & Co., working cutlers, were at 79 St. Paul's Churchyard c. 1823–37. Henry Verinder was at the same address 1839–51 – in the latter year described as a manufacturing cutler. In 1857 Mrs. Emma Verinder is listed at the same address.

In 1922 Henry Verinder, cutler, was at 17A Ludgate Hill.

22.66 WADDEN

The following entries appear in the London directories:

John Wadden, hairdresser, 13 Chester Place, Old Kent Road, S.E. (1862–3), 285 Old Kent Road, S.E. (1864–79).

Thomas Wadden, umbrella manufacturer, 357 Goswell Road (1871–8), 349 Goswell Road (1879–87).

Thomas Wadden, hairdresser, 294 Upper Street, N. (1884–6), 172 Upper Street, N. (1887–1901).

It is probable that Thomas Wadden produced hair dye at his umbrella works in Goswell Road when launching his own, or a relative's, hair-dressing business c. 1884–6. He does not appear under 'Hair Dyers' in the Trades directories. This countermark also occurs on European bronze coins – see 22.221 in Table 2 below.

22.67 (WAR CRY)

On 19 October 1882 Frank Lasham, a bookseller of 61 High Street, Guildford, wrote to the Royal Mint objecting to having received a shilling with a Salvation Army advertisement on both sides. This was apparently a War Cry paper sticker, although the exact wording is not known. As with other similar enquiries, the Mint gave no opinion on the legality of this. The Attorney-General gave his views to the Master of the Mint, C. W. Fremantle, in a letter of 28 October, as mentioned in the introduction above.

The Salvation Army was founded by William Booth (1829–1912) in 1878 as the East London Christian Mission. The first weekly issue of 'The War Cry and Official Gazette of the Salvation Army' appeared on 27 December 1880. Directories show the following entries for the Salvation Army:

1883–7 101 Queen Victoria Street, E.C., 8 and 9 Paternoster Square, E.C.

1889 101 Queen Victoria Street only.

1890–1900 101 Queen Victoria Street, E.C. and 98, 100, 102 Clerkenwell Road, E.C.

The Army's Headquarters are still at 101 Queen Victoria Street, E.C.4, although the premises were blitzed in 1941.

In September 1882, 'The War Cry' was up-graded to two issues per week with a considerable amount of publicity exhorting Salvationists to push circulation. It is likely that the paper label was an example of local initiative in response to the appeal and that other coins then current, including bronze, were similarly treated.

By the mid 1880's, 21 editions of 'The War Cry' were produced throughout the world, including one in Welsh fortnightly. In March 1888, the editorial offices moved from 96 to 58 Southwark Street. Circulation of the 16 page paper was then 260,000. It was printed on three Marinoni machines at Fieldgate Street. In February 1890, when circulation had reached 300,000, the offices moved to 98 and 100 Clerkenwell Road, and in September 1896 to the Army Headquarters at 101 Queen Victoria Street. For further information on the Salvation Army at this time see the five-volume 'History of the Salvation Army' by Arch. Wiggins and Robert Sandall.

22.68 WARNER

The following entries appear in the London directories:

1806 Edw. Warner, brass founder, Little New Street, Shoe Lane; John Warner, brass and bell founder, 5 Blackfriars Road.

1818–36 John and Robert Warner, brass founders, 8 Crescent, Jewin Street.

1837–48 John Warner & Sons, brass founders, 8 Jewin Crescent.

1853 John Warner & Sons, brass, bell and cock founders, fire, garden, deep well and beer engine pump and watercloset manufacturers, braziers, tea urn, bath, lamp and standard weight and measure makers, copper, tin, zinc, lead and galvanized iron merchants, 8 Crescent, Jewin Street.

1870–2 John Warner & Sons, bell and brass founders to Her Majesty, brass finishers, cock founders, hydraulic engineers, braziers and coppersmiths, manufacturers of brass and iron pumps, patent annular sail wind engines, patent water closets, high pressure cocks, copper, tin, zinc and galvanised iron merchants, 8 Jewin Crescent.

1879 As above, but at 27 Jewin Crescent. Foundry and works: Walton on the Naze, Essex. No mention of zinc.

1880–91 As above, but shown as The Crescent Foundry.

1892 As above, but John Warner & Sons Ltd.

1900 As above, but at 2 Jewin Crescent.

1910 As above, but with additional entry for works at Spelman Street, Spitalfields.

1922 John Warner & Sons Ltd., bellfounders, Spelman Street, E.1.

1953 John Warner Ltd., Ironfounders. The Foundry, Stepney Causeway, E.1.

The countermark must date from the period between 1861 – the date of the coin, and 1898 – the date of Waters' article. It is difficult to be more precise, except that the probable date of issue was before 1879 – zinc was mentioned in the firm's advertisements in the 1860's and 1870's.

22.69 WG

This is probably a trader's piece, dating from c. 1780–1820. Among gunmakers, possible issuers are William Golding (1770–1820) and William Green (5 generations – 1711–1864).

22.70 WHITEHOUSE

61 Great Tower Street seems to have been the location of the Corn Meter's Office during the 1820's (Robson's 1823 Directory) and again from the mid 1830's (Robson's 1835, 1836 and 1838 Directories). Holden's 1811 Directory shows the Corn Meter's Office at 61 Great Tower Hill. John Smiton was clerk. Ten Corn Meters were elected 'in trust for the City for four years.' In 1817 there was a gap between numbers 59 and 63, while the 1833 directory shows the 'City Arms' (see the reverse of this engraved piece!), landlord C. Searle, at number 61. The 1834 directory shows a gap between numbers 60 and 62. From 1842 to 1848, J. Hurcomb, clerk to Corn Meter's Office, is shown at 61 Great Tower Street, while simply the Corn Meter's Office is listed in the 1851 directory. C. Whitehouse does not appear at all – he may have been an earlier clerk, or some other employee.

22.71 WILLIAMS

Thomas Williams, cutler, 14 West Smithfield, first appears in the London directories in 1834, possibly having transferred his business from 105 Union Street, Southwark, where a cutler of the same name is listed 1823–33. In 1851 and 1853 he is listed as a butchers' cutler at 14 Smithfield. Subsequent directory entries are as follows:

1859 Butchers' cutler and scale maker, 14 Smithfield.

1862, 1877 address shown as 14 West Smithfield, E.C. and 7 Bank Buildings, Metropolitan Cattle Market, N.

1880 address as above and Gee Street, Goswell Road, E.C.

1882 address shown as 8 and 14 West Smithfield, otherwise as 1880.

1886 as 1882 except not shown at 7 Bank Buildings.

1890 Butchers' cutlers, 79 Charterhouse Street, E.C., 8 and 14 West Smithfield, 59 and 61 Gee Street and Great Arthur Street.

1896 address shown as 8 and 11 West Smithfield, 79 Charterhouse Street, and 59 and 61 Gee Street.

1910 8 West Smithfield, 79 Charterhouse Street, 59 and 61 Gee Street, 16 Norman's Buildings, St. Lukes.

1915, 1925 8 West Smithfield, 79 Charterhouse Street, 57, 59 and 61 Gee Street.

1930 79 Charterhouse Street.

1935 described as butchers' outfitters, 57 Gee Street.

1939 described as butchers' engineer, Smithfield Works, Graces Road, S.E.5.

The countermark probably dates from c. 1834–53.

22.72 (WOOLWICH ARSENAL OR DOCKYARD)

These countermarked coins seem to have served as stores checks at Woolwich Arsenal or Dockyard during the Napoleonic Wars. The Naval Dockyards at Deptford, Chatham, Portsmouth and Sheerness issued similar pieces. Holden's 1811 Directory shows T. Burnett, storekeeper at Woolwich Dockyard. In 1839 William Stace was storekeeper, and William Jones deputy storekeeper at the Royal Arsenal.

23 Middlesex
Uxbridge

23.1 PITKIN

On 30 January 1882, Carrick & Coles, wholesale and retail drapers, tailors etc. of 30 and 31 High Street, and 57–60 Windsor Street, Uxbridge, wrote to the Master of the Royal Mint asking about the legality of affixing paper labels to coins as they were thinking of doing it for advertising purposes. Enclosed with the letter was one of Henry Pitkin's labels. As in similar cases, the firm were merely referred to the 1861 Act.

24 Norfolk
Acle

24.1 SPRINGALL

Edward Springall, smith and victualler, The Crown, Acle, appears in White's 1845 Directory.

24.2 LYNN

In the absence of an initial, this countermark is assumed to originate from Kings Lynn, commonly known as Lynn or Lynn Regis in the nineteenth century.

Norwich

24.3 GILLHAM

Robert Gillham, whitesmith, is listed in Pigot's 1830 Directory at St. Martin's Lane. In 1839 and 1845 he is described as a mill bill maker at the same address.

24.4 GRIFFIN

This countermark is attributed to Norwich as, in three instances, it appears on Norwich tokens. The issuer might be William Griffin, joiner and builder, of St. Andrew's Street (1845), and Cow Hill (1854). Alternatively it could have been issued by the Griffin Inn, King Street, where licensees were John Phillips (1801), Thomas Smith (1822–3), Samuel Vince (1839), and William James (1845, 1854).

24.5 PARKERSON

I. C. Parkerson, corn and coal merchants, 18 St. Martin's by Palace Street, and John Parkerson, house-bell hanger and venetian blind maker, 9 Hungate Street are listed in Thomas Peck's 1801 Directory. Bailey's 1784 Directory shows the latter in King Street. Pigot's Directories for 1822–3 and 1830 list Francis Parkerson, venetian blind manufacturer and bell hanger, Princess Street. The countermark was probably issued by John Parkerson before 1822.

25 Northamptonshire
Oundle

25.1 BROOKSHAW

The Northamptonshire Record Office have not been able to trace this trader. He does not appear in directories for 1816–17, 1823, 1824, 1841 or 1847.

Guilsborough

25.2 NEALE and READ

Guilsborough, with a population of 939 in 1841, had two blacksmiths in 1847 – Robert Read and William Loydell, according to the Post Office Directory for that year. There are no further entries for Read – Whellan's 1849 Directory shows William Loydell and James Wormleighton, blacksmiths. It is possible that G. Neale was Read's or Loydell's predecessor.

Peterborough

25.3 RICKMAN

Alexander James Rickman, ironmonger, of 2 Cowgate, Peterborough, appears in directories between 1874 and 1901, but not in those for 1847 and 1920 – the nearest years available outside this period. From 1884 he is shown as living in Priestgate. The countermark must date from before 1906, as in that year the coin was presented to the British Museum by Dr. Parkes Weber.

Weedon

25.4 MILITARY STORES DEPOT

A depot was established at Weedon in 1803 – as far from the coast as possible in view of the threatened French invasion. It included a pavilion built for George III, and is sometimes known as the Weedon Royal Arsenal. Holden's 1811 Directory shows Joseph Wheeler, store-keeper, Weedon-beck. Made into a fort in 1831/2, it was found, somewhat belatedly, that the place had no natural defences! 350 men were stationed there in

1884, when the Commissary of Military Stores was George Henry Everard. There was a serious fire at the depot in 1889. The check probably dates from the mid nineteenth century – it is difficult to be more precise.

26 Northumberland

26.1 ALNWICK

In the absence of initials this is assumed to represent the town rather than a surname. There are no clues as to the identity of the issuer. However the possibility that it is a brand mark cannot be ignored.

Newcastle

26.2 BELL

Although no town is shown on this engraved coin, the arms – three castles – are those of Newcastle upon Tyne. John Bell appears in the Newcastle Directories as follows:

1782 Land surveyor, east end of the Low Friar Chare, or at Mr. Charnley's, Bookseller.
1790 Surveyor, Westmoreland Street.
1795, 1801 Bookseller and surveyor, Union Street.
1811 John Bell, Snr., Union Street, John Bell, Jnr., Quayside.

The piece probably dates from about 1811.

26.3 ELLIOTT

The countermark is dated 1814. Similar struck farthings exist – see Davis nos. 33–38. The 1821 directory lists John Elliott, tobacconist, Quayside.

26.4 LEIGHTON & TEMPERLEY

Directories show the following entries:

1824 Nicholas Temperley, grocer and tea dealer, Sandhill; N. Temperley, cheese, butter and bacon factor, Folly Wharf.
1827–8 John Leighton, whitesmith, Church Street, Gateshead; Nicholas Temperley, wholesale cheesemonger, butter and bacon factor, Folly Wharf and Hexham, field seedsman, 21 Old Butcher Market. In 1827, Nicholas Temperley is also shown at 30 Vine Lane.

Neither trader appears in the directories for 1811 or 1833. The combination of whitesmith and tea dealer, cheesemonger or seedsman seems an odd one, and this may not be a true trader's piece.

26.5 YELLOLEY

This countermark was described as a modern forgery in the Cokayne sale catalogue (1946), where it is attributed to Scotland. However Ouseburn is a district of Newcastle upon Tyne, where Yellowley (sic) is a fairly common surname. Mitchell's Directory for 1801 shows Robert Yellowley, pottery, Ouseburn. He is not listed in Pigot's 1826 Directory. Thus the trader, at least, is authentic.

27 Nottinghamshire
Nottingham
27.1 CHEETHAM
Directories show Mr. Cheetham, tailor, Greyfriar-gate (1799) and George Cheetham, tailor, at the same address (1814–32). The countermark is dated 1790 and may be of the 'hatch match or dispatch' variety rather than a true trader's piece.

28 Oxfordshire
Bicester
28.1 CARTHEW
William Carthew, working cutler, Market End is listed in Pigot's Directories for 1824, 1830 and 1844. James Carthew, cutler, appears in Holden's 1811 Directory and Underhill's Biennial Directory for 1816–17. William was, presumably, his son.

Great Tew
28.2 S.G
The issuer of this early shop ticket has not been identified. An entry for Samuel Greaves, school-master and post office appears in Kelly's Post Office Directory for 1847. Greaves may have been related to the issuer.

Oxford
28.3 BUCKLAND
Thomas Buckland, chimney sweeper, is shown at 34 Castle Street, Oxford, in Kelly's Post Office Directory for 1847, and Dutton, Allen & Co.'s 1863 Directory. The latter lists Thos. Buckland jun., photographer, 13 Castle Street, who also appears in the 1869 Post Office Directory. The countermark probably dates from the 1840's.

28.4 ROBINSON
There are no entries for Robinson in Holden's Triennial Directory 1805–7. William Robinson appears as a whitesmith of All Saints parish in the Poll Book for 1818 and as an ironmonger in 1825. Pigot's 1823–4 Directory shows James Robinson, cutler, Corn Market, while the issues for 1830 and 1844 list John Robinson, working cutler, at the same address. Pigot's 1844 Directory and Slater's 1851 Directory show the address as 46 Corn Market. There are several varieties of this fairly common countermark, which probably dates from c. 1825–50. Two varieties at least (28.4C and E, with additional countermark crown/VR) presumably date from after 1837.

30 Shropshire
Alberbury
30.1 PARR
Thomas Parr, or 'Old Parr', was born in Alberbury about 1483 and died in London in 1635, killed, according to the surgeon William Harvey, by the London air! He is commemmorated by a farthing token issued for the Old Man Inn, St. James' Market, Westminster (Williamson 2532). There were several public houses named 'The Old Parr's Head' in London in the nineteenth century – e.g. in 1857 at 166 Aldersgate Street, 1 Cross Street, Islington, and 4 Little Knightrider Street. Parr's Life Pills, said to be concocted from a secret recipe handed down by Old Parr, were widely advertised in the 1840's. The recipe was purchased by Herbert Ingram and Nathanial Cooke from Thomas Roberts, a Manchester druggist, soon after 1834. They moved to 9 Crane Court, London, mainly to advertise, in 1842. The partnership was dissolved in 1848.

Parr's cottage at the Glyn, Alberbury was restored in the early 1900's and destroyed by fire in 1959.

The countermark is fairly worn, but less so than the coin. It is assumed to date from the second half of the eighteenth century. It has no direct advertising message – probably, therefore, an inn, or Parr's Life Pills can be discounted as issuers. It closely resembles the top half of the touch of Robert Parr, a pewterer. (See Cotterell, op. cit., p. 278, and London Touch Plate no. 352.) He lived 1703–77. Cotterell quotes Berrow's Worcester Journal of 29 January 1767: 'Died, Mrs. Parr, aged 74, wife of Mr. Parr, an eminent pewterer in Greek Street, and a lineal descendant of the famous Old Parr who lived to the age of 152 years . . .'. The countermark may be un-official use of one of Parr's touch punches or, alternatively, it is just possible that such pieces were issued as souvenirs to visitors to the cottage. However attribution must remain, for the moment, uncertain. For further information see the Dictionary of National Biography, and H. E. Forrest's 'Handbook to Old Parr's Cottage'.

Broseley
30.2 SOUTHERN
The Rodens, established in 1681, were celebrated Broseley tobacco pipe makers who introduced the 'churchwarden' and 'London straw' models – i.e. very long stemmed clays. Alfred Dunhill states ('The Pipe Book', p. 173) that 'the Roden business was taken over by a Mr. Southorn (sic) who received honourable mention for his pipes at the Exhibition of 1851. In 1868 he introduced steam power into his factory, and was then enabled to produce one and a half million pipes a year.' The following entries occur in directories:

1828, 1835 William Southern (manufacturer of the most superior quality of pipes).
1859 William Southern & Co. (of the noted Regalia or Cigar Pipe and of the superior quality of fancy Broseley and Dutch pipes) Broseley.
1856 Joseph Southern, King Street, Broseley.
1859 Joseph Southern, Broseley Wood.

The countermark is probably early nineteenth century, and reversed for sealing. It was apparently well worn when noted by Batty (1872).

Ludlow
30.3 BOWYER
This countermark probably dates from the 1850's or 1860's. It is listed by Batty, writing in 1868. Directories show that Anthony Bowyer was at the Pheasant Inn in 1856 and 1863, Martha Bowyer in 1870. The Pheasant Inn was in Old Street. See also 15.5 above.

30.4 HARDING

There are two possible issuers for this counter-mark, which probably dates from the 1830's. Directories show:

1822–3 T. Harding, 'Green Dragon', Corve Street.
1828–9, 1834 Thomas Harding, 'Hop Pole', Mill Street, Ludlow.
1835 James Harding, 'Clive's Arms', Whitcliffe, Ludlow, and beer retailer, Corve Street.
1859 James Harding, 'Raven', Sandpits.

See also 15.5 above.

30.5 MASSEY

Francis Massey appears in directories at Bull Ring 1828–56. The 1859 entry is for M. Massey & Son at the same address. See also 15.5 above, and 39.1 and 50.1 below.

30.6 THOMAS

John Thomas was at 'The Fox', Upper Gaolford, Ludlow in 1856 and 1859 but does not appear in any other of the available directories between 1797 and 1870. See also 15.5 above.

31 Somerset
Bath
31.1 HOOPER'S ARMS

The Hooper's Arms and Brewery is listed in the 1833 Bath Directory at 1 Highbury Terrace under Jas. Simpkins; it does not appear in the 1826 and 1829 directories. The Simpkins family continued there until 1866. In the 1890's the name changed to the Highbury Brewers, continuing until 1913. In 1928 no public house is recorded at that address.

31.2 THOMAS

Rate books show William Thomas living in Cock Lane 1775–86, but no trade is mentioned. In 1791 Joseph Thomas, cutler, Borough Walls is listed. He may have been the issuer of the countermark as Cock Lane was a passage leading from Upper Borough Walls. Thomas does not appear in local directories or poll books 1820–50, but is listed in the Universal British Directory for 1793.

31.3 (UNKNOWN TRADER)

On 17 April 1884, Mr. W. H. Winwood of 11 Cavendish Crescent, Bath, wrote to the Royal Mint enclosing a halfpenny with an advertisement stuck on the obverse – one of two received in change that morning at the Post Office. The halfpenny was returned to him and the trader's name was not mentioned: it is possible that an example of the label will turn up.

Curry Rivel
31.4 LOCK

This countermark is tentatively attributed to Curry Rivel, usually spelt Curry Rivell in the 19th century – i.e. the apparent reading CURRY RIVA.L. (both countermark and coin are worn) is assumed to be CURRY RIVELL. Lock is a common surname there and appears in directories as follows:

1861 William Lock, baker and shopkeeper.
1866 William Lock, junior, baker and shopkeeper.
1875 Walter Lock, watchmaker. William Lock, junior, baker, shopkeeper and Post Office.

There were also several farmers of this name. Directories have been checked for 1830, 1840, 1842, 1844, 1859, 1861, 1866, 1875, and 1883. Throughout the period other drapers and/or grocers are listed, but none is named Lock. Perhaps this trader was active during one of the long periods with no directory cover – e.g. 1845–58.

31.5 HAMBRIDGE

This could be either a place-name or a surname, but, in the absence of an initial, has been assumed to be the former. In 1901 Hambridge, 4 miles south west of Langport, had a population of 554. It was, perhaps, issued by a local blacksmith – see 24.1 above.

31.6 TAUNTON

In the absence of an initial this is assumed to be the place-name, not a surname. It is possible that the countermark represents half of a maker's mark – e.g. the following gunsmiths were active in Taunton in the early nineteenth century: T. Parkhouse, High Street (1823–40); John Burnell, South Street (1820–40); Thomas Goldsworthy, Fore Street (1800–39).

32 Staffordshire
Darlaston
32.1 WILKES

This is overstruck rather than countermarked. Such pieces are not uncommon in the nineteenth century token series (cf. Davis, Gloucestershire 16, Staffordshire 74, Somerset 105) although it is unusual to be able to identify the original coin.

Job Wilkes issued tokens dated 1812 and 1813, and appears in directories as follows:

1818 gun lock manufacturer, Bilston Street, gentleman, Bilston Street.
1828–9 (armament) contractor, gun lock maker, Bilston Street.
1834 Bilston Street.
1851 bolt, latch and bed screw makers, Bell Street.
1860 builder, Foster Street.

His Bilston Street premises later became a public house – the 'Bradford Arms'.

Fazeley
32.2 WRIGHT

Wright does not appear in the directories for 1793, 1818, 1822–3 or 1829. In the Calendar of Wills, Samuel Wright, a victualler, died in 1803 – possibly he was a relation of the issuer. Robert Peel, the Lancashire cotton manufacturer, established, about 1790, mills at Fazeley for cotton spinning and calico printing. Canals also brought prosperity to the area – the Birmingham & Fazeley Navigation Company dates from 1790. By 1801 the population was 905 and by 1811 1,165. Peel's cotton mills closed about 1841 and were taken over by William Tolson Ltd., about

1847 for use as a tape factory. It is probable that H. Wright was connected with the textile industry, even if only indirectly, as a trader who became established due to its presence and the needs of its labour force. White's 1851 Directory shows Cooke and Wright, cotton spinners, Old Mill.

Lichfield

32.3 WOODWARD

There is no entry for Woodward in the few available directories. Being dated as well as engraved this is probably of the 'hatch, match or dispatch' variety rather than a true trader's item.

Wednesbury

32.4 ELWELL

Edward Elwell, edge tool maker, forge, appears in the 1834 directory, but is not listed in those for 1793 and 1818. In 1851 he was living at Wood Green, while Edward Elwell junior is shown as a spade, shovel and edge tool manufacturer at Forge Works. As late as 1924 Edward Elwell is still listed as an edge tool manufacturer at Wednesbury Forge. The countermark probably dates from c. 1830–50.

33 Suffolk
Bury St. Edmunds

33.1 BURY WORKHOUSE

Jesus College, in College Street, was founded by Edward IV in 1480 for a warden and six associate priests. It was still shown as a college on the 1748 map, but by an Act of 1746 the two parishes of Bury were united for the support of their poor, and by 1804 the college buildings formed part of the workhouse. Pigot's 1830 Directory shows Samuel and Hannah Sale, governor and governess of the workhouse in College Street. In 1839 Thomas Bruce was master, Susan Bruce matron, and John Priest, relieving officer. In 1841 the population of Bury was 12,544, and there were 93 inmates in the workhouse. The following is an extract from White's Suffolk Directory for 1844, p. 602: 'Its Workhouse, in College-street, was built many years ago, and has room for 200 inmates, and had about 170 in March 1843, but its average number is about 100. Its expenditure for the support of the poor, in 1837, was £6,627. Six Guardians are elected for each of its two parishes. John Cambridge, Esq., is the Union Clerk; and Mr. Thomas Legge is Master of the Workhouse'.

33.2 PARKER

Carey says (p. 75) that Parker had a shop at Bury St. Edmunds (1800–30) and made boxlock and flintlock pocket pistols. He appears as a gunsmith in the Universal British Directory (1793), but no address is shown. Benjamin Parker, gunmaker, is listed in directories at (30) Church-gate Street (1824, 1830, 1839) and 9 Chalk Lane (1844, 1855). Charles Parker, gunmaker, presumably related to Benjamin, appears at (18) Abbeygate Street (1824, 1830, 1839). T. Parker, probably Benjamin's father, is listed as a gunsmith at Church Gate Street in Bailey's 1784 Directory.

Hadleigh

33.3 MARJORAM

Pigot's 1824 Directory shows J. Coates, whitesmith and gunsmith, at Hadleigh. James Marjoram, gunsmith, Market Place, appears in the 1830 issue. Richard Marjorom (sic), gunmaker, High Street, Wickham Market is listed in White's 1844 Directory of Suffolk. There are other Marjorams at Aldeburgh, Benhall and Charsfield but no other R. Marjoram. The only gunsmith in Hadleigh at the time was Henry Cocksedge, High Street. It is probable that Richard Marjoram was the son of James and preceded Cocksedge at Hadleigh before moving to Wickham Market. The countermark probably dates from the 1830's. Cocksedge was at Hadleigh in 1839.

Ipswich

33.4 BENNETT & BROOKES

On 30 December 1881, Bennett & Brookes wrote to the Royal Mint asking if it was illegal to affix their circular paper advertisements to new bronze pence. The Mint merely referred them to the 1861 Act. The firm, previously owned by J. V. Gregory, were wholesale and retail dealers in tea, coffee, fruit, spices, and English and Foreign provisions at 35 Tavern Street. In 1899 Walter Bennett, grocer, was at 16 Tavern Street, and Bennett & Co., wine and spirit merchants, were at 31 Tavern Street.

33.5 SMITH

William Smith, cutler, appears in the Poll Books of 1832 and 1835 for St. Matthew's Parish. He is also listed in the directories for 1830, 1839 and 1844 at St. Matthews Street. Subsequent entries are:

1855 Wm. Smith, cutler and trussmaker, Westgate Street.
1864 Smith & Son, cutlers, 59 Westgate Street.
1868 Fredk. Smith, cutler, 59 Westgate Street.

The countermark probably dates from the 1830's or 1840's.

34 Surrey
Charlwood

34.1 SQUIRE

This trader has not been identified. Squire is still a common surname in this part of Surrey.

Farnham

34.2 ROBINSON

From about 1822–32 William Robert Robinson was landlord of the 'Royal Oak', East Street. He may well have been a small landowner and hop-grower, as were most people of property in Farnham at that time. It is probable that he was a cooper as well as a publican. By 1839 he had conveyed the 'Royal Oak' to Frederick Tobias Robinson whose major enterprise by the 1860's was cooperage. In the view of the curator of the Farnham Museum, the countermark may be a form of hop token.

Guildford

34.3 I.C

Two possible issuers, both blacksmiths, are listed in local directories as follows:

1832 Isaac Coleman, blacksmith, Catherine Hill.
1839 John Chandler, smith and farrier, 10 North Street.
1844 John Chandler & Son, smith and farrier, 52 North Street.
1847–50 Mrs. Chandler & Son, same address.

The countermark probably dates from the 1830's or 1840's.

35 Sussex
Brighton

35.1 SHAW

Thomas Shaw, cook and confectioner, is listed in the 1839–40 directory at 39 Old Steine. William Shaw, pastrycook and confectioner, appears at the same address 1843–64. After 1864 the entry is for William Shaw, lodging-house keeper, 53 Regency Square. By 1864, 39 Old Steine had been swallowed up by the two hotels on either side of it. The countermark probably dates from c. 1843–55.

35.2 BROADHURST

In the absence of an initial this piece is assumed to originate from the hamlet near Horsted Keynes, although it could, of course, be a surname. It is described in the H. D. Gibbs sale catalogue as a 'Workhouse Prison Token' which seems most unlikely.

Chichester

35.3 BARKER

Robert Barker, jeweller and silversmith, is listed in directories at East Street 1823–33. By 1826–7 he is also described as a cutler, at the Cross, and in 1839 the entry is for jeweller, silversmith and cutler at the Cross. In 1845 John Barker, silversmith, was at East Street. The countermark probably dates from c. 1826–39. Robert Barker, cutler, no address shown, is also listed in Underhill's Biennial Directory for 1816–17.

35.4 BLAKE

R. Blake has not been traced. John Blake was a cutler in South Street, and appears in directories 1823–45. It is possible that R. Blake was a cutler before 1823.

35.5 BUDDEN

James Budden was a smith in Orchard Street, appearing in directories 1823–51. By 1855 Mrs. Charlotte Budden is listed at the same address. The 1826–7 entry describes Budden as a smith and bellhanger; by 1845 he is listed as a whitesmith. The other names appearing on one variety of this piece, Stinton, and Hanworth, do not seem to have been those of Chichester traders. Nor has a trader named Stinton been traced in Hanworth, Middlesex.

Rye

35.6 TISANOLD

There is no trace of a Rye trader or resident named Tisanold in the available Sussex directories, and it is possible that this is a joke piece: TIS AN OLD RYE.

Waldron

35.7 (LIONS GREEN FARM)

In the absence of any public house called 'The Lion' or any family of Green in the nineteenth century directories under Waldron, or on the tithe map of 1841, it is assumed that this piece was issued in the settlement of Lions Green, a mile to the east. The tithe map shows a house with a barn which may well have been called Lions Green Farm, and the countermarked coin may well have served as some form of farm or market check. Hops were grown on a large scale in the area, so another possibility is that the piece is a hop token.

36 Warwickshire
Birmingham

36.1 ATKIN & SONS

This firm is listed in the Birmingham directories as follows:

1835 (Wrightson & Webb's) Aaron Atkins (sic), manufacturer of saws, joiners' tools, and elastic steel busks, 35 Barford Street.
1839 (Robson's) Atkin & Son, saw and joiners' toolmakers, Barford Street; Aaron Atkins (sic) & Son, saw and joiners' toolmakers, gimlet and steel busk makers, 96 Barford Street.
1847 (Slater's) Aaron Atkin & Son, joiners' toolmakers, 96 Barford Street.
1849 (White's) Aaron Atkin & Sons (sic), saw, plane and joiners' tool manufacturers, 117 Barford Street.
1850 (Post Office) Atkin & Sons, saw, plane and joiners' tool manufacturers, 58 Ludgate Hill and 97, 115, 116 and 117 Barford Street, Cheapside.
1852–3 (Slater's) Atkins & Sons, saw makers, 117 Barford Street and 50 Ludgate Hill.

The countermark probably dates from c. 1839–47.

36.2 BOWN

Although no town is shown on this piece, Summer Lane is in Birmingham, and Bown is listed in the directories as follows:

1878 William Bown, horse clipper manufacturer and sewing machine shuttle manufacturer, 308 Summer Lane.
1884, 1888 William Bown, horse clipper, sewing machine shuttle and attachment and bicycle and tricycle fittings manufacturer, 308 Summer Lane.
1894 William Bown Limited, horse clipper maker, 308 Summer Lane.
1904 William Bown Limited, cycle fittings manufacturers, 130 Brearley Street.

The countermark probably dates from c. 1875–90.

36.3 BIRMINGHAM SMALL ARMS AND METAL COMPANY LTD.

The Birmingham Small Arms Co. Ltd. was originally registered in 1861. William Tranter, the famous gunmaker and patentee, was a founder shareholder, and a director in the firm's early years. On 3 February 1873 the company was re-registered as the Birmingham Small Arms and Metal Co. Ltd., with subscribed capital of £203,150. On July 1 1896 the firm sold its ammunition works and metal rolling mills in order to specialise in military and sporting rifles and cycle components. Later, on 23 September, the company was reconstructed and re-registered, the name being changed late in 1897 to the Birmingham Small Arms Company Ltd. By 1968, the company had authorised capital of £10,703,150, and four main product headings: motorcycles, central heating, metal components and general engineering. Directories show the address of the arms factory as Small Heath, with Benjamin McKay secretary and manager (1870), followed by Major-General W. M. H. Dixon, R.A., C.B. (1875, 1880), when the firm also had cartridge and metal mills at Adderley Park. The countermark is probably the mark used on rifles made under government contract in 1874, or of 1874 model.

Coventry

36.4 WILKINS

The legend on the reverse of this piece – 'When this you see remember me' is typical of those used on 'love tokens' c. 1770–1830. However, the fact that a trade and town, and no date, are included on the obverse, justifies its listing here. The reverse message is, of course, equally appropriate for use on a shop or advertisement ticket!

Unfortunately, directory cover of Coventry during this early period is not good, and Wilkins has not been traced in the directories for 1784, 1791, 1805–7, 1818–20, 1822, 1835, 1842 or 1851. A Joseph Wilkins, poulterer, dealer in game, and fishmonger, Market Place, is listed in Pigot's 1835 Directory.

Warwick

36.5 SIMMONS

Alexander Simmons, watch and clockmaker, later described also as a jeweller, is listed in directories from 1842 to 1874. His address is shown as West Street – by 1874 as 10 West Street. The countermark probably dates from before the 1853 Act.

38 Wiltshire

Salisbury

38.1 SARUM

This is assumed to be the mark of a Salisbury trader, possibly a cutler. Ten cutlers are listed in Pigot's 1830 Directory:

William Baech, Catherine Street.
James Bennett, Market Place.
Jane Botley, Market Place.
Charles Fox, Milford Street.

Zachariah Hill, Castle Street.
Jno. & Geo. Mackrell, Blue Boar Row.
John Nash, Silver Street.
James Phillips, Blue Boar Row.
Henry Shorto, Queen Street.
William Snook, Catherine Street.

'SARUM' does not appear to be a Sheffield mark, although '_{SARUM}G' was used in 1797 by Robert Hinchsliffe, fine scissors maker, of 36 Cheney Square, Sheffield.

39 Worcestershire

Kidderminster

39.1 MASSEY

Massey does not appear in the directories for 1783, 1794, 1805, 1805–7, 1809, 1820, 1835, 1837, 1840–2, 1850–1, 1855 or 1860. It is possible that he was connected with the Ludlow firm of wine merchants (see 30.5 above) – Francis Massey 1828–56 at the Bull Ring. However, the style of this piece is late eighteenth or early nineteenth century and it is perhaps more likely that there was some connection with Elizabeth Massey of Abergavenny (see 50.1 below). See also 15.5 above.

Moseley

39.2 TODD

Joseph Moss Todd is shown in directories as victualler of the 'Fighting Cocks', Moseley, 1854–60. In Kelly's 1854 Directory, he is also described as a cutler. In 1868 and 1872, he appears as a farmer at King's Heath, Birmingham. The countermark probably dates from the early 1850's, the forget-me-not being, presumably, Todd's trade mark.

Worcester

39.3 BRIDGES

J. Bridges, Worcester and Gloucester carrier, Quay, is listed in the 1820 directory but not in those for 1835, 1837, 1840–2, 1850–1, 1855 or 1860. However, Joshua Bridges, victualler, appears in the 1840 and 1854 directories at the King's Head, St. Johns. The piece probably dates from about 1820.

39.4 HIGGINS

The following entries appear in the Worcester directories:

1790–4 John Higgins, victualler, Green Man, Tything; James Higgins, tailor, Tything.

1820 James Higgins, tailor, Green Man and Still, The Tything.

The style of this piece is 1820 rather than 1790, but there are no other clues for dating it. By 1828/9 William Underhill was at the Green Man.

40 Yorkshire

Beverley

40.1 MOORE

There is no directory for 1800; that for 1823 shows Thomas Moore, hosier, toy and hardware dealer, Market Place. Moore does not appear in the 1840 or subsequent issues. It is not clear whether this Thomas Moore was the issuer, or a relative.

Bradford
40.2 WORKHOUSE
Duffield says these countermarked pieces took the place of the Bradford penny after a fire in 1813 destroying the dies. It should be noted, however, that the countermarks also occur on silver coins.

It is possible that these tokens were contemporary with those countermarked by the Keighley Overseers of the Poor in 1818 to pay paupers (see below). The cost of diesinking was thus avoided.

Keighley
40.3 OVERSEERS OF THE POOR
Davis says these pieces were issued by Keighley Overseers of the Poor to pay the paupers in 1818. It is not certain that the addition of numbers or initials was the work of the Overseers. It is usual to find both the Bradford and Keighley countermarks on Union Copper Company pennies, though other types occur. A Select Committee reported in July 1842 on 'allegations as to the management of the poor in the Keighley Union'. At this time there were 57 paupers in the workhouse, where the Master (appointed 1 April 1828) was Joseph Waterhouse.

Kingston-upon-Hull
40.4 EXTON or REXTON
This piece came to Mr. Banks from Kingston-upon-Hull and it is assumed that the countermark was issued there. Neither surname has been traced in directories, poll books or voters' registers 1790–1860, but the cover of these documents is not comprehensive.

Rotherham
40.5 (STEEL, TOZER & HAMPTON)
'Phoenix' was one of the trade marks of Steel, Tozer and Hampton (now Steel, Peech and Tozer), who, in 1881, were at Phoenix Bessemer Steel Works, Ickles, Rotherham. However, this is an extremely common brand mark in the metal trades, and it is not possible to be certain about the attribution of this piece.

Scarborough
40.6 HILL
Hill does not appear in the directories for 1784, 1823, 1840, 1846 or 1855. It is likely that he was active in the late eighteenth century.

Settle
40.7 HARGREAVES
Hargreaves (or Hargraves) was the name of a well-known local family of watch and clock makers – William 1710–30, Thomas 1770–95 and c. 1822–3, and John (of Duke Street) c. 1837–41. The latter was also an engraver. William Hargrave, grocer and butcher, is listed in Baines' 1822 and 1823 Directories, and it is possible that this engraved piece was issued in his name. The

alternative is some relative of the clockmaking family, in which case this may not be a trader's item.

Sheffield
40.8 (EDGAR ALLEN & CO.)
The trademark of £ · s · d within a diamond was granted by the Cutlers' Company to Edgar Allen & Co. Ltd. in 1870. Earlier, in 1733, they had been granted the mark of a fleur de lis above a letter K above a large figure 9. Directory entries are:
1875 manufacturers and export merchants, cast steel of all descriptions, tools made from steel and iron, Well Meadow Steel Works.
1890 address shown as Imperial Steel Works, with Steel Furnaces, File and Saw Works at Minerva Works, Cross George Street.
1922 Imperial Steel Works.

40.9 BEST
This countermark has been tentatively attributed to Thomas Best, the Sheffield cutler, who appears in directories as follows:
1805–7 Thomas Best, table and plated knife manufacturer, 28 Eyre Street.
1817 Thomas Best, manufacturer of table knives and silver-plated cutlery, Howard Street.
1828 As 1817, but at 45 Howard Street.
1833, 1837 John Thomas and James Best, table knife manufacturers and merchants, 46 Howard Street.
1841, 1845 as above, but at 12 Howard Street.

40.10 BINGHAM
James Bingham is listed in the Sheffield directories as follows:
1833 razor manufacturer, 8 New Church Street.
1837 as above, house Broomspring Lane.
1841 razor manufacturer, between 17 and 19 New Church Street, house Crook's Cottage.
1845 warehouseman, top of Broomspring Lane.
1852 warehouseman, top of Spring Lane.
1856 clerk, 130 Spring Lane.
1859 razor manufacturer, house 130 Broomspring Lane.
1864 clerk, 130 Spring Lane.
The countermarked piece presumably dates from c. 1833–41.

40.11 BRAMALL
Bramall is not listed as a mark in the Sheffield directories for 1787 and 1797. However it is a Sheffield street name (Bramall Lane) and a common surname in the town – hence its inclusion here. The name appears in directories as follows:
1797 Thomas Bramall, pocket knife cutler, Malin-bridge.
1841 John Bramall, filesmith, 13 South Parade.
1845 Thomas Bramall, file manager, 15 Talbot Street.
1849 James Bramall, penknife manufacturer, 18 Duke Street; John Bramall, file etc. manufacturer (Fisher & Bramall), 78 Hoyle Street.

1852 John Bramall, table knife cutler, 27 Monmouth Street; James Bramall, spring knife cutler, 18 Duke Street; William Bramall, saw manager, 27 Paternoster Row.

1859 John Bramall, cutler, New Saville Street; John Bramall, steel converter, refiner, manufacturer of improved cast steel engineering and machine files, circular saws etc., Saville Works, Mowbray Street; Lewis Bramall, pen blade maker, Daisy Bank Street, Philips Road.

The countermark probably dates from the period 1840–60.

40.12 BRISCOE

William Briscoe & Son, merchants (Wolverhampton) are listed in the 1845 and 1849 Sheffield directories at 37 Victoria Street (J. S. Warner, agent). Wm. Briscoe & Sons (sic), merchants, St. John's Square., Wolverhampton, appear in Robson's Commercial Directory 1839 and White's Staffordshire Directory 1851. Briscoes were obviously associated with Hiram Cutler of Sheffield, hence the two (unofficial) countermarks on the same coin. Cutler appears in the Sheffield directories as follows:

1828 Hiram Cutler, merchant, house Broomspring.

1837 Hiram G. Cutler, merchant, steel converter and saw, edge-tool, file, and table, shoe and butcher knife manufacturer, Castle Hill, house Broomhill.

1841 As above, but house Glossop Road.

1845 As above, but house Springfield.

1849, 1857 (No entry in 1854) Hiram Cutler, Son, and Chambers, Castle Hill.

1860 Hiram Cutler, merchant and manufacturer, house Broomhill House, 343 Glossop Road.

1864 Chas. Chambers & Co., late H. Cutler, Son & Chambers, Castle Hill Works, established by Thomas Weldon in 1780.

The countermark probably dates from the mid-1840's.

40.13 BROOMHEAD

In Gales and Martin's 1787 Directory, 'Broomhead' is shown as the mark of Broomhead, Hinchsliffe and Co., manufacturers of pen and pocket knives, razors, and table knives, of Brinsworth's Orchard. The 1797 directory lists Broomheads & Rutherford, factors and manufacturers of table knives, Court 22, No. 7 Far Gate, but no mark is shown. The other countermarks on this piece – daggar, maltese cross, ΓYAS (TYAS?). QUIT and ELAM, have the appearance of Sheffield marks (cf. EYAM, in 1797 the mark of Robert Skidmore & Son, fine scissor maker, 7 and 8 Carver Street), but it has not proved possible to associate them with particular traders.

40.14 CADMAN

Luke Cadman, razor maker, was at Fargate in 1774 and used the trade mark 'BEN GALL' By 1787 he was described as a cutler and had moved to Norfolk Street, using the mark 'BENGALL'. While Cadman is a fairly common name in the Sheffield metal

trades there is no further mention of this trademark in directories until the late nineteenth century – e.g. the 1891 and 1915 entries are for Thomas Radley Cadman & Sons, 211 St. Mary's Road, razor manufacturer, established 1748, trade mark 'BENGALL'. The countermark probably dates from the late eighteenth century.

40.15 CARR

John and Riley Carr, steel refiners and saw manufacturers, of Bailey Lane Works, Bailey Lane, are listed in the Sheffield directories 1833–1951. In 1833 they were described as merchants, steel refiners and saw, file, edge tool, tobacco knife, spiral edges and ledger blade manufacturers. In 1845, 1860 and 1864 the address is shown as 41 Bailey Lane. By 1884 they had become steel converters and refiners, engineering machine, saw and file manufacturers. By 1891, and probably earlier, they were using the trade mark of a dog pointing left, with 'STANCH' below. The countermark must date from between 1861 – the date of the coin, and 1877 – the date it was noted by Batty.

40.16 CONGREVE

James Fox, Love Street, and Charles Congreve, Arundel Works, were both active as 'merchants' c. 1830–45, although directories give no indication of the commodities in which they dealt. Sanderson probably refers to Sanderson Bros. and Co. who adopted this title about 1830 and had a shear steel works at Attercliffe Forge. By 1915 they had become Sanderson Brothers and Newbould, and are now Sanderson Kayser.

40.17 (DUNGWORTH)

'1772' was the mark of Jonathan Dungworth, cutler, maker of common pocket and pen knives, listed in Gales and Martin's 1787 Directory at Meadow Street, Sheffield. The coin has a Sheffield provenance. In John Robinson's 1797 Directory Dungworth appears as a pocket knife cutler at 6 Edward Street, with the same mark.

40.18 ELLIN

The following entries appear in the Sheffield directories:

1825 Thomas Ellin & Co. (late Oldale and Ellin), manufacturers of table knives and forks, and all kinds of shoe, bread, butcher, carving and spear point knives, bottom of Arundel Street.

1833, 1837 Thomas Ellin & Co., table knife works, foot of Arundel Street, and steel rollers, Vulcan Works, South Street.

1841 Thomas Ellin & Co., merchants, and manufacturers of steel, table, butchers' and cook knives, Vulcan Works, and table knife works, 273 Arundle (sic) Street.

1852, 1864 Thomas Ellin & Co., merchants, steel converters, and table, butcher and cook knife etc. manufacturers, Silvester Works, 273 Arundel Street, and forgers, rollers etc., Vulcan Works, Hereford Street.

1868 As 1852, 1864, but with Corporate Mark 'VULCAN'.

1876, 1884 Thomas Ellin & Co., manufacturers of pen, pocket and table knives, razors, scissors, steel files, edge tools, saws, and general merchants, Sylvester Works, Sylvester Street. Trade mark 'VULCAN'.

The countermark probably dates from before the 1853 Act.

40.19 FENTON

Directory entries are as follows:

1856 (White's) Fenton & Shore, merchants and cutlery &c. manufacturers, 46 Division Street. Joseph Fenton (Fenton & Shore), house, 85 Broomhill Road.

1864 (White's) Joseph Fenton and Sons, merchants and cutlery manufacturers, Essex Works, 88 Scotland Street.

1868 (White's) as above, but described as merchants and manufacturers of pen, pocket, table and butchers' knives &c.

1876, 1879 (White's) Joseph Fenton & Sons, merchants and manufacturers of crucibles, cast steel castings, steel, files, saws, pen & pocket, table, shoe and butchers' knives, razors, scissors &c., Sykes Works, Eyre Street, Matilda Street, and Bridge Street.

1893 (Post Office) J. Fenton & Sons, cutlery manufacturers, 40 Matilda Street.

The firm was still at this address in 1922.

This unofficial countermark probably dates from the last quarter of the nineteenth century.

40.20 FIELD

Alfred Field & Co., merchants, 66 and 67 Parade, are listed in the Birmingham directory for 1865, but do not appear in the Sheffield directories until the 1870's:

1876 Alfred Field & Co., table, spring and butchers' knives and razors, merchants and manufacturers, 23 Westfield Terrace and Birmingham and Liverpool. E. M. Dickinson, agent.

1884 Alfred Field & Co., manufacturers and merchants of pen, pocket, table and butchers' knives, razors, scissors etc. 23 Westfield Terrace. M. Ward and B. H. Bates, agents. (Trade mark shown as a swan's head.)

1887 Alfred Field & Co., American merchants, 23 Westfield Terrace.

1893 Alfred Field & Co., cutlery manufacturers, manufacturers of pen, pocket, table, butchers' spear, dagger and hunting knives, razors, scissors etc., Continental Cutlery Works, 23 Westfield Terrace.

1897 Alfred Field & Co., manufacturers of cutlery, razors, scissors and electroplated goods and general merchants, Continental Works, 23 Westfield Terrace. (see 40.27 below).

1922 Alfred Field & Co. (Sheffield) Ltd., cutlery manufacturers, 23 Westfield Terrace.

It is difficult to be precise about the dating of this countermark, but the most likely period is the 1870's, when the firm had just set up business in Sheffield.

40.21 GROVES

Richard Groves, saw maker, Trinity Street is listed in the 1787 directory, and by 1797 is shown at 1 Bottom of Snow-hill. By 1817 the firm was known as Richard Groves and Sons, saw manufacturers, of Allen Street. In 1828 the entry is for saw manufacturers, steel converters and refiners, manufacturers of cast steel patent turned circular saws and of patent bronzed ladies' busks. Subsequent entries are:

1833, 1837 saw and steel busk manufacturer and steel refiners, Snow Lane.

1841 file, saw and steel manufacturers, 71 Snow Lane and 207 Moorfields.

1845, 1860 Bee Hive Works, 71 Snow Lane.

1854 Snow Lane, Moorfields and Gibraltar Street.

1864 71 Snow Lane and 73 Allen Street.

1884 manufacturers of circular &c. saws, steel files and edge tools, Henry Street and Snow Lane.

The countermark probably dates from before 1830.

40.22 HALL

W. Hall appears in the Sheffield directories as follows:

1817 William Hall, engravers' toolmaker, Scotland Street.

1825 William Hall, file manufacturer, Porter Street. Cast steel drawer, engravers and fancy trimming toolmaker, 57 Pea Croft.

1833 William Hall, file, saw and edge tool manufacturer and steel converter, 61 Porter Street.

1837 William Hall, razor etc. manufacturer, Sharrow Moor, merchant, steel refiner, and file manufacturer, 61 Porter Street

1841, 1845, 1849, 1852 William Hall, merchant, and table knife and razor manufacturer, 45 Eyre Street (Hall & Colley, 1852; 43 Eyre Street, 1845, 1849, 1852). William Hall, manufacturer of files, edge tools etc., 54 Porter Street (described as merchant, steel refiner, and file, saw, edge tool and table knife manufacturer 1845, 1849, 1852).

1856 William Hall (now Charles), merchant, and file, steel, saw, edge tool and table knife manufacturers, Alma Works, Pool Square, 96 Fargate.

1859 as 1856, but address shown as Alma Works, Barkerspool Square.

1868 address shown as Alma Works, Pool Square, corporate mark, 'W. HALL' $\frac{}{2865}$

1887 manufacturer of steel files, edge tools, saws etc., address as 1868.

1897 steel manufacturer, Alma Works, Pool Square, Barker's Pool.

1900, 1904 manufacturer of files, tools, saws, steel and general merchant, address as 1897.

1917, 1922 William Hall (Sheffield) Ltd., steel manufacturers, Alma Works, Matilda Lane.

The countermark probably dates from the 1840's when William Hall was at Porter Street.

40.23 HORN

William Ibbotson Horn & Co. appear in the Sheffield directories as follows:

1833 Steel file, saw, edge tool, scythe, fender and cutlery manufacturer and agents for the Ore-ground iron, 18 Bridge Street and Wisewood House, Pitsmoor.

1841 Merchant and manufacturer, Wisewood House, Pyebank; works, Bridge Street.

1845 67 Bridge Street.

1857, 1860 67 Bridge Street and tilters and rollers, Wisewood.

1864 65 Bridge Street.

The firm was taken over by Joshua and Robert Dodge about 1875. In 1884 the directory entry is for W. I. Horn & Co. (now Josh. & Robt. Dodge Lim.) 65–67 Bridge Street. By 1915 'W. I. HORN & CO.' was one of the trade marks of W. K. & C. Peace Ltd., Eagle Works.

40.24 HUNTSMAN

Benjamin Huntsman was born in 1704, and settled in Doncaster as a clockmaker. Not satisfied with the quality of steel for springs, he made experiments and in 1740 moved to Handsworth, near Sheffield, where he invented crucible or cast steel. The Sheffield cutlers refused to work a material so much harder than ordinary steel, so Huntsman exported his output to France. Alarmed by the preference shown by both English and French consumers for cast steel cutlery, Sheffield tried and failed to get the export of cast steel prohibited. Huntsman, who had not patented his process, stayed in Sheffield despite tempting offers to move to Birmingham. The cutlers adopted cast steel but tried by all manner of industrial espionage to find out the process of manufacture. Huntsman did his best to hide this by working only at night, but eventually Walker, a Greenside ironfounder, discovered the secret while warming himself near the furnace, disguised as a tramp. In 1770, Huntsman moved to large new premises at Attercliffe. He died in 1776, and the business was carried on by his sons. The 'B. HUNTSMAN' mark (illustrated in an advertisement of 1891) was imitated by others – e.g. J. C. Fischer of Schaffhausen c. 1814. The firm moved from Huntsman steel works, Attercliffe in 1899 and are now at Coleridge Road. For further information see 'Dictionary of National Biography' and 'A Brief History of the Firm of B. Huntsman Ltd. 1742–1930' (1930).

40.25 MANNING

This countermark must date from between 1862 – the date of the coin – and 1877 – the date noted by Batty. Thomas Manning & Co., manufacturers of the improved endless bandsaw etc., are listed in Algar's 1859 Directory at Upper St. Philip's Road. The firm does not appear in the issues for 1857 or 1860. It is, therefore, likely that this is an unofficial countermark, a brand-marking punch falling into the wrong hands after the firm had ceased to exist.

40.26 (MARSDEN & BEETEN)

The (Crown) PEKIN trade mark was used by Marsden & Beeten and appears in White's 'Hardware Trade Marks' (1892) and the 'Register of Trade Marks of the Cutlers Company' (1919). The firm is listed in the local directories as follows:

1893 Marsden & Beeten, saw, steel and file manufacturers, Newcastle Street (not listed 1887).

1900 Marsden & Beeten, manufacturers of steel, files, saws, hammers etc., Carr Lane, and Middlesex Works, Newcastle Street.

Entries cease in 1931. In 1900 the firm was also using the mark 'J. W. & Cº, ESTABLISHED 1823' round a file within an incuse diamond.

40.27 MOILLIET & GEM

The Sheffield directories show entries for Moilliet & Gem, merchants, 6 Eyre Street (and at Birmingham), Thomas Ingall, agent, from 1852 to 1856. Subsequent entries are for Edward Gem & Co., merchants and manufacturers, 6 Eyre Street, and Charlotte Street, Birmingham, Thomas Ingall, agent (1859, 1868). In 1879 the firm were described as merchants and manufacturers of cutlery, 4–6 Eyre Street, and in 1888 as general merchants at 9 Eyre Street. By 1896 they were at Continental Works, 23 Westfield Terrace, described as 'merchants and manufacturers of pen, pocket, butchers' & table knives & electro-plated goods &c.' (see 40.20 above).

The Birmingham directory for 1888 lists Edward Gem & Co., hardware and general merchants, 27 Charlotte Street.

40.28 MORTON

The following entries appear in the Sheffield directories:

1859, 1868 William Morton, spring knife manufacturer, Darnall.

1879 William Morton, manufacturer of scissors, razors, & table, pen, pocket & sportsmen's knives, & nail, champagne &c. nippers, Old Rockingham Works, 175 Rockingham Street.

1888, 1896 William Morton, cutlery manufacturer, 175 Rockingham Street.

1905, 1922 Wm. Morton & Sons, pen, pocket, sporting & table knife manufacturers, 175 Rockingham Street.

The Spa Hotel, Boscombe, Bournemouth, is listed in Stanford's Hampshire Guide for 1881, but not in Baedecker's 1910 issue.

Clearly, William Morton had a contract for cutlery for this hotel, and the countermarked coin was an unofficial trial of the brand and hotel punches. Since the coin only has a small degree of wear, the piece probably dates from c. 1875–90.

40.29 NEWBOULD

This countermark has been attributed to Samuel Newbould & Co., the Sheffield tool and steel manufacturers who appear in directories as follows:

1787, 1797 Samuel Newbould, edge toolmaker, Sheffield Moor.

1805–7 Samuel Newbould and Co., saw, fender, edge tool, wool shears and steel manufacturers, Sheffield Moor. At the same time William

Newbould and Sons, merchants and manufacturers (and silver platers) were at South Street.

1817, 1828 Samuel Newbould & Co., edge tool,
shear, fender and steel manufacturers, South
Street.

1833, 1837 Samuel Newbould & Co., saw, edge
tool and wool shear manufacturers, steel converters and merchants, South Street Bridge.

1841 As above, Bridgefield Works, 170 South
Street.

1845 As above, also tilters and forgers, Loxley
Works.

1854, 1860, 1864 As above 170 South Street.

1884 Samuel Newbould & Co. Ltd., edge tool,
files, steel and saw manufacturers, Newhall
Road.

By 1915 the firm had amalgamated with
Sanderson Brothers & Co.

The countermark probably dates from the
early nineteenth century.

40.30 PEACE BROTHERS

This firm is listed in directories between 1787 and
1876 as follows:

1787 Joseph Peace, file smith, Scotland Street.
Mark: a diamond above two fleurs de lis.

1797 Joseph Peace & Son, file smiths, 92 Scotland
Street.

1817 William & Samuel Peace, file manufacturers,
Scotland Street.

1825 W. & S. Peace, file manufacturers, 78
Scotland Street.

1828 W. & S. Peace, file and steel manufacturers,
Garden Street.

1833 William Peace, file manufacturer and steel
refiner, 9 Garden Street.

1837 Sarah Peace (late William) file manufacturer
and steel refiner, 8 Garden Street.

1841 Sarah Peace (late William), file manufacturer,
48 Garden Street.

1841, 1845 William Peace, file manufacturer and
Mrs. Sarah 55 Garden Street.

1849 Peace, Kirby & Co., steel converters and
manufacturers of files, edge tools etc., 55
Garden Street.

1852 W. H. & E. Peace, file, saw, tool and steel
manufacturers, 43 Garden Street.

1854 Peace Brothers, steel file and saw manufacturers, Garden Street Works.

1860 Peace Bros., file, saw, steel &c. manufacturers and merchants, 55 Garden Street.

1864, 1876 As above. Advertisements show the
firm's corporate mark of a letter P with a
diamond above, a fleur de lys below to left and
right, all in a circle (granted 1770).

The countermark probably dates from the
1850's.

40.31 PEACE & CO.

No firm using the style 'S. Peace & Co.' has been
traced in nineteenth century Sheffield directories.
There are, however, four possibilities:

1. Samuel Peace, saw and truss manufacturer,
and steel refiner, 5 Smithfield (1822), shown as
cast steel refiner (1825).

Charles and Samuel Peace, same address
(1833).
C. & S. Peace & Co., merchants, steel con-
verters, and saw and scythe manufacturers,
Eagle Works, Russell Street (1837, 1841).
(S. Peace & Co.' only just fits on the coin –
perhaps a C. & S. Peace & Co. punch was used.)
Ibbotson, Peace & Co., Eagle Works, 84 Russell
Street (1845), later Peaces, Spafford & Co.,
same address (1856).
W. K. Peace & Co. (1859), William, K. and
Charles Peace, Eagle Works, Mowbray
Street (from 1864).

2. S. Peace & Sons, merchants, and steel, file,
saw, scythe, and James Cam's edge tool auger
manufacturers, Burnt Tree Lane, and 9 Forge
Lane (1845, 1847).
Joseph Peace & Co., saw, file, edge tool manufacturers, 9 Forge Lane (1849, 1856), later at
Merchant Works, Neepsend (1864 and 1893).

3. Samuel Peace, file manufacturer, Jericho
(1849, 1856).

4. John & Charles Peace, file manufacturers, 101
Peacroft (1864).
Samuel Peace & Sons (late J. & C. Peace), 101
Peacroft and 115 Scotland Street (1867–8), by
1876 at Wellmeadow Steel Works, 54 Well-
meadow Street.

The countermarked coin was probably
produced by an employee of C. & S. Peace & Co.
in the 1840's, though could conceivably have
been used as some sort of works check.

40.32 (REVEL)

Abraham Revel, Little Common, is listed under
makers of common pocket knives, using the mark
'EPHOD' in Gales and Martin's 1787 Directory.

40.33 SANDERSON & KIRK

Sanderson and Kirk, saw manufacturers, Carver
Lane, are listed in the directories for 1816–17 and
1817. By 1821 John Sanderson, saw manufacturer,
(without Kirk), appears at Carver Street, with a
house in Button Lane. He was no doubt related to
William Sanderson and Sons, manufacturers of
every description of cutlery, of Carver Forge
Works, Carver Street, listed in the 1870 directory.

40.34 SMITH & HAWKSLEY

The following entries appear in the Sheffield
directories:

1841 H. & J. Smith, merchants, steel converters,
manufacturers of files and spring knives,
scissors etc., 112 and 114 Rockingham Street.

1845 Smith & Hawksley, razor manufacturer,
114 Rockingham Street.

1849 Smith & Hawksley, razor manufacturer, 118
Rockingham Street.

1852, 1856 Smith & Hawksley, razor and spring
knife manufacturers, 24 Lambert Street.

1859, 1860 Smith & Hawksley, merchants, and
manufacturers of razors, table knives, pen and
pocket knives etc., 24 Lambert Street. Smith
& Hawksley also have an advertisement in the
1859 issue.

The firm is not listed in the 1864 directory.

40.35 SORBY

Robert Sorby, edge tool maker, first appears in the 1828 directory at Union Street. Subsequent entries are as follows:

1833 merchant and edge tool, saw, patent scythe and hay knife manufacturer, 2 Union Street.

1837 description as above, also steel refiners, Carver Street.

1841, 1845 Robert Sorby & Son, manufacturers of edge tools, saws, patent scythes and sickles, and general merchants, 2 Carver Street.

1854, 1884 Robert Sorby & Sons, 2 to 10 Carver Street.

1940 Robert Sorby & Sons Ltd. (Regd. Nov. 1923), tool makers, Kangaroo Works, Woodseats.

The firm are still in business at Kangaroo Works, 803/817 Chesterfield Road.

William and Joshua Edmundson & Co., manufacturers and general house furnishing ironmongers were at 35 Capel Street, Dublin, 1831-2. The firm became Joshua Edmundson & Co. of 35–36 Capel Street, and were still operating in 1900.

The countermark probably dates from the 1830's. There was possibly some form of association between the two firms, although this is unlikely. See 98.1 below.

40.36 SPENCER

This countermark cannot be definitely attributed but is assumed to have been issued by Matthias Spencer & Sons who appear in directories as follows:

1805-7 John Spencer, file manufacturer, Peacroft.

1817 Matthias Spencer & Son, file manufacturers, Peacroft.

1828 as above, steel converters and refiners, manufacturers of files, edge tools, saws, etc, 50 Peacroft.

1833 as above, 51 Peacroft.

1837 as above, 50 Peacroft.

1841, 1845 as above, 107 Peacroft.

1854, 1857, 1860 M. Spencer & Sons, file and edge tool manufacturer, 107 Peacroft.

1864, 1872 John R. Spencer & Son, merchants and steel file, edge tool, cutlery, steel shovel, wire etc. manufacturers, Albion Steel Works, 107 Peacroft.

1884 Matthias Spencer & Sons, as above.

Alternative possibilities are William Spencer & Son, merchants and steel file, cutlery etc. manufacturers, Kingston Steel Works, Malinda Street (1864-83) or Walter Spencer & Co., Midland Steel Works, Rotherham (formerly of Sheffield – corporate mark granted 1777), manufacturers of files and sole makers of the Diamond Cast Steel (1871-91).

The countermark probably dates from the 1830's.

40.37 (SPURR)

'SPUR' was the mark of Peter Spurr, pen and pocket knife maker, of Church Lane, Sheffield, listed in the 1774 and 1787 directories. In Pigot's 1818-20 Directory, Peter Spurr is described as a razor maker, merchant, lancet and phleme manufacturer, factor and manufacturer in Arundel Street. By 1822-3 the entry is for Peter Spurr and Sons.

40.38 STU . . .

This countermark cannot be attributed, but is assumed to have been issued by one of the many Stubbs engaged in the Sheffield metal trades. The number (74) could be a brand mark – numerals were often used for this purpose – or could mean that the piece served as a pay or tool check. A possible issuer might be: George Stubbs, edge tool maker, 10 Orchard Lane (1834).

40.39 THOMPSON

This again is difficult to attribute, as the name is a common one. The issuer is assumed to be William Thompson, living at Upperthorpe and described as a saw manufacturer in the 1837 directory. Subsequent entries are:

1839 steel converter and refiner, 115 and 117 Scotland Street.

1841 steel converter and refiner and manufacturer of files, 115 Scotland Street, house, Upperthorpe.

An alternative might be James Thompson, cutlery manufacturer living at 31 Charles Street (1833), and listed as James Thompson & Son in 1837.

40.40 TILLOTSON

This trader is listed in directories as follows:

1817, 1824 John Tillotson, table knife cutler, merchant, manufacturer, factor, Coalpit Lane.

1828-9 John Tillotson & Co., as above.

1834 Thomas and John (junior) Tillotson, as above 47 Coalpit Lane.

1842 Thomas and John Tillotson, as above, 56 Coalpit Lane.

1849 Thomas Tillotson, merchant, 40 Suffolk Road, house, Sharrow Lane; listed under 'merchants' at Columbia Works, 34 Suffolk Road.

1856 Thomas Tillotson & Co., merchants, Columbia Place, 40 Suffolk Road.

1859 As above, Suffolk Road.

1864 No entry.

The countermark dates from c. 1849-59.

40.41 TWIGG etc.

Twigg is a very common name in the Sheffield metal trades, but Twigg Bros. & Co. have not been traced in directories. Broomhall Works, Broomhall Street, were occupied by Henry Thompson, a manufacturer of all kinds of edge and joiners' tools, in 1876 and 1880.

Levison & Sherman have not been traced in Sheffield directories: Michael Levison was a jewellery hawker at 24 Pond Hill in 1849 and the name Sherman does not appear at all.

Fenton & Marsdens are listed as follows:

1841 Fenton & Marsden, merchants and manufacturers of edge tools, joiners' tools, braces and bits, saws, screw boxes, skates etc., 245 Rockingham Street, house Ecclesall.

1845 Fenton & Marsdens (late Maw & Staleys), as above but at 51 Bridge Street.

1849 Fenton & Marsdens, now Marsden Brothers & Silverwood, skate manufacturers to Prince Albert, 51 Bridge Street.

1854 Marsden Brothers & Co. (late Fenton & Marsdens), Bridge Street works 'skate manufacturers to Her Majesty and the Royal Family'.

1870 Marsden Brothers & Co., Bridge Street works, merchants and manufacturers of edge and joiners' tools, skates etc.

The countermark probably dates from the mid-1840's.

40.42 TYZACK

This firm appears in the Sheffield directories as follows:

1868 William Alexander Tyzack, traveller, 141 Cemetary Road.

1876 William Alexander Tyzack & Co., manufacturers of cast, shear, bar, spring and sheet steel, files, saws, scythes, machine knives &c., Stella Works, Hereford Street.

1879 described as manufacturers of paper knives, steel, files, saws, scythes and machine knives, same address.

1893 W. A. Tyzack & Co., steel, file, saw, tool, machine knife and scythe manufacturers &c., Stella Works, Hereford Street, and Upper Slack, Penistone Road and Walkley Bank.

Tyzack & Co. were still at Stella Works in 1922.

40.43 (WARBURTON)

A cross above 'LISBON' was the mark of Thomas Warburton, razor maker, listed in directories at Coalpit Lane (1774), Burgess Street (1787) and Charles Street (1828-9).

40.44 WARD & PAYNE, T. TURNER & CO.

Directory entries are as follows:

1825, 1833 David Ward & Son, merchants and manufacturers of edge tools, engravers' and joiners' tools, saws, skates and steel refiners, Portobello Street.

1837 David Ward & Son, edge and joiners' tool manufacturers, Portobello Street. Henry Payne, edge tool maker, 10 Westfield Terrace.

1841 David Ward & Co., manufacturers of edge and joiners' tools, saws and skates, and steel refiners, 95 and 97 Trippet Lane. Henry Payne, edge tool manufacturer, Trippet Lane.

1845 Ward & Payne, merchants, and edge and joiners' tools, saw, skate and steel manufacturers, Ward Works, 110 West Street, and 89 Portobello Street.

In 1852, the address is shown as 110 West Street only. By 1856 the firm were using the corporate mark of two crossed hammers over an anvil between W and P. In 1888 they were at 106 to 114 West Street, and in 1896 at West Street, and Limbrick Works, Hillsborough.

Thomas Turner set up business in 1802, and by 1825 was listed in the Sheffield directory as Thomas Turner & Co., merchants and manufacturers of table and pocket knives, files, tools

&c., steel refiners, 38 Norfolk Street. Subsequent entries are:

1833 Turner, Yeomans & Yates, Suffolk Road.

1837-1915 Thomas Turner & Co., manufacturers of cutlery &c., Suffolk Works, Suffolk Road.

The unofficial countermarks on this coin probably date from c. 1875-1900.

40.45 WRAGG

While Wragg is a name common in the Sheffield trades, it seldom occurs with the initial 'H'. The issuer of this countermark is assumed to be one of the following:

1841 Henry & William Wragg, pen knife manufacturers, Lydgate.

1849 Henry Wragg, pen and pocket knife manufacturer, Lydgate.

1852 Henry Wragg, pen and pocket blade and surgical instrument maker, Balm Green; Henry Wragg, shopkeeper and spring knife manufacturer, Lydgate.

1854 Henry Wragg, pen and pocket blade maker, Pool Square, Fargate.

1857, 1860, 1864 Henry Wragg, razor etc. manufacturer (Wm. Wragg & Sons, 7 Lambert Street), house, 48 Meadow Street.

It is probable that the countermark was issued by Henry Wragg of Lydgate in the 1840's.

40.46 YATES

W. Yates is listed in directories as follows:

1856 William Yates, saw manufacturer, house, Hillfoot; Yates & Wood, saw and machine knife makers, 12 Wicker Lane.

1868 William Yates, house, 207 St. Philip's Road; Yates & Wood, saw manufacturers, Wicker Lane.

1884 William Yates, saw manufacturer (Yates & Wood), house, 59 Montgomery Terrace Road; Yates & Wood, saw and machine knife manufacturers, Wicker Lane.

York

40.47 DRINGHOUSES

This piece is discussed in my note in the Bulletin of the Token Corresponding Society, volume 1, no. 11 (July 1973), p. 257-8.

Dringhouses, a parish 1½ miles south west of York, had a population of 156 in 1821, 342 in 1851 and 659 in 1901.

By the 1830's, the few traders are included under York in the local directories. Apart from a shopkeeper and wheelwright (1823), a boot and shoemaker (1848-9) and butcher (1848-55), and up to three innkeepers, the only significant occupations in the first half of the nineteenth century seem to have been market gardening and brick and tile making.

It seems likely that the countermarked coin served either as a truck ticket or a load ticket in connection with the brick and tile industry. The punch used may well have been also employed for marking tiles – said to be of good quality in the 1857 Post Office Directory. It probably dates from before 1850.

Among the principal manufacturers were the brothers John, Edward and George Simpson of Dringhouses Moor, who are listed in the 1848, 1849 and 1857 directories. Others include: James Dalby, brick and tile maker, and surveyor of the York and Tadcaster Road (1823); Henry Bookless, brickmaker (1834); William Cropper, brickmaker (1841); John Carr, brickmaker (1848, 1849); Mrs. Mary Carr, brickmaker (1857); Thomas A. Wilkinson, brick and tile maker (1848, 1849, 1855); John Wright, market gardener and brick maker (1857).

40.48 HARRISON
This trader has not been traced. The countermark could, of course, be a Sheffield brand mark. In York the only remote possibility is William Harrison, blacksmith, North Street (1834).

40.49 PRINCE
John Prince, ironfounder, High Ousegate, appears in the directories for 1798, 1805, and 1809–11. Prince & Glover, iron and brass founders, and furnishing ironmongers, were at High Ousegate 1818–20, but had disappeared by 1822. By 1828 Harwood & Dale, iron and brass founders, were at 22 High Ousegate.

WALES

48 Glamorgan
Swansea
48.1 JOYCE
By 1830 Swansea was a flourishing seaport with considerable domestic and foreign trade, and had 'one of the most safe and beautiful harbours in the kingdom' (Pigot's Directory 1830). This helps explain the presence of a French coin; add to this the fact that no cutler named Joyce has been traced in any other town and we have a reasonable basis for attribution. Joyce appears in the directories as follows:
1844 James Joyce, working cutler, Wind Street (not listed 1835–6).
1851 James Joyce, cutler, College Street.
1858, 1859 as above, but address shown as 5 College Street.
1868 as above, but address shown as 28 Goat Street.
By 1875 James Joyce was living at 20 Page Street. The countermark probably dates from the 1840's.

48.2 LOCK
Lock is not a common name in the Swansea directories, and appears as follows:
1868 James Lock, boot and shoe merchant, Victoria Road (not listed 1859).
1871 James Lock, Orange Tree Inn, Orange Street (Matthew David was licensee in 1875.)
1873–4 James Lock, beer retailer, 4 York Street. (Frederick Lock, boot and shoe maker, was at this address in 1875.)
1880–1910 James Lock, bootmaker, 16 Greenfield Street.
1901 Charles Lock, grocer, 94 Gorse Lane.

The countermark probably dates from before 1880, either 1860–7, when no directories are available for study, or the early 1870's, when James Lock seems to have changed his occupation frequently. Alternatively, the piece could have been issued earlier in the century, as directory cover is far from comprehensive; only the following issues have been studied: 1822–3, 1830, 1835–6, 1844, 1848, 1849, 1851, 1852, 1854, 1858, 1859.

50 Monmouth
Abergavenny
50.1 Massey
Elizabeth Massey, dealer in wine and spirits, is listed in Holden's Triennial Directory for 1811. No address is shown. See also 15.5, 30.5 and 39.1 above. There is no entry for Massey in Pigot's 1822–3 Directory.

SCOTLAND

54 Aberdeenshire
Kemnay
54.1 ANDREW
Cornwall's New Aberdeen Directory, 1853, lists William Andrew, farmer, tenant of Willbush. In the Valuation Rolls for 1859, 1880 and 1884 he is shown as tenant of Greenkirtle. From 1893 the entry is for William Leslie Andrew, farmer, tenant of Greenkirtle. There were no traders named Andrew in Kemnay during this period, so it is probable that the countermarked coin served as a market check or token. The only other possibility is a pay check or truck ticket for a worker in one of the local quarries; with Rubislaw, Kemnay had the most important granite quarries in Aberdeenshire – Paradise Hill, Whitestones, Leschangie and Tom's Forest employed about 300 men in the 1860's.

55 Angus
Dundee
55.1 BUTCHART
Andrew Butchart, grocer and spirit merchant of 56 Overgate appears in directories from 1860–1 to 1867–8. The countermark was issued to meet a local shortage about 1860 during the period of changeover from copper coinage to bronze. Similar countermarks by Dundee traders are found on metal discs – see 'G.G.R.' in Spink's Numismatic Circular 1933, p. 131. Andrew Butchart was followed by Alexander Butchart, also a grocer and spirit merchant, at 74 Overgate (1869–70), 57 Overgate (1870–1 to 1877–8), 27 Overgate (1878–9) and 57 Overgate (1880–1).

57 Ayrshire
Ayr
57.1 YOUNG
J. & T. Young were engineers, millwrights, founders and boilermakers, and appear in directories from 1851 to 1888 at Vulcan Foundry,

Newton Green, Ayr. The firm's advertisements also appear in directories. They made mills and threshing machines; the maker's plate of one of the latter, from Beoch Mill near Maybole, is now in the National Museum of Antiquities, Edinburgh – see John Butt, 'The Industrial Archaeology of Scotland' (1967) p. 38. The countermarked coin was probably used for a pay or tool check, or, possibly, a truck ticket.

Catrine

57.2 CATRINE COTTON WORKS
Returning to his estate at Ballochmyle in 1786 after a long spell in India, Claud Alexander looked for some outlet in industry. He decided to build a cotton spinning mill at Catrine, using the River Ayr for power. There was nothing at Catrine then except a blacksmith's shop and a meal mill, and a village had to be built for the workers, together with schools and a library. Alexander formed a partnership with David Dale, the Glasgow merchant, who, with Richard Arkwright, had started the New Lanark cotton mills (see below) in 1785. The first mill was built in 1787 and a second followed in 1790. By 1793 the village population had reached 1350. The partnership lasted until 13 April 1801, when the mills were purchased by Kirkman Finlay. Shortly afterwards Archibald Buchanan came from the Ballindalloch cotton mill at Balfron, Stirlingshire (see below) to be resident manager. At this time the works were considerably extended. In 1827, Archibald Buchanan was still acting manager. Pigot's 1837 Directory shows James Finlay & Co. as proprietors of the mills, Alex. Buchanan (sic) resident partner, John Barclay manager of the cotton works and James Barclay manager of the bleach works. Archibald Buchanan died in 1841 and Kirkman Finlay a year later. The mills were offered for sale in 1844 but there was no buyer and they continued to be owned by James Finlay & Co. For further information see S. A. H. Whetmore in British Numismatic Journal, vol. XXVIII 1955-7, p. 643-4, Butt, op. cit., p. 66-7 and 'James Finlay & Company Limited, Manufacturers and East India Merchants 1750-1950', published privately in 1951. The countermark probably dates from c. 1795-1805, and is better known on Spanish dollars (Davis 55-7). The pieces were probably used as truck tickets, although this countermark on copper may well have been a trial piece for the silver issues.

60 Bute
Rothesay

60.1 ROTHESAY COTTON MILLS
James Kenyon, a Sheffield engineer, found himself restricted in England by Richard Arkwright's patent for the waterframe and decided to move to Scotland. In 1778, encouraged by the Earl of Bute, he planned a large cotton spinning complex at Rothesay, and his first mill, of 1,000 spindles, was opened the following year. The town, long a centre of fine linen manufacture, had a good supply of child and female labour, while the nearby port of Greenock imported raw West Indian cotton. Plentiful local water power was available. Kenyon brought some of Arkwright's workmen with him to make sure of success. However he sold the mills in 1785, the first of many changes, owners being, successively, David Dale, Messrs. Dugal & J. Bannatyne, and Messrs. Anderson, Fullerton and Dunlop. The mills were bought by William Kelly and Robert Thom in 1813 during a period of general depression in the Scottish economy. Kelly, an inventor, came from New Lanark, where he had been David Dale's manager; Thom was a civil engineer. Butt says (op. cit., p. 65) Kelly 'carried New Lanark-style labour relations to Rothesay, built workers' houses, and paid in tokens which could only be spent at the company shop, which far surpassed other private retailers in the town with its quality and range of services'. If these are the countermarked silver and copper tokens listed by Davis (numbers 61–67), it is clear that they are strictly truck tickets rather than tokens.

Kelly retired and sold out to Thom in January 1826. Thom brought a Mr. Struthers into the firm – listed in Pigot's 1837 Directory as Thom & Struthers, Rothesay Cotton Mills; the labour force was then upwards of 400. Later, Duncan Salmond, with Struthers, purchased the works and became sole owner when the latter retired. For their first fifty years the mills prospered and three more were built. At their peak over 1,000 people were employed and there were 1,000 looms and 50,000 spindles. The 1874 directory shows Doig & Co., cotton cloth manufacturers, High Street. By 1886 only one mill was working. It was still in operation in 1900, but was later used as a store and stable until destroyed by fire in 1955. At least two of the other mills still exist, though are not working. The last cotton worker, a woman, died in 1961 aged 92. See also Butt, op. cit., p. 64-5 and Whetmore, op. cit., p. 629 for additional information on these mills.

62 Clackmannan
Alloa

62.1 ALLOA COLLIERY
As early as 1623 there were drift mines near Alloa, and the coal industry prospered in the eighteenth century with coastal traffic to Leith. A steam pump was in use in 1764 and an iron railway replaced the wooden wagon-way in 1785 – see Butt, op. cit., p. 89. In its early history the Alloa Colliery was developed and managed by the Earls of Mar. John Francis Erskine, who succeeded to the Mar estates about 1773, was fortunate in having the services of Alexander Bald, one of the best mining engineers in the country, to help him run the colliery – he was appointed superintendent in 1774. The firm was progressive for its period, the Alloa Colliers' Fund being created in 1775 – see Whetmore, op. cit., p. 629-30. Many other improvements were also introduced. Bald died in 1823, so the Earl of Mar, unable personally to supervise the pits, devised a scheme for handing the work over to

trustees who would run the collieries for and on behalf of his family. Shortly before his death in 1825, the deed for this scheme was completed and active direction of the pits vested in Robert Bald, Alexander's son, and Robert Jamieson the Mar estate factor, who was expected to consult the earl on major questions of policy. In 1835 a number of prominent businessmen in Alloa took over the lease of the Alloa Colliery, forming the Alloa Coal Company, while Bald leased various other collieries from the earl. Later Bald's leases passed to the Company also. The 1827 'Edinburgh, Leith, Glasgow and North British Commercial and Literary Advertiser' lists J. Mackie, Alloa Colliery Co., while Pigot's 1837 Directory shows Alloa Colliery Office, Shore, with John Craich, manager and James Mackie, agent. The group's remaining collieries are now owned by the National Coal Board. See John L. Carvel's 'One hundred years in coal, the history of the Alloa Coal Company' (privately printed, 1944) for further background on this firm.

It is clear from the report of the select committee appointed in 1842 to examine the payment of wages that the truck system was very common in the mining areas of Scotland, and it is probable that these countermarked pieces were used as truck tickets. Similar countermarks occur on false Spanish dollars – see Davis 67, 68.

63 Dumfries
63.1 LOCHMABEN

This piece is described as a transportation token in Seaby's 'Coin and Medal Bulletin' for January 1971, though this seems unlikely. Dumfries Museum has a similar specimen, but nothing is known locally about it. Lochmaben is a small market burgh with a population of about 1,000. Main industries in the late eighteenth and nineteenth centuries were flax growing, linen weaving and quarrying – sandstone from Corncockle quarry was used for many Glasgow buildings. In view of the prevalence of the truck system in the rural areas of Scotland noted in the report of the select committee in 1842, it is probable that this countermarked piece served as a truck ticket in one of the local industries. Alternatively it could be a market token.

64 Dunbarton
Dumbarton
64.1 G.L

Presumably issued by a trader with initials G.L, this piece is similar in style to the other Scottish early nineteenth century countermarked tokens or truck tickets. Directory cover in this period in Scotland is extremely sparse. It is suggested that the issuer might be a Lang or Laing – a common name in the area at the time. Pigot's 1837 Directory lists a George Lang, boot and shoe maker, and Robert Laing, grocer, merchant, general dealer, wine and spirit merchant and agent for Larn-lime and for Lossit distillery, Islay, High Street. The town had a harbour, and main industries of stone

quarrying, ship building (four yards), distilling brewing, tanning, iron founding and rope making. Until 1831 it had been a centre for the manufacture of crown glass, in which 300 men had been employed.

71 Lanarkshire
Glasgow
71.1 CUMMINGS

This countermark is similar to lot 151 in the Cokayne sale. Lots 148–150 have a large star as well as DC. The coins in these lots are dated 1707, 1789, 1803, 1806. D.C., according to the sale catalogue, are the initials of David Cummings, 27 Brunswick Street, Glasgow. The countermarks presumably date from about 1810. Directories show Hill, Cumming & Co., linen-printers, warehouse Macnair's land, Trongate by no. 31 (1787, 1789), P. Cumming, shoe shop (1817), P. Cumming & Son, shoe shop, Brunswick Place (1823) and John Cumming & Co., manufacturers, 5 Ingram Street (1826). Brunswick Street and Place run from Trongate to Ingram Street.

New Lanark
71.2 LANARK COTTON MILLS

Richard Arkwright and David Dale went into partnership in April 1785 and started to build a cotton mill at New Lanark. This started production the following year. Arkwright soon left, but a second mill was built in the summer of 1788 and was almost complete when the first building was destroyed by fire. Within a few years others were constructed and when four were operating they employed 1,334 workers. With William Kelly as manager, water power was successfully applied to Crompton's spinning mule – in 1790, see Butt, op. cit., p. 69–70. In 1799 Dale sold the mills to the Chorlton Twist Company of which Robert Owen was the managing partner. Owen came to New Lanark to manage the mills, and married Dale's daughter Caroline.

The Lanark Mills became the largest spinning establishment in Britain and at the same time was the scene of a far-sighted social experiment in housing, factory management and education. In 1816 about 1,700 of the population of 2,297 actually worked in the mills, which received about 20,000 visitors between 1815 and 1825, including Grand Duke Nicholas of Russia.

Owen gradually withdrew from the business after 1825 and left in 1829. Robert Owen & Co. had become the New Lanark Twist Co. by 1830, and Pigot's 1837 Directory lists Walker & Co., cotton spinners, New Lanark and Miller Street, Glasgow. In 1881, Mr. Henry Birkmyre, a member of the family which controlled the Gourock Rope Co. Ltd., and Mr. R. G. Somerville, then Provost of Port Glasgow, became part owners of the Lanark Mills. The Lanark Spinning Company continued thus until 1903 when it became a wholly owned subsidiary of the Gourock Rope Work Co. Ltd. – see Whetmore, op. cit., p. 640.

One mill was burned down in 1882, and not rebuilt. 170 of the factory houses remain and have been preserved by the New Lanark Association, formed in 1963.

The countermarks probably date from before 1813 when William Kelly left to manage the Rothesay Cotton Mills (see above) and were almost certainly used as truck tickets. Similar countermarks occur on silver coins (see Davis 83–87) and on leaden or zinc uniface discs. (Cokayne lot 168.)

The pieces in the David McFarlan collection and the National Museum of Antiquities, Edinburgh, are on brass, not copper flans, and H. E. Manville (op. cit., note 35) concludes that they are 'buttons'. However both Davis (no. 88) and Cokayne (lot 167) list the countermark on Scottish bodles, so it seems likely that the two types exist.

72 Midlothian
Cramond
72.1 J.S

John Sproxton was at the Cramond Ironworks 1864–5, but is not listed in the 1857–8 or 1869–70 directories. William Cadell Sons & Co. are listed in Edinburgh directories at Cramond Ironworks, Royal Exchange 1839–51, but had moved to Cramond by 1857. The Cramond Iron Co. is listed at Cramond and Holytown in 1877.

Edinburgh
72.2 WILKISON

The Edinburgh firm of Wilkison or Wilkinson, gunsmiths, appears in directories as follows:

1790–2 Anthony Wilkison, gunsmith, Fountain Well.

1793–1802 Anthony Wilkinson, as above.

1803–4 as above, and opposite Black Bull Head, Leith Walk. House: Baron Grant's Close.

1804–5 address shown as Netherbow.

1805–6 to 1809 address shown as 4 Greenside Street.

1809–10 to 1817–8 5 Greenside Street, House Baron Grant's Close.

1818–9 to 1820–1 James Wilkinson, 14 Greenside Street.

1821–2 to 1825–6 James Wilkison, 5 Greenside Street.

1826–7 to 1829–30 James Wilkison, gunmaker in ordinary to His Majesty, 5 Greenside Street, house, 21 Leith Street.

It is clear that this countermark is a gunmaker's stamp, probably issued in the 1820's. It may be a shop ticket or, possibly, a truck ticket, but is unlikely to be a trade token as suggested by Davis.

72.3 YETTS

Lieut. John Yetts of the Royal Navy, is listed at Springfield, Leith Walk in the 1801 and 1804–5 directories. In 1810 he was a captain at Jamaica Street, and in 1817–20 he is again shown as a Lieutenant at 51 Hope Park End. This implies that the piece could be a love token – common among sailors. However there is no date or message, which is unusual with love tokens. As Yetts

is an alternative form of Yates it is quite possible that the piece is a trader's item – e.g. John Yates, boot and shoe maker, 4 Roxburgh Place (1832). It is assumed to date from c. 1775–1835.

Leith
72.4 LEITH MILLS

It is not possible to be certain about the attribution of this countermark. There are at least three possible issuers: Leith Sawmills; Dickson, Ferguson & Davidson (1839–40), Ferguson, Davidson & Co. (1843–77) – by 1877 at 251 Great Junction Street and Albert Street.

Leith Flour Mills, stated in the National Encyclopaedia, 1868 to be 'the most extensive and complete in the country'. In 1869 the mills, in Commercial Street, were owned by Alexander and Robert Tod.

Leith Saw Mills: Edwin Hughes, saw maker, was granted a patent in March 1857 for face plate ground circular saws. He advertised in Slater's 1860 Directory of Scotland, and would have had to hand the necessary punches for producing this piece.

73 Morayshire
73.1 ELGIN

In the absence of an initial, this is assumed to represent the town rather than a surname. The piece was probably issued by a blacksmith or ironmonger.

77 Perthshire
Deanston
77.1 & 77.2 ADELPHI COTTON WORKS or
DEANSTON COTTON MILLS

These cotton spinning mills were erected in 1785 on the south bank of the River Teith to the west of Doune by John Buchanan of Carston and his brothers, formerly linen yarn merchants with connections in Manchester. At that time they employed about 700 workers – see First Statistical Account of Scotland, Vol. 20, 1798 (Parish of Kilmadock), p. 52. John's brother Archibald was recalled from the mill at Cromford, Derbyshire, where, since 1783, he had been apprenticed to Sir Richard Arkwright, to act as manager. In this predominately agricultural area, Archibald Buchanan had difficulties in maintaining the labour force, which led to financial troubles. Whetmore, op. cit., p. 642–3 quotes an advertisement in the London 'Sun' for 10 January 1794 announcing the sale of cotton mills in 'Deanstoun, commonly called Adelphi . . . all belonging to the sequestered estate of James and Archibald Buchanan & Co.' After leaving Deanston, Archibald Buchanan joined James Finlay & Co. Ltd., becoming manager of the Ballindalloch Cotton Works, Balfron (see below) in 1798 and of the Catrine Cotton Works (see above) about 1801. In December 1794 there was a fire at the works; at this time the owners were Joseph, Samuel and William Twigg. The First Statistical Account of Scotland shows that Benjamin

Flounders was manager for an English company at this time. Presumably this was Twigg as Flounders, a Yorkshire quaker, certainly bought the works early in 1794. After about 12 years he was followed by a Mr. Glen, who retired shortly afterwards a poorer man – see Whetmore, op. cit.

In 1808 the mills were bought by Kirkman Finlay, who appointed as manager James Smith, a nephew of Archibald Buchanan. The firm continued Flounders' policy of having no public houses in the village – see Butt, op. cit., p. 67. Smith built a new village at Deanston, and, being an engineer of great mechanical ability, began the reorganisation of the mills. This took him until about 1820, after which there was a period of expansion. A dam was constructed over the Teith and two waterwheels became operational in 1830.

Pigot's 1837 Directory lists under 'cotton spinners and manufacturers by power' James Finlay & Co., Deanston, James Smith managing partner. The same source mentions that a Deanston friendly society was established in 1795. The Second Statistical Account of Scotland, Vol. 10 1845, p. 1233 states that 'Deanston Cotton Works employ above 1,100 persons and contain the most perfect machinery in the kingdom'.

Appearing before the Select Committee enquiring into payment of wages in 1842, James Smith said that his establishment always paid in current coin and that the truck system did not operate there. It is probable, however, that the truck system applied at the mills before 1808 and that these countermarked pieces are truck tickets. The Adelphi countermarks seem to be the earlier, probably all dating from before 1794. Similar countermarks occur on silver coins – see Davis 89, 93.

Lochearnhead

77.3 MCLAREN
Pigot's 1837 Directory lists James M'Laren, blacksmith, and John M'Laren, grocer, linen draper and shopkeeper, both of Lochearnhead. Possibly this countermark was a joint effort by these country traders or their forbears. The village was the centre of a large rural area. In such agricultural regions of Scotland, according to the report of the select committee in 1842, the truck system operated extensively, and it is probable that these pieces are truck tokens. John McLaren continues to be listed in the 1852 and 1861 directories.

Perth

77.4 PERTH
This may well be a cutler's mark. Pigot's 1837 Directory lists the following Perth cutlers:
John Bell, 32 Skinnergate
James Macgregor, 64 George Street
Walter Marshall, 77 High Street.

78 Renfrew
Paisley
78.1 MCLEAN
John McLean was a grocer, tea and spirit dealer at 6 Cotton Street, Paisley in 1812 and 1813. He does not appear in Pigot's 1821–3 Directory. Probably he ran a truck shop for one of the local industrial firms. The countermark is better known on Spanish dollars – see Lingford sale Lot 774.

78.2 MORRIS
This countermark is also known on Spanish silver dollars 1806, 1812 – see Cokayne 193, Gibbs 363, and Davis (addenda) 113B (110B in Spink's Numismatic Circular' 1906 column 9138). John Morris was, presumably, a merchant, but it has not proved possible to find him in local directories or other records.

Mr. Purvey is unfortunately unable to trace the source of information which enabled him to insert ST86A in his catalogue.

Port Glasgow
78.3 CRIGHTON
Robert Crighton was a grocer of King Street, Lions Lane in the early nineteenth century. In 1821–3 he is listed in Pigot's Directory at Church Street. In Fowler's Directories 1831–5 he is shown as Crighton's & Co., general grocers, wine and spirit merchants, King Street and Lyons Lane. Creighton & Co. (sic), grocers and spirit dealers, King Street, are listed in Pigot's 1837 Directory. The countermark is better known on Spanish dollars – see Davis 77. Only one specimen of Crighton's countermark and one each of McLean's and Morris' have come to light on copper coins, and it is possible that they are trial pieces for the silver issues. Alternatively they may be low denomination truck tickets.

Renfrew
78.4 RENFREW VICTUALLING SOCIETY
Wrongly described in both the H. D. Gibbs Sale Catalogue (lot 275) and Emil Szauer's article (op. cit., no. 41) as 'A Renfrew Society', it is clear from the Gibbs plate that the legend is 'RENFREW Vᵀ SOCIETY'. There is a record of a Renfrew Victualling Society, High Street, Renfrew, owned by a Mr. J. Brown. The Society went out of business in 1828. Such friendly societies, or 'Box Clubs' as they were commonly called, were a feature of the early nineteenth century – see F. Willson Yeates' note in Spink's Numismatic Circular, April 1912, col. 13519. Examples are the Galston Society, the Paisley Society, the Balfron Victualling Society (q.v.), and the Deanston Friendly Society. The countermark could be a token, shop ticket or truck ticket. John Brown, grocer, is listed in Pigot's 1837 Directory.

83 Stirlingshire
Balfron
83.1 FRUIT
This is assumed to be a token or truck ticket issued in connection with the Ballindalloch Cotton Mills (q.v.), the major employers in Balfron. It is not clear whether Fruit was the surname of the issuer or if the token or ticket was valid for fruit. Pigot's 1837 Directory gives no clues.

83.2 BALFRON VICTUALLING SOCIETY

This is also assumed to be a token or truck ticket issued in connection with the Ballindalloch Cotton Mills (q.v.). On such 'Box Clubs' see Renfrew Victualling Society, above, and F. Willson Yeates, op. cit. Pigot's 1837 Directory lists under 'grocers & shopkeepers' the Balfron Economical Society, possibly the same body or its successor. The entry is in capital letters, the other grocers etc. listed being in small print, possibly indicating that they formed the Society. For the record the other names are: John Brown, Andrew Graham (also a spirit dealer), William Lawson, James Lockhart, Duncan M'Naught, Janet M'Ouat, Jane Main, Peter Marshall and Thomas Scott.

83.3 ZUILL

As with 83.1 and 83.2 this is assumed to have been issued in connection with the Ballindalloch Cotton Mills (q.v.). Zuill is not a common surname – there are four in the current GPO Telephone Directory for West Scotland. Pigot's 1837 Directory lists Robert Yuill, baker, Balfron, possibly an alternative spelling of Zuill. This trader is also listed in Slater's 1852 Directory.

83.4 BALLINDALLOCH COTTON WORKS

This countermark was attributed by Davis to Elginshire but this is clearly incorrect in the light of directory evidence and has been shown to be so by F. Willson Yeates in Spink's Numismatic Circular, April 1912, col. 13519 and A. J. MacLean in Seaby's Coin and Medal Bulletin, May 1965, p. 168.

Whetmore says, op. cit., p. 643, that Robert Dunmore, laird of Ballindalloch, established a calico works on his property in 1780, but this was not a success. In 1789 he introduced a colony of cotton workers into the parish and built a few houses for letting. A cotton mill was erected on the banks of the Ettrick, in partnership with James & Archibald Buchanan & Co., and was completed by June 1790 – see J. Guthrie Smith 'Strathendrick and its inhabitants from Early Times' (Glasgow 1896) p. 263. Balfron village grew up from 1790 on the other bank of the Ettrick following the building of the mill and the institution of a printfield and bleachfield by 1796. These works were more successful than Dunmore's previous enterprise, and are said to be the first mills in Scotland worked entirely by women. In 1792, 390 were employed and the value of the goods manufactured was £7,676 – see Smith, op. cit. By 1796, 105 new houses had been built.

The Ballindalloch Cotton Mill Co. was purchased by Kirkman Finlay in 1798. Archibald Buchanan came from Deanston (q.v.) to join James Finlay & Co. and was manager at Ballindalloch until about 1801 when he left for a similar position at the Catrine Cotton Works (q.v.).

Pigot's 1837 Directory lists James Finlay & Co., cotton spinners, Ballindalloch Works, William Miller, manager. The same source says of the town and mill: 'the houses are, for the most part, well built, and very nearly all whitewashed – the appearance of the place is that of cleanliness

and respectability. The Ballindalloch cotton spinning works, the property of Messrs. Finlay and Co., furnish employment to a considerable number of the inhabitants, chiefly females, whose general clean and healthful appearance may be ascribed to the salutary regulations enforced in the establishment of this respectable firm.' The mills were bought by Robert Jeffreys & Sons in 1844 for a nominal price – both trade and population declined steadily in Balfron throughout the nineteenth century. The mills continued operating until 1893, passing at some time to H. W. Pottock & Co. The building was purchased by Sir Archibald Orr-Ewing in 1898 and demolished.

The countermarked coins were probably used as truck tickets. The countermark also occurs on silver – see Davis 71.

Fintry
83.5 CULCREUCH MILL

In 1794 sites were being feued for workers' houses along the south side of the street in the Newton of Fintry – see Stirlingshire: An Inventory of the Ancient Monuments, H.M.S.O. 1963, p. 324. The reason was the foundation of a cotton spinning mill by Peter Spiers of Culcreuch, a member of the well-known Elderslie family. The Spiers family lived at Culcreuch Castle 1769–1890. At the time of the First Statistical Account of Scotland (1796) the mill contained 20,000 spindles and employed 260 people. Pigot's 1837 Directory lists Culcreuch Cotton Company, cotton spinners, Fintry, and Capt. Alex. Graham Speirs under gentry. There is no mention of Thomas Whyte, and it is not clear whether he was manager of the works or in charge of the local truck shop.

The mill was not a commercial success. It was too far from a supply of coal, and cotton and yarn had to be carried to or from Glasgow, 18 miles, over hilly roads. It was possibly in use for a time as a saw mill, but by 1896 was definitely closed – see Smith 'Strathendrick', p. 261. The building is still standing.

Similar countermarks, without 'THOS WHYTE', occur on silver coins – see Davis 114, 115.

83.6 MCNEE

This is assumed to be a token or truck ticket issued in connection with the Culcreuch Cotton Mill. The trader has not been identified and does not appear in Pigot's 1837 Directory. The countermark also occurs on silver – see Lingford sale, lot 779, Gibbs sale, lot 369, although its first appearance was at the Lingford sale (1950).

86 Wigtownshire
86.1 CARTY

Attribution of this countermark must remain uncertain. It has been assumed to represent the place-name but could equally be an Irish surname in view of its source (Szauer, op. cit., no. 446).

The harbour at Carty Port was rebuilt by the Earl of Galloway in the early years of the nineteenth century, chiefly for the import of lime and fertilisers and export of agricultural produce. It could, therefore, be some form of harbour ticket or loading tally. At about the same period a tile works was established there, and is still operating under different ownership.

IRELAND, NORTHERN

88 Armagh
88.1 Armagh

This is an enigmatic countermark – perhaps issued by a local trader for county circulation, and possibly connected with local linen manufacturing. In the latter event it could be a truck ticket. Alternatively it could have been issued by a county building or authority, e.g. the County Gaol in Barrack Street, or County Infirmary in Abbey Street. The countermark also occurs on the obverse of a George IV crown of 1822 (Szauer 180), and so must date from the 1820's or later. W. A. Seaby ('Catalogue of Ulster Tokens etc', nos. AR: V1–2) suggests, in view of the worn state of the coins, that the countermark dates from the mid- or late nineteenth century. However, there is ample evidence of countermarks dating from the 1830's or 1840's on very worn 1797 pennies. See 116.1 below for a similar countermark.

Portadown
88.2 OVEREND

This is an example of a silver token (Davis 28) being struck on a copper coin. It was first reported, by Davis, in Spink's Numismatic Circular, June 1906, col. 9138.

Davis, quoting from the Monthly Chronicle, Ireland, for February 1758, states that John Overend, merchant, died at Portadown in 1758.

There are no directories for the early eighteenth century, but the following nineteenth century entries are of interest:

1814 (Leet's) William Overend Esq., Edenderry, Portadown.
1824 (Pigot's) John Overend under 'spirit stores and public houses'; William Overend under 'grain merchants'.
1846 (Slater's) John Overend, corn merchant, Bridge Street, also commissioner for taking affidavits.

89 Down
Ballylenahan or Ballylenaghan
89.1 MCCLURE

It is difficult to find any sound trading or advertising reason for the over-striking of an early eighteenth century piece (Davis 18) on a Glasgow token issued 56 years later. Perhaps the dies fell into the hands of counterfeiters.

There are no early directories to throw any light on McClure. Leet's 1814 Directory shows that Ballylenaghan was a Post town on Belfast Townland. Davis lists the original piece under Antrim but mentions that Aquilla Smith was unable to locate the name Ballyloghnegany, which occurs in the Index Locorum of the Ulster Inquisitions.

Down or Downpatrick
89.2 SOMERVILL, SUMMERVILL

Here again one is defeated by lack of early directory cover. There are no Somervills listed under Downpatrick in the 1824 or 1846 directories. The attribution is not entirely satisfactory: see G.G.R. in Spink's Numismatic Circular, April 1933 (who suggests Doune, Perthshire) and 109.1 below. The origin of these pieces is also discussed by W. A. Seaby in 'Catalogue of Ulster Tokens etc.', nos. DN:V18–19.

90 Fermanagh
90.1 Enniskillen (Inniskilling)

'VI–D' probably refers to the 6th Dragoons, a regiment originally raised in the town in support of William III. The possibility exists, however, that the countermarked piece was intended to be used as a 6d. token. Enniskillen was a garrison town, and Pigot's 1824 Directory gives the following description: 'At the western extremity of the town are the barracks with suitable accommodations for five companies of foot with another barrack for artillery in time of war, but used at present as a military hospital.' If it was issued by the 6th Dragoons, the countermarked coin may have served as some form of stores check or tally – cf the Woolwich Arsenal or Dockyard checks. It is possible that a button-maker's punch was used to manufacture this piece; flat buttons were used for officers until c. 1820–30, and for men until 1855.

91 Londonderry
Moneymore
91.1 ALLEN

David Allen is listed in local directories for 1858 and 1868, but had disappeared by 1880. He was an agent for an Agricultural Insurance Company as well as a manufacturer of agricultural equipment. W. A. Seaby of the Ulster Museum, Belfast, suggests that these countermarked pieces were used by David Allen as liquor tokens or 'subs' (advances) for his outworkers. If so, they are, strictly, truck tickets. Alternatively, they may have had some advertising significance. The museum has 28 examples of this countermark in its collection.

92 Tyrone
Fintona
92.1 DOUGHERTY

Edward Dougherty, butcher, is listed in the 1892 directory. In Slater's 1894 Directory he appears as Edward Doherty. Examination shows that the 'A. HAUGHTON' countermark was added later, but neither Dougherty nor Haughton appear in Kelly's 1906 Directory, which lists James Cassidy and William Mitchell, butchers. W. A. Seaby, no. TY:VII, op. cit., dates the Dougherty countermark c. 1894–1905.

93 Carlow
Bagenalstown

93.1 TIERNEY

Bagenalstown, or Bagnalstown, is not listed in Pigot's 1824 Directory. In nearby Leighlinbridge, two miles to the north, only one apothecary, Terence O'Reilly, is shown. By 1841 Bagenalstown, with a population of 2,225, had overtaken Leighlinbridge – population 1,748 and was becoming a small town. In Slater's 1846 Directory, the following entries appear:

Apothecaries:

Bagenalstown: Joseph Beard, Francis Malcolmson, Charles Scott.

Leighlinbridge: William Hutchinson, Walter Charles Pierce.

Other traders:

Hugh and Peter Tierney, boot and shoe makers, Leighlinbridge.

Mary Tierney, straw bonnet maker, Bagenalstown.

Patrick Tierney, grocer and salt merchant, Bagenalstown.

It is probable that this engraved piece was produced by Patrick Tierney or one of his relatives c. 1830–50.

94 Cavan
Cavan

94.1 MURRAY

The 'Cavan Herald' for Tuesday, 21 September 1824 records the marriage the previous Thursday of Mary Anne, daughter of John Murray, watchmaker. Pigot's Directory for the same year lists John Murray, merchant, Main Street. In 1838, John Murray was one of the last freemen to be admitted – see T. S. Smyth's 'Civic History of the town of Cavan' (Browne & Nolan, 1938). Robert Murray, gunmaker, Bridge Street, appears in Slater's 1846 Directory, with Michael Murray, boot and shoe maker, Half Acre, and John Murray, watch and clock maker, Main Street. Thus the countermarked coin could have been issued by John Murray, a merchant and, presumably, a watch maker, or, perhaps more likely, by Robert Murray using his gunmaker's name punch.

96 Cork
Cork

96.1 BUCKLEY

John J. Buckley, engraver, is listed in the 1871 and 1893 directories at 35 George's Street. He does not appear in the 1867 issue. The address is shown as 35 George Street in the 1894 and 1906 directories. By 1912, no. 35 is listed as vacant, and in 1913 the premises were occupied by a newsagent. The street is now named Oliver Plunkett Street, and no. 35 is still used for the sale of newspapers. The countermark, presumably intended as a shop or advertisement ticket, and an illegal issue, dates from c. 1904–11.

98 Dublin
Dublin

98.1 BIGGER

John Bigger, cutler, does not appear in Pigot's 1824 Directory but is listed in subsequent directories as follows:

1834 manufacturing cutler, 25 Bolton Street.

1835 cutler, same address.

1836–8 36 Bolton Street.

1839–43 41 Bolton Street.

1844–9 6 North King Street. In 1844 his premises were rated at £35.

Countermark 98.1B has the address 36 Bolton Street, indicating that it was issued c. 1836–8, and also the name Jas. Ireland, Belfast. James Ireland appears in Belfast directories as follows:

1819 James Ireland, copper and tin-smith, 23 Corn Market.

1824, 1835 ironmonger, 19 Cornmarket.

1839 ironmonger, copper and tin plate manufacturer and japanner, 19 and 21 Cornmarket.

1843 sheet iron manufacturer, hardware, house furnishing and ironmongery work, 17 Cornmarket, residence, 3 Adelaide Place.

1846 ironmonger, 17 and 19 Corn Market.

By 1858 William McNeill, house furnisher and ironmonger is shown at 17 Corn Market, presumably having bought out the Ireland business.

It is unlikely that Bigger and Ireland were associated in any way. Probably Ireland countermarked one of the Bigger pieces to serve as one of his shop tickets, perhaps in the 1840's – Ireland's countermark is certainly less worn than Bigger's. See 40.35 above for a similar example.

98.2 CHRISTIAN

Cole Alley led off Meath Street in Dublin. John Christian, grocer, appears at 51 Meath Street in the 1795 directory, while Mary Christian is shown at the same address in 1804 and 1806.

98.3 DELAHOYD

Baillie says that De la Hoyde was a member of the Clockmakers' Company and made cylinder watches at Dublin 1786–96. The 1784 directory lists Bernard Delahoyd, watchmaker at 4 Cockhill. He was at 81 Dame Street in 1795 and 1804. The initial in Szauer's illustration of this countermark is not clear, and could be a B rather than R. The surname is uncommon, and the issuer, if not Bernard Delahoyd, was presumably related to him. The name does not appear in Pigot's 1824 Directory, but Richard Delahoyd, greengrocer, 127 Townsend Street, and Robert Delahoyd, druggist, 81 Queen Street are listed in Slater's 1846 Directory. Robert Delahoyd was at 76 Queen Street in 1836 and 1840. In view of the date of the coin and the question of access to punches, Bernard Delahoyd seems the most probable issuer.

98.4 (Crown) DUBLIN

This mark has not been traced to a particular trader. It is a clear case of the use of a firm's brand-marking punch, though whether for a shop ticket or unofficially is not certain.

98.5 GEALE & MACBRIDE

The following entries appear in the Dublin directories:

1792 Ebenezer Geale, ironmonger, 193 Abbey Street; Thomas Macbride, hardware merchant, 27 W. New-row.

1795 Ebenezer Geale, ironmonger, 193 Abbey Street; Thomas Macbride, hardware merchant, 20 Bridge Street.

1804 Ebenezer Geale, ironmonger, 7 Aston's Quay (also thus in Holden's 1805-7 Directory); Thomas McBride, hardware merchant, 33 Pill Lane.

1806-10 Geale & M'Bride, wholesale and retail ironmongers, 17 Westmorland Street.

1817 Ebenezer Geale, wholesale and retail ironmonger, 17 Westmorland Street.

The firm is not listed in the 1819 directory. The countermark dates from not earlier than 1806 or later than 1816.

98.6 GRIFFIN

Michael Griffin, shoemaker, is listed in Pigot's 1824 Directory at 86 Great Britain Street, Dublin. No other M. Griffin has been traced in Dublin or other Irish towns in the early nineteenth century. An Irish issuer seems probable, as the countermark is known only on Irish coins and tokens.

98.7 KAVANAGH

This well-known firm of gunmakers made percussion pistols and revolvers, and appear in the Dublin directories as follows:

1824 William Kavanagh, gunmaker, 4 Upper Ormond Quay.

1846 William Kavanagh, gunmaker, 11 Dame Street; William Kavanagh & Son, gunmakers to his Excellency the Lord Lieutenant and gunpowder office, 4 Lower Ormond Quay.

1861 William & James Kavanagh, gunmakers and gunpowder merchants, 12 Dame Street.

1870 as 1861, and factory Dame Lane.

1880 William Kavanagh, as 1870, and residence 8 Richmond Street N.

1890, 1900 William Kavanagh & Son, 12 Dame Street.

1906 William Kavanagh, gunmaker (William Kavanagh & Son), Mount Town House, Kingstown.

The countermark probably dates from the 1890's and is almost certainly unofficial.

98.8 KEOGH

This piece was initially attributed to Dublin on the basis of the current distribution of the surname Keogh and of towns with streets named Summer Hill. Edward Keogh, hairdresser, is listed in directories at 75 Summer Hill from 1902 until at least 1935. He was preceded by J. Mangan (1900-1) and Patrick Hagerty (1890, 1895), also hairdressers. Keogh's premises were rated at £15 until c. 1915, thence at £18. Not until the 1930's does Keogh appear in the commercial or trades sections, being hitherto confined to the street directories. This is the latest example of a paper label on a coin known to me, probably dating from c. 1901-10.

98.9 MCMAHON

The following entries appear in the Dublin directories:

1840 Christopher Toner, house painter, 30 Pill Lane.

1842, 1844 James M'Mahon, cutler, 30 Pill Lane.

1846 James M'Mahon, cutler, 28 Pill Lane, residence 36 Constitution Hill.

1847, 1848 James M'Mahon, cutler, 28 Pill Lane.

1850 28 Pill Lane, vacant; James M'Mahon, cutler, 51 Pill Lane, and Constitution Hill.

McMahon is not listed in the 1863 directory. The countermark dates from c. 1846-8.

98.10 OSBORNE

Joseph Osborne, cutler, 10 Fade Street, is listed in Pigot's 1824 Directory. George Osborne, cutler and surgical instrument maker, 55 South Great George's Street, appears in directories 1839-60. The latter was probably the issuer.

98.11 VICKERS

Pigot's 1824 Directory lists Peter Vickers, gunmaker, 10 Aungier Street, who was probably the issuer of this countermark although, in the absence of a town name, this cannot be proved. Vickers was a common name in the Sheffield metal trades, and, had not an Irish coin been involved, one would have said this was the most likely source – e.g. 'VICKERS' was the mark of William Vickers, scissorsmith, Sims Croft, Sheffield, in 1787.

99 Galway
Galway

99.1 BLAKE – MENLOUGH CASTLE

Leet's 1814 Directory lists Val. Blake Esq,. Meulo (sic), Galway, and Sir John Blake, Bart., Meulo Castle. Sir John Blake appears at Meulo House and Valentine Blake at Meulo Castle in Pigot's 1824 Directory. Slater's 1846 Directory shows Sir Valentine Blake, Bart., M.P. at Menlo Castle, while the 1894 issue, under Oranmore, Co. Galway, states: 'On the banks of Lough Corrib is Menlough Castle, the seat of Sir Valentine Blake, Bart, J.P., built in 1300.'

The Blakes were great landowners in Galway, and at Ballyglunin Estate, south of Tuam, M. J. Blake issued truck tickets or tokens – see A. E. J. Went 'Truck tickets or tokens of M. J. Blake' in Numismatic Society of Ireland Occasional Papers, No. 7 (1969).

The Menlough Castle piece was also issued as a struck ticket (Davis 1, p. 223, Batty 3891). Both the struck and countermarked varieties were clearly used as truck tokens to pay workpeople on the estate.

108 Mayo
Hollymount

108.1 MALVERNBURY

Attribution of this countermark is only tentative. Malvernbury does not appear to occur as a place name, even in Worcestershire. Hollymount is a village in Co. Mayo on the river Robe 8 miles south west of Claremorriss. Leet's 1814 Directory lists, besides the latter, eight properties named Hollymount in as many Irish counties.

No house or individual named Malvernbury is listed under Hollymount in Slater's 1894 or Kelly's 1906 Directories.

109 Meath
Hill of Down
109.1 MITCHELL
Both this countermark and that of Mrs. Summervill (see 89.2 above) are akin in style to the early nineteenth century Scottish issues. In neither case can one be entirely happy about their attribution, but in the absence of any early directory or other evidence to the contrary, Davis' conclusions must be allowed to stand.

109.2 Trim
The countermark is assumed to represent the place name – the county town of Meath. Of Trim, Thom's 1880 Directory says 'it contains a union workhouse and two good hotels but little trade is carried on in the place'. Also in the town were hospitals, schools, a Saturday market, barracks, and the Meath County Gaol. The issuer is unknown.

111 Offaly (Kings)
Birr or Parsonstown
111.1 EGAN
Mr. W. Bergin of Birr informs me that Benedict Egan was a hardware merchant and gunmaker about 1830, still active in 1854.

Slater's 1846 Directory lists Patrick Egan, cutler and gunsmith, Grave Yard, while Benjamin Egan, cutler, High Street, appears in the 1894 issue.

116 Westmeath
116.1 Athlone
Athlone, on the River Shannon was, in the nineteenth century, the military headquarters for the West of Ireland, with a large stores depot and accommodation for 2,000 troops. It also had linen manufacturers, distilleries, flour mills, and tan yards. 'ATHLONE' has not been traced as a metal trades brand mark, so the piece may have served as a military stores check, but could equally have been a local shop ticket. See 88.1 above for a similar countermark. There is also the possibility that both these countermarks were issued for political purposes.

Kilbeggan
116.2 GEOGHEGAN
The following entries appear in directories:
1846 James Geoghegan, shoe maker.
1894 Joseph Geoghegan, butcher and grocer; James Geoghegan, farmer, Sureen.
1906 Mrs. Geoghegan, grocer; James Geoghegan, farmer, Sureen.

The piece was probably issued by Joseph Geoghegan as a shop ticket in the last quarter of the nineteenth century.

120 Jersey
120.1 MOLLET, SULLIVAN
The rather sparse nineteenth century directory cover for St. Helier indicates the following possibilities:
1845 J. Mollet, boot and shoe maker, New Street; J. Sullivan, fancy and toy dealer, jeweller etc., Halkett Place.
1852 Clement Sullivan, chemist and druggist, 6 Queen Street.
1874 Mrs. Mollet, grocer, 18 Hillary Street; C. Sullivan & Co., tea dealers, 15 Halkett Place; George Sullivan, grocer and baker, 20 Sand Street; James Sullivan, Bell Tavern, 2 Wesley Street.
1884 Mrs. Mollet, grocer, 18 Peter Street; Mrs. Sullivan, grocer, 2 Grove Place; J. Sullivan, The Eagle, 39 Lower Bath Street.
1896 G. Sullivan, baker, 15 Albert Street.
1898 Walter P. Mollet, provision merchant, 14B New Street. (In 1896 F. Jeandron was at this address, and in 1903, Ingram & Kelly, paper hangers); Mrs. Mollet, grocer, 18 Peter Street (until at least 1903, had gone by 1907); George Sullivan, shopkeeper, 8 Columbus Street; Mrs. Mary Sullivan, grocer, 16 Union Street (until at least 1907, Miss Elson Sullivan, grocer, in 1911).

In neighbouring Guernsey, William J. D. Mollet, family grocer, tea, coffee and provision merchant, was at 32 Bordage Street, St. Peter Port c. 1898–1911.

The countermark was probably issued in St. Helier c. 1875–1900. In the absence of Mrs. Mollet's initials it is difficult to be more precise.

122 Unattributed names
122.5 ADAMS
The tiger is assumed to be Adams' brand mark, but the issuer has not been traced.

122.10 BAGSHAW
Bagshaw is a common name in the Sheffield metal trades, but this initial and the crowned E and I marks have not been traced. The following patents are in the name of S. Bagshaw:
No. 4576, 26 July 1821, making vases, urns, basins and other ornamental articles.
No. 5232, 8 August 1825, manufacturing pipes for conveyance of water, gas, and other fluids.
No. 6708, 6 November 1834, filter for water or other liquids.

The countermark is, presumably, Bagshaw's brand mark used unofficially.

122.12 BALL
Ball was, presumably, a trader, but has not been identified.

122.15 BAXTER
This is probably a public house check. The issuer has not been traced. It is likely that a flan rather than a coin has been used, so the eligibility of this piece is doubtful.

122.20 BEDFORD
Bedford Bros. were gunsmiths in London about 1865; John Bedford was a Sheffield merchant and manufacturer of steel, files, etc. c. 1845–54. However the cock brand mark cannot be attributed with certainty to either of these traders. There are no patents in the name of G. Bedford before 1852.

122.25 BEST
The brand mark of an incuse B and a lion has not been traced. The issuer is unlikely to have been a Sheffield firm. For BEST's (crown) see 40.9 above.

122.28 BOWKER
The name is uncommon, and it is probable that the two pieces listed were issued by the same trader. There is no likely London issuer of this name in the directories for 1817, 1834, 1836 or 1842.

122.29 BRADLEY
No steel manufacturer named Bradley, of Bridgwater Hill, has been traced in Birmingham, Bristol, Manchester or Sheffield directories for the first half of the nineteenth century, nor has any connection with Bridgwater, Somerset been found.

122.30 BRIGDEN
The crown was a common brand mark in the nineteenth century – see 123.10 below. The issuer of this piece has not been traced.

122.32 BROADFOOT
This countermark is included as it appears, from the same punch, on two pieces from different sources. The issuer is unknown, and has not been traced in London, Sheffield or Manchester directories.

122.33 BROTHERS & CO.
No firm named Brothers & Co. has been traced, and this is probably only part of a brand marking punch. The most likely issuer is a steel or tool manufacturer, e.g.
1868 Taylor Brothers & Co., boiler plates, locomotive, carriage and waggon tyres, Clarence Iron and Steel Works, Leeds; Wilks Brothers & Co., ironmongers, whitesmiths, successors to Joseph Wilks, 40 and 42 Furnival Road, Corn Exchange, Sheffield; Marsden Brothers & Co., edge and joiners' tools, Bridge Street Works, Sheffield.
1887 Sanderson Brothers & Co. Ltd., Attercliffe Steel Works, Sheffield; Jowett Brothers & Co., steel manufacturers, Union Street, Sheffield; Marsh Brothers & Co., steel manufacturers, Pond Works, Pond Street, Sheffield; Marsden Brothers & Co., steel manufacturers, Bridge Street.

The keyhole (?) brand mark is not listed in the Corporate and Trade Marks section of the Sheffield directories for 1900 and 1917.

122.35 BRYAN
Conceivably a doctor's check – M.B. being the abbreviation for Bachelor of Medicine. Equally, this could be a 'Love Token'.

122.40 CAMPBELL & CO.
There are no clues as to the origin of this countermark, which could be a pay or tool check.

122.42 CAST STEEL
This is a clear example of unofficial use of a firm's brand marking tools. Any one of a number of Sheffield firms could have been responsible following the invention by Huntsman (see 40.24 above) of the cast steel process.

122.45 CITY PRISON
It is ironic that an unidentified prison has apparently issued an illegal countermark!

122.50 CLARK, F. & T.
This piece has been included because the '&', indicates a firm. London, Manchester and Sheffield directories have been checked for F. & T. Clark without success. Alternatively, it is possible that the countermark is a 'love token'.

122.55 CLARK, JOSEPH
This name is a very common one, but possible issuers appear in directories as follows:
Birmingham:
1842 Bed screw maker, 28 John Street.
London:
1836 Saddler and harness maker, 1 St. James Place, Hampstead Road.
1836–8, 1842, 1857 Fishing rod and tackle manufacturer, 11 St. John's Lane.
Sheffield:
1817 Britannia Metal Manufacturer, North Street (in 1821 at 21 Lambert Street).
Sheffield seems most likely, but the 'T<>' mark has not been traced.

122.58 CONCINNUM, THE
This is, presumably, a brand mark. The issuer has not been identified.

122.60 COTTON
Montague Guest (No. 1413) classes this as a toll ticket, but does not attempt to identify the issuer. It is more likely that it was issued by a trader named Cotton at a place named M— Bridge. It has not proved possible to say which theory is correct, though the following locations have been considered – Menai Bridge, Anglesey, Matlock Bridge, Derbyshire, Markham Bridge, Newark, and Malin Bridge, Sheffield. The name Cotton is particularly common in the Midlands.
William Cotton was the holder of patents 9392 (13 June 1842) for manufacture of weighing machines, and 11255 (22 June 1842) for knitting machinery.

122.65 COLLETTE

This piece is of doubtful eligibility for inclusion, since, apart from the fact that it is engraved on an English penny, there is no evidence that it is of British origin. It could, for example, equally be French or Belgian. It is assumed that 'Crypto-conchoidsyphonostomata' relates to a manufactured product, but this need not be so. Charles Collette does not appear in the 1875 London Directory, although Collette & Collette, solicitors, are listed in both the 1875 and 1890 issues at 23 Lincolns Inn Fields, W.C.

122.68 DAVIS

The crown was a common brand mark in the nineteenth century – see 123.10 below. Carey op. cit. lists William Davis, a Birmingham gunmaker 1790–1834, who is a possible issuer of this countermark. However, Holden's 1811 Directory has Wm. Davies (sic), gunmaker, Summer Street, while other Birmingham directories do not show him as a gunmaker, but as follows:
1818, 1821 William Davis, bullet and shot mould maker, Moat Row.
1835 William Davis, gun stocker, 13 Court, Weaman Street.
1839 Address shown as 84 Weaman Street.

122.70 DEAKON

No traders named Deakon have been traced, and the entry in the Gibbs Sale Catalogue (lot 165) is presumably a misprint for Deacon or Deakin. Directories indicate the following possibilities:
Birmingham:
c. 1815–25 William Deakin, gunmaker, also F. Deakin, gunmaker c. 1815.
Glasgow:
1826 Deakin & Co., button warehouse, 88 Trongate.
London:
1870 Solomon Deacon, builder and patentee of improvements in tops, caps and wind guards for the cure of smoky chimneys, 59 Alma Street, New North Road, N.
Sheffield:
1814–15 George Deakin & Co., scissor makers, Green Lane.
c. 1828–45 James & Thomas Deakin, in 1833 described as 'merchants & patentees & manufacturers of the East India buffalo horn knobs for door & drawer handles, 5 Change Alley; cast steel cutlery and boot heel manufacturers and iron and steel dealers, Pond Hill'.
c. 1854–57 George Deakin & Co., table cutlery manufacturers, in 1854 at 48 Eyre Street.
c. 1857–84 Joseph Deakin & Sons, in 1861 at 78 Green Lane and described as 'manufacturers of Patent Electro Silver Plated and Britannia Metal tea and coffee services, Corporate Mark 3573'. By 1864 they were at Spring Street Works.
The following patents were filed in the names of Deacon and Deakin up to 1852:
Deacon, Benford:
No. 3664, 13 March 1813, improved fireplaces and bricks.

Deacon, Henry:
No. 10686, 22 May 1845, plate glass etc.
No. 11384, 24 September 1846, construction of flattening kilns.
Deacon, James & Thomas:
No. 5753, 14 January 1829, handles, knobs etc., from horns and hoofs of animals.
Deacon, William Archer:
No. 4403, 1 November 1819, boots, shoes and clogs from materials other than those normally used.
Deakin, Francis:
No. 3603, 23 October 1812, cases or sheaths for knives etc.
No. 4724, 9 November 1822, holster cases etc.
No. 4759, 18 February 1823, pianofortes etc.
No. 4785, 22 April 1823, furniture for mounting umbrellas and parasols.
Deakin, Thomas:
No. 3427, 1 April 1811, kitchen ranges.
No. 3890, 7 March 1816, portable kitchen.
No. 3975, 15 June 1816, stove, grate etc.
No. 9417, 12 June 1842, harnass (sic) parts.
No. 11540, 21 January 1847, construction and arrangement of machinery for cutting, stamping and pressing.
No. 13130, 12 June 1850, machinery and apparatus for rolling metals and making metal tubes.
This is probably an unofficial countermark by James and Thomas Deacon (or Deakin) of Sheffield (c. 1830–45) or Thomas Deakin (c. 1847–50).

122.72 DE MILT, GIBSON and WALKER

The traders whose punches were used for this unofficial piece have not been traced.

122.74 DOLLARD

This is probably an Irish shop ticket, but cannot be definitely attributed. A possible issuer might be James Dollard, vintner (Ship Inn?), 11 Cork Hill, Dublin (c. 1822–30). The piece is included as more than one example is known from the same punch.

122.75 DRIVE

'DRIVE' was the mark of William Hague, manufacturer of pen and spotted knives, of Dungworth, Sheffield in 1787. Hague is listed as a pocket knife cutler in the 1797 directory, but his mark is not shown. This is only one of a number of possible explanations of this countermark, which could even have been issued for political purposes.

122.76 DUNGFORD and WOODWARD

This is probably another example of an unofficial countermark by an employee of a firm in the metal trades. No trace of the firm(s) has been found in London directories 1842/50/56/62/67/72/77/83 or Sheffield directories 1833/37/41/45/52/56/64.

122.78 DURHAM

This is clearly a brand mark using the common nineteenth century device of a crown. Possible issuers include the following:
Edinburgh:

c. 1809–50 William Durham, clockmaker.
London:
1832 William Durham, cutler, 261 Regent Street.
1836 Robert Durham, coal merchant, same address.
1842 Robert Durham, cutler and razor maker, same address.
1857 Thomas Durham, engraver, 19 Rathbone Place, Oxford Street.
Sheffield:
1841 Joseph Durham, steel converter, Edgerton Street.

122.80 EASTERN CUTLERY COMPANY
This firm has not been traced in Birmingham, London, Manchester or Sheffield directories.

122.81 EDDY
The issuer of this early nineteenth century piece has not been identified. He is not listed in the London directories, at any rate up to 1835.

122.83 FITZ-P
This is probably an Irish shop ticket for a trader named Fitzpatrick. At least two examples are known, presumably from the same punch.

122.85 FLETCHER
The only Fletcher traced in the Sheffield directories is Robert Fletcher (jun.), white metal smith, 50 Talbot Street (1876), although the issues for 1864, 1884, 1893 and 1897 have been checked. A white metal smith would be unlikely to manufacture cast steel, so this pay check must remain unattributed.

122.88 FORREST
This countermark is included as it appears, from the same punch, on two pieces from different sources. A possible issuer is George Forrest, the London brass and gun metal founder, lamp manufacturer and gas fitter. In 1851 Forrest (of Hughes & Forrest) was at 32 New Street Square, Fetter Lane, and 1862–74, as George Forrest and Son, at 5 and 6 Nevills Court, Fetter Lane. This attribution is, of course, only tentative.

122.90 GEE & SON
This firm has not been traced in Birmingham, London or Sheffield directories. In Manchester, however, the name is a common one, and, as the piece is listed by Batty, it is possible it was issued in the Manchester area. Directories indicate the following possibilities:
1838 Charles Gee, pawnbroker, 154 Chapel Street, Salford.
1861 Charles Gee, bootmaker, 46 Higher Chatham Street, Chorlton on Medlock.
If Batty misread a G for a C, the following firm could be the issuer:
1850 Giles Gee & Sons, manufacturers of nankeens etc., 3 Duke Street, Cannon Street (works, Kearsley).
1861 ditto, cotton spinners and manufacturers of nankeens, same address but mills, Stoneclough.

1879 as 1861 but Manchester address moved to 27 Fountain Street.

122.95 GIBSON
It has not, so far, proved possible to identify this trader. Two tentative possibilities are Solomon Gibson, who made earthenwares in Liverpool c. 1816 (see Godden, p. 271), and Samuel Gibson, brass and german silver caster in general, Thomas Street, Sheffield (c. 1854). As Batty, who recorded the piece, came from Manchester, a location in the north of England is not unlikely.
Gibson, although an inventor, had not filed any patents up to 1852.

122.100 GILPIN
A possible issuer might be William Gilpin, senior, & Co., bar iron, steel and edge tool manufacturers, Churchbridge and Wedges Mills, Cannock, listed in the Staffordshire directories for at least 1850–1922. The 1860 Post Office Directory states (p. 525) that 'these works are in a flourishing state, and give employment of some hundreds of workmen'. Gilpin was awarded a prize medal at the 1862 International Exhibition, and a silver medal at Paris in 1867 'for the superiority of the manufacture of edge tools'. The name is also fairly common in the West Riding of Yorkshire.

122.103 HAMPSTEAD ROAD
While this is probably a London piece, it cannot be firmly attributed there as Hampstead Roads exist elsewhere, e.g. Liverpool. A possible London issuer might be William Heath, listed in directories as follows:
1832 ironmonger, 7 Adams Row, Hampstead Road.
1836 ironmonger, 14 Hampstead Road.
1842–7 furnishing ironmonger, 13 Hampstead Road.
No cutlers are listed in Hampstead Road, London, during the period 1825–50.

122.105 HANDCUT
This is another clear case of unofficial use of a firm's brand-marking punches by a workman.

122.107 HILDICK
This name is uncommon, and has not been traced in the London directories. Some innkeepers and shopkeepers named Hildick are listed in the Birmingham directories 1850–70. A possible issuer might be Aaron Hildick, listed in the Sheffield directories as follows:
1864 Aaron Hilldie (sic), tool maker, Wicker Lane.
1868 Aaron Hildick, edge tool manufacturer, Wicker Lane, house 11 Nursery Lane. His advertisement shows him as a manufacturer of plough bits, grooving, moulding, rabbeting and all kinds of plane irons and light edge tools at 57½ Bridge Street.
1876 address shown as 57½ Bridge Street, house 11 Nursery Lane.
1879, 1896 as above, but house 45 Melrose Road, Burngreave Road.

1900, 1910 described as edge and joiners' tool manufacturer, 57½ Bridge Street and Court 7, Brightmore Street.

1922 address shown as Rutland Street.

The use of a crown was very common in nineteenth century brand marks – see 122.78 above and 123.10 below.

122.108 HOBSON

This piece is included as the same punch has been used for at least two, and probably three examples. In each case the same type of coin has been used. One, in the author's collection, was incorrectly described in Seaby's Coin and Medal Bulletin, January 1971: 'TP353 T. HOBBS (sic) engraved on Middlesex halfpenny 1794'.

It has not proved possible to attribute this countermark to a particular town. No T. Hobson is listed in the Brighton directories for 1824, 1839, 1843, 1846 or 1848. London directories have the following entries:

1796 Thomas Hobson, boot and shoe maker, 26 James Street, Covent Garden.

1797 Thomas Hobson, shoe warehouse, same address.

1805, 1808 Tho. Hobson, 'The Puncheon', 1 Rose and Crown Court, Moorfields.

1811 Thos. Hobson, merchant, 1 Jeffrey's Square; Thos. Hobson, leather cutter, 13 Grays Inn Lane; Thos. Hobson, last and patten maker, 1 Rose Street, Soho (a possible issuer); Thos. Hobson, leather cutter, 68 Shadwell High Street; Thos. Hobson, potato dealer, Spitalfields Market.

Gales and Martin's 1787 Sheffield Directory shows 'HOBSON' as the mark of Thomas Hobson of Bradfield, manufacturer of spotted knives.

122.110 IN HOC SIGNO VINCES

This motto – 'by this sign shalt thou conquer' is found on the coins of Portugal. However, the arms on this piece are not those of Portugal and it is likely that a brand marking punch has been used unofficially, perhaps by a gunmaker.

122.120 KELLY

There is little doubt that this is an Irish shop ticket. However the name and initial are an extremely common combination and the piece is virtually impossible to attribute. One possible issuer with access to punches is Thomas Kelly, tool cutter and engraver, 34 Bow Street, Dublin (1806). A number of Dublin shoe makers would also qualify. At least three examples of this countermark are known, apparently from the same punch.

122.125 LEE

No patent in the name of A. Lee has been traced in the period 1617–1852. Abner Cowell Lea (sic) was granted patent number 2569 on 2 January 1802 for manufacturing the furniture for umbrellas and parasols.

122.127 LIP SALVE

See F. Sherwood Taylor 'The Century of Science', second edition, London 1941, p. 202: in 1840 'lipstick did not exist, but lard which had been dyed with annatto (the colour used on a Dutch cheese) was often used as a lip-salve. Cosmetics were, however, very little used by respectable Englishwomen of the middle classes before the nineteen-twenties'.

122.132 MINIFIE

R. Minifie does not appear in the 'Alphabetical Index of Patentees of Inventions 1617–1852', or in Underhill's Biennial Directory 1816–7 (metal trades) under Birmingham, Dublin, Edinburgh, Glasgow, London, Manchester or Sheffield. The crown was a common brand mark in the nineteenth century, see 123.10 below.

122.135 MITCHELL

A running fox was a common brand mark in the metal trades in the nineteenth century, but it has not proved possible to confirm that it was used by a J. Mitchell.

A possible issuer might be Joshua Mitchell, the Sheffield edge tool manufacturer, who appears in directories as follows:

1837 21 Bernard Street, Park.

1860 65 Duke Street, Park.

1864 69 Duke Street, Park.

The piece is described as a hunting ticket in Seaby's Coin and Medal Bulletin, January 1971 (TP 476) – this seems unlikely.

122.150 OLYMPIC BRACE, THE

This is another example of an unofficial issue. The manufacturer of the 'Olympic Brace' has not been identified, and does not appear in Buck & Hickman's 'General Catalogue of Tools and Supplies' (1935), or in White's 'Hardware Trade Marks' (1892).

122.152 OSBORN

This countermark is included as it occurs from the same punch on a halfcrown of 1688 and a 'cartwheel' twopence of 1797. The state of wear of the coins (halfcrown nearly fine, twopence very fine), and the particular coins involved, indicate an issue date early in the nineteenth century, possibly during the 1811–2 token period when regal silver and copper were in short supply in many areas. Assuming this, and that the issuer had his own punches to hand, directories indicate the following possibilities:

Birmingham

1808 (Holden's) Henry Osborn, sword cutler and accoutrement maker to His Majesty, Bordesley.

1816–7 (Underhill's) Osborn and Gunby, sword cutler, accoutrement and gun makers to His Majesty, His Royal Highness the Prince Regent, and the Honourable East India Company, Bordesley.

Cork

1808 (Holden's) John Osborn, hardwareman, Castle Street.

1816–7 (Underhill's) John Osborn, London, Birmingham, and Sheffield Warehouse, Castle Street.
London
1811 (Holden's) Geo. Osborn, cabinet maker and upholsterer, 136 Tottenham Court Road.
Geo. Osborn, umbrella maker, 3 Holborn-Bars.
Henry Osborn & Co., sword manufacturers to His Majesty, 82 Pall Mall.
Wm. Osborn & Edw. Ovenden, goldsmiths, 6 Staining Lane, Wood Street, Cheapside.

122.155 PARKER, PARKES or PARNELL
This is presumably a public house check, and probably Irish. However it has not proved possible to attribute it to a pub named the Swan in London, Belfast, Cork, Dublin or Limerick in the early nineteenth century.

122.158 PATENT & AXLE 1246
This is evidently not a patent number, at any rate before 1852: in the first series of patents (1617–1852), number 1246, granted 4 March 1780, reads as follows: 'A grant unto James King, of Newcastle upon Tyne, merchant, of his new invented British barillia, for the making and manufacturing of crown window glass, broad window glass, and glass bottles, and also for the manufacturing of soap and allum . . .'. For a countermark by an axle-tree maker see 22.35 above.

122.160 PATENT
Another 'punch-happy' unofficial countermark, in the case of 122.160A on an already overstruck token (Dublin: Davis 52 on Davis 22–4).

122.162 PERRY
This is included as two examples are known from the same punch. Almost certainly the pieces are Irish shop tickets, although the issuer cannot be definitely identified. A possibility might be James & Henry Perry, ironmongers and hardware merchants, 27 Pill Lane, Dublin (1818–1830), by 1840 J. H. & J. Perry & Co., 27 and 28 Pill Lane.

122.165 POTTS & CO.
Since this piece is listed by Batty it may originate from the north of England. No company of this name has been traced in London, Manchester or Sheffield.

122.170 Q(UARTE)RN LOAF
This is clearly a truck ticket valid for a quartern loaf at a firm's truck shop.

122.171 RACKHAM'S(?) PATENT
No-one named Rackham appears in the alphabetical list of patentees 1617–1852. In the London directories for 1835 and 1836, Jno. Rackham is listed as a coach builder at 14 Long Acre, and E. Rackham as a corset manufacturer at 36 Bury Street, St. James'. The name Rackham does not appear clearly on this piece, which must remain unattributed.

122.173 RAVANAGE(?) FOUNDRY
The reading of the first word of this countermark as 'Ravanage' is by no means certain, and this piece must remain unattributed, at least until further examples turn up.

122.175 RICHARDS
An open hand is a common mark on 'Old Sheffield' plated articles. However the name Richards is scarce in Sheffield in the nineteenth century, and it has not been possible to attribute the countermark to this town or elsewhere.
Theophilus Richards held patent no. 8592, dated 5 August 1840, for machinery for cutting or sawing wood.

122.180 ROSS & CO.
This countermark cannot be definitely attributed. There are several entries for Ross & Co. in London directories, including the following:
A. Ross & Co., merchants, 3 Copthall Court (1806).
Alexander Ross & Co., merchants, Leadenhall Buildings, Gracechurch Street (1818).
A. Ross & Co., Army clothiers, 28 Castle Street, Leicester Square (1818, 1827).
Daniel Ross & Co., merchants, 46 Lime Street (1818).
Ross & Co., wine merchants, 349 Strand (1827).
Ross & Co., boot and shoe warehouse, 16 Shoreditch (1832).
I. Ross & Co., hatters and hat manufacturers, 45 Old Street Road., St. Lukes (1832, 1836/7).
Alex. Ross & Co., wine and spirit merchants, 42 St. Mary Axe (1842).
Andrew Ross & Co., scotch and irish linen factors, 5 Mitre Court and 1 Feather Court, Milk Street (1842).

122.185 RUSSELL
The crest countermarked on this coin is that of the Russells, Dukes of Bedford, although other Russells have similar crests. It is possible that the piece served as a truck ticket on one of the Bedford estates. John Russell, sixth Duke of Bedford, 1766–1839, had extensive estates in Bedfordshire, Devonshire and London. He was one of the leading agriculturalists of his day, and succeeded to the dukedom in March 1802. For further information see the 'Dictionary of National Biography'.

122.186 SALT
This piece may have served as a dock or load ticket for salt, cf 122.195 below.

122.187 SHIPDEM
The two possibilities here are, firstly, that the piece is a love token to mark the engagement or marriage of James Shipdem and someone named A. Tinker, or, secondly, and more likely, that it was issued by James Shipdem, who was a tinker in 1742.

122.188 SINGER & CO.
The letters of this countermark have been individually punched, so, while the piece may be unofficial, a firm's brand marking punch has not been used. The piece may have served as a pay or tool check. Among possible issuers, the following appear in the London directories:

Alfred Singer & Co., brownstone, crucible &c. potter, Vauxhall, from at least 1842 until 1866. In 1850 the entry is for brownstone and chemical potters, and patent mosaic pavement manufacturers. In 1856 the style is Singer and Green, in 1860 Alfred Singer, the '& Co.' reappearing by 1866 when the address is shown as Vauxhall High Street.

Marchant, Singer & Co., letterpress, copperplate and lithographic printers, 1 Ingram Court, Fenchurch Street, EC, c. 1850–80. The entry is for Marchant, Singer & Smith at the same address 1842–4 and the address is shown as 47 St. Mary Axe in 1885 and 1890.

The Singer Manufacturing Company, patent sewing machines, George Baldwin Woodruff, manager, 147 Cheapside, EC (1867–85). The address is shown as 39 Foster Lane, EC and 17 Chiswell Street, EC by 1890.

Singer & Co., bicycle manufacturers, 21 Holborn Viaduct, EC (1879–80), 17 Holborn Viaduct, EC (1885, 1890).

J. Singer & Co., fur merchants, 5 Greenfield Street, Commercial Road East, E, and 11 Queen Victoria Street, EC (1890).

122.190 SMITH BROTHERS
Although the issuer of this piece was probably a Sheffield firm of cutlery or edge tool manufacturers, this cannot be proved. Sheffield directories show the following entries:

1837 Smith, Henry & John, merchants, and file, table, pen and pocket knife, scissor and steel manufacturers, 95 Rockingham Street.
Smith, Jas., & Brother, merchants, table knife manufacturers (mark, Extra), and steel refiners, Coalpit Lane.
1841 Smith, H. & J., merchants, steel converters, manufacturers of files, table and spring knives, scissors etc., 112 and 114 Rockingham Street.
1845 Smith, Henry & John, merchants, and steel, file, and cutlery manufacturers, 112 Rockingham Street.
1879 Smith, William Hemsworthy, merchant, and manufacturer of table and pocket cutlery, scissors, saws, files, edge tools &c., 25 Carver Street, and New York.
1896 Smith, R. & J., brothers, iron, steel and general merchants, 18 Park Station, Victoria Arches, Furnival Road, and Castle Hill.

122.192 SPRING STEEL
This unofficial countermark was probably produced by an employee of a Sheffield steel firm.

122.195 2 STONE
Dock tickets were struck in Liverpool in the nineteenth century – see Davis & Waters' 'Tickets and Passes of Great Britain and Ireland' (Leamington Spa, 1922), p. 333, no. 22 (Load of Ballast) and 24 (Load of Stone). One possibility is that this countermarked piece served as a similar dock ticket for two loads of stone.

Alternatively it could be a check, tally or receipt for a weight of two stones of a particular commodity.

122.200 H. STREET
The only justification for including this piece is that it could be a ticket or check valid in the H(igh) Street of a town. It is, however, quite possible that H. Street is a trader's name, or the name of a private individual.

122.202 SUN
This piece was probably issued in connection with a public house named the 'Sun'.

122.203 TAGART and TERNAN
This piece is included as two examples of the V. Tagart countermark are known from the same punch. The coins probably served as Irish shop tickets, though it is not possible to identify the issuers. The following entries appear in the Dublin directories:

William Taggart, grocer, 37 Townsend Street (1810–27) (spelt Tagart from 1821).
James Ternan, baker, 143 North King Street (1818–19).
John Ternan, victualler, 7 Camden Street (1836).
Wm. Tagert (sic), surgeon, 21 French Street (1840).
John Ternan, surgeon, 5 Prussia Street (1840).

122.205 TAYLOR
The following patents are filed in the name of I. Taylor up to 1852:

Isaac Taylor, junior, No. 5040, 20 November 1824, cock or tap for drawing off liquids.
Isaac Taylor, No. 12248, 21 August 1848, preparing and engraving surfaces; construction of cylinders adapted for engraving; machinery for printing and ornamenting surfaces.

In addition, various J. Taylors held 33 patents up to 1852.

'J. TAYLOR & SON' was one of the marks of Taylor Brothers, manufacturers of saws, steel, files, edge tools, machine knives etc., Adelaide Works, Sheffield c. 1854–70, and it is possible that this firm was the issuer.

122.210 TULLY
From both the name and the address, this countermark ought to originate from Cumberland or south west Scotland, but the issuer has not been identified. A check of current telephone directories for the British Isles shows 569 entries for Tully, of which 292 are concentrated as follows: Newcastle on Tyne, 59 Central London 58, Eire – outside Dublin 44, Dublin 39, Edinburgh 30, S.W. Essex 21, N.E. Surrey 21, Northern Ireland 20. However, no Maryport Street has been traced in these areas or any other, although there is a Mary-le-port Street in Bristol. As the piece was known to Batty, it may well originate from the north of England.

122.225 WARD
It is assumed that this piece was issued by or for P. Ward and that 'IS' signifies one shilling. However the significance of 'BICH:O:W:A:GALAS:' is far from clear. 'GALAS' could be an abbreviated form of Galashiels, Selkirkshire, but no trader named Ward is listed in the directories for 1837, 1860 or 1866.

122.230 WARRANTED
Another unofficial countermark, possibly by an employee of a Sheffield cutlery firm.

122.235 WARRANTED CAST STEEL
The brand-marking punches of a number of steel firms could have been used for this unofficial countermark, and it is clearly impossible to make a definite attribution. However at least one Sheffield firm did use the phrase 'warranted cast steel' in their advertisements: 'William Turner & Son, manufacturers of Warranted Cast Steel for turning tools, taps, dies, burrs, chisels, punches, cold sates, shear blades etc. etc. Warranted double shear steel for welding, spring and blister steel, warranted cast steel files, Caledonia Steel & File Works' (1890).

122.237 WARRANTED PATENT etc.
Another unofficial countermark, possibly by an employee of a firm of machine makers.

122.238 WATSON
It is assumed that Os. Watson was a gunmaker, but he does not appear as such in any lists of gunmakers known to me or in the early nineteenth century London directories.

122.240 WILK
The name Applebeck sounds Cumbrian in origin, but has not been traced as a place-name in Cumberland, Westmorland or elsewhere. As a date is also countermarked on this piece, it is probable that this is a 'love token'. However it is possible that Applebeck is the name of a farm or road, in which case the coin could be some form of farmer's check or tally; this is the only justification for including this piece in the list.

122.245 Wᴹ SON
This piece, probably Irish in origin, is only included because the countermark might be an abbreviation of W . . . m and Son, thus indicating that it was issued by a trader.

122.250 YATE
This countermark is similar to the marks found on plated goods and cutlery, but it has not proved possible to attribute it to a specific trader.
Possible issuers include William Yates, who was registered at the Sheffield Assay Office as a silversmith in 1878 (see Jackson, op. cit., p. 437) and is listed in the 1884 directory as a silver ferrule maker at 217 Rockingham Street, Sheffield.
Another possibility is John Yates, spoon maker (Britannia metal etc.), 38 Coleshill Street Birmingham (1847).

123 Unattributed Marks and Initials

123.10 A (crown)
It was common practice in the nineteenth century and earlier to incorporate a crown in trade and brand marks. This was particularly common in the metal trades, but was not confined to Sheffield, which, from 1773, used a crown as its town mark on silver goods. The Trade Marks Act of 1938 prohibited the use of the British Royal or Imperial Crowns in trade marks.
A common pitfall is to attribute such countermarked pieces to the West Indies. There is absolutely no legislative or other documentary evidence to support such attributions, as Pridmore has shown in his work on the coins of the West Indies. It should also be noted that copper coin was disliked in this area, the natives preferring silver and billon. Some of these pieces may have been used as shop tickets.

123.15 A (fleur de lis) I
This is assumed to be a brand mark and may be Irish. It is possible it served as a token.

123.20 A (fleur de lis) L
These pieces were almost certainly used as tokens or shop tickets in Ireland in the early nineteenth century.

123.30 (crown) B
See 123.10 above.

123.35 (crown) BC
See 123.10 above.

123.36 B.E.W. CO.
This firm has not been identified.

123.37 (corkscrew) BH
In style this is similar to many Sheffield cutlers' marks of the late eighteenth century. However this particular mark has not been traced in the 1787 and 1797 directories.

123.40 (crown)
See 123.10 above.

123.50 (crown) CH
See 123.10 above.

123.55 D (fleur de lis) H
This early countermark is assumed to be a brand mark. The piece may have served as a token.

123.57 DM
This countermark is included as it is known, from the same punch, on two pieces. Also the countermark is in the same position on each coin – below the truncation. A third piece has slightly smaller lettering, but again the countermark is placed at the base of the coin. The pieces may well have served as Irish 'slap' tokens – cf Szauer 92 (see Appendix 2).

123.60 (winged dog seated)
This is probably a crest or badge rather than a brand mark. The piece may have served as a truck or estate token.

123.65 DW (within a sunken crown)
See 123.10 above.

123.68 (elephant)
This could be the unofficial use of a brand-marking punch, or a hotel or pub check. See 22.3 and 22.59 above.

123.75 (crown) ES
See 123.10 above.

123.76 (crown) E.S.
See 123.10 above.

123.78 EW and Maltese Cross
It is assumed that this is a brand mark, but the issuer has not been identified. See 123.115 below.

123.80 (crown) F
See 123.10 above. A crowned F was the mark of Foad, a gunmaker in Tewen Street, London, about 1690. (See Carey, op. cit.)

123.85 (crown) F.B
See 123.10 above.

123.87 (fleur de lis, crescent and figure 9)
These are all common Sheffield cutlers' marks but have not been traced in combination in the 1787 and 1797 directories.

123.88 (fleur de lis and crescent)
See 123.87 above.

123.90 (crown) G
See 123.10 above.

123.92 (crown) GAN
See 123.10 above. This is probably a cutler's mark, but does not appear in the Sheffield directories for 1787 (Gales and Martin's) or 1797 (John Robinson's), both of which contain lists of marks.

123.94 G.E.Sca 1793
The same punch has been used to countermark the two pieces in the author's collection. The purpose and issuer are unknown. It is possible that the letter G stands for 'Guaranteed' and that E.Sca (perhaps E.Sea) are the initials of a trader. It is interesting to note that the seventeenth century Bath farthing was, presumably, still in circulation in 1793.

123.96 G & P
The '&', and the fact that this piece is counter-marked, not engraved, indicate that it was issued by a firm.

123.98 (crown) G.R (broad arrow) and 2 sceptres in saltire, crowned.
See 123.10 above. The broad arrow is, of course, a government mark, while the crowned sceptres were used by, among others, William Ketland, the Birmingham gunmaker. Ketland had a London shop, and his mark, or a variation on it, became the Birmingham proof mark in the early nineteenth century. This is assumed to be 'punch happy' work by a gunmaker with a government contract.

123.100 (crown) G.R
According to the Bliss sale catalogue (lot 1000) this piece was countermarked 'probably to guarantee it as a two ounce weight', but see 123.10 above. Cokayne (lot 96) lists 'three copper pieces' with this countermark.

123.105 (crown) G.R
See 123.10 above. Ray Byrne and Jerome H. Remick in 'The Coinage of Jamaica' (1966), p. 34 list a penny of 1806 with (crown)/GR on the obverse and another of 1797 with a larger variation of the same countermark on the reverse. The authors consider the pieces to be contemporary forgeries used in Jamaica c. 1800–35.

123.108 (griffin passant)
This is the crest of Earl Fitzwilliam, the landlord of the Brameld family who made Rockingham pottery in Swinton, Yorkshire. The Bramelds adopted the crest as their brand mark on bone china c. 1826–42. William Wentworth Fitzwilliam (1748–1833) was Lord Lieutenant of Ireland in 1795, and, in 1806, President of the Council. He had large estates in Ireland and Yorkshire. It is possible that this piece is some form of truck or estate ticket, although it may be unofficial.

123.110 (griffin's head)
This is probably a brand mark, although it could be a crest. If the latter, the piece could be a truck or estate token.

123.112 (plume) GS
This is probably another example of the unofficial use of a brand marking punch.

123.115 H.D and Maltese Cross
It is assumed that this is a brand mark, but the issuer has not been identified. See 123.78 above.

123.119 (crown) I
See 123.10 above.

123.120 (crown) I
See 123.10 above.

123.122 (crown) IB
See 123.10 above.

123.123 (crown) ID
See 123.10 above.

123.125 (crown) II
See 123.10 above.

123.128 I.S

This countermark is included as it is known, from the same punch, on both sides of two pieces. It is not known whether I.S signifies the initials of a trader or 'one shilling'.

123.130 (crown) IS

See 123.10 above.

123.132 (crown) I.S

See 123.10 above.

123.135 (crown) ISR

See 123.10 above.

123.136 (crown) I, SR and 3

See 123.10 above. This piece may well have served as a pay check, and have some connection with 123.135 above.

123.140 (crown) IW

See 123.10 above.

123.142 (crown) I.Y

See 123.10 above.

123.144 JB

This countermark is included as it is known from the same punch on two pieces. It may have served as a token, perhaps in Ireland.

123.145 (crown) JB

See 123.10 above.

123.146 JB

209 of these pieces are discussed, and 191 described, in Michael Dolley's 'A parcel of counter-marked early nineteenth-century farthings Irish'. (Numismatic Society of Ireland Occasional Papers 15–16, 1973). An additional farthing, believed to be from the same source, is in Mr. A. G. Davies' collection. The author's specimen, in contrast to the 210 known farthings, is a countermarked penny of 1797. The countermark has indeterminate prickings in the face of the die above the letters JB, and, more clearly, but crudely, the date '1811.' below.

Besides the primary JB/1811 countermark, secondary (incuse) countermarks occur on 14 of the pieces catalogued by Dolley as follows:

1. CR on reverse, Irish farthing 1806 (JB on obverse).
2. HE on reverse, Irish farthing 1806 (JB on obverse).
3. HI on obverse, Irish farthing 1806 (JB on obverse).
4. M on reverse, Irish farthing 1806 (JB on obverse).
5. QURPI(?) on reverse, Irish farthing 1806 (JB on reverse) – partially beneath the primary countermark.
6. R on reverse, Irish farthing 1806 (JB on obverse).
7. SK(?)/ASN(?) on obverse, Irish farthing 1806 (JB on reverse).

8. –UX on obverse, X on reverse, farthing 1806 (JB on reverse).
9. W on obverse, farthing 1806 (JB on reverse).
10. W on obverse, Irish farthing 1806 (JB on obverse) – beneath the primary countermark.
11. X on reverse, Irish farthing 1806 (JB on obverse).
12. X on reverse, Irish farthing 1806 (JB on reverse).
13. X(?) on reverse, Irish farthing 1806 (JB on obverse).
14. (an asterisk) on reverse, Irish farthing 1806 (JB on reverse).

In view of the amount of wear on the Anglo-Irish farthings of 1806 (average weight 4.10 g., compared with prescribed standard of 4.36 g.,) Dolley suggests that they may have been counter-marked after the Irish pieces were demonetised in 1826. This demonetisation was less effective in Ireland than in England, where Irish coins were accepted reluctantly or not at all. His theory is that the coins were sold in England as scrap copper, perhaps about 1830, the purchaser using them as blanks for truck tickets destined for premises in Lancashire or Yorkshire, but not circulating them because of the passing of the 1831 Truck Act. This leaves unexplained the date 1811 on the countermark, unless either it is not intended to be read as a date or it refers, as Dolley suggests, to the date of a firm's foundation. Were it not for the wear on the coins, one might be tempted to suppose that these pieces served as tokens for a short time about 1811 until proper dies for a token issue had been prepared, when they were recalled. Copper tokens were issued in the early nineteenth century by a number of traders with initial JB:

Gloucestershire: Cheltenham
    John Bastin, Penny 1812 (Davis 14).
    John Bishops & Co., Penny 1812 (Davis 15).
Middlesex: Walworth Road
    James Bean, Farthing 1814 (Davis 8).
Northumberland: Newcastle
    John Bell, Farthing 1815 (Davis 18–24).

It should, however, be remembered that copper coins wear far more easily than our modern bronze issues, and that, in the early nineteenth century, such low denomination coins had considerable use.

123.150 (crown) JC

See 123.10 above.

123.155 J.C.C PATENT 5535

The issuer of this piece has not been traced. A possibility might be J. C. Campbell, who held British and United States patents for revolving firearms in 1863. In the earlier series of patents (i.e. before 1852), patent 5535 was granted on 4 August 1827 as follows: 'A grant unto Peter Burt, of Waterloo Place, in the parish of Saint Ann, Limehouse, in the County of Middlesex, mathematical instrument maker, in consequence of a communication made to him by a certain foreigner residing abroad he is in possession of 'An invention of an improved steam engine'; six months'.

123.160 JDV
This countermark is included as it is known from the same punch on two pieces, both very worn. One could be an English or Irish token, with a seated female on one side. However it could equally be an octavo of Jalisco State, Mexico (1856-62), although JDV does not seem to be one of the recognised Hacienda or Revolutionary countermarks. While attribution to the British series could, therefore, be incorrect, a possible issuer might be the trader who countermarked a worn copper coin 'MR. J D (V)ALLENTIN' (Szauer 87). Joseph Valantine (sic) was a cutler of 44 New Road W., Dublin, in 1830, and is a possible alternative.

123.165 JFR
This is probably a brand mark, but could be a love token.

123.170 J.H
I am informed by Charles P. O'Neill that James Hannan, a spirit dealer of 133 Shankhill Road, Belfast, countermarked brass gaming counters with the initials J.H and 1D or ½ c.1858-78. The letters on this piece are much larger, and the position of the stop varies, though the possibility that the issuer was the same cannot be entirely ruled out. See also W. A. Seaby 'Catalogue of Ulster Tokens etc.' nos. AN:827-9. Another possibility might be J. Hammond of Ellenden, Hawkhurst – see Seaby's Coin and Medal Bulletin, February 1973, HT 144(a). (JH/2 countermarked on thin copper flan to serve as a hop token).

123.175 (bucket) J-K
This well-produced countermark probably dates from the early nineteenth century, and could be a cowman's or dairyman's 'shop' ticket.

123.180 J:R
The issuer of this piece, presumably a shop ticket, and before c. 1850, has not been traced.

123.182 (crown) J.S
See 123.10 above.

123.183 J.T
The issuer of this countermark, which occurs on at least four pieces, was probably an Irish trader.

123.185 (Justice holding scales)
This is a device appropriate to the issuer of a shop ticket, though it could be just a brand mark.

123.188 JW & CO
This piece is tentatively included, although the issuer may not be British. The countermark is reversed, probably for sealing.

123.190 JW, DJ(?), J.T, JR, AMJ
These appear to be silversmiths' or cutlers' marks, but the issuers have not been identified. Jackson, op. cit., p. 617 shows that the mark JR was registered in Dublin in 1876 by a silversmith named J. Redmond.

123.195 (crown) K
See 123.10 above.

123.200 (crown) L
See 123.10 above.

123.205 (crown) LN
See 123.10 above.

123.208 (man in moon)
This is assumed to be a brand mark, but the issuer has not been identified.

123.210 M
The countermark is included as it is known from the same punch on five pieces. Moreover, the countermark occurs in three instances to the left of the bust on the obverse of farthing-size coins in EF condition. On the regal farthing, the countermark is on the centre of the bust.

123.211 MB
This countermark is included, as Christopher Brunel reports that he has seen two examples, presumably from the same punch.

123.212 M.G
The issuer of this countermark, which occurs on at least two pieces, was probably an Irish trader.

123.215 M.I
The issuer of this countermark, which occurs on at least three pieces, was probably an Irish trader.

123.225 (crown) (mushroom-like device)
See 123.10 above.

123.230 (crown) N
See 123.10 above. V. Guilloteau in 'Monnaies Françaises' (1942) attributes this mark to the Napoleonic Occupation of Santo Domingo (1802-3) – see also Craig 44. It will be noted that one of the pieces listed by Guilloteau is dated 1807.

123.232 (crown) NB
See 123.10 above.

123.238 OK and SS
This is assumed to be an Irish trader's piece, as at least two examples are known from, presumably, the same punch. For other SS countermarks see 123.333 below, and Appendix 2.

123.240 O.W
Similar, but not identical countermarks on silver coins are recorded in Spink's Numismatic Circular as follows:
1. IW/WARRANTED/DEC. 1790/28G in an oval indent on obverse William III half-crown, Chester mint. (April 1907, col. 9761).
2. OW/WARRANTED/1792 in an oval on reverse William III half-crown, Chester mint. (July 1927, col. 346).
These countermarks, and those on the copper pieces, have the air of official stamps, perhaps

Office of Works(?). If so it seems likely that they have been used unofficially – certainly no other reason is apparent. Although one of the coins involved, the Anglesey penny, weighed, on issue, 32 grammes (and the countermark shows 32G), the supposition that these pieces may be weights can be dismissed – the weights of the other coins do not correspond with the countermarks, and grains, rather than grammes were in use in England in the 1790's.

In 1785, the staff of the Office of Works consisted of 2 resident clerks, 2 assistant clerks, 6 clerks of works, a 'keeper of all the engines', 2 other engineers, 10 labourers in trust, 4 constant carpenters, master bricklayer, master plumber, office keeper, messenger, 8 constant labourers and gate keeper. (See Sir Harold Emmerson, 'The Ministry of Works', London, 1956, p. 16). They were concerned with the maintenance of Royal palaces, houses, parks and roads, and came under professional, rather than lay control, in 1796.

123.245 (owl-like device)
This countermark appears to have been formed by a 'B' in relief in a serrated indent next to an incuse 'B'. It probably served as an Irish trader's token or shop ticket.

123.250 (crown) P
See 123.10 above.

123.255 (crown) P/(crown) WH
See 123.10 above.

123.270 (pipe)
A pipe was a common form of brand mark, particularly in the metal trades. The mark was used by the following manufacturers, among others:
(2 short straight tobacco pipes, crossed):
William Webster, Whiteley Wood, Sheffield, maker of spotted knives (1787).
(curved, long-stemmed tobacco pipe):
W. & H. Hutchinson, 76 Norfolk Street, Sheffield, manufacturers of surgical, veterinary and dental instruments, sole manufacturers of the true pipe razors (1844).
(straight-stemmed tobacco pipe):
William Twigg, scissor maker, Wicker, Sheffield (1787).
Samuel Walker, spotted knife maker, Sowden, Sheffield (1787).
(straight-stemmed tobacco pipe, IR to left):
William Mullins, sickle maker, Ford, Sheffield (1787).
(straight-stemmed tobacco pipe, diamond to right):
John Newton, penknife maker, Sharrowmoor, Sheffield (1787).

123.275 (plume of three feathers)
Fairbairn's 'Book of Crests' (4th edition 1892) lists 30 families employing this device as their crest, apart, of course, from the Prince of Wales. Alternatively this may be another example of the unofficial use of a brand marking punch.

123.280 (railway locomotive)
The locomotive countermarked on the George IV penny has the 2-2-2 wheel arrangement and appears to be of a type built about 1850. It could be a brand mark – a similar device was used c. 1876 by Turton Brothers & Matthews of Phoenix Steel Works, Wentworth Street, Sheffield, merchants and manufacturers of steel, files, saws, edge tools etc.

123.285 R. CO
The issuer of this countermark has not been identified.

123.290 RD 459419
Board of Trade Design Registration numbers were introduced in January 1884. Design number 459419 was registered in 1905.

123.291 R & G
The '&', and the fact that this piece is countermarked, not engraved, indicate that it was issued by a firm.

123.293 R (fleur de lis) N
This piece, like 123.20 above, may have served as a token or shop ticket, perhaps in Ireland, in the early nineteenth century.

123.295 (Royal Arms)
This is assumed to be an unofficial countermark by a workman of a firm in the metal trades holding a royal warrant. The Royal Warrant Holders Association was established in 1840 and incorporated in 1895. For a similar piece see 11.2 above.

123.297 R.S & CO.
The issuer of this piece may be Irish. The use of a star as a brand mark was not uncommon. A possible issuer might be Richard Southall & Co., the early nineteenth century Birmingham gunmaker, at any rate if this is an unofficial issue rather than a shop ticket.

123.300 (crown) RW
See 123.10 above. This mark was used by R. Wilson, the London gunmaker, c. 1780.

123.305 RY
This countermark is included as there are at least five known instances from the same punch. The pieces are assumed to be early nineteenth century tokens or shop tickets with a very local circulation. In each case the countermark is on the reverse of the coin.

123.310 (crown) S
See 123.10 above.

123.313 (shamrock)
It is assumed that this is a brand mark, though the issuer has not been traced. Another possibility is that the piece may have been issued for political purposes.

123.315 (crown) SD
See 123.10 above. Among gunmakers, possible issuers might be:
Samson Davis, 4 East Smithfield, London (1832–50).
S. Deacon, Monmouth (c. 1835).
Samuel Dixson, Leicester (1800–32).
This piece, and 123.320 below, are discussed in 'Token Corresponding Society Bulletin 1971/2, No. 2 (p. 44), No. 3 (p. 63) and No. 4 (p. 82).

123.320 S.D/2.6
See 123.315 above. This piece is almost certainly a truck ticket for two shillings and sixpence. The issuer has not been traced.

123.325 ·S·/3.6

123.326 3 6
These are probably truck tickets for three shillings and sixpence.

123.330 S. D/13.6
The Portuguese gold coin of half a moidore was current in Ireland in the late eighteenth century for thirteen shillings and sixpence. This counter-marked piece probably served as a coin weight.

123.332 (crown) SS
See 123.10 above.

123.333 SS
The issuer of these common countermarks is assumed to be an Irish trader of the late eighteenth century. A number of examples are listed by Szauer, presumably from the same punch. See also 123.238 above, and Appendix 2.

123.334 (shield)
Engraved shields on coins usually signify private pieces or love tokens. This countermarked example may have had a wider use. Unfortunately it is not clear whether the device in the first quarter is a dagger or a tall fleur de lis. If the former, the arms of the City of London seem indicated, if the latter, the arms of Elias Ashmole, the antiquary, or of the Leinhams, Purton, Metham or Rochfort families. Alternatively this could be a case of the use of unauthorised arms as a brand mark. Both coin and countermark are considerably worn.

123.336 (stag trottant)
Fairbairn's 'Book of Crests' (4th edition, 1892) lists 114 families who employ this device. As the piece is countermarked rather than engraved, it may have served as a truck ticket on one of these estates. Alternatively it may be another case of the unofficial use of a brand marking punch, or even a worn livery button.

123.338 (swan)
This is another example of an unofficial counter-mark. Many firms used a swan as a brand or trade mark in the nineteenth century – e.g. Francis Newton & Sons, table knife manufacturers, Portobello Works, 127 Portobello Street, Sheffield (c. 1876), Howell & Co., file manufacturers, Brook Works, Sheffield (c. 1876).

123.342 (crown) TB
123.345 (crown) TE
123.353 (crown) TS
123.354 (crown) TS
123.355 (crown) T.S
See 123.10 above. TB could be Thomas Barnett, a London gunmaker under government contract c. 1750–1835.

123.360 (crown) T.W.
See 123.10 above. This is the corporate mark of Thomas Wilkinson & Son, who by 1971 had become William Whiteley & Sons (Sheffield) Ltd., Phoenix Works, 29 Rockingham Street. However, the mark may well have been used by other traders.

123.380 (crown) V/(crown) P
These are the View and Proof marks respectively of the Gunsmith's Company. The piece is discussed by F. Pridmore in Spink's Numismatic Circular August/September 1954 columns 339/340.

123.385 (crown) V
See 123.10 above.

123.390 (crowned harp) VR 249
The mark of a crowned harp was used by the following traders:
Armstrong & M'Birney, pottery factory, Belleek, Co. Fermanagh. The firm was formed in 1857. This mark was used c. 1863–80. The partners died in 1885, and the firm continued operating in a smaller way. (See Godden, op. cit., p. 67, no. 325).
Wingfield, Rowbotham & Co., 82 Tenter Street, Sheffield and 321 High Holborn, London W.C., 'manufacturers of the celebrated harp and crown cutlery, cast, shear, mining, blister and spring steel, files, saws and machine knives. Solid cast steel engineers' hammers and Mill bills and general merchants' (Sheffield Directory 1890).

123.392 (crown) VR and T
See 123.10 above. This is an unusual example of a French coin countermarked unofficially in England, presumably after 1837.

123.395 (lion) W (male head)
Almost certainly these are silver or plate marks. The male head is probably that of George III, George IV, or William IV – denoting that Excise Duty had been paid. This mark was introduced in 1784-5. The lion passant is the sterling silver mark.

123.397 (crown) W
See 123.10 above.

123.398 (crown) w
See 123.10 above. This piece was included with the colonial section of the Bliss collection, presumably because, at one stage, almost any heart-shaped mark on a coin was attributed to Martinique.

123.400 (crown) WB
See 123.10 above. Monica Bussell assumed the piece to be a hop token issued by Sir Walter Wheeler Berry, KBE, of Gushmere, Selling, Faversham, Kent, but there appears to be no basis for this attribution. (See Seaby's Coin and Medal Bulletin, January 1973, HT 142).

123.403 (crown) WC
See 123.10 above. This piece was attributed to West Coast, Sierra Leone, in the Gibbs sale catalogue. There is no documentary evidence to support the official countermarking of copper coins with this mark. Pridmore discusses the West African countermarks in depth in Spink's Numismatic Circular, February 1954, columns 59–64. The piece is either a concoction, or, more likely, a brand mark.

123.405 (horse rampant) WC
This could be either a brand mark or a crest. If the latter, the piece may be a truck or estate ticket.

123.408 WF
This may be a silversmith's mark, but the issuer has not been identified.

123.410 (wheatsheaf and sickle)
Since this is countermarked rather than engraved, it has been assumed to be a brand mark rather than a love token. There is also the possibility that it could be a public house check.

123.412 W.H.J
The issuer of this piece, which probably dates from the late nineteenth century, has not been traced.

123.414 WII
This early piece is included as two examples are known from the same punch. The countermarked coin may have served as a token or shop ticket, perhaps in Ireland.

123.415 W&JS.S
The issuer of this piece has not been identified.

123.417 WM and I
This is assumed to have been issued by a trader with initials WM. The 'I' could signify 1 penny, 1 shilling, or 1 pint, load or bushel etc. – i.e. the piece could be a token, hotel check, dock ticket or hop token.

123.419 W & T.E
The '&', and the fact that this piece is countermarked, not engraved, indicate that it was issued by a firm.

123.420 (crown) WW
See 123.10 above.

123.430 (crown) X
See 123.10 above.

MORE NEWS THAN ALL THE OTHER WEEKLY NEWSPAPERS COMBINED.

LLOYD'S
WEEKLY
LONDON NEWS

IS THE CHEAPEST, LARGEST, AND BEST FAMILY NEWSPAPER,

Containing SIXTY LARGE COLUMNS of the very LATEST INTEL-
LIGENCE from all parts of the World, at the extraordinary Low Price of

ONE PENNY!

SALE, 500,000!   SALE, 500,000!

Printed by Hoe's Fast American Printing Machines (manufactured expressly
for this Journal), at the rate of 50,000 per hour.

LLOYD'S PAPER MILLS,
AT BOW BRIDGE, LONDON,

Were erected at an enormous cost for this Newspaper, covering Four Acres
of ground; each Paper-Making Machine making One Hundred feet run, or
Five Hundred square feet of Paper per minute! Paper Mills of equal
magnitude are also erecting at Sittingbourne, Kent.

☞ *Upwards of Two Hundred Thousand Acres of Land in Africa are
employed growing fibre for the manufacture of Paper for the above-mentioned
Journal.*

SOLD IN EVERY PART OF THE GLOBE.

Advertisement for Lloyd's Weekly Newspaper (1866).
See 22.28 in Table 1.

BY

His Majesty's Royal Letters Patent,

FOR AN

Improvement on Axletrees.

W. MASON,

PATENTEE & MANUFACTURER,

No. 22,

CASTLE-STREET EAST, OXFORD-MARKET,

LONDON.

The Improvements on Axletrees.

1st. There are four long Reservoirs in the Centre of the Box, which contain a greater quantity of Oil (than usual) that is always circulating round the Arm, which will prevent the Wheel ever sticking fast, and runs with considerable more ease.

2nd. The Fixtures are such as to prevent the possibility of the Wheel coming off.

3rd. To let out the Wheel when travelling on bad roads with perfect safety.

PORTRAIT OF OLD PARR
attributed to Rubens, and copied on wrapper of
"Parr's Life Pills."

MARSDEN BROTHERS AND CO.,

PRIZE MEDAL.   PRIZE MEDAL.

BRIDGE STREET WORKS,
SHEFFIELD,
MERCHANTS,
AND MANUFACTURERS OF

EDGE AND JOINERS' TOOLS,
ENGRAVERS' TOOLS,
And of the celebrated Cast Steel

BRIGHT ELASTIC HAY, MANURE & DIGGING FORKS,
Garden Shears, Horticultural Tools, Pen, Pocket, and Table Cutlery, Razors, Scissors, &c.

SKATE MANUFACTURERS
(By Special Appointment)
TO HER MAJESTY AND THE ROYAL FAMILY.

Table 1 issuers: Pegler, Mason, Parr, Marsden.
See 14.4, 22.35, 30.1, 40.41, 122.33.

TABLE 2 LIST OF COUNTERMARKS ETC.
ON EUROPEAN BRONZE COINS

KEY: Column A: Countermarked (C), or with printed paper affixed (P).
Column B: Incuse (I) or relief (R).
Column C: Obverse (O) or reverse (R).
Column D: Purpose: Advertisement ticket (A), pay or tool check (P), unofficial (U).
S: Author's article in Seaby's Coin & Medal Bulletin, December 1970, March and April, 1973.
SNC: Spink's Numismatic Circular.
† Not known or illegible.

NUMBER	LEGEND	A	B	C	D	COIN TYPE	SOURCE REFERENCE	APPROX. DATE
ENGLAND								
14 *14.201	**HAMPSHIRE** REMBRIDGE (curved)/YORK HOTEL/ SANDOWN (curved) Large plain letters	C	I	O	A	France: 5c 1854K	S2.1B (R. N. P. Hawkins)	1879–95
14.202	DEAR & SONS (curved)/GROCERS/ SHANKLIN I.W (curved) Medium plain letters	C	I	†	A	France: 5c 1854	S2.11B (Duffield 1543)	1878– 1906
		C	I	R	A	Italy: 10c 1867H	D. G. Vorley	
16 16 201	**HERTFORDSHIRE** THE/WINE LODGE/WARE Medium letters with serifs	C	I	O	A	Luxembourg: 10c 1855A	D. G. Vorley	1906–10
18 18.201	**KENT** SILVESTER/PILOT/GRAVESEND Medium plain letters	C	I	R	A	France: 5c 1876† (pierced 12 o'c)	D. G. Vorley	1899
22 *22.201	**LONDON** BAKER'S (curved)/CARTES DE VISITE/ 28 JUBILEE SᵀE (curved) 1st line medium letters with serifs 2nd line slightly smaller plain letters 3rd line medium plain letters	C	I	O	A	France: 10c 1865BB	S1.1C (J. G. Scott) Waters 9	1872–98
*22.202	BORWICK'S (curved)/BAKING/POWDER (curved) Large plain letters	C	I	O	A	France: 10c 1853† ,, 1853B ,, 1854BB ,, 1854K ,, 1854W ,, 1854† ,, 1855† ,, 1856A	D. G. Vorley J. G. Scott S1.2A (J. G. Scott) Dr. G. H. L. Bullmore J. G. Scott D. G. Vorley C. Brunel J. G. Scott	1880's
		C	I	R	A	,, 1856W	J. G. Scott	
		C	I	O	A	France: 5c 1855†	D. G. Vorley	
		C	I	O	A	France: 10c 1871A	S1.2E (Dr. G. H. L. Bullmore	
		C	I	O	A	Italy: 10c 1863	J. G. Scott	
		C	I	2XO 1XR	A	Luxembourg: 10c 1870	J. G. Scott	
*22.203	SEE BRAHAM'S (curved)/ADᵛᵀ/IN/ + POSTAL GUIDE + (curved) Very small plain letters	C	I	R	A	France: 10c 1855K France: 10c 1872A	S1.13A (S. Perry) S1.13E (J. G. Scott)	1882–5
22.204	BUTCHER/BRUSH MAKER/KING'S ✠ Medium plain letters	C	I	O	A	France: 10c 1865BB	D. G. Vorley	1877–97

NUMBER	LEGEND	A	B	C	D	COIN TYPE	SOURCE REFERENCE	APPROX. DATE
*22.205	.CLAPHAM. (curved)/OBSERVER (curved) Medium plain letters, forming a circle	C	I	O	A	France: 10c 1854D	S1.14A (J. G. Scott)	1880's
						,, 1855 MA monogr.	J. G. Scott	
		C	I	O	A	France: 5c 1856BB	C. Brunel	
		C	I	R	A	France: 10c 1865BB	D. G. Vorley	
		C	I	†	A	Italy: 5c 1867M	Lickey Coins, Oct. 1973 No. 2048	
*22 206	Colman's/Mustard Medium letters with large initial capitals	C	I	O	A	France: 10c 1872K	S1.3E (J. G. Scott)	1880's
*22.207	At the/'DAILY'/WORMWOOD ST./ BROAD ST./E.C. within circle Quality ※ Attention ※ Economy ※ Expedition ※ around circle All within circle, printed on yellow paper label	P	–	O	A	France: 10c 1853–65K	S1.17A or C (C. Brunel)	1880's
*22.208A	DIX/GAS/LAMP MAKER/CLERKENWELL (curved) 1st line large letters with serifs Remainder small plain letters Overall height of countermark approx. 12mm	C	I	O	A	France: 10c 1853B	S1.4A (J. G. Scott) (D. G. Vorley)	After 1883
						,, 1854K	D. G. Vorley	
						,, 1855A (anchor)	J. G. Scott	
						,, 1855B (anchor)	R. A. Merson	
						,, 1855BB	D. G. Vorley	
						,, 1855BB (anchor)	National Museum of Wales	
		C	I	O	A	France: 5c 1854A	S1.4B (C. Brunel)	
						,, 1854K	J. G. Scott	
						,, 1854W	D. G. Vorley	
						,, 1856K	British Museum	
		C	I	O	A	France: 10c 1862BB	S1.4C (J. G. Scott)	
B	Similar but 2nd, 3rd and 4th lines in medium plain letters	C	I	O	A	France: 10c 1854BB	D. G. Vorley	
						,, 1856A	C. Brunel	
						,, 1856K	J. G. Scott	
	Overall height of countermark 16–17mm	C	I	O	A	France: 10c 1863BB	British Museum	
						,, 1865BB	Dr. G. H. L. Bullmore cf. Waters 10	
22.209	DREW & SON'S (curved)/BISCUITS Medium plain letters	C	I	O	A	France: 10c 1853A	D. Lord S1.15A (P. Verret)	1880's
						,, 1854K		
*22 210A	EMPIRE (curved)/IMMENSE/SUCCESS/ THEATRE (curved) Small letters with serifs	C	I	O	A	France: 10c 1852A	S1.5(i)A (Dr. G. H. L. Bullmore)	1884
						,, 1853A	Seaby: Stock	
						,, 1853†	P. Verret	
						,, 1854A	J. G. Scott	
						,, 1854W	D. G. Vorley	
						,, 1855A (anchor)	R. A. Merson	
						,, 1855BB	Spink: Stock	
						,, 1855D (anchor)	J. G. Scott	
						,, 1855†	C. Brunel	
						,, 1856K	Nat. Museum of Wales	
						,, 1856W	P. R. Davies J. G. Scott	
						,, (1852-7)A	D. G. Vorley	
		C	I	O	A	France: 10c 1872†	S1.5(i)E (Duffield 1545) cf. Waters 14	

For key to column headings, please refer to page 123.

NUMBER	LEGEND	A	B	C	D	COIN TYPE	SOURCE REFERENCE	APPROX. DATE
* B	EMPIRE/THEATRE/IMMENSE/SUCCESS Large letters with serifs Two lines on obverse, two on reverse	C	I	O&R	A	France: 10c 1854A	S1.5(ii)A (J. G. Scott)	1884
						,, 1854K	R. A. Merson	
						,, 1854W	J. G. Scott	
						,, 1855B (anchor)	Nat. Museum of Wales	
						,, 1856B	Spink: Stock	
						,, 1856K	Whelan: Stock Sept. 1972	
						,, 1857MA monogr.	J. L. Herrick	
		C	I	O&R	A	,, 1857W France: 10c 1861K	C. Brunel S1.5(ii)C (J. G. Scott)	
						,, 1863K	D. G. Vorley	
		C	I	O&R	A	France: 10c 1872†	S1.5(ii)E (C. Brunel)	
		C	I	O&R	A	Italy 10c 1862M	D. G. Vorley	
						,, 1866T	J. G. Scott (ex Alec Clunes)	
		C	I	O&R	A	Luxembourg: 10c† Utrecht	S1.5(ii)M (R. N. P. Hawkins) cf. Waters 13	
*22.211	A. T. GIRDLER Small letters with serifs	C	I	O	A	France: 10c 1855B (Dog)	S1.16A (J. G. Scott)	1873–1921
22.212	G. B. GOODMAN/PATENTEE/LONDON Small (1st & 3rd lines) and medium (2nd line) plain letters	C	I	R	A or U	France: 10c 1853BB	D. G. Vorley	
*22.213	GOTHARDS/COALS Medium plain letters	C	I	O	A	France: 5c 1885A	S1.6 (C. Brunel) cf. Waters 11	1880's
*22.214	HERON'S/DOUGLAS/WHISKEY Large letters with serifs	C C C	I I I	R R R	A A A	France: 10c 1855D France: 10c 1865BB Italy: 10c 1866H	D. G. Vorley S1.7C (J. G. Scott) S1.7G (J. G. Scott) cf. Waters 12	1875–83
22.215	HYMAN/LONDON	C	I	†	A	France: 5c 1857†	S1.8B (Duffield 1544)	
*22.216	MAY'S/WASHING/POWDER Very large (1st line) and large (2nd & 3rd lines) plain letters	C	I	O	A	France: 10c 1853W ,, 1855BB (dog) ,, 1855W ,, 1856A	J. G. Scott S1.9A (J. G. Scott) J. H. Mulholland C. Brunel J. G. Scott	1880's
						,, 1856B ,, 1856K ,, 1856W ,, 1857W	Seaby: Stock J. G. Scott D. G. Vorley (2) J. G. Scott	
22.217	NYMAN/LONDON Very small letters with serifs	C	I	O	A or U	France: 10c 1853A	J. G. Scott	1877–94

For key to column headings, please refer to page 123.

NUMBER	LEGEND	A	B	C	D	COIN TYPE	SOURCE REFERENCE	APPROX. DATE
*22.218A	PEARS'/SOAP. Large plain letters Stop after SOAP.	C	I	O	A	France: 10c 1853A	S1.10(i)A (J. H. Mulholland)	1884-5
						,, 1853B	J. G. Scott	
						,, 1853BB	J. G. Scott (2)	
						,, 1853D	D. G. Vorley	
						,, 1853MA monogr.	J. G. Scott	
						,, 1853W	P. R. Davies	
						,, 1854A	J. G. Scott	
						,, 1854B	C. Brunel Dr. G. H. L. Bullmore J. G. Scott	
						,, 1854BB	J. G. Scott	
						,, 1854D	J. H. Mulholland	
						,, 1854MA monogr.	J. G. Scott	
						,, 1854W	A. G. Davies	
						,, 1854†	J. H. Mulholland P. Verret	
						,, 1855A	A. G. Davies	
						,, 1855B	C. Brunel	
						,, 1855BB	D. G. Vorley	
						,, 1855D (anchor)	J. G. Scott	
						,, 1855MA monogr.	D. G. Vorley	
						,, 1855W	P. Verret, D. G. Vorley	
						,, 1855W (anchor)	J. G. Scott (2)	
						,, 1856A	J. G. Scott (3)	
						,, 1856B	J. G. Scott (2) C. Brunel	
						,, 1856BB	P. R. Davies P. C. Wright	
						,, 1856D	A. G. Davies	
						,, 1856W	Nat. Museum of Wales J. H. Mulholland, D. Lord	
		C	I	R	A	France: 10c 1854BB	J. G. Scott	
		C	I	O&R	A	France: 10c 1854D	J. G. Scott	
		C	I	O	A	France: 5c 1855MA monogr.	S1.10(i)B (C. Brunel)	
		C	I	O	A	France: 10c 1861BB	S1.10(i)C (C. Brunel, D. G. Vorley)	
						,, 1861†	C. Brunel	
						,, 1862K	J. G. Scott	
						,, 1863BB	J. H. Mulholland	
						,, 1864K	Lee E. Harvey	
						,, 1864†	D. G. Vorley	
		C	I	O	A	France: 10c 1870A	'Coins & Medals' Dec. 1968	
						,, 1871A	R. A. Merson	
						,, 1872A	Spink: Stock J. G. Scott (2)	
						,, 1872K	J. H. Mulholland	
						,, 1872†	D. G. Vorley	
						,, 1873A	C. Brunel	
						,, 1873K	S1.10(i)E (J. G. Scott)	
						,, 1874†	P. Verret	
						,, 1880A	J. G. Scott	
						,, 1883A	C. Brunel	
*	Variety: (i)Much larger, thicker letters [See note below]	C	I	O	A	France: 10c 1856B	J. G. Scott	
	(ii) Ƨ instead of P	C	I	R	A	France: 10c 1854K	J. G. Scott	

For key to column headings, please refer to page 123.

NUMBER		LEGEND	A	B	C	D	COIN TYPE	SOURCE REFERENCE	APPROX. DATE
*	B	PEARS'/SOAP Large plain letters No stop after SOAP	C	I	O	A	France: 10c 1852A	J. G. Scott	1884–5
							,, 1853B	National Museum of Wales	
							,, 1853D	J. G. Scott	
							,, 1854A	J. G. Scott	
							,, 1854W	J. G. Scott	
							,, 1855B	C. Brunel	
							,, 1855BB	British Museum	
							,, 1855W	J. H. Mulholland	
							,, 1855W (dog)	Dr. I. H. Taylor	
							,, 1856D	S. Perry, J. G. Scott	
							,, 1856MA monogr.	British Museum C. Brunel J. G. Scott	
							,, 1856W	J. G. Scott D. G. Vorley	
			C	I	R	A	France: 10c 1855A (dog)	Jean M. White	
			C	I	O	A	France: 10c 1861A	D. G. Vorley (2)	
							,, 1861BB	D. G. Vorley	
							,, 1862A	S1.10(i)C (J. G. Scott)	
							,, 1863BB	J. G. Scott	
			C	I	O	A	France: 10c 1872†	D. G. Vorley	
		Variety: (i) Taller lettering [See note below]	C	I	O	A	France: 10c 1854BB	Nat. Museum of Wales	
		(ii) ꟼ instead of P	C	I	O	A	France: 5c 1853D	J. G. Scott	
*	C	PEARS'/SOAP Large letters with serifs No stop after SOAP	C	I	O	A	France: 10c 1853BB	S1.10(ii)A (J. G. Scott)	1884–5
							,, 1853MA monogr.	P. R. Davies	
							,, 1853W	D. G. Vorley	
							,, 1854A	Nat. Museum of Wales	
							,, 1854B	J. G. Scott	
							,, 1854BB	F. Banks R. A. Merson	
							,, 1854D	R. A. Merson	
							,, 1854K	'Coins & Medals' Dec. 1968 J. G. Scott	
							,, 1854MA monogr.	J. G. Scott (2)	
							,, 1854W	D. G. Vorley	
							,, 1855B (dog)	J. G. Scott	
							,, 1855B (anchor)	S. H. Dixon	
							,, 1855BB (anchor)	J. G. Scott	
							,, 1855D	Charles Dobie	
							,, 1855K	C. Brunel J. H. Mulholland	
							,, 1855W	C. Brunel	
							,, 1855W (dog)	J. G. Scott	
							,, 1856A	J. G. Scott (2)	
							,, 1856K	J. H. Mulholland	
							,, 1856MA monogr.	J. G. Scott	
			C	I	O	A	France: 5c 1854W	S1.10(ii)B (J. G. Scott)	
							,, 1855A (dog)	C. Hanson	
							,, 1855B (anchor)	J. G. Scott	
							,, 1855MA monogr.	D. G. Vorley	
							,, 1855W	D. G. Vorley	

For key to column headings, please refer to page 123.

NUMBER	LEGEND	A	B	C	D	COIN TYPE	SOURCE REFERENCE	APPROX. DATE
		C	I	O	A	France: 10c 1861A „ 1861K „ 1863BB „ 1864BB „ 1864†	J. G. Scott S1.10(ii)C (J. G. Scott) G. N. Robbins Nat. Museum of Wales D. G. Vorley	
		C	I	O	A	France: 5c 1861† „ 1862A	D. G. Vorley S1.10(ii)D (C. Brunel)	
		C	I	O	A	France: 10c 1872A „ 1873K „ 1878A „ 1884A	S1.10(ii)E (Ulster Museum) J. G. Scott J. G. Scott R. N. P. Hawkins	
		C	I	O	A	Italy: 10c 1866H	S1.10(ii)G (C. Brunel)	
*22.219A	RACING/OPINION/1ᴰ Large plain letters	C	I	O	A	France: 10c 1856W	S1.11(i)A (J. G. Scott)	1881
* B	RACING/ƆPINION/1ᴰ Large plain letters First O in OPINION is reversed C	C	I	O	A	France: 10c 1855B (anchor)	S1.11(ii)A (J. G. Scott)	1881
		C	I	O	A	France: 5c 1853W „ 1855B (dog) „ 1856A	S1.11(ii)B (J. G. Scott) J. G. Scott P. Withers: stock P. R. Davies	1881
*22.220	CIGARS/G. STONARD/EALING Large plain letters	C C	I I	O R	A A	France: 10c 1854BB Italy: 10c 1866N	S1.12A (J. G. Scott) S1.12G (J. G. Scott)	1888
*22.221	WADDEN'S (curved)/HAIR DYE | 2/6 | GOSWELL Rᴰ (curved) Medium plain letters	C	I	O	A	France: 5c 1854K	C. Hanson	1884–6
34 *34.201	SURREY HERBERTS (curved)/RUNEMEDE/ALES/ EGHAM (curved) Medium plain letters	C	I	R	A	France: 10c 1870A	C. Hanson	1878–82
*34.202	COX/CHEMIST/WOKING Large letters with serifs	C	I	O	A	France: 10c 1854K „ 1854W	S5.1A (J. G. Scott) C. Brunel	1887
35	SUSSEX							
35.201	HUGH BROˢ/AIR Sᵀ /BRIGHTON 1st and 2nd line medium plain letters 3rd line small letters with serifs	C	I	O	A	France: 10c 1855A (anchor)	D. G. Vorley	1886–9

For key to column headings, please refer to page 123.

Note: Pears' Soap countermarks
It is clear that, in order to produce these pieces quickly, a number of different punches were used. As a result there are several varieties of both plain and serif'd letter countermarks, the variables being the height of the letters in each word, the overall width of each word, and the distance between words as follows: (mm)

| TYPE | PEARS' | | SOAP | | Distance between base of PEARS' |
	Height	Width	Height	Width	and top of SOAP
A	4–5	18–18.5	3–4	12.5–13.5	3–4
A (i)	6	25	5	16	4.5
B	4	18–18.5	3.5–4	13–14	3–3.5
B (i)	5	18.5	4.5	14	3
C	3.5–4	18–19	3–3.5	12–14	2–2.5

NUMBER	LEGEND	A	B	C	D	COIN TYPE	SOURCE REFERENCE	APPROX. DATE
*35.202A	H. E. MITCHELL (curved)/EDGE TOOL/ GRINDING MILLS/4. NORTH ROAD/ BRIGHTON (curved) 1st and 5th lines small letters with serifs 2nd, 3rd and 4th lines small plain letters	C	I	O	A	France: 10c 1853A " 1854† " 1855K " 1855† " 1856K " 1856MA monogr.	J. G.Scott D. Lord Charles Dobie S3.1A (Brighton Museum) D. G. Vorley C. Brunel	1870–99
		C	I	O	A	France: 5c 1856†	S3.1(i)B (Brighton Museum)	
		C	I	O	A	France: 10c 1862A " 1865A	S3.1(i)C (R. N. P. Hawkins) Brighton Museum	
* B	MITCHELL/SAW MAKER/BRIGHTON Small letters with serifs	C	I	O	A	France: 10c 1853A " 1854A " 1854† " 1855A (dog) " 1855BB " 1855† (dog) " 1856K	S3.1(ii)A (J. G. Scott) Seaby:stock C. Brunel C. Brunel Brighton Museum J. G. Scott D. G. Vorley	1870–99
		C	I	O	A	France: 5c 1854B " 1855A (dog) " 1856W	D. G. Vorley Jean M. White S3.1(ii)B (Brighton Museum)	
		C	I	†	A	France: 5c 1864BB	Lickey Coins March 1973 No. 2820	
		C	I	O	A	Italy: 10c 1867OM	S3.1(ii)G (J. G. Scott)	
	Variety: (i) W.H.D Small plain letters on reverse	C	I	O	A	France: 5c (1853–5)W	R. N. P. Hawkins	
35.203	G. MOODY (curved)/GOOD BEDS/ 33 UPPER SAINT/JAMES ST (curved)/ BRIGHTON 1st and 4th lines large letters with serifs 2nd and 3rd lines large plain letters 5th line small plain letters	C	I	R	A	France: 10c 1856†	S3.2A (Brighton Museum) SNC June 1970 7548	after 1883
*35.204	TILLEY'S/COALS/BRIGHTON Medium plain letters	C	I	O	A	France: 10c 1854BB " 1856B " 1856K " 1856†	D. G. Vorley S3.3A (J. G. Scott) C. Brunel C. Brunel	after 1882
		C	I	R	A	France: 10c 1854† " 1854A " 1854K " 1856MA monogr.	Brighton Museum J. G. Scott J. G. Scott Seaby: Stock	
		C	I	O	A	France: 5c 1854K	S3.3B (Brighton Museum) D. G. Vorley	
		C	I	R	A	France: 10c 1862†	S3.3C (Brighton Museum)	
		C	I	O	A	France: 5c 1864†	S3.3D (Brighton Museum)	
		C	I	R	A	Italy: 5c 1861M	D. G. Vorley	
*35.205	CLIFT (curved)/PIANOS/EASTBOURNE (curved) Large plain letters	C	I	O	A	France: 10c 1853BB " 1855†	S3.11A (Dr. G. H. L. Bullmore) Brighton Museum	after 1877
		C	I	O	A	France: 10c 1862BE	D. G. Vorley	

For key to column headings, please refer to page 123.

NUMBER	LEGEND	A	B	C	D	COIN TYPE	SOURCE REFERENCE	APPROX. DATE
35.206	FEAIST'S/BREAD Large plain letters [Attributed to Hastings]	C	I	O	A	France: 10c 1853BB	S3.21A (J. L. Herrick)	
UNAT- TRIBUTED 122	NAMES							
*122.501	(Crown)/ARNOLD (curved) Large letters with serifs	C	I	R	A or U	France: 10c 1855BB	S4.1A (J. G. Scott)	
*122.505	ATKINSON Large letters with serifs	C	I	R	A or U	Italy: 10c 1867H	S4.2G (J. G. Scott)	
*122.520	STRAWBERRY (curved)/CABANE'S/ TOOTHPASTE (curved) Medium plain letters	C	I	O	A	France: 10c 1854D „ 1856A „ 1856D	J. G. Scott S4.6A (C. Hanson) D. G. Vorley	
122.527	HOME/BREWED/ALES/GARDEN/GATE Medium (1st, 2nd & 3rd lines) and slightly larger (4th & 5th lines) plain letters	C	I	R	A	France: 5c 1855W	D. G. Vorley	
122.530	J. HOOD Large plain letters	C	I	O	A or U	France: 5c 1861BB	A. G. Davies	
122.540	G. MARSH (twice) Medium letters with serifs	C	I	O	A or U	France: 10c 1872A	J. G. Scott	
*122.545	J. NICOLLE Large letters with serifs	C	I	O&R	A or U	France: 10c (1855-7)A	J. G. Scott	
*122.550	OSBORNE/PATENT Small plain letters	C	I	O	A or U	Italy: 10c 1867OM	S4.4G (J. G. Scott)	
122.552	PATENT/WIRE QUILTED/SOLES Medium plain letters	C	I	O	A or U	France: 10c 1857W	D. G. Vorley	
*122.560	A ROEULX. Medium letters with serifs	C	I	O&R	A, P or U	France: 10c 1861A	J. G. Scott	
*122.570	SAPOL Large letters with serifs	C	I	O	A or U	Italy: 5c 1862N	J. G. Scott	
122.573	THE SELBORNE (curved)/10703/PATENT CLIP (curved) Small plain letters	C	I	O	A or U	Portugal: 20 reis 1884	D. G. Vorley	
122.575	THOS SIMS Small letters with serifs	C	I	R	A or U	France: 10c 1872†	D. G. Vorley	
123	INITIALS AND/OR BRAND/TRADE MARKS							
*123.650	(Fleur de lis)/M Large plain letter	C	I	O	U(?)	France: 10c 1857A	S4.3A (J. G. Scott)	
*123.680	PB/A CO. Large plain letters	C	I	R	A, P or U	France: 10c 1854K	S4.5A (R. N. P. Hawkins)	
123.700	S.A.D C^O L Large plain letters	C	I	R	A, P or U	Italy: 10c 1866M	D. G. Vorley	
	Variety: (i) 2 incuse on reverse	C	I	O	A, P or U	Portugal: 20 Reis 1883	N. D. A. Andison	

For key to column headings, please refer to page 123.

NOTES ON THE ISSUERS OF PIECES
LISTED IN TABLE 2

ENGLAND

14 Hampshire
Sandown

14.201 REMBRIDGE

Henry Charles Rembridge, of York Hotel, Wilkes Road, appears in street directories 1879–95. By 1898, the hotel had changed hands. There is still a York Inn in York Road.

Shanklin

14.202 DEAR

Clement Dear was established in 1840 at Ventnor, and appears in the Ventnor directory of 1871. In 1878, there is an entry in the Shanklin directory for Dear and Thomas, Grocers, Bakers and Agents for W. & A. Gilbey's Wines and Spirits, High Street, Shanklin (and Ventnor). The entry continues until 1906.

16 Hertfordshire
Ware

16.201 THE WINE LODGE

Lionel Cox, The Wine Lodge, 102 High Street, Ware, is listed in the Post Office Directories for 1906, 1908 and 1910, but not in the 1902 and 1912 issues. This is about twenty years later than most of the countermarked pieces in this series.

18 Kent
Gravesend

18.201 SILVESTER

Directory entries are as follows:

1890 George Silvester, shopkeeper, 138 Parrock Street. Henry Augustus Silvester, master mariner, Springhead, Southfleet.

1899–1900 George Silvester, pilot, 3 Park Place, Milton Road.

1907 George Silvester, Rockleigh, Darnley Road.

In Kelly's Gravesend Directory for 1899–1900, Silvester is one of 117 pilots listed. Capt. A. Ronaldson is shown as 'ruler of pilots, Pilot Station, Terrace Pier, Royal Pier Road'.

22 London

22.201 BAKER

Gabriel Augustine Baker worked as a photographer at 28 Jubilee Street, E., off Mile End Road, from 1872 to 1898.

22.202 BORWICK

George Borwick, of Morven, Torquay, was born in 1806. He founded the famous baking powder firm, George Borwick & Sons Ltd., in 1842. In 1880, Borwick had premises at 24 Chiswell Street, E.C., and 134 Upper Thames Street, E.C. He died in 1889, leaving £259,000. His son, Robert Hudson Borwick (1845–1936), a director of the firm, was knighted in 1916 and raised to the peerage in 1922. Borwicks later became a subsidiary of H. J. Green and Co. Ltd. of Brighton, and are now owned by the Pillsbury Co., of Minneapolis, U.S.A.

22.203 BRAHAM

Frank Braham was the Postmaster at Tabernacle Square Post Office, E.C., and made machinery for perforating the initials of firms and others on all kinds of revenue and postage stamps as a safeguard against theft. Such perforations also served as advertisements. Cost was 1d. per sheet. Perforating of postage stamps to prevent theft was recommended by the Post Office in the Post Office Guide and is still practised to a limited extent. Braham's advertisement appears 1882–5; similar advertisements, slightly earlier, appear for Francis A. Hancock of Wood Street Post Office and Steam Printing Works, Moor Lane E.C.

In the London street directories, Frank Braham appears as follows: perforating press maker, 51 Hoxton Square, N. (1882), 51 Hoxton Square and 8 Tabernacle Square, E.C. (1883–4), 51 Hoxton Square and 142 Tabernacle Street, E.C. (1885); perforating press maker and perforator (initial) of postage stamps, 51 Hoxton Square, N. and 93 Tabernacle Street (1886–90) (91 Tabernacle Street in 1891); 91 Tabernacle Street and 47 Rivington Street, E.C. (1892–4), 91 Tabernacle Street and 11 Rivington Street (1895–8), 91 Tabernacle Street and works, Rivington Street (1899–1901).

22.204 BUTCHER

Charles Butcher, brushmaker, is listed in the London directories at 116 Kings Cross Road, W.C. from 1877 to 1885, and at 179 in the same road from 1886 to 1897. The 1876 issue shows Lane Osmond, brushmaker at 116 Kings Cross Road, while that for 1898 lists Bushnell & Sons, corndealers, at 179 and 181 Kings Cross Road.

22.205 CLAPHAM OBSERVER

The Clapham Observer, Tooting and Balham Times was founded in 1868 by William Baldwin and is still in progress. Issue No. 50 appeared on 1 May 1869. A weekly paper, the Clapham Observer was printed and published by Baldwin from his office at 152 Manor Street, Clapham, S.W. from 1868 until at least 1889. By 1893 his premises were at 65 High Street, Clapham, and were still there when William Baldwin died about 1903. For an account of Baldwin see 'William Baldwin, late editor and proprietor of the Clapham Observer', by Rev. Arthur Mursell (1903). The paper was still in the family in 1922 – Edmund Baldwin, printer and publisher, 83 High Street, Clapham – but was sold shortly afterwards. It is now owned by South London News Group Ltd. – a member of the United Newspapers Limited Group – News Buildings, Crystal Palace, S.E.19.

It is not possible to be precise about the date of the countermark, which seems more likely to have been used in a promotional campaign in the 1880's rather than to mark the paper's debut in 1868.

22.206 COLMAN

Jeremiah Colman, aged 27, left a flour mill in Bawburgh in 1804 and set up on his own in a windmill at Norwich. He moved to Stoke Mill, 4 miles south of Norwich, in 1814, when he started producing mustard. Jeremiah had no sons of his own, but eleven nephews (who played together as a cricket team). One of these, James Colman, he took into partnership, and two others were sent to London when an office was opened there about 1824. Carrow Mill, Norwich, was opened in 1857. Colmans became a limited company in 1896, and, because of their joint interest in starch, formed a trading merger with Reckitt & Sons of Hull in 1938. A new company, Reckitt & Colman Holdings Ltd. was formed in 1954. The London office, the probable source of this countermark, was at various premises over the years: the first London directory entry for J. & J. Colman is at Symons Wharf, Tooley Street in 1824, moving to Southwark Square, Borough by 1827–8, then to 8 Cloak Lane 1829–32. From 1835 to 1848, Colmans were at 1 Dowgate Hill, and in 1851 at 9 College Hill. Between 1855 and 1866 they were at 26 Cannon Street, and 2 New Corn Exchange, Mark Lane, and at 108 Cannon Street and 2 New Corn Exchange 1867–93. In 1892–3, the firm was also at 7 Old Ford Road, and from 1894 to 1903 at 108 Cannon Street only. Between 1907 and 1946, Colmans were at 108 Cannon Street and 76/77 Wapping Wall; from 1947 to date certain staff have been at the Reckitt Head Office at 40 Bedford Square.

22.207 'DAILY'

Although the 'Daily' probably belongs to the early 1880's, no firm or building identifiable as such has been found in the London directories 1870–1910. It is possible that the trader occupied premises in Wormwood Street for only a short time. This use of a paper label on a European bronze coin is unusual.

22.208 DIX

Street directories show the following entries: Richard Dix, tinplate worker, 93 White Lion Street, Pentonville, N., and 128 St. John Street Road, E.C. (1875), George Thomas Dix, tinplate worker at latter address (1880), George Richard Dix, Gas Lamp Manufacturer, 124, later 124 and 180, later 350 and 412 St. John Street, E.C. (1883–1909).

22.209 DREW

The first entry I have found for this firm in the London street directories is for William George Drew, wholesale biscuit maker, 166, 167, 201 Shadwell High Street, E. (1855–6). Subsequent entries are: licensed victuallers' biscuit baker 166 and 167 Shadwell High Street (1857–9), 165, 166 and 167 Shadwell High Street (1861). By 1870 the firm had become Drew and Son, and in 1880, still at the same address, were described as manufacturers of biscuits &c. for licensed victuallers, hotel proprietors and refreshment contractors. From the early eighties, the entry is for 'biscuit manufacturers', and it is probably from this period that the countermark dates.

By 1891, Drew and Son, biscuit manufacturers, were at 181 Queen Victoria Street, E.C. and 165–7 Shadwell High Street, and Meredith and Son, biscuit manufacturers, were at 69 Christian Street, Commercial Road East, E. In 1892 the entry is for the now familiar Meredith and Drew, 181 Queen Victoria Street and 165–7 Shadwell High Street. Later addresses are 165–7 Shadwell High Street (1900), 158–9, 163–70 Shadwell High Street (1907–10), 158–170 Shadwell High Street (1915), 158–178 (1921), 158–174 (1930), The Highway, E.1. (1949–53), Murray House 43/46 Beach Street, Barbican, E.C.2 (1967–71). The firm now form part of United Biscuits (Holdings) Ltd. of Edinburgh and have no knowledge or record of the countermark.

22.210 EMPIRE THEATRE

The Empire Theatre, Leicester Square, was opened on 17 April 1884 by Nichols (Daniel Nicholas Thévenon), proprietor of the Café Royal. The theatre was built on the site of Savile House, home of two Princes of Wales in the eighteenth century, later rebuilt as an exhibition gallery, Eldorado Music Hall, and Café Chantant. This second building had been destroyed by fire on 28 February 1865. The Empire was not a success as a theatre, and reopened as a Music Hall in December 1887. It became a theatre again in 1918, and was demolished and rebuilt as a cinema in 1927. The countermark was probably made in 1884 to launch the new theatre, whose first manager was H. J. Hitchins.

22.211 GIRDLER

Since this countermark consists of a name only – i.e. no trade or town, it is difficult to be completely certain about its attribution. However, the circumstantial evidence is fairly convincing: of 89 Girdlers in the current GPO telephone directories, 15 are in the London postal area, 11 in north east Surrey, 8 in Guildford, 18 in Reading, and 5 elsewhere in the London area – the remaining 49 U.K. directories producing only 32 entries. London is thus a strong probability.

The London street directories for the period 1870–1920 show a maximum of 6 and minimum of 2 Girdlers in any one year. There is only one A. T. Girdler, as follows: Arthur Thomas Girdler, Chemist, 16 Deptford Broadway, S.E. (1873–7), Dentist, at same address (1878–80); Dentist, 59 Deptford High Street, S.E. (1881–3); Dentist, 469 New Cross Road, S.E. (1884–99), 439 New Cross Road (1900–21).

It is not possible to assign the countermark to any particular period of Girdler's activity, which covers nearly 50 years.

The following entries appear in the alphabetical list of patentees 1617–1852:

George Goodman, No. 8640, 24 September 1840, manufacture of mourning and other dress pins.

George Goodman junior, No. 14099, 29 April 1852, ornamenting japanned metal and papier-mache wares.

No G. B. Goodman has been traced in the London directories 1875–1910.

22.213 GOTHARD

Charles Gothard and Co., Coal and Coke Merchants, 1864–1911, started at the Midland Railway Coal Depot, Agar Town, N.W. Later, they established a depot at Amelia Street, Walworth, S.E. By 1900, the firm had several branches, but their head office remained at St Pancras. There is still a coal merchant of the same name active: J. Gothard and Sons, of Chesterfield.

22.214 HERON

Heron and Sons were wine merchants at 40 Mark Lane, E.C. (1861), 37 Ely Place, E.C. (1864), and 158 New Bond Street, W. (1865–72). William Charles Heron was a wine merchant at 90 Queens Road, Bayswater, W. (1875–83). This countermark cannot thus be later than 1883.

22.215 HYMAN

Attribution of this countermark is uncertain. A probability is David Hyman, wholesale rag merchants, founded 1840, in 1880 at Iron Wharf, Thornhill Bridge, 135 Caledonian Road, N., or his sons Israel and John Hyman, rag and metal merchants, Britannia Street, Kings Cross Road, W.C., and Wicklow Street, Kings Cross Road, W.C., established in 1861. The firm, who are still in business at 9 Brewery Road, N.7., have not been able to confirm this. See also 22.217 below.

22.216 MAY

Henry May appears in street directories as follows: Washing Powder Maker, 4 Princes Street, Fitzroy Square, W. (1867), 6 Goodwin Street, Barnsbury, N. (1869), Bride Street, Barnsbury, N. (1870), and at the same address, described as a Washing Crystal Manufacturer, from 1878. By 1885, he had moved to Fakenham Street, Metropolitan Cattle Market, N., and the following year was at Goodinge Road, N. By 1890, the entry is Henry May & Co., washing powder, extract of soap and starch glaze manufacturers, and milk and cream preservative makers, at the same address. In 1901 and 1904 the firm was at 14 Fakenham Street, Goodinge Road, Cattle Market, N., and were described as extract of soap and starch glaze manufacturers, starch and match importers. The entry ceases by 1907.

22.217 NYMAN

Directory entries are as follows:

1875–6 Henry Neyman (sic) & Sons, surgical instrument makers, 6 Kirby Street.

1877–81 Henry Nyman & Sons, surgical instrument maker, 6 Kirby Street, Hatton Garden, E.C.

1883–92 No entries.

1893–4 Henry Nyman, surgical instrument maker, 33 Charles Street, Hatton Garden.

The countermark, which could be unofficial, thus dates from c. 1877–94.

It is interesting that Duffield 1544 reads HYMAN/LONDON – see 22.215 above. Both Hyman and Nyman are Jewish names. This may be coincidence, or just possibly a mistaken reading by Duffield's contributor.

22.218 PEARS

Andrew Pears, a Cornishman, started making soap in 1789. His transparent soap dates from 1807. He moved from a barber's shop in Gerrard Street to a factory at 55 Wells Street, off Oxford Street, and in 1835 took his grandson Francis into the business. From 1838, Francis carried on alone. In 1862, the Lanadron Works were opened at Isleworth. About the same time, Thomas J. Barratt married Francis Pears' eldest daughter, having met her at 'an Academy of Dancing and Deportment in the West End'; a salesman with ingenious ideas on advertising, he became, in 1865, London Manager for Pears, and joint proprietor, with Francis, and Andrew, Francis' son. The firm's big expansion came after Francis' retirement in 1875, when Barratt was free to develop his advertising ideas. He thought up puzzles, optical illusions, sky advertisements, and other devices to focus public attention on Pears' Soap, as well as normal press and poster advertising, at home and abroad, particularly in the United States. Some famous examples are: 'He won't be happy till he gets it' (baby in the bath); 'Good morning! Have you used Pears' Soap?'; Harry Furniss' drawing of a tramp in 'Punch', April 1884: 'Two years ago I used your soap, since when I have used no other'. He bought Millais' painting 'Bubbles' for £2,200 to mount an advertising campaign. In this climate, one of intense competition among soap firms following the repeal of the excise tax on soap in 1853, Barratt saw the advertising possibilities of the foreign bronze coins circulating freely in the 1880's: it was not illegal to deface coins except those of the realm. He imported 250,000 such pieces and countermarked them 'PEARS' SOAP', putting them into circulation by means of a host of distributors, who sold them to London bus-conductors at fourteen for a shilling. The countermarking must have been done between 1884, the latest countermarked coin I know of, and 22 May 1885, when a question was asked in the Commons about these pieces. The great majority of coins countermarked in this way were French. However, one example on an Italian 10c is known – see Table 2 above. The countermark also occurs on both sides of a Luxembourg 10c of 1870 – see J. & S. Whitmore list, March 1973, no. 2823, though it is not known which variety is involved. In 1865 Pears' had a depot at 91 Great Russell Street, spreading, by 1885, to number 38 opposite, before a new palatial headquarters and art gallery were built in the late 1880's at 71, 73 and 75 New Oxford Street.

A. & F. Pears became a Limited Liability Company in 1892, with Barratt as Chairman and Managing Director. In 1914, Pears became a subsidiary of Lever Brothers Ltd., and in 1929 was one of the founding companies of Unilever.

22.219 RACING OPINION

Racing Opinion was a newspaper published from 26 April 1881 to 10 March 1922. In 1886 the paper's office was at 26 Bouverie Street, E.C. The advertisement tickets may have been a promotional stunt when the paper started.

22.220 STONARD

George Stonard, tobacconist, lived at 3 Pembridge Cottages, Blandford Road, Ealing, London W., and appears in street directories for 1888 and 1889. In 1894–6, the entry at this address is for Mrs. Stonard, no tobacconist mentioned. The countermark was probably made about 1888.

22.221 WADDEN

The following entries appear in the London directories:

John Wadden, hairdresser, 13 Chester Place, Old Kent Road, S.E. (1862–3), 285 Old Kent Road, S.E. (1864–79).

Thomas Wadden, umbrella manufacturer, 357 Goswell Road (1871–8), 349 Goswell Road (1879–87).

Thomas Wadden, hairdresser, 294 Upper Street N. (1884–6), 172 Upper Street N. (1887–1901).

It is probable that Thomas Wadden produced hair dye at his umbrella works in Goswell Road when launching his own, or a relative's, hairdressing business c. 1884–6. He does not appear under 'Hair Dyers' in the Trades directories. This countermark also occurs on English coins – see 22.66 in Table 1 above.

34 Surrey
Egham
34.201 HERBERT

A. Herbert, West Egham, appears in Arnold's West Surrey Court Guide (1876). Abraham Herbert, brewer, High Street, is listed in the 1878 directory, while in 1882 the entry is for Abraham Herbert & Co., brewers, at the same address, Herbert does not appear in the 1887, 1890 or 1895 directories.

Woking
34.202 COX

Frank Cox, chemist, is listed under Woking in Kelly's Surrey Directory for 1887, but no address is shown. He does not appear in the issues for 1878, 1882, 1890 or 1891. Arthur Cox, storekeeper and general dealer was at Ripley, Woking station in 1882 – an address previously occupied (1878) by a chemist, Thomas Garlike. It is possible that Arthur Cox was related to Frank Cox.

35 Sussex
Brighton
35.201 HUGH BROS.

Page's 1886 Directory lists Hugh Bros., plumbers' supply stores, at 6 Air Street, Brighton. In Pike's 1888 Directory the firm is listed also at 54 St. James's Street, while in Kelly's 1889 issue the entry is for Hugh Brothers, hardware dealers, at 6 Air Street only. The firm does not appear in the 1885 directory, and in 1892, W. J. Macdonald, music seller, is shown at 6 Air Street, and there is a gap between numbers 52 and 59 St. James's Street.

35.202 MITCHELL

H. E. Mitchell, saw and tool maker, was at 12 High Street, Brighton, in 1870. He appears in street directories as H. E. Mitchell at 4 North Road, between 1872 and 1893, and as H. E. Mitchell & Co. Ltd., at the same address from 1894 to 1899. The premises are now occupied by J. B. Bennett & Co. Ltd., tool merchants.

35.203 MOODY

G. Moody was in business at 33 Upper Saint James Street from 1883 to 1898. Before this, he was at 71 Edward Street, and, after 1898, at 125 Gloucester Road.

35.204 TILLEY

Tilley Bros., corn, flour, seed and coal merchants, appear in street directories from 1882 to 1923 as local merchants, at 11 and 161–2 Lewes Road, 133 London Road, 4 Ann Street and 104 Church Street – the addresses vary slightly through the years. The entry is for seedsmen in 1924 at 117 Western Road, and in 1925 at The Granaries, Davigdor Road. In 1885 the entry is for W. Tilley & Son, coal merchants and carriers, 11 and 159a Lewes Road.

Eastbourne
35.205 CLIFT

M. B. Clift ran a music warehouse at 4 Gildredge Road. The firm appears in street directories from 1877 to 1940.

Hastings
35.206 FEAIST

John Feaist first appears in the Hastings directories in 1865 as owner of a general shop at Robertson House, Halton. By 1867, the entry is John Feaist, baker, 21 Castle Road. In 1884, the address is given as Rock Bread factory, Castle Road. The firm branched out, and by 1929 had 3 premises besides offices and factory at 32, 34 and 36 Castle Hill Road; in 1939, there were 6 premises. Between 1940 and 1964, the firm appears as Henry King and Feaist. By 1966 some of the premises were occupied by Duncan Foster Ltd., and others were sold. In the late nineteenth century, Feaist's were frequent and enterprising advertisers in the local directories.

122 Unattributed Names

122.501 ARNOLD

This issuer is unknown, but it is probable that the piece was issued by a firm, rather than a 'punch-happy' workman using the firm's trade mark unofficially.

122.505 ATKINSON

It is probable that this piece was issued by J. and E. Atkinson Ltd., perfumers, established 1799, formerly of 24 Old Bond Street, London, and now at 45 Portman Square. The firm have not been able to confirm this, but they were prolific advertisers in the 1880's, and closely associated with Pears; it is very likely that Atkinson followed the Pears practice.

122.520 CABANE

It is surprising and disappointing that it has not, thus far, proved possible to attribute this interesting countermark. At least one piece was obtained 'with a large quantity of worn Victorian pennies from a scrap metal dealer' in the London area. (C. Hanson).

However, there is no trace of any Cabane or C. A. Bane in the London street directories 1856–1915, London suburban directories 1880–1908, or in the catalogues of the Army and Navy Stores 1880–1908.

122.527 GARDEN GATE HOME BREWED ALES

It seems likely that this is the name of a brand, or of a public house brewing its own beer, rather than that of a firm. No firm of this name could be traced in the Stock Exchange Year Book for 1880, 1885 or 1890, 'The noted breweries of Great Britain and Ireland', by Alfred Barnard (1889–91), or Dring and Fage's 'Almanac and Brewers' Directory' for 1873–8. No public house called the 'Garden Gate' is listed in the London or Suburban directories 1888/1900.

122.530 HOOD

Among the few possible issuers listed in the London directories are the following:

1877 James Hood, bootmaker, 356 Commercial Road East, E.

1877, 1880 James Hood, coffee rooms, 8 Tottenham Street, Tottenham Court Road, W.

1880 (Suburban, South) John Hood, tobacconist, Widmore, Bromley.

122.540 MARSH

This is a common surname, and it has not proved possible to identify the issuer.

122.545 NICOLLE

This could be a French countermark, although it has an English provenance, which is the only justification for its inclusion here. The surname occurs occasionally in the London directories, and is very common in Paris. It is also found in the Channel Islands, where possible issuers might be:

St. Helier (Jersey):

1852 Joshua Nicolle & Co., merchants and ship-owners, 13 Commercial Buildings, Pier.

1884, 1896 Nicolle & Co., coal merchants, Commercial Buildings, 22 Pier.

1874 Joshua Nicolle, builder and contractor, importer of Portland and Roman cement, drain pipes, chimney pots etc., 11 Hue Street.

1884, 1896, 1898, 1903, 1907, 1911 Joshua Nicolle, builder, bricklayer, plasterer, 11 Hue Street.

St. Peter Port (Guernsey):

1852 John Nicolle, confectioner, 25 Mill Street.

1903 John Nicolle, shopkeeper, New Paris Road (until at least 1911).

122.550 OSBORNE

A possible issuer is Osborne and Co., brass, bronze, copper, gun metal and german silver founders, white metal, phosphor bronze, manganese bronze and solder manufacturers and merchants, 11 Great Garden Street, Whitechapel, London E. They were prolific advertisers in the 1880's and held at least one patent. Another candidate might be E. M. Osborne, Patent medicine vendor, of 26 Thavie's Inn, Holborn E.C. (1880), and 65 Hatton Garden E.C. (1885).

122.552 PATENT WIRE QUILTED SOLES

The issuer of this countermark has not been traced in the London directories.

122.560 ROEULX

This piece has an English provenance, otherwise one would dismiss it as part of the French series of countermarks on French and other European bronze coins. The name does not appear in London, Guernsey, Jersey or Brighton directories 1880–1930, or in current directories for Paris, Brussels, Antwerp or Amsterdam. The case for including the piece here must remain, for the moment, non-proven.

122.570 SAPOL

This is assumed to be a trade or brand mark, but cannot be attributed to a particular trader. Like the piece above, this could be part of the French series of countermarks. The Army & Navy Stores catalogue for 1907 has an entry under 'Soaps (plain)' for 'Sapolio (for cleaning), 2 tablets 0/6½d., doz. tablets 3/-, case 17/9'. 'SAPOLIO' was the brand name in 1887 of household cleaning soap manufactured by Enoch Morgan's Sons' Co., 31 Snow Hill, London E.C.1, frequent advertisers in the 'Illustrated London News'.

122.573 SELBORNE PATENT CLIP

The manufacturer of the Selborne Patent Clip has not been traced in Birmingham, London or Sheffield directories for the late nineteenth century.

122.575 SIMS

No town is shown, so it is difficult to attribute this countermark. In the London directories, possible issuers are:

Thomas Sims, baker, 191 Devon's Road, Bromley, E. (1880–7).

Thomas Sims, masonic jeweller, 75 Little Britain, E.C. (1895–1900).

123 Unattributed Marks and Initials

123.650 M

This could be unofficial use of a firm's trade mark or, possibly, a gambling machine token.

123.680 PBA CO.

A possible issuer is P. B. Advertizing Co. Ltd.' 130 Fleet Street, London E.C. (1913), and 42 Old Broad Street (1914).

Another possibility is a maker of automatic machines: R. N. P. Hawkins reports some more recent brass and white metal discs – gambling machine tokens with 'P.B.A. Co.' and large figure 1 or 2, each side. In this case, the piece is more likely to be a gambling machine token than an advertisement ticket – these are usually of earlier date.

123.700 S.A.D. CO L

A possible issuer might be S. A. Daniell Ltd., listed in the London directories as follows:

1884 S. A. Daniell (Birmingham), stocks, dies, taps, ratchet, braces, etc., also copying, embossing and general presses, first prizes Sydney and Melbourne, James Gibb & Co., agents, 23 St. Mary Axe E.C.

1888, 1892 as 1884, but London address shown as 99 Fenchurch Street.

1894 no London address shown – Lion Works, Birmingham only.

1895 as 1894 with additional entry for Samuel Allen Daniell, toolmaker, 10 Wormwood Street.

1896 S. A. Daniell, copying presses etc., Lion Works, Birmingham and 10 Wormwood Street.

1897, 1898 S. A. Daniell Ltd., as above.

1902 S. A. Daniell Ltd., copying presses, screw stocks and dies, taps, screwing machines, engineers tools etc., Lion Works, Birmingham and 10 Camomile Street.

1922 S. A. Daniell Ltd., ironfounders, engineers' tool, screwing machine and copying press makers, 10 Camomile Street, E.C.3 and Edward Street, Parade, Birmingham.

Pears' Soap

"MATCHLESS FOR THE COMPLEXION."

Advertisement for Pears' Soap (1882).
See 22.218 in Table 2.

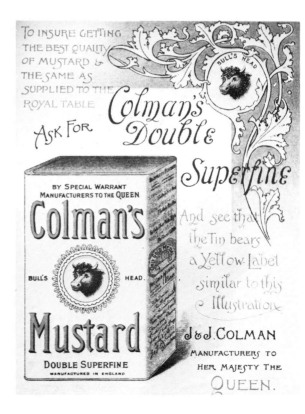

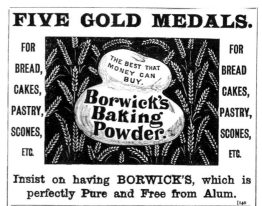

Table 2 issuers : Braham, Colman, Feaist, Borwick, Empire Theatre.
See 22.203, 22.206, 35.206, 22.202, 22.210.

TABLE 3: LIST OF ALUMINIUM ADVERTISEMENT RINGS APPLIED TO BRITISH BRONZE COINS

KEY   Column A   Diameter of ring (mm).   SCMB Seaby's Coin & Medal Bulletin.
            Column B   Coin central (C) or offset (O).   †   Not known or illegible.
            Column C   Obverse (O) or reverse (R).

NUMBER	LEGEND	A	B	C	COIN TYPE	SOURCE REFERENCE	APPROX. DATE
22 22.301	LONDON *ALEXANDRA THEATRE* (curved)/ ALADDIN (curved) Large letters with serifs *KEEP ME AND YOU NEVER GO BROKE Large letters with serifs forming a circle	37.5	C	R O	Farthing 1909	Alec Clunes (SCMB Aug. 1972 TP515) Birmingham Museum	1909–17
22.302	.GOOD LUCK FROM A. J. BRANCH. (curved)/ "FORESTERS" (curved)/PERRY VALE, FOREST HILL (curved) 1st line (except FROM) medium plain letters, remainder small, plain letters KEEP ME AND YOU WILL NEVER BE BROKE within horseshoe 1st, 2nd, 7th and 8th words large letters with serifs 3rd, 4th, 5th and 6th words medium plain letters J.R.G. [= J. R. Gaunt & Son] below	38	C	R O	Farthing 1937	J. G. Scott	late 1930's
*22.303	VISIT CROCKERS DRAPERY EXHIBITION (curved)/ FRIDAY ST /EC. 1st line large letters with serifs 2nd and 3rd lines medium plain letters within scroll panel below KEEP ME AND NEVER GO BROKE Large letters with serifs within horseshoe Shamrock below	38	C	O R	Farthing 1908	A. Watson Token Corres. Soc. Bull. 5	1930's
*22.304	.HOOPER STRUVE'S. (curved)/MINERAL WATERS (curved) 1st line large letters with serifs 2nd line medium plain letters KEEP ME AND YOU WILL NEVER BE BROKE within horseshoe 1st, 2nd, 7th and 8th words large letters with serifs 3rd, 4th, 5th and 6th words medium plain letters J.R.G. below	38	C	R O 	Farthing 1919 Farthing 1927 Farthing 1934 Farthing 1939 Farthing †	J. G. Scott C. Brunel Birmingham Museum Canada Dry Ltd. Dr. G. H. L. Bullmore J. G. Scott R. N. P. Hawkins	1936–9
*22.305	.LOCARNO DANCE HALL. (curved)/ STREATHAM HILL, S.W.2 (curved) 1st line medium letters with serifs 2nd line medium plain letters KEEP ME AND YOU WILL NEVER BE BROKE within horseshoe 1st, 2nd, 7th and 8th words large letters with serifs 3rd, 4th, 5th and 6th words medium plain letters J.R.G. below	36	C	R O	Farthing 1922	Jean M. White	after 1930

NUMBER	LEGEND	A	B	C	COIN TYPE	SOURCE REFERENCE	APPROX. DATE
*22.306A	TO ENSURE PROSPERITY IN BUSINESS USE THE (curved)/SMITH (curved)/PREMIER TYPEWRITER (curved)/GRAND PRIX—PARIS 1900. (curved)/14 GRACECHURCH ST. LONDON (curved) Small plain letters except SMITH (medium) W & CO. below GOOD (shamrock, horseshoe, wishbone) LUCK Small plain letters	32	O	R O	Farthing 1902	J. L. Short Token Corres. Soc. Bull. 5	1902–7
B	SMITH REMINGTON PREMIER TYPEWRITER GOOD (shamrock, horseshoe, wishbone) LUCK	†	†	O R	Farthing 1901	SCMB Jan. 1971 TP484	1921–40
35 35.301	SUSSEX (SHERRY'S AMUSEMENT ARCADE BRIGHTON) [Legend uncertain]	†	†	†	Farthing †	S. Perry Token Corres. Soc. Bull. 6	after 1920
120 *120.301	JERSEY .GOOD LUCK FROM CHELSEA HOTEL GLOUCESTER ST. (curved)/JERSEY (curved) 1st line medium plain letters with large initial letters 2nd line large plain letters KEEP ME AND YOU WILL NEVER BE BROKE within horseshoe 1st, 2nd, 7th and 8th words large letters with serifs 3rd, 4th, 5th and 6th words medium plain letters [Attributed to St. Helier]	38	C	R&O O&R R&O	Farthing 1938 Farthing 1950 Farthing 1954	R. N. P. Hawkins Token Corres. Soc. Bull. 6 Dr. G. H. L. Bullmore C. Brunel J. G. Scott	mid 1950's

For key to column headings, please refer to page 139.

NOTES ON THE ISSUERS OF PIECES LISTED IN TABLE 3

ENGLAND

22 London

22.301 ALEXANDRA THEATRE

The Alexandra Theatre was located on the west side of Stoke Newington Road between the junctions with Wiesbaden Road and Princess May Road, and was opened on 29 December 1897. The first proprietor was F. W. Purcell. In 1906 it was temporarily renamed the Palace Theatre of Varieties, with H. T. Dudley Bennett as director (1907), followed by Walter de Frece (1908–9). From 1909 to October 1920, the Alexandra Theatre was under the control of Oswald Stoll, of Stoll Theatres. It was a cinema for a short time about 1917. One of the first productions was Cinderella (Christmas 1909). It is probable that this aluminium ring dates from this period. Directories show that the managers at this time were as follows: G. E. Williams (c. 1911–16), John Morland (1917), James A. Tupman (1918), and George Arthur Morley (1919–20).

The next period of management lasted from October 1920 to January 1931. The programme included a yearly pantomime directed by Florrie Ford. Gracie Fields made her debut at the Alexandra in 1922 in 'Mr. Tower of London'. Managers were John Binmore (1921) and Arthur W. Pearce (also lessee, 1922–31).

In 1931 the building became a cinema, also catering for stage shows, circuses and revues. It was leased by M. Dent (1932–3). It closed for a time about 1935, reopening in 1939 with a Tom Walls season. After closure during the war, the theatre had reopened for musicals by the end of 1944. Jack Solomons had a boxing booth there for a time. Throughout this period (c. 1934–46) the theatre was owned by Alexandra Theatre (lessees) Ltd. In 1947 a Yiddish Theatre company took over (P. W. Spellman). At the end of 1948 the building was condemned but patched up. It came under new management in February 1950 but was finally closed in October the same year.

22.302 BRANCH

Alfred James Branch is listed in the Post Office London Directories at the 'Mason Arms', 31 Union Road, Newington Causeway, S.E.1 1912–34, where he followed James Walter Gomm. From 1935 to 1951 he is shown at the 'Forester's Tavern', 53 Perry Vale, Forest Hill, S.E.23, where he took over from Joseph Mudge. Mrs. N. A. M. Branch appears at the same address 1952–8. The aluminium ring was made by J. R. Gaunt & Son, and probably dates from the late 1930's.

22.303 CROCKER

This long-established City firm appears in the London directories as follows:

1812 Crocker W. & J., printers and warehousemen, 86 Watling Street.

1823 Crocker & Jardine, as above.

1839 Crocker, Jonathan & Son, warehousemen, 51 Friday Street and 85 Watling Street.

1841 Crocker, Jonathan & Son, warehousemen and calico printers, 85 and 86 Watling Street, and 51 Friday Street, Cheapside.

1851 Crocker, Jonathan & Albert, 85–86 Watling Street, 51–53 Friday Street.

1862 as above but 84–87 Watling Street, 50–54 Friday Street.

1872 Crocker, Sons & Turner, 81–87 Watling Street, 50–54 Friday Street.

1880, 1890, Crocker, Sons & Co., as above.

1900, 1910 Crocker, Sons & Co. Ltd., wholesale Manchester warehousemen, calico printers etc. 50–54 Friday Street.

1920 Crockers Ltd., warehousemen as above.

1930–9 Crockers Ltd., exporters and warehousemen, as above.

1940–1 Hayes, Candy & Crockers Ltd., warehousemen and export merchants as above.

1942–5 Hayes, Candy & Crockers Ltd. (of 54 Friday Street) Haycand Mill, Waterside, Macclesfield – presumably the London premises had been bombed.

1946–70 as above, variously described, including 'merchant converters' (1960), at 86 Marylebone High Street.

1971 as above, piece goods wholesalers, 15/17 Gt. Marlborough Street, W.1.

The aluminium ring probably dates from the 1930's.

22.304 HOOPER STRUVE

Directory entries are as follows:

1839 William Hooper, chemist, 24 Russell Street, Covent Garden.

1846 William Hooper, operating and dispensing chemist, 7 Pall Mall East.

1852–72 William Hooper, chemist and manufacturer of Brighton seltzer and other waters, 7 Pall Mall East and 55 Grosvenor Street, W. Laboratory: Mitcham.

1882 Hooper & Co., mineral water warehouse, 19 Phoenix Street, Soho, W.C.

1895 Hooper & Co., chemists &c., 7 Pall Mall East, Whitcomb Street, 55 Grosvenor Street, 11 Whitfield Street.

1896–1920 Hooper, Struve & Co. Ltd., chemists, 7 Pall Mall East, mineral water manufactory, 11 Whitfield Street.

1923 Hooper Struve & Co. Ltd., table water manufacturers and chemists, 7 Pall Mall East; factory and offices 11 Whitfield Street, chemists 26 Davies Street.

1925 Hooper Struve & Co. Ltd., table water manufacturers, 26 Charlotte Street, W.1., 11 Whitfield Street, 26 Davies Street.

1930–52 Hooper Struve & Co. Ltd., table water manufacturers, 26 Charlotte Street, W.1, 11 Whitfield Street.

1953–66 as above but address 112 St. Paul's Road, N.1.

The firm also appear in Brighton directories c. 1905–58 as Hooper Struve & Co. Ltd., mineral water manufacturers, Park Hill.

These aluminium rings formed part of an advertising campaign which started in 1936 and ran continuously until the outbreak of war. Several thousand pieces of this sort were produced (by J. R. Gaunt & Son of Birmingham and London) and distributed by the Hooper Struve sales force to members of the trade. The firm are now owned by a subsidiary of Bass Charringtons Ltd. – Canada Dry (UK) Ltd., of Ealing, to whom I am indebted for this information.

22.305 LOCARNO DANCE HALL

Directories show that this dance hall, at 158 Streatham Hill Road, S.W.2, was owned by Locarno (London) Ltd. 1931–59. From 1960 Mecca Ltd., Dance Hall, appears at the same address, while the current (1972) entry is for Locarno Dance Hall (Mecca Ltd.).

The aluminium ring was produced by J. R. Gaunt & Son of Birmingham and London, and probably, like the Hooper Struve pieces, dates from the late 1930's.

22.306 SMITH PREMIER TYPEWRITERS
SMITH REMINGTON TYPEWRITERS

Some doubt must remain attached to piece no. 22.306B – it could be merely an inaccurate description of no. 22.306A.

Remington's were associated with Smith Premier 1921–40 before taking them over, but have no knowledge or record of no. 22.306B, though they have full information on the specially struck advertisement tickets of 1895–7. (See R. N. P. Hawkins in Spink's Numismatic Circular, February 1963, p. 25 and Seaby's Coin and Medal Bulletin, March 1968, p. 94.)

The firms appear in directories as follows:

Smith Premier Typewriter Co.

1900–07 The Smith Premier Typewriter Co., 14 Gracechurch Street, E.C.

1908–30 The Smith Premier Typewriter Co. Ltd., Smith Premier House, 6 and 7 Queen Street, Cheapside, E.C.4.

1933–4 as above at 4 St. Pauls Churchyard, E.C.4.

1935–9 also at 102–106 Tabernacle Street, E.C.2.

1940 4 St. Pauls Churchyard and Commonwealth House, 1–19 New Oxford Street, W.C.1.

1944–47 see below.

Remington Typewriters

1900 Remington Standard Typewriter (Wyckoff, Seamans & Benedict, manufacturers and proprietors) 100 Gracechurch Street, E.C.

1905 Remington Typewriter Co., 100 Gracechurch Street, E.C. and 263 Oxford Street, W.

1910-25 Remington Typewriter Co. Ltd., 100 Gracechurch Street, and 4 St. Pauls Churchyard.

1930 address shown as 100 Gracechurch Street and 83 Regent Street.

1933 100 Gracechurch Street only.

1934 100 Gracechurch Street, works and accounts depts., 102-104 Tabernacle Street, E.C.2.

1935 100 Gracechurch Street, 102, 104, 106 Tabernacle Street, E.C.2 and Shell Mex House, Victoria Embankment W.C.2.

1937-9 100 Gracechurch Street.

1940 Commonwealth House 1-19 New Oxford Street, W.C.1.

1944-7 Remington Rand Ltd. (Remington & Smith Premier Typewriters) 1-19 New Oxford Street, W.C.1.

1948-60 Remington Rand Ltd., as above.

1961 to date (1972) Remington Rand Division, Sperry Rand Ltd., 65 Holborn Viaduct, E.C.1.

The makers of these pieces (W. & Co.) are assumed to be Warrington & Co., of Garrick Street, London, who were certainly active during the period of issue – i.e. c. 1902-7 (see R. N. P. Hawkins in Seaby's Coin and Medal Bulletin, July 1968, p. 250).

35 Sussex
Brighton

35.301 (SHERRY'S AMUSEMENT ARCADE)

Directories show the following entries:

1920 Sherry's Dancing Academy, Middle Street and 78 West Street.

1925-40 Sherry's Palais de Danse, same address.

1947-51 Sherry's Dance Hall (Sherry's (Brighton) Ltd.), 78 West Street and Middle Street.

1954-66 Ritz Roller Rink (Sherry's (Brighton) Ltd.), 78 West Street.

1966 Sherry's Bar, public house, 7 Middle Street.

1972 Sherry's Dixieland Show Bar, 7A Middle Street.

In the absence of more specific information on the legend of the piece, it is not possible to say more than it must have been issued after about 1920 at or in connection with Sherry's Palais de Danse.

120 Jersey
St. Helier

120.301 CHELSEA HOTEL

Directory entries are as follows:

1915 William Henry Ford, boarding house, 11 Gloucester Street.

1923 Mrs. Lilian Curry, boarding house, 11 Gloucester Street.

1927-36 Chelsea Private Hotel (Mrs. Quenault, proprietress), 11 Gloucester Street.

1939 Chelsea Private Hotel, 11 Gloucester Street Manager, R. Binnington.

1949 Chelsea Hotel, Gloucester Street, Manager, R. Binnington.

1959 as above, Manager B. T. Binnington.

1969 Chelsea Private Hotel, 11 Gloucester Street,

The advertisement rings probably date from the mid 1950's and must thus rank among the most recent of the English series of these pieces, although there are some later American examples. They are very similar to the Hooper Struve pieces, and may have been produced by J. R. Gaunt & Son, although the specimens I have seen do not bear the initials J.R.G.

INDEX TO TABLES 1, 2, AND 3

FOR ALPHABETICAL LISTS OF OTHER COUNTERMARKED NAMES AND INITIALS SEE APPENDICES I AND 2

ISSUER OR MARK	TABLE	NO.
A, and crown	I	123.10
Abbey, Cutler, Bedford	I	1.1A
Abbey, Gunmaker, Bedford	I	1.1B
Abbey, Gunmaker, St. Ives	I	17.1
Adams, W. and tiger	I	122.5
Adelphi Cotton Work	I	77.1
AI and fleur de lis	I	123.15
AL and fleur de lis	I	123.20
Alexandra Theatre	3	22.301
Allen D, Moneymore	I	91.1
(Allen, Edgar & Co., Sheffield)	I	40.8
Alloa Colliery	I	62.1
Alnwick	I	26.1
AMJ	I	123.190
(anchor)	I	40.18
(anchor) and (pipe)	I	123.270H
Anderson, Robt., London	I	22.1
(Andover)	I	14.1
Andrew, W, Kemnay	I	54.1
Applebeck	I	122.240
Armagh, Co.	I	88.1
Arnold, and crown	2	122.501
Athlone	I	116.1
Atkin & Sons, Birmingham	I	36.1
Atkinson	2	122.505
B	I	116.2
B, and crown	I	123.30
Bagshaw, S. and crowned E or I	I	122.10
Baker's Cartes de Visite	2	22.201
Balfron Fruit	I	83.1
Balfron Vict. Society	I	83.2
Ball, F.	I	122.12
Ballindalloch Cotton Work	I	83.4
Barker	I	122.40
Barker, cutler, Chichester	I	35.3
Barnes, Canterbury	I	18.1
Barron Patent	I	22.2
Bartleet & Sons	I	22.3
(Bath)	I	31.3
Baxter, C, IS	I	122.15
BC, and crown	I	123.35
Bedford, G, and cock	I	122.20
Bell, John, bookseller, Quay	I	26.2
Bennett, W, Hackney	I	22.4
Bennett & Brookes, Ipswich	I	33.4
Best, W. B., Poole	I	10.3
Best, and lion	I	122.25
Best's, and crown	I	40.9
B.E.W. Co.	I	123.36

ISSUER OR MARK	TABLE	NO.
BH, and corkscrew	I	123.37
BICH: O: W: A: GALAS: and IS	I	122.225
Bigger, Dublin	I	98.1
Bingham, James, Newchurch St., Sheffield	I	40.10
Blake, R., Chichester	I	35.4
Blinkhorn, J., Holbeach	I	21.3
Blunt, London	I	22.5
Bolsover	I	8.1
Bond, London	I	22.6
Borwick's Baking Powder	2	22.202
Boscombe Spa Hotel	I	40.28
Bowker, S.	I	122.28
Bown, Wm., 308 Summer Lane, Birmingham	I	36.2
Bowyer, Ludlow	I	30.3
Bradford Workhouse	I	40.2
Bradley Cast Steel, Bridgwater Hill	I	122.29
Bradshaw, ticket porter, Custom House	I	22.7
Braham	2	22.203
Bramall	I	40.11
Branch, A. J., "Foresters", Forest Hill	3	22.302
Bridges, Joshua, Worcester	I	39.3
Brigden	I	122.30
Briscoe, W., & Son	I	40.12
Broadfoot, W. H.	I	122.32
Broadhurst	I	35.2
Brookshaw, Oundle	I	25.1
Broomhead	I	40.13
Brothers & Co., cast steel	I	122.33
Bryan, M., M.B.	I	122.35
B.S.A. & M. Co.	I	36.3
Buckland, Thos., chimney sweeper, Oxford	I	28.3
Buckley, J. J., Cork	I	96.1
Budden, Jas., Chichester	I	35.5
Bunyar, Maidstone	I	18.4
Burch, waterman, Pauls Wharf	I	22.8
Bury W.house	I	33.1
Butchart, A.	I	55.1
Butcher, brushmaker, King's Cross	2	22.204
BW	I	22.281
C, and broad arrow	I	18.3
Cabane's Strawberry Toothpaste	2	122.520
Cadman, L.	I	40.14
Campbell & Co.	I	122.40
Cark Cotton Works	I	19.1
Carr, J. & R.	I	40.15
Carthew, Bister	I	28.1
Carty	I	86.1
Cast Steel	I	122.42, 122.80

ISSUER OR MARK	TABLE	NO.
Fletcher, R., warranted cast steel	1	122.85
Fletcher, Tho., Liverpool	1	19.2
(fleur de lis and crescent)	1	123.88
(fleur de lis, crescent, and figure 9)	1	123.87
Forrest	1	122.88
(Founders Company)	1	22.17
Fox, James	1	40.16
Fruit, Balfron	1	83.1
G, and crown	1	123.90
GAN, and crown	1	123.92
Garden Gate, home brewed ales	2	122.527
GB, and T. Corns, Bear Town	1	9.1
G.C	1	22.40A
Geale & Macbride, Dublin	1	98.5
Geall, Dorchester	1	10.1
Gee, C. & Son	1	122.90
Geoghegan, Jn., Kilbeggan	1	116.2
G. E Sca, 1793	1	123.94
GG, Manchester	1	19.7
Gibson, S., inventor	1	122.95
Gibson	1	122.72
Gillham, R., Norwich	1	24.3
Gilpin, V. dges Mills	1	122.100
Girdler, A. T.	2	22.211
G.L., Dumbarton	1	64.1
Goodman, G. B., patentee, London	2	22.212
Gothard's Coals	2	22.213
Gover, I., Crediton	1	9.2
G & P	1	123.96
G.R., and crown	1	123.105
G.R., and crown	1	123.100
G.R., crown, and broad arrow	1	123.98
GR and crown, Thirteen & Sixpence	1	123.330
GR and crown, Tower	1	22.63
Graham, Exeter	1	9.3
Greaves, I., London	1	22.18
Green, J., Bristol	1	13.2
Green, Culver St., Colchester	1	12.1
(griffin passant), and J.DD	1	123.108
(griffin's head)	1	123.110
Griffin, M. (Dublin)	1	98.6
Griffin (Norwich)	1	24.4
GR, Keighley	1	40.3B
Groves, Sheffield	1	40.21
GS and plume	1	123.112
G.W.R., loco. & carr. dept., Windsor	1	2.2
Hall, B., Bristol	1	13.3
Hall, John Parker, London	1	22.19
Hall, W., cast steel	1	40.22
Hambridge	1	31.5
Hamilton, A., 106 Fenchurch St.	1	22.20

ISSUER OR MARK	TABLE	NO.
Hampson, Mary & Son, Manchester	1	19.8
Hampstead Rd.	1	122.103
Handcut	1	122.105
Hanworth	1	35.5
Harding, Ludlow	1	30.4
Hargreaves, W., Settle	1	40.7
Harrison, York City	1	40.48
Hatchetts Hotel, Piccadilly	1	22.21
Haughton, A.	1	92.1
Hayes, dentist, Mays Buildings	1	22.22
Hayward, Tewksbury	1	13.6
HB, Buxton	1	8.2
H.B	1	122.175
H & C	1	22.25
H,D, and Maltese Cross	1	123.115
Hems & Son, London	1	22.23
Henson, J., Tidd Gote	1	21.5
Herberts Runemede Ales, Egham	2	34.201
Heron's Douglas Whiskey	2	22.214
Higgins, Worcester	1	39.4
Hildick, and crown	1	122.107
Hill, hatmaker, Scarbro	1	40.6
Hobson, T.	1	122.108
(Hoddesdon Brewery)	1	16.1
Hollymount, Malvernbury	1	108.1
Holy	1	40.34
Home Brewed Ales, Garden Gate	2	122.527
Hood, J.	2	122.530
Hooper Struve's Mineral Waters	3	22.304
Hooper's Arms, Bath	1	31.1
Hooper, John, Sevenoaks	1	18.6
Horn, W. I., & Co., Sheffield	1	40.23
(Horse rampant), and WC	1	123.405
H. Street	1	122.200
H.T	1	122.100
Hugh Bros., Air St., Brighton	2	35.201
Hundley, London	1	22.24
Hunt, W., and crown	1	18.7
Huntsman, B.	1	40.24
Huxley & Ching	1	22.25
Hyman, London	2	22.215
I, and crown	1	123.119,
		123.120
I, and pipe	1	123.270G
IB, and crown	1	123.122
I.B, and pipe	1	123.270E
I.C, Guildford	1	34.3
ID	1	122.74
ID, and crown	1	123.123
II, and crown	1	123.125
Ingall	1	122.5

ISSUER OR MARK	TABLE	NO.
In Hoc Signo Vinces, and standing angel	I	122.110
Inniskilling, and VI.D	I	90.1
IP	I	22.28A
IP, Poole	I	10.2
Ireland, Jas., Belfast	I	98.1
I.S	I	123.128
IS, and crown	I	123.130
I.S., and crown	I	123.132
ISR, and crown	I	123.135
I, SR, crown, and 3	I	123.136
IW, and crown	I	123.140
I.Y, and crown	I	123.142
J.A.R, London	I	22.47
JB	I	123.144
JB, and crown	I	123.145
JB, 1811	I	123.146
JB, J.B, and Brigden	I	122.30
JC, and crown	I	123.150
J.C.C Patent 5535	I	123.155
J.DD, and griffin passant	I	123.108
JDV	I	123.160
J.F.R, and horseshoe	I	123.165
J.H 1s	I	123.170
JJ., Cork	I	96.1C
JK, crown, and bucket	I	123.175
JM, Keighley	I	40.3C
Johnson, 101 Great Titchfield St.	I	22.26
Joyce, cutler	I	48.1
JR	I	123.190
J:R 2D	I	123.180
J.S, Cramond	I	72.1
J.S, and crown	I	123.182
J.T	I	123.183,
	I	123.190
(Justice holding scales)	I	123.185
JW & CO	I	123.188
JW	I	123.190
K, and crown	I	123.195
Kavanagh, W., & Son, Dublin	I	98.7
Keighley	I	40.3
Kelly, T.	I	122.120
Keogh, E, 75 Summer Hill	I	98.8
(Keyhole)	I	122.33
Kilburn	I	22.27
L, and crown	I	123.200
Lanark Cotton Mills	I	71.2
Lane, W., Gloucester	I	13.5
Lateman, Sileby	I	20.1
Lee, A., patent	I	122.125
Leighton, John, Newcastle	I	26.4

ISSUER OR MARK	TABLE	NO.
Leith Mills	I	72.4
Levison & Sherman	I	40.41
(lion)	I	123.395
(lion) and Best	I	122.25
Lip Salve	I	122.127
Lisbon, and Portuguese Cross	I	40.43
Lloyd & Co., London	I	22.29
Lloyd's Penny Sunday Times	I	22.28
Lloyd's Weekly Newspaper	I	22.28
LN, and crown	I	123.205
Locarno Dance Hall	3	22.305
Lochmaben	I	63.1
Lock, A., draper & grocer, Curry Rivell	I	31.4
Lock, J., Swansea	I	48.2
London	I	22.30
London, London	I	22.31
London, and crown	I	22.32
Looker	I	22.33
Lovett, James, Derby	I	8.3
Lr. House Tavern, Church	I	19.3
£.s.d within diamond	I	40.8
Lund, W., 24 Fleet St.	I	22.34
Lynn	I	24.2
M	I	123.210
M, and fleur de lis	2	123.650
(male head)	I	123.395
Malvernbury, Hollymount	I	108.1
Manchester, and GG	I	19.7
(man in moon)	I	123.208
Manning, T. & Co., Sheffield	I	40.25
Marjoram, R., Hadleigh	I	33.3
(Marsden & Beeten, Sheffield)	I	40.26
Marsh, G.	2	122.540
Mason, W., Patent, London	I	22.35
Massey, Abergavenny	I	50.1
Massey, Kidderminster	I	39.1
Massey, Ludlow	I	30.5
May's Washing Powder	2	22.216
MB	I	123.211
McClure, Allex, Bellylonaghan	I	89.1
McLaren, Dun., Lochearn	I	77.3
McLean, J., Paisley	I	78.1
McMahon, cutler, 28 Pill Lane	I	98.9
McNee, Robert, Fintry	I	83.6
Menlough Castle, 6D	I	99.1
Merit Sheffield	I	40.41
M.G	I	123.212
M.I script	I	123.215
Mildwater	I	22.36
Mil(ne), Io, attorney, Manchester	I	19.9
Minifie, R, and crown	I	122.132
Mitchell, H. E., Brighton	2	35.202A

ISSUER OR MARK	TABLE	NO.
Mitchell, I., H. Down	I	109.1
Mitchell, J., and fox	I	122.135
Mitchell, sawmaker, Brighton	2	35.202B
Moilliet & Gem, warranted	I	40.27
Mollet, W.	I	120.1
Moncrieffe, Fs.	I	22.37
Moody, G., Brighton	2	35.203
Moody, Reading	I	2.1
Moore, Tho., Beverley	I	40.1
Morrall's Needles, A.	I	22.38
Morris, John, Paisley	I	78.2
Mortimer, H. W.	I	22.39
Morton, William, Sheffield	I	40.28
M.S.D., Weedon, and broad arrow	I	25.4
Murray, Cavan	I	94.1
(mushroom-like device), and crown	I	123.225
N, and crown	I	123.230
NB, and crown	I	123.232
Neale, G., Gilsbro	I	25.2
Nevill's Patent Lentils	I	22.40
Newbould & Co.	I	40.29
Nicolle, J.	2	122.545
Noakes & Holborow, London	I	22.41
Nyman, London	2	22.217
(oak tree)	I	22.42
OK	I	123.238
Olympic Brace, The	I	122.150
Ord, J.	I	40.2
Osborn	I	122.152
Osborne, Dublin	I	98.10
Osborne Patent	2	122.550
Overend, John, Portadown	I	88.2
O.W Warranted, Dec. 1790 32.G	I	123.240A
O.W Warranted, Dec. 1790 28	I	123.240B
(owl-like device)	I	123.245
P, and crown	I	123.250,
		123.255,
		123.380
Pacey, A., Alford	I	21.1
Parker, B., Bury	I	33.2
Parker or Parkes, W., Swan	I	122.155
Parkerson, I.	I	24.5
Parr, Tho.	I	30.1
Partridge, Richard, Cranfield	I	1.2
Patent	I	122.160
Patent & Axle 1246	I	122.158
Patent wire quilted soles	2	122.552
Pay's Hotel, W.	I	22.43
Payne, cutler, Aylesbury	I	3.1
PBA Co.	2	123.680

ISSUER OR MARK	TABLE	NO.
Peace Bros., Sheffield	I	40.30
Peace, S., & Co.	I	40.31
Pears' Soap	2	22.218
Pegler, Southampton	I	14.4
Pekin, and open crown	I	40.26
Pendleton	I	19.11
Penny Newsman	I	22.44
Percy St., London	I	22.45
Perry, H.	I	122.162
Perth	I	77.4
Philadelphia, Dm.	I	11.2
Philipps, chemist, Plaistow	I	12.2
Phoenix, 1881	I	40.5
Pidcock, London	I	22.46
(pipe with curved stem, and heart)	I	13.5
(pipe)	I	123.270
(pipes)	I	123.270
(pipe) and (anchor)	I	123.270H
(pipe) and I	I	123.270G
(pipe) and I.B	I	123.270E
Pitkin, Henry A., Uxbridge	I	23.1
(plume)	I	123.275
(plume), and GS	I	123.112
PO, and broad arrow	I	14.2
(Portsmouth Dockyard)	I	14.2
Potter, Amos, Hairdresser, Exon	I	9.4
Potts & Co.	I	122.165
Pridie, cutler, engraver, Windsor	I	2.3
Prince, York	I	40.49
PS	I	122.72
Qrn Loaf	I	122.170
quit	I	40.13
RA, Poole	I	10.2
Racing Opinion, ID	2	22.219
Rackham's (?) improved patent	I	122.171
(railway locomotive)	I	123.280
Ravanage (?) Foundry	I	122.173
Rawfor, Thos., Derby	I	8.4
R. Co	I	123.285
RD 459419	I	123.290
Read, R., Gilsbro	I	25.2
Rembridge, York Hotel, Sandown	2	14.201
Renfrew Vt. Society	I	78.4
(Revel, Abraham)	I	40.32
Rexton, T., K: H	I	40.4
R & G	I	123.291
Richards, T. and hand	I	122.175
Richardson, W.	I	21.2
Richards, Wood & Co., London	I	22.48
Rickman, Peterboro'	I	25.3
RN and fleur de lis	I	123.293

ISSUER OR MARK	TABLE	NO.
Tisanold, Rye	1	35.6
Todd, J. M., Moseley	1	39.2
Tome	1	8.1B
Tower, and GR, crown	1	22.63
Townsend, cutler, Hereford	1	15.3
Tregellas	1	6.1
Trim	1	109.2
TS, and crown	1	123.353, 123.354
T.S, and crown	1	123.355
Tully, Maryport St.	1	122.210
Tupling, W., Grimsby	1	21.2
Turner, T., & Co., Sheffield	1	40.44
T.W., and crown	1	123.360
Twigg Bros. & Co.	1	40.41
Tyas	1	40.13
Tyzack, W. A., & Co., Stella Works	1	40.42
Underwood	1	22.64
V, and crown	1	123.380, 123.385
Verinder	1	22.65
Vickers, and SS	1	98.11
VR, and crowned harp, 249	1	123.390
VR, T, and crown	1	123.392
W, and broad arrow	1	22.72
W, and crown	1	123.397, 123.398
W, a male head, a lion	1	123.395
Wadden's Hair Dye 2/6, Goswell Rd.	1	22.66,
	2	22.221
Waldron Green, and lion	1	35.7
Walker	1	122.72
Warburton, Manchester	1	19.10
(Warburton, Thomas)	1	40.43
(War Cry)	1	22.67
Ward, P.	1	122.225
Ward & Payne, Sheffield	1	40.44
Warners, London	1	22.68
Warranted	1	122.230
Warranted Cast Steel	1	122.235
Warranted Patent upon an improved principle	1	122.237
Watling, wines & spirits, Leominster	1	15.5
Watson, Os.	1	122.238
WB, and crown	1	123.400
WC, and crown	1	123.403
WC, and horse rampant	1	123.405
WF script	1	123.408
WG, London	1	22.69
WH, and crown	1	123.255
W.H.D	2	35.202B
(wheatsheaf and sickle)	1	123.410
Whitehouse, C., 61 Gt. Tower St.	1	22.70
W.H.J, 6D	1	123.412
Whyte, Thos., Culcreuch Mill	1	83.5
WII	1	123.414
Wilk, John, Applebeck	1	122.240
Wilkes, Job, Darlaston	1	32.1
Wilkins, Henry, pinmaker, Coventry	1	36.4
Wilkison, Edinburgh	1	72.2
Williams	1	122.40
Williams, T., 14 Smithfield	1	22.71
Wine Lodge, The, Ware	2	16.201
W & JS. S	1	123.415
WM, and I	1	123.417
Wm Son, J.	1	122.245
Woodward	1	122.76
Woodward, S., Lichfield	1	32.3
(Woolwich Arsenal or Dockyard)	1	22.72
Wragg, H., Sheffield	1	40.45
Wright, H., Fazeley	1	32.2
W&T. E	1	123.419
WW, and crown	1	123.420
WW, Keighley	1	40.3D
X, and crown	1	123.430
X, Dentist, Chester	1	5.1
Yate	1	122.250
Yates, W.	1	40.46
Yelloley's Pottery, Ouseburn	1	26.5
Yetts, Jo, Edinb.	1	72.3
Young, J & T, Ayr	1	57.1
Zuill, Balfron	1	83.3

KEY

Column A	Incuse (I) or relief (R).
Column B	Obverse (O) or reverse (R).
Column C	See Note.
SCMB	Seaby's Coin & Medal Bulletin.
SNC	Spink's Numismatic Circular.
†	Not known or illegible.

COUNTERMARK	A	B	COIN TYPE	SOURCE REF.	C
P ABBOTT Small letters with serifs	I	O	Penny 1797	C. Brunel	
J. ABEY ZZ	I I	O R	Penny George III	Andrews 1005	
E. ADAMS	I	†	Halfpenny 1799	Batty 3940A	
ADAMS Medium letters with serifs	I	R	Penny 1797	A. G. Davies	
J. ADKIN	I	O&R	Twopence 1797	Andrews 1006	
S. ALLEN	I	O	Halfpenny 1806	Batty 3948a	
ALLINSON Medium letters with serifs	I	R	Isle of Man Halfpenny 1830 (Davis 14–15)	C. Brunel	
T. ARCHER Medium letters with scrifs	I	O	Penny 1886	J. G. Scott	
T. ARNOLD Medium letters with serifs (and W.P/E. HARRIS)	I	O	Irish Halfpenny 1805	J. G. Scott	
B...r in notched oval	R	†	Irish Halfpenny George III	SNC Apr. 1897	
BAGSHOW Medium plain letters in rectangular indent	R	2XO 1XR	Halfpenny William III	SCMB Jan. 1971 TP321	
BAILEY	I	R	Halfpenny George II	Batty 3957 I	
E. BAILY Large letters with serifs	I	O	Irish Halfpenny 1805	J. G. Scott	
BALDWIN Large letters with serifs	I	O	Halfpenny 1806/7	C. Brunel	
J. BARTON/(flower)	I	†	Barnsley Penny (Davis 75–8)	SNC Nov./Dec. 1920	1
S. BATES (3 times)	I	†	Penny 1797	Gibbs 159	

COUNTERMARK	A	B	COIN TYPE	SOURCE REF.	C
BAYN	I	O	Cronebane Halfpenny 1789 (D & H 43 etc.)	Batty 3826A	
BEASLEY in rectangle	†	†	Dublin Farthing (D & H 394)	Szauer 43	
BEASLEY and SS Medium letters with serifs	I	†	Farthing †	Szauer 44a	
C. BELL	I	O	Irish Halfpenny 1805	Batty 3970B	
S. BELLFIT AND LIBERTY LIBERTY	I I	O R	Halfpenny George II	Batty 3971	
F. BENNETT Large letters with serifs	I	O	Penny 1797	J. G. Scott	
W. B..NETT twice forming a cross	I	O	Penny 1797	Charles Dobie	
W. BENNETT and R. SWA. BRIC forming a cross Medium letters with serifs	I	R			
G. BEVAN Medium letters with serifs	I	O	Penny 1863	Seaby	
I BIELBY Medium letters with serifs	I	O	Penny 1826	Seaby	
J. BIGGIN Medium letters with serifs	I	O	Penny 1863	J. G. Scott	
BIRCH twice Small letters with serifs	I	O	Farthing 1806	C. Brunel	
Jˢ BIRD	I	†	Irish Halfpenny George II	Batty 3972	2
BLAKE	I	O&R	Halfpenny 1806	Batty 3973A	
BLANC Medium letters with serifs	I	O	Evasion Halfpenny 177? Jacobus Omancs	C. Martin	

COUNTERMARK	A	B	COIN TYPE	SOURCE REF.	C
J. BLYTON	I	O&R	Twopence 1797	Chitty 71	
J. BLYTHON	I	†	Twopence 1797	Andrews 1018	
	I	O&R	Twopence 1797	Andrews 1019	
H. BOYLE and (flower spray)	I	O&R	Halfpenny 1807	Szauer 169	
W. BRAITHWAITE	I	O&R	Halfpenny 1799	Batty 3976C	3
R. BREEZE	I	O&R	Irish Halfpenny 1822	Batty 3976D	4
J. BRIGS Medium letters with serifs	I	2XO 1XR	Penny 1797	J. G. Scott	
A. BROAD Medium letters with serifs	I	IXO 2XR	Penny 1797	J. G. Scott	
BROWN Small letters with serifs	I	O	Halfpenny 1772	J. G. Scott	
T. BROWN Medium letters with serifs	I	O	Halfpenny 177?	J. G. Scott	
W. BROWN	I	†	Penny 1797	Andrews 1023	
J. BUFTON Medium letters with serifs in serrated rectangular indent	R	O&R	Halfpenny 1799	C. Brunel	
I. BULLEY Medium letters with serifs	I	O	Penny 1806/7	Seaby	
(B)URNETT Medium plain letters	I	O	Irish Halfpenny 1723	J. G. Scott	
BURTON Small letters with serifs	I	O	Penny 1806/7	C. Brunel	5
E. BURY Large letters with serifs (Large spoked wheel device)	I	R	Penny 1806/7	Charles Dobie	
	I	O			
A. BUSH in rectangle Large letters with serifs	R	O&R	Penny 1806/7	C. Brunel	
J. BUTCHER	I	†	Penny 1841	Andrews 1028	
CANIF (and IM obv.) Small letters with serifs	I	O&R	Penny 1797	J. G. Scott	6
Cape Medium letters	I	R	Penny 1797	J. G. Scott	
J. CARTER Medium letters with serifs	I	O&R	Penny 1862	J. G. Scott	
CHANT Small letters with serifs	I	7XO 7XR	Irish Penny 1805	J. G. Scott	7
CHILDS	I	R	Halfpenny 1807	Batty 4001C	
T. CLARK Large letters with serifs	I	R	Penny 1797	Seaby	
ADAM (curved)/CLARKE (curved) Medium letters with serifs	I	R	Carmarthen Halfpenny (D & H 5)	C. Brunel	
J. CLEMMET (Spray of flowers) above, (double spray) below	I	†	Isle of Man Penny	Andrews 1044	
J. CODY Medium letters with serifs	I	O	Irish Halfpenny 1774–82	Szauer 80	
P. COFFEY Large letters with serifs	I	R	Halfpenny 1770–5	Szauer 76	
W. COLE Medium letters with serifs	I	O	Halfpenny 1775	J. G. Scott	
J. COOPER Medium letters with serifs	I	O	Penny 1806/7	Birmingham Museum	
S. COT Very large letters with serifs (and TBC obv.)	I	R	Penny 1797	J. G. Scott	
C. H. COX Medium plain letters	I	R	Halfpenny 1862	C. Brunel	
M. COX	I	O&R	Halfpenny 1746	Batty 4047C	8
W. COX/C Large letters with serifs	I	O	Penny 1797	J. G. Scott	
S. CRAIG	I	†	Irish Halfpenny 1822	Duffield 1496	
CRIB	I	12XO	Halfpenny 1745	Batty 4048	9
I. CRISTY In oblong depression	R	†	Halfpenny George II	Duffield 1527	
CROXON	I	†	Twopence 1797	Andrews 1057	
CROXSON	I	†	Penny George III	Andrews 1058	

For key to column headings and abbreviations, please refer to page 150.

COUNTERMARK	A	B	COIN TYPE	SOURCE REF.	C	COUNTERMARK	A	B	COIN TYPE	SOURCE REF.	C
DALRY (also LLOYD WEEKLY, &c)	I sic	† O & R	Penny George III	Andrews 1071a		FENNELL 'Small and thin' letters	I	R	Camac Halfpenny 1792	Batty 3493C	
DAVEY	I	R	Halfpenny 1806	Batty 4051A	10	FERGUSON Very large letters	I	†	Penny 1797	P. R. Davies	
T. DAVIS	I	†	Penny 1797	Andrews 1077, Chitty 76		I. FISHER Small letters with serifs	I	O	Twopence 1797	Seaby	
S. DAWE in 2 lines	I	†	Penny George III	Andrews 1078		J. C. FISK Medium letters with serifs	I	O & R	Penny 1806/7	J. G. Scott	16
DAYKIN Small letters with serifs	I	O	Halfpenny 1746	J. G. Scott		I. FLANAG(AN) W.H	I I	O R	Irish Halfpenny 1781	Batty 4090A	
DEANSTON in 2 lines Very large letters	I	†	Penny 1797	R. N. P. Hawkins	11	R. FORD Medium letters with serifs	I	O & R	Halfpenny 1807	J. G. Scott	
E. DENNIS Medium letters with serifs	I	O	Irish Halfpenny 1781	Szauer 73 Batty 4053	12	E. FRENCH	I	R	Halfpenny George IV	Batty 4093D	
DISON Medium letters with serifs	I	O	Irish Halfpenny 1772	Szauer 79		J. FRY (4 times) Medium letters with serifs in serrated rectangular indent	R	O	Penny 1797	A. G. Davies	
DISPAT(CH) In notched oblong	†	†	Halfpenny †	Gibbs 163	13	A. FYFE	R	†	Penny 1807	Duffield 1485	
H. DODD Large letters with serifs	I	R	Penny 1797	J. G. Scott		R. GAIR J.F	I	R	Halfpenny 1806	Batty 4095	
W. DOIBY	†	†	Irish Halfpenny 1751	Gibbs 278		T. GARDNER Large letters with serifs	I	O	Penny 1797	J. G. Scott	
I. DOLLARD Small letters with serifs	I	R	Dublin Halfpenny token 1794 (D & H 251–67)	Szauer 69	14	W. GEORGE Medium letters with serifs	I	IXO 2XR	Penny 1797	C. Brunel	
DOWLING/20 Small letters with serifs	I	R	Irish Halfpenny 1773	P. R. Davies	15	GIBBENS Small letters with serifs	I	6xO 3XR	Penny 1797 (pierced)	J. G. Scott	
W. DOWNS	I	O	Dublin Halfpenny token 1795 (D & H 7)	Batty 3664		W. GIBBS (and A. SMITH) A. SMITH Small letters with serifs	I I	O R	Penny 1831	J. G. Scott	
W. DREW	I	†	Halfpenny 1806	Batty 4057		C. GIBSON	I	R	Halfpenny 1806	Batty 4183A	
W. DUNCAN Medium letters with serifs	I	R	Penny 1797	J. G. Scott		S. GILLET	I	O	Coventry Halfpenny 1793 (D & H 238–45)	Batty 2535	
I. DUNG	I	O	Irish Halfpenny 1780	Batty 4065		*II T. GILLETT T.G	I	†	Halfpenny †	Ashmolean Museum	
M DUNN Medium italic capitals with serifs	I	O	Penny 1797	J. G. Scott		W. GILPIN	I	O & R	Halfpenny 1806	Batty 4183C	
R. EVANS	I	R	Halfpenny 1799	Batty 4075A		W. GILSON	I	R	Halfpenny 1807	Batty 4183B	

For key to column headings and abbreviations, please refer to page 150.

COUNTERMARK	A	B	COIN TYPE	SOURCE REF.	C
H. GODDARD (6 times) (and T. JUDD twice) Medium letters with serifs	I	O&R	Penny 1806/7	Charles Dobie	
H. GODDARD (twice) Medium letters with serifs	I	O&R	Connecticut cent 1787	Charles Dobie	
GOOD (crude) Large letters with serifs	I	R	Penny 1890	J. G. Scott	
T. GOODMAN/P Medium letters with serifs	I	O	Halfpenny 1774	J. G. Scott	
J. GRATY Medium letters with serifs	I	R	Sheffield Penny 1813 (Davis 138)	J. G. Scott	
M. H. GREEN Large letters with serifs	I	O&R	Halfpenny 1799	A. G. Davies	
GROS	R	†	Halfpenny William III 1486	Duffield	
JOHN GUNTON (crude) Large letters with serifs	I	R	Halfpenny 1799	British Museum	
S GUY	I	O	Halfpenny 1807	Batty 4236	
HAMBILTON Large letters with serifs	I	R	Irish Halfpenny George III	Szauer 65	
HAMBILTON W/TAYLOR Medium letters	I I	R O	Halfpenny 1770–5	Ashmolean Museum	
HANCOCK	I	O	Halfpenny 1717	Batty 4237D	
J. HAND	I	†	Penny 1797	Andrews 1274	
T. C. HANDLER (and I. MITCHELL on other side)	I	†	Halfpenny George III	SNC Jan./ Feb. 1921 Col. 82 89460	
HARD	I	16XO 25XR	Halfpenny George III	Batty 4237E	17
HARDING Medium letters with serifs	I	O	Farthing 1840	J. G. Scott	
E. HARRIS Medium letters with serifs (and W.P/T. ARNOLD)	I	O	Irish Halfpenny 1805	J. G. Scott	
J. HARRISON	I	O&R	Halfpenny 1806	Batty 4250	
J. HARRO . . . (N?) Medium letters with serifs J H Large letters with serifs	I I	R O	Halfpenny 1806/7	C. Brunel	
R. HARVEY Large letters with serifs (and J. WINNALS obv.)	I	O&R	Newark Penny 1811	J. G. Scott	
HAWKSWORTH in 2 lines	I	O	Halfpenny George II	Batty 4252	
G. HAYTON/HAYTON/G. HAYTON Small (1st & 3rd lines) and large (2nd line) letters with serifs	I	O&R	Halfpenny 1799	J. G. Scott	
MARTIN HAYWOOD	I	O	Halfpenny 1862	Batty 4445	
O: HEADEN Medium letters with serifs in serrated indent	R	O	Irish Halfpenny 1775–82	Szauer 62	
R. S. HEDLEY	I	R	Dublin Penny 1814 (Davis 22–4)	Batty 886	
A HERBERT	I	O	Irish Halfpenny 1781	Batty 4254	
R. HICKS Small letters with serifs in horseshoe shaped indent (also P incuse obv., wavy line and X incuse rev.)	R	O&R	Farthing Charles II	Charles Dobie	
S. HILL Medium letters with serifs	I	R	Halfpenny 1806	J. G. Scott	
J. HOGAN Medium letters with serifs	I	O	Dublin Halfpenny 1794 (D & H 216 etc.)	J. G. Scott	
J. HOLLIDAY Large plain letters	I	O	Penny 1834	C. P. C. Parish	
J. HOLLOWAY Large letters with serifs	I	O	Penny 1807	J. G. Scott	
HOLTS Four times forming a square. Medium letters with serifs Figures 1–12 forming a clock, time 12.25	I I	O R	Penny 1797	Birmingham Museum	
F. HOMER	I	O&R	Halfpenny 1694	Batty 4262	

For key to column headings and abbreviations, please refer to page 150.

COUNTERMARK	A	B	COIN TYPE	SOURCE REF.	C
R. HOPE Medium letters with serifs	I	O	Frederick, King of Prussia Farthing-size Medalet	C. Brunel	
HOUSTON Large letters with serifs	I	R	Irish Halfpenny 1805	Spink	
HOWARD Very small letters with serifs	I	O	Manchester Halfpenny 1793 (D & H 135h)	P. R. Davies	
T. HOWELL	I	†	Penny 1797	Chitty 77	
T. HOWITT	I	†	Penny George III	Andrews 1111	
T. HOY Medium letters with serifs	I	O	Penny 1797	J. G. Scott	
SAMUEL/HOYLAND	†	†	Halfpenny Charles II or William III	SNC Nov. 1905	
I. HUGHES Medium letters with serifs	I	R	Penny 1826	Charles Dobie	
1234567890011120 forming a circle	I	O			
T. HUNT Small italic capitals with serifs	I	R	Penny 1797	J. G. Scott	
T. HYNES Medium letters with serifs	I	O	Irish Halfpenny 1775–82	Szauer 63	
A. INGRAM	I	†	Cronebane Halfpenny 1789 (D & H 3 etc.)	Batty 3785A	
P INGRAM Medium letters with serifs	I	O&R	France: 2 Sols 1792BB	J. G. Scott	
BEN: IOHNSON Within ornamental compartment	†	†	Halfpenny †	SNC Nov./Dec. 1920	18
ISIS 'many times'	I	O&R	Penny †	Szauer 170	19
T. JACKS Medium letters with serifs	I	R	Irish Halfpenny 1783	Szauer 226	
H. JAMES Large letters with serifs	I	†	Penny 1797	J. G. Scott	
JARVIS (twice)	I	O	Halfpenny 1799	Batty 4306D	

COUNTERMARK	A	B	COIN TYPE	SOURCE REF.	C
J. JEFFERAY	I	O&R	Halfpenny 1799	Batty 4306F	
BEN: JOHNSON 'Radiated letters within a sunken ornament'	R	R	Halfpenny George II	Batty 4317A	18
J. JOHNSON Medium letters with serifs, and TREES (twice) Slightly smaller letters individually punched	I	O	Twopence 1797	S. London dealer May 1973	
I.Iones Medium letters in serrated indent	R	O	Flint Penny 1811 (Davis 7 etc.)	Birmingham Museum	
J. R. JONES	I	R	Halfpenny 1806	Batty 4318	
T. JONES Medium letters with serifs	I	O&R	Penny 1873	Seaby	
J. JORDAN	I	O	Halfpenny 1807	Batty 4318D	
I. J..D Large letters with serifs (and H. WIGGALL)	I	R	Penny 1862	J. G. Scott	
S. JUDD Large letters with serifs (and W. MORTON ? obv.)	I	R	Penny 1866	J. G. Scott	
T. JUDD (twice) (and H. GODDARD 6 times)	I	O&R	Penny 1806/7	Charles Dobie	
W. JULER	I	†	Penny George III	Andrews 1127	
A. KAY in rectangular indent with stippled background Large letters with serifs	R	R	Penny 1825	J. G. Scott	
KEENA Large plain letters	I	†	Halfpenny †	Szauer 34	
J. KELLY	I	†	Penny George III	Andrews 1130	
T. KELLY	I	†	Halfpenny 1806/7	Chitty 78	20
I. KEY Medium letters with serifs	I	4xO 3xR	Irish Penny 1805	Seaby	
I.K Large letters with serifs	I	O			
N. KEYS (and CL or T)	†	†	Halfpenny George II	Gibbs 155	
GEORGE KIRK	†	†	Penny 1797	Bliss 824	

For key to column headings and abbreviations, please refer to page 150.

COUNTERMARK	A	B	COIN TYPE	SOURCE REF.	C
W. KITSON Small letters with serifs	I	R	Halfpenny 1770–5	J. G. Scott	
T KNIGHT Medium letters with serifs	I	O	Halfpenny 1806	J. G. Scott	
V. LARKING	I	†	Dublin Halfpenny 1792 (D & H 355 etc.)	Batty 3605A	
J. LAW Medium letters with serifs	I	O	Penny 1797	Seaby	
I/LEACH	†	†	Halfpenny 1749	Gibbs 152	
T LEE (twice) Large letters with serifs	I	O	Penny 1797	C. Brunel	
THOMAS LEWES Large crude letters with serifs individually punched	I	IXO 2XR	Halfpenny †	C. Brunel	
also RP/LT	I	O			
W. LEWIS Large letters with serifs	I	O	Penny 1797	Birmingham Museum	
J. LEY Large letters with serifs	I	O	Warwickshire Halfpenny 1787 (D & H 340–8)	J. D. Stott	
LINEKER Medium letters with serifs	I	O&R	Penny 1797	J. G. Scott	
C. LINEKER Medium letters with serifs	I	2XO			
LIN/LEY Small letters with serifs in sunken serrated oval	R	O	Halfpenny 1799	A. G. Davies	21
S. LLOYD	I	O&R	Halfpenny 1806	Batty 4394E	
LOFT Medium letters with serifs	I	O	Irish Halfpenny 1805	A. G. Davies	
I. LORD Medium letters with serifs in serrated rectangular indent	R	R	Halfpenny George II	J. G. Scott	
IL Large letters with serifs in serrated rectangular indent	R	O			
I LOVE in rectangular indent	R	†	Halfpenny George II	Duffield 1528	

COUNTERMARK	A	B	COIN TYPE	SOURCE REF.	C
W. LOWE (script)	I	O&R	Halfpenny 1806	Batty 4418	
H. LUCAS Medium letters with serifs	I	O	Farthing 1675	J. G. Scott	
LUML/LEY Large crude letters with serifs	I	R	Halfpenny 1806	J. G. Scott	
MᶜHARDY Large letters with serifs	I	R	Penny 1797	J. G. Scott	
S. MACNAY Medium letters with serifs	I	O	Penny 1797	Seaby	
D MAHON and W.H.	I	†	Halfpenny 1770–5	Batty 4428B	
J. MAIN Large letters with serifs	I	O&R	Penny 1797	Seaby	
J. MANTLE	I	O&R	Halfpenny 1806	Batty 4428C	
MASON/✠/A/T Small letters with serifs	I	†	Halfpenny †	Szauer 230	
R. MATHEWS	I	O	Halfpenny 1806	Batty 4454	
T MAW Large letters with serifs	I	R	Irish Halfpenny 1805	J. G. Scott	
MᶜCONNELL Large plain letters	I	R	Penny 1872	J. G. Scott	
CON McG	†	†	Voce Populi Halfpenny 1760	Duffield 516	
B/MENEZES Small letters with serifs 6 Fleurs de lis above and below all in rectangular indent	R	†	Halfpenny †	J. G. Scott	
I (or J) MILLER Large letters with serifs	I	O	Penny 1860	C. Brunel	
I. MITCHELL in an oblong indent (and T. C. HANDLER on other side)	R	†	Halfpenny George III	SNC Jan./Feb. 1921 Col. 82 8946c	
I. MONDAY (twice) Small letters with serifs (and W.R obv.)	I	O&R	Penny 1797	Parsons p. 22 fig. 10	
E MONK Large letters with serifs	I	O	Halfpenny	C. Brunel	
z/ (bell)	I	2XR	†		

For key to column headings and abbreviations, please refer to page 150.

COUNTERMARK	A	B	COIN TYPE	SOURCE REF.	C	COUNTERMARK	A	B	COIN TYPE	SOURCE REF.	C
R. MOORE Large letters with serifs in serrated rectangular indent	R	O	Halfpenny 1799	Seaby		J. OXLEY Large letters with serifs I. OXLEY (twice) Small plain letters	I I	O R	Penny 1797	J. G. Scott	
I MORRISS Large crude plain letters	I	O	Penny 1860	Seaby		W. PALFREMAN	I	R	Halfpenny 1806	Batty 4514	
MOULDS	I	†	Halfpenny 1861	Batty 4468A		R. PARKE Medium letters with serifs in rectangular indent	R	†	Irish Halfpenny George III	Szauer 66	25
R. T. MUR(PHY) MURPHY Large plain letters	I I	O R	Penny 186(?)	J. G. Scott		R. PARKE	† †	†	Halfpenny †	Gibbs 157	25
W. NAISH Medium letters with serifs in rectangular indent (and large incuse C)	R	O	Penny 1797	A. G. Davies		W. PARKER	I	R	Halfpenny 1806	Batty 4513B	26
						M. PARTRIDGE (twice) Small letters with serifs	I	R	Penny 1806/7	J. G. Scott	
NEEDHAM Medium letters with serifs	I	R	Halfpenny George II	C. Brunel		H. PEEBLES Large letters with serifs (and WP rev.)	I	O	Penny 1797	J. G. Scott	
NEILL (twice) Medium letters with serifs	I	R	Guernsey 4 Doubles 1830	C. Brunel		W. PEGG Medium letters with serifs	I	O&R	Halfpenny 1799	J. G. Scott	
B. NEWMAN Medium letters with serifs	I	O	Penny 1797	Seaby		W. PETTY Large letters with serifs in serrated rectangular indent	R	O	Halfpenny George II	J. G. Scott	
L. NORTH Medium letters with serifs (and E. B, I. ROBERTS)	I	3XO 4XR	Penny 1806/7	A. G. Davies		J. POPE Large letters with serifs	I	O&R	Halfpenny 1775	J. G. Scott	
R. NURSE	I	†	Penny †	Andrews 1177		S. POYNER Large letters with serifs	I	R	Penny 1797	J. G. Scott	
R. OAKLEY Large letters with serifs	I	O	Penny 1807 (pierced at centre)	C. Brunel		W. PRESTON Small letters with serifs in serrated rectangular indent	R	O&R	Halfpenny George II	J. G. Scott	
OATES Small plain letters	I	O	Halfpenny 1774	C. Brunel		W. PRICE Large letters with serifs	I	R	Penny 1797	J. G. Scott	
OLIVER (curved) Very large letters with serifs	I	O	Twopence 1797	SNC Dec. 1972 p. 455	22	QUINN	I	O&R	Farthing George IV	Batty 1609	
O'NEILL Small letters with serifs	I	O	Irish Farthing 1806	Szauer 148	23	W. RAMSBOTAM Medium letters with serifs	I	R	Penny 1797	J. G. Scott	
I. OTIW in 3 lines H	I I	R O	Halfpenny William III	Batty 4305B		J. REESE Large letters with serifs	I	O	Penny 1797	J. G. Scott	
OULSDAL	I	O&R	Liverpool Halfpenny 1791	Batty 598	24	I. REEVES Large letters with serifs	I	R	Twopence 1797 (pierced 12 o'c)	Baldwin	
R. OWEN/OWEN Large letters with serifs	I	R	Penny 1797	J. G. Scott		G. REILLY F (six times)	I I	O R	Halfpenny †	Szauer 168	
						J. RIDLEY	I	†	Penny 1797	Andrews 1197	

For key to column headings and abbreviations, please refer to page 150.

COUNTERMARK	A	B	COIN TYPE	SOURCE REF.	C
RIS . . . Large letters with serifs	I	O	Irish Halfpenny 1782	Szauer 75	
ROBERTS	I	O&R	Penny 1797	Andrews 1198	
I. ROBERTS Medium letters with serifs in serrated rectangular indent (and E. B, L. NORTH)	R	R	Penny 1806/7	A. G. Davies	
ROBINSON/1848/ E. ROBINSON/VV Medium (1st & 3rd lines) and large (2nd & 4th lines) letters with serifs	I	O	Irish Penny 1822	C. Brunel	
T. ROBINSON (twice) Medium letters with serifs	I	O&R	Birmingham Penny 1812 (Davis 74–77)	C. Brunel	
T. ROBINSON Medium letters with serifs (different punch)	I	O&R	Penny 1797	C. Brunel	
J. ROSE Small letters with serifs ww (large)	I I	O&R R	Irish Penny 1805 (pierced at centre)	C. Brunel	
D. ROWE/D.R Medium letters with serifs	I	R	Suffolk Halfpenny 1793 (D & H 16)	C. Brunel	
W: ROWNEY Medium letters with serifs	I	O&R	Halfpenny (George I?)	J. G. Scott	27
I. RUSSEL(L) Medium letters with serifs	I	O&R	Yorkshire Halfpenny 1812 (Davis 150)	C. Brunel	
J. RUSSELS Large letters with serifs	I	O	Halfpenny 1799	J. G. Scott	
S. SCHOFIELD	I	O&R	Halfpenny 1770–5	Batty 4617A	
L. E. SEYMOUR Small letters with serifs	I	O	Penny 1841–60 (silvered)	Charles Dobie	
I. SHANK (curved) Small letters with serifs	I	R	Halfpenny 1799	J. G. Scott	
W. SHORT Medium plain letters	I	O	Penny 1870	J. G. Scott	

COUNTERMARK	A	B	COIN TYPE	SOURCE REF.	C
W. SIMONS 1800 I B	I I	R O	Penny 1797	Duffield 341 and SNC Dec. 1908	
SMALLBONE Medium letters	I	†	Penny 1806/7	S. H. Dixon	
A. SMALLEY. (curved) Medium letters with serifs round rim	I	O	Penny 1797	J. G. Scott	
A. SMITH Small letters with serifs (and W. GIBBS obv.)	I	O&R	Penny 1831	J. G. Scott	
F. SMITH Medium letters with serifs	I	R	Counterfeit Halfpenny George III	J. G. Scott	
H SMITH	I	R	Halfpenny 1806	Batty 4748A	
J. SMITH Medium letters with serifs	I	4XO 2XR	Penny 1797	J. G. Scott	
W. SMITH Large letters with serifs	I	O	Penny 1855	J. G. Scott	
SOMMER Small letters with serifs	I	O	Halfpenny 1770–5	Charles Dobie	
I. STALEY within indented serrated rectangle	R	O	Farthing 1799	Batty 2556	
STANLEY Medium letters with serifs	I	O	Penny 1825	Ashmolean Museum	
STEEL (3 times)	I	R	Halfpenny 1799	Batty 4856A	28
S. STOKEL(EY) Medium letters with serifs	I	O	Halfpenny 1806/7	Dr.G.H.L. Bullmore	
I/STOW Large letters with serifs	I	O	Farthing 1770–5	C. Brunel	
STUART Medium letters with serifs	I	R	Irish Halfpenny George II	J. G. Scott	
J. STUBBINGS Medium letters with serifs	I	R	Irish Halfpenny 1805	C. Brunel	
E. STURGES Medium letters with serifs	I	O	Penny 1797	Seaby	
HENRY/SUTTON Medium plain letters	I	O	Penny 1797	J. G. Scott	

For key to column headings and abbreviations, please refer to page 150.

COUNTERMARK	A	B	COIN TYPE	SOURCE REF.	C
R. SWA. BRIC (and W. BENNETT, q.v.)	I	R	Penny 1797	Charles Dobie	
SYKES/SPRING ON	I I	O R	Halfpenny George II	Batty 4874	29
R. C. S .. TO . . . ON Medium letters with serifs	I	O	Penny 1806/7	J. G. Scott	
TALBOT	I	O&R	Halfpenny 1799	Batty 4876B	
TALBOT Medium letters with serifs	I	R	Penny 1797	C. Brunel	
J. TAYLOR	I	O	Halfpenny George III	Batty 4878B	
JOHN/TAYLOR	†	†	Irish Halfpenny 1769	SCMB Jan. 1971 TP331	
W/TAYLOR HAMBILTON Medium letters	I I	O R	Halfpenny 1770–5	Ashmolean Museum	
TEASDALE Medium plain letters	I	O	Penny 1862	J. G. Scott	
C. TERRY Very small letters with serifs	I	2XO 4XR	Birmingham Workhouse Penny 1812	C. Brunel	
W.ᴹ TEW Very small letters with serifs	I	2XO	Penny 1797	J. G. Scott	
E. THACKER Small letters with serifs	I	R	Penny 1797	C. Brunel	
THOMAS Medium letters with serifs	I	R	Penny 1797	C. Brunel	
THYNES (See T. HYNES)	I	O	Irish Halfpenny 1782	Batty 4882	
TOOMER Medium letters with serifs in serrated rectangular indent	R	O	Penny 1806	J. G. Scott	
T. TORR Large letters with serifs	I	O&R	Penny 1797	J. G. Scott	
W. TURNBULL Medium letters with serifs	I	O	Penny 1797	J. G. Scott	
T. TURNER	I	R	Halfpenny George II	Batty 4906F	

COUNTERMARK	A	B	COIN TYPE	SOURCE REF.	C
THᴼˢ TYZACK (twice) Small letters with serifs	I	O&R	Penny 1797 (pierced with 6mm hole)	A. G. Davies	
H. UNDERWOOD HW	I	R	Halfpenny 1806	Batty 4907B	
MR, J D (V)ALLENTIN	†	†	'Worn copper coin'	Szauer 87	30
L. WALTON 1735	† †	O R	Clifton token 1735	Duffield 514	
WARD Medium letters with serifs in serrated rectangular indent	R	O	Halfpenny 1774	J. G. Scott	
T. WATKINS Small letters with serifs	I	R	Halfpenny 1806/7	J. G. Scott	
WATKINSON (twice) Small letters with serifs	I	O	Penny 1797	Birmingham Museum	
WATSON	I	O	Halfpenny 1799	Batty 4964F	
WATSON Medium letters with serifs	I	O	Halfpenny 1806 (pierced)	J. G. Scott	
WATSON Medium letters with serifs in serrated rectangular indent/ W* Large letter with serifs	R I	O	Halfpenny 1807	J. G. Scott	
WEATHER Large letters with serifs	I	R	Halfpenny 1862	C. Brunel	
WEBSTER	I	R	Hull Halfpenny 1791 (D & H 17–21)	Batty 2820A	31
WERSTER (sic)/3 Medium letters with serifs	I	O	Hull Halfpenny 1791 (D & H 17–21)	A. G. Davies	31
WHEATLEY Large letters with serifs	I	O	Penny 1797	A. G. Davies	
EDWARD/(WH)ITEHE(AD) Small letters with serifs	I	R	Irish Halfpenny 1723	J. G. Scott	
H. WIGGALL Medium letters with serifs (and I . J .. D)	I	R	Penny 1862	J. G. Scott	

For key to column headings and abbreviations, please refer to page 150.

COUNTERMARK	A	B	COIN TYPE	SOURCE REF.	C
H. WILD Medium letters with serifs	I	O&R	Halfpenny 1807	J. G. Scott	
WILM. THOM	†	†	Halfpenny †	Szauer 167	
R. WILSON Medium letters with serifs in serrated rectangle	I	R	Halfpenny 1799	C. Brunel	
S. WILSONNS (curved) (twice)	I	†	Halfpenny †	Szauer 59	
B WINDSOR Large letters with serifs	I	O&R	Halfpenny 1799	J. G. Scott	
J. WINNALS (and R. HARVEY) Medium letters with serifs	I	O	Newark Penny 1811	J. G. Scott	

COUNTERMARK	A	B	COIN TYPE	SOURCE REF.	C
WOOD	I	O&R	Halfpenny George II	Batty 5056	32
WOOD	†	†	Halfpenny †	SNC Nov./ Dec. 1920 Col. 527 88101	32
B/WRIGHT Medium letters with serifs in serrated indents	R	R	Twopence 1797	C. Brunel	
S. WRIGHT (twice) Medium letters with serifs	I	R	Penny 1797	J. G. Scott	
J. YATES	I	O	Halfpenny 1806	Batty 5058K	33
Σ YATES Medium letters with serifs	I	O	Penny 1797	J. G. Scott	33

For key to column headings and abbreviations, please refer to page 150.

NOTES ON THE NAMES LISTED IN APPENDIX 1

1 James Barton was a clockmaker in Sheffield c. 1825. It will be noted that the coin in question is a Barnsley token.
2 James Bird was a cutler and gunmaker in St. Nicholas Street, Ipswich, in 1844.
3 William Braithwaite was a clockmaker in Hawkshead (Lancs.) c. 1820.
4 Robert Breeze was a gunmaker in Market Place, Great Yarmouth, in 1844.
5 Burton – this countermark possibly represents the town, although it is a very common surname.
6 Canif – this may be a cutlery brand mark.
7 Chant – this may be a brand mark.
8 Matthew Cox was a gunsmith in Yeovil c. 1840.
9 Crib – this may be a brand mark.
10 W. Davey was a gunsmith in Norwich c. 1835.
11 Deanston – this countermark is quite different in type from the Deanston Cotton Mill pieces – see 77.2 in Table 1 above.
12 E. Dennis – the two countermarks listed may be from the same punch, but this cannot be confirmed.
13 Dispa(tch) – this is possibly some form of factory or office check.
14 I. Dollard – see 122.74 in Table 1 above.
15 Dowling is a common Dublin name.
16 J. C. Fisk – Fisk was a common name in Suffolk – see White's 1844 Directory.
17 Hard – this may be a brand mark.
18 Ben: Iohnson, Ben: Johnson – the two countermarks listed may be from the same punch, the description in one case being inaccurate. 'Ben Johnson' could be a brand mark or the name of an inn.
19 Isis – this may be a brand mark.

20 T. Kelly – see also 122.120 in Table 1 above.
21 Linley is a name common in the Sheffield metal trades – e.g. S. & R. Linley, established in 1772, manufacturers of scythes, hay and straw knives and nails, in 1875 at Clough Works.
22 Oliver – the photograph appears to be of a cartwheel penny rather than a twopence. The piece was reported by E. J. Hankinson, of the Rhodesia Numismatic Society, as follows: 'The Cartwheel was one of a number of coins in the possession of a retired Indian Army officer, Thomas Bird Craig (69) living in Salisbury. The collection was of no particular importance and was kept in a bag. Craig himself was a recluse and an eccentric. On April 26th 1972, three Africans broke into Craig's home in Hatfield, Salisbury, and murdered the old man. They pleaded Not Guilty at the trial and claimed they merely wanted to keep him quiet whilst they stole. It was shown that one of them strangled the old man whilst the juveniles tied his hands and feet. In sentencing the murderer to death and the two juveniles who were with him to 8 Cuts and Reformatory, the Judge said he was satisfied that they had a constructive intent to kill. The coins were produced in evidence by the C.I.D. as having been found in possession of the accused and identified by a house servant of Craig's as having been the property of the old man, thus tying in the accused with the crime.'
23 O'Neill – see also Irish silver 'slap' tokens, Szauer 191, 221, Davis 128.
24 Oulsdal – this may be a brand mark.
25 R. Parke – the two countermarks listed may be from the same punch, but this cannot be confirmed.

26 William Parker, gunsmith, had a shop in Holborn, London 1790–1840, and was the founder of a famous firm of gunmakers, who continued as Parker, Field & Co. 233 High Holborn (1840–50) and Parker, Field & Sons (1850–86).

27 W. Rowney – there is no trace of Rowney as a London trader in a sample of 26 directories 1770–1880 at roughly 4–5 year intervals.

28 Steel – this may be part of a brand mark – e.g. 'Cast Steel'.

29 Sykes, Spring – this may be part of a brand mark – e.g. 'Sykes Spring Steel'. Sykes & Co. made tableknives at Pinston Lane, Sheffield c. 1787.

30 J. D. (V)allentin – this may be the issuer of the JDV countermark – see 123.160 in Table 1 above.

31 Webster, Werster – the two pieces listed may be the same, Batty's description possibly being inaccurate.

32 Wood, impressed, occurs on small china figures, and is the mark of Ephraim Wood, Niles Street Works, Burslem, c. 1805–30.

33 J. Yates & Co., edge tool makers, are listed in the Birmingham directory for 1847 at Pritchett Street.

KEY   Column A   Incuse (I) or relief (R).   SCMB   Seaby's Coin & Medal Bulletin.
        Column B   Obverse (O) or reverse (R).   SNC   Spink's Numismatic Circular.
        Column C   See Note.   †   Not known or illegible.

COUNTERMARK	A	B	COIN TYPE	SOURCE REF.	C
A Large letter with serifs	I	O	Halfpenny George II	Aylesbury Museum	
A Large letter with serifs in square indent	R	R	Halfpenny George II	Szauer 88	
A.A (crude) Large letters with serifs	I	O	Farthing George IV	A. G. Davies	
A19 I.C	I I	R O	Halfpenny 1806	Batty 4303B	
AB	†	†	Farthing 1775	SCMB Jan. 1971 TP336	
AB Large letters with serifs	I	O	Halfpenny 1807	Seaby	
AC/GI Large letters with serifs	I	R	Penny 1927	C. Brunel	
A.E Very large letters with serifs	I	†	Irish Penny George IV	Szauer 60	
A.F./33 Medium letters with serifs	I	†	Twopence (?)	C. Brunel	
AH Crude plain letters in rectangular indent	R	†	Farthing token†	Lothian: D & H p. 443 69, 70	
A.H.	I	R	Poole Halfpenny 1795 (D & H 6)	Batty 161	
AJ and L and 7-pointed star J and five 7-pointed stars Large letters with serifs	I I	O R	Penny 1797	J. G. Scott	
AK	†	†	Dublin token (W354)	Szauer 23	
AK	I	R	Voce Populi Halfpenny 1760	P. Withers	
AR Very large letters with serifs	I	R	Irish Penny George IV	C. Brunel	
A (crossed branches) R in oval indent	R	†	Halfpenny 1883	Duffield 1526	

COUNTERMARK	A	B	COIN TYPE	SOURCE REF.	C
A.W in rectangular indent	R	O	Irish Halfpenny 1805	Batty 3957A	
A.W	I	R	Halfpenny 1770-5	Batty 3957a	
A.Y (crude) Large letters with serifs in rectangular indent	R	R	Halfpenny George II	Seaby	
B Large letter with serifs	I	O	Halfpenny 1697	J. G. Scott	
B Large letter with serifs	I	O	Halfpenny George II	J. G. Scott	
B Large letter with serifs	I	†	Halfpenny †	J. G. Scott	
B Large letter with serifs	I	O	Halfpenny 1770-5	J. G. Scott	
B Large letter with serifs in serrated rectangular indent	R	O	Warwick-shire Halfpenny 1790 (D & H 385 etc.)	Seaby	
B Large letter with serifs	I	O	Dublin Halfpenny 1792 (D & H 29 etc.)	J. G. Scott	
B Medium letter with serifs	I	O	Canterbury Halfpenny 1795	Seaby	
B Large letter with serifs	I	R	Penny 1919	J. G. Scott	
B G and W Very large letters with serifs	I I	R O	Halfpenny 1799	J. G. Scott	
B LDR in oblong	I R	R O	Penny †	Gibbs 454	
BB Large letters with serifs	I	O	Irish token Halfpenny† (D & H ?)	Szauer 91	
BB Very large letters with serifs each side of 4mm hole	I	R	Penny 1860 (bronze)	J. G. Scott	
*/B Small letter with serifs	I	O	Halfpenny 1717	C. Brunel	

COUNTERMARK	A	B	COIN TYPE	SOURCE REF.	C
Ʈ(£?)B (twice) Very large letters with serifs	I	†	Halfpenny †	Szauer 233	I
B/IW/6 Large letters with serifs (Cross fleury)	I	O	Halfpenny †	C. Brunel	
	I	R			
BxP. Large letters with serifs in rectangular indent	R	O	Anglesey Halfpenny 1791 (D & H 436–42)	J. G. Scott	
B S Medium letters with serifs	I	R	Penny 1806/7	C. Brunel	
BW Medium letters with serifs	I	O&R	Penny 1797	C. Brunel	
B/WV Large letters with serifs	I	O	Halfpenny George II	J. G. Scott	
C/51 Large letter with serifs (and FW rev.)	I	O	Penny (1860–94?)	Seaby	
C Large letter with serifs (and W. NAISH in relief)	I	O	Penny 1797	A. G. Davies	
C (twice) Large letter with serifs	I	O	Halfpenny 1799	J. G. Scott	
C (and SS obv.)	I	R	Irish Farthing George II 1760	Szauer 161	
CB Large letters with serifs in serrated rectangular indent	R	†	Halfpenny †	Birmingham Museum	
CB in rectangular indent	R	O	Halfpenny George II	Batty 4021A	
CB Medium letters with serifs	I	O	Halfpenny 1913	J. G. Scott	
CEF in circular indent	R	R	Early Irish Halfpenny George III	Batty 3999B	
CE Large crude letters with serifs	I	R	Middlesex Halfpenny (D & H 369)	J. G. Scott	
CF Medium letters with serifs	I	O	Penny 1863	J. G. Scott	
CG Large letters with serifs	I	O	Penny 1861	J. G. Scott	

COUNTERMARK	A	B	COIN TYPE	SOURCE REF.	C
CH	I	R	Evasion Halfpenny 1774 (Atkins 375 var.)	Batty 4693A	
C.H.	I	O	Halfpenny 1799	Batty 3999D	
C.H.O Small letters with serifs	I	O	Irish Halfpenny 1805	C. Brunel	
CL Large letters with serifs	I	O&R	Halfpenny †	Szauer 234	
C.M	I	R	Irish Halfpenny 1805	Batty 3999C	
C.M Large letters with serifs in serrated rectangular indent	R	O	Penny 1826	Numismatist June 1954	
CP Large letters with serifs	I	O	Penny 1797	Seaby	
cTo in serrated oval indent	R	†	Penny 1797	Gibbs 160	
C.V.E.P Large letters with serifs	I	†	Halfpenny †	C. Brunel	
CW Large plain letters	I	O&R	Halfpenny 1806/7	J. G. Scott	
D	I	O	Irish Farthing 1744	Szauer 159	
D Large letter with serifs in shaped indent	R	R	Norwich Halfpenny (D & H 23A)	Seaby	
D Large letter with serifs	I	O	Penny 1797	J. G. Scott	
D Large letter with serifs	I	O	Farthing 1822	Charles Dobie	
D Large letter with serifs	I	IXO 4XR	Penny 1871	J. G. Scott	
D Medium letter with serifs (and w obv.)	I	R	Penny 1797	J. G. Scott	
D.B (twice) forming a cross Large letters with serifs	I	O	Halfpenny 1799	J. G. Scott	
D.K Large letters	I	O	Halfpenny 1799	Batty 4054A	
DM	I	†	Halfpenny 1721	Szauer 92	2

For key to column headings and abbreviations, please refer to page 161.

COUNTERMARK	A	B	COIN TYPE	SOURCE REF.	C
DM. Large letters with serifs (twice)	I	O&R	Penny 1806	Baldwin	2
DN Large letters with serifs	I	O	Halfpenny 1724	J. G. Scott	
DP (and large rosette obv.) Large letters with serifs	I	O&R	Twopence 1797	Szauer 55	
DP Very large crude letters with serifs (also engraved rev. TN script)	I	2XO 1XR	Penny 1797	J. G. Scott	
D/R Large letters with serifs	I	O	Middlesex Halfpenny 1795 (D & H 346)	C. Brunel	
D.R Medium letters with serifs (and D. ROWE)	I	R	Suffolk Halfpenny 1793 (D & H 16)	C. Brunel	
DW 'within a sunken Figure' (SPENCES PLAN)	R / I	R / O	Irish Halfpenny 1723	Batty 4790	
E Very large letter with serifs	I	†	Halfpenny †	J. G. Scott	
E Medium letter with serifs	I	O?	Halfpenny 1770–5?	J. G. Scott	
E Very large letter with serifs in notched circular indent	R	O	Penny 1797	J. G. Scott	
E Very large narrow letter with serifs	I	O	Isle of Man Halfpenny 1830 (Davis 20)	J. G. Scott	
E Very large letter with serifs (and T rev.)	I	O	Penny 1936	J. G. Scott	
EB Medium letters with serifs (and NK obv.)	I	R	Penny 1853	Baldwin	
E.B Medium letters with serifs (and L. NORTH, I. ROBERTS)	I	O&R	Penny 1806/7	A. G. Davies	
ECR Large letters with serifs	I	O	Penny 1806/7	J. G. Scott	
ED Large letters with serifs	I	O	Irish Halfpenny 1782	Szauer 93	
ED Large crude plain letters in rectangular indent	R	1XO 2XR	Penny 1797	Num. Soc. of Ireland enquiry July 1973	
E.D Medium letters with serifs	I	O	Farthing 1806	J. G. Scott	
EEB Large letters with serifs	I	R	Halfpenny 1860–94 (pierced 12 o'c)	J. G. Scott	
EH	I	†	Halfpenny 1770–5	Batty 4070F	
E.H Medium letters with serifs	I	R	Irish Halfpenny 1805	J. G. Scott	
EKB Large letters with serifs	I	R	Early Irish Halfpenny George III	C. Brunel	
EL in a heart-shaped indent	R	†	Halfpenny	Gibbs 156	
EP Script in oval indent	R	†	Counterfeit Halfpenny George III	Batty 5237	
EP Large letters with serifs	I	†	English token Halfpenny† (D & H ?)	Szauer 94	
ES Large letters with serifs	I	5XO 5XR	Twopence 1797	J. G. Scott	
ES Large letters with serifs	I	R	Staffordshire Halfpenny 1794 (D & H 16a)	SNC Oct. 1972 9795	
EW Large letters with serifs in serrated rectangular indent	R	R	Penny 1797	J. G. Scott	
EW Medium letters with serifs	I	1XO 2XR	Halfpenny 1799	J. G. Scott	
F 'several times' Medium letter with serifs	I	O&R	Irish Halfpenny 1723	Ashmolean Museum	
F Large letter with serifs	I	R	Francis McMinn token 1760	Szauer 50	
F Large letter with serifs	I	O	Halfpenny 1770–5	J. G. Scott	

For key to column headings and abbreviations, please refer to page 161.

COUNTERMARK	A	B	COIN TYPE	SOURCE REF.	C
F in notched square indent	R	†	Irish Halfpenny 1769	Gibbs 279	
F	I	O	Kent Halfpenny 1794 (D & H 28)	Batty 441	3
F (6 times) (and G. REILLY obv.)	I	R	Halfpenny †	Szauer 168	
F Very large letter with serifs	I	O	Halfpenny 1806/7	J. G. Scott	
(Maltese cross)/F.	I	†	Halfpenny 1799	Duffield 1488	
.F.	†	†	Halfpenny †	SNC Nov./Dec. 1920 Col. 527 88096	
F/20 Large letter with serifs	I	O&R	Halfpenny 1799	A. G. Davies	
FD	†	†	Irish Farthing 1760	Duffield 1550	4
F.I.	I	†	Halfpenny 1807	Duffield 1490	
FK Medium letters with serifs	I	O	Penny 1886	J. G. Scott	
½ (incuse) F/K N̲ J Large letters with serifs in rectangular indents	I&R	†	Farthing/disc †	C. Brunel	
FS Large letters with serifs	I	R	Hull Halfpenny 1791 (D & H 17–21)	Seaby	
FS (and S on rev.) Large letters with serifs	I	O	Irish Farthing 1806	Szauer 147,241	
FW Large letters with serifs in serrated rectangular indent (and 11 incuse over W)	R	O	Halfpenny 1775	J. G. Scott	
FW Large letters with serifs in serrated rectangular indent	R	O	Early Irish Halfpenny George III	C. Brunel	
FW Medium letters with serifs (under JB)	I	O	Halfpenny 1723	J. G. Scott (see 123.144 in Table I above)	

COUNTERMARK	A	B	COIN TYPE	SOURCE REF.	C
FW Large letters with serifs (and C/51 obv.)	I	R	Penny (1860–94?)	Seaby	
F and Y Large letters with serifs	I	O	Halfpenny 1799	J. G. Scott	
G	I	†	Halfpenny 1806	Duffield 1061	5
GB in indented rectangle	R	O&R	Halfpenny 1806	Batty 4095A	
G.B Large letters with serifs	I	1XO 4XR	Halfpenny 1806/7	C. Brunel	
G.B Very large letters with serifs in serrated rectangular indent	R	R	Halfpenny 1807	A. G. Davies	
GD Medium letters with serifs	I	O	Farthing 1806	J. G. Scott	
GE/F Large crude letters with serifs in circular notched indent	R	†	Halfpenny †	J. G. Scott	
GEH/SH Large letters with serifs	I	O	Twopence 1797	J. G. Scott	
GEH/S with serifs	I	R			
GG Large letters with serifs	I	O&R	Twopence 1797	Baldwin	
GH Large letters with serifs	I	O	Halfpenny George II	Szauer 95	
G.N Large letters with serifs	I	O	Penny 1873	Seaby	
GO Medium letters with serifs	I	4XO 3XR	Penny 1797	J. G. Scott	
G.O Large letters with serifs	I	O			
G.R Large letters with serifs	I	2XO 1XR	Penny 1797	C. Brunel	
GS Large letters with serifs	I	R	Penny 1797	A. G. Davies	6
GS Large letters with serifs	I	O	Farthing 1821	A. G. Davies	6
GS Large letters with serifs	I	R	Penny 1831	C. Brunel	6
GW Very large letters with serifs	I	R	Penny 1797	J. G. Scott	
G and W Very large letters with serifs (and B on rev.)	I	O	Halfpenny 1799	J. G. Scott	

For key to column headings and abbreviations, please refer to page 161.

COUNTERMARK	A	B	COIN TYPE	SOURCE REF.	C
H (I.OTIW on reverse)	I	O	Halfpenny William III	Batty 4305B	
H Medium letter with serifs	I	O	Glasgow Halfpenny 1791 (D & H 9a)	C. Brunel	
H Large letter with serifs	I	O	Brighton Halfpenny 1794 (D & H 2)	Seaby	
H Large letter with serifs	I	O&R	Penny 1797	J. G. Scott	
H Small letter with serifs	I	O	Halfpenny 1799	J. G. Scott	
H	†	†	Penny 1806	Andrews 1101, Chitty 107	
↓/H/18 Medium plain letter	I	R	Farthing 1918	C. Brunel	7
H23 Large letter with serifs	I	O	Halfpenny 1900	J. G. Scott	
H/↓/47 Medium plain letter	I	2XO 2XR	Farthing 1913	J. G. Scott	7
H.B Large letters with serifs in serrated rectangular indent	R	O	Dublin Penny 1816 (Davis 25–33)	C. Brunel	
HB Large letters with serifs in square indent	R	O	Halfpenny 1770–5	Birmingham Museum	
4/HD in a circle	I	O&R	Halfpenny George II	Batty 5146	
H.H Large letters with serifs in serrated rectangular indent	R	O	Penny 1806	J. G. Scott	
HH (or HH) Very large crude letters with serifs	I	O	Penny 1797	A. G. Davies	
HI (or IH) Large letters with serifs	I	O&R	Penny 1806	C. Brunel	
.H.I (or I.H.) Large letters with serifs in serrated rectangular indent	R	O	Halfpenny 1806/7	C. Brunel	
HI (or IH) Large letters with serifs	I	O	Flint Penny 1813 (Davis 7–15)	City Museum, St. Albans	
IH (or HI) Very large letters with serifs (and ⊕ on reverse)	I	O	Birmingham Threepence 1813 (Davis 34–35)	C. Brunel	
HK Very large letters with serifs (and K2R on reverse)	I	O	Irish Penny 1805	Jean M. White	
HP Medium letters with serifs	I	2XO IXR	Middlesex Halfpenny 1795 (D & H 914)	A. G. Davies	
HP Large letters with serifs	I	R	Penny 1797	J. G. Scott	
HP Large letters with serifs in heart-shaped indent	R	R	Halfpenny 1724	A. G. Davies	
HRH monogram in serrated circle (7.5mm) (and rosette incuse obv.)	I	R	Halfpenny 1770–5	Szauer 109	
HS (or SH) Medium letters with serifs in four-sided indent	R	O	Halfpenny 1770–5	C. Brunel	
HS (or SH)	†	R	Dundee Halfpenny 1796 (D & H 16a)	Batty 3263	
HW	R	O	Halfpenny	Gibbs 173	
RY/HW	I	R	†		
HW (and H. UNDERWOOD)	I	R	Halfpenny 1806	Batty 4907B	
H W Very large letters with serifs	I	O	Penny 1797	C. Brunel	
I Large letter with serifs (and V or A reverse)	I	O	Farthing 1740	Ashmolean Museum	
I Large letter with serifs	I	O	Warwickshire Halfpenny 1791 (D & H 432 etc.)	Seaby	
I Large plain letter	I	O	Halfpenny 1806	J. G. Scott	
I. Small plain letter in boot-shaped indent (3 times)	R	O&R	Halfpenny 1799	J. G. Scott	
.I.	†	†	Halfpenny †	SNC Nov./Dec. 1920 Col. 527 88096	

For key to column headings and abbreviations, please refer to page 161.

COUNTERMARK	A	B	COIN TYPE	SOURCE REF.	C
IA Small letters	I	†	Halfpenny George II	SNC June 1906 9157	8
IA and 1771	I	†	Halfpenny †	Szauer 235a, 235b	
IA	†	R	Anglesey Halfpenny 1789	Batty 3047, Duffield 334	
I·A in a square (twice)	†	†	Halfpenny †	SNC Nov./Dec. 1920 Col. 527 88099	
I.A (or J.A)	†	†	Anglesey Halfpenny	SNC Dec. 1908 11079–80	
IB in a heart	†	†	Farthing 1694	SNC June 1906 9157	
IB/97 Large letters with serifs	I	O	Irish Halfpenny 1782	J. G. Scott	
IB	†	†	Warwickshire Halfpenny 1788 (D & H 336)	SCMB Jan. 1971 TP346	
IB Large letters with serifs	I	R	Warwickshire Halfpenny 1788 (D & H 381–4)	J. G. Scott	
IB Large letters with serifs	I	O&R	Penny 1797	J. G. Scott	
IB (or JB) Very large crude letters with serifs (and SB on reverse, large letters with serifs)	I	O	Penny 1797	J. G. Scott	
IB (crude) (and W. SIMONS 1800 reverse)	I	O	Penny 1797	SNC Dec. 1908 and Duffield 341	
IB	I	O&R	Anglesey Halfpenny 1791 (D & H 386 etc.)	Batty 3058	
IB Large	I	O&R	Anglesey Halfpenny	SNC Dec. 1908 and Duffield 331	
IB	I	O	Halfpenny 1799	Batty 4303a	

COUNTERMARK	A	B	COIN TYPE	SOURCE REF.	C
IB Very large letters with serifs	I	O	Penny 1797	Baldwin	
IB Medium letters with serifs	I	O&R	Penny 1797	Baldwin	
IB Very large letters with serifs	I	R	Penny 1797	Seaby	
I.B.	†	†	Imitation Halfpenny George III	Duffield 958	9
I.B Very large letters with serifs in serrated rectangular indent	R	R	Penny 1797	Baldwin	
I·B Large letters in square indent	R	R	Penny 1797	Ashmolean Museum	
I:B In notched square indent	R	†	Halfpenny George III	SNC April 1897	
I.B Large crude letters in rectangular indent (and IR incuse 2 x obv., I x rev.)	R	O	Halfpenny 1799	C. Brunel	
I.B Medium letters with serifs in serrated rectangular indent (twice)	R	O	Sheffield Penny 1813 (Davis 139)	Charles Dobie	
I.B.P. in rectangular indent	R	O	Halfpenny 1775	Batty 4303A	
I.C Small letters with serifs in square indent	R	I	Hereford Token (W7)	John Parry	
IC Large letters with serifs	I	O	Halfpenny George I	J. G. Scott	
IC Large letters with serifs	I	O	Halfpenny 1735	J. G. Scott	
IC Large letters with serifs	I	O	Halfpenny George II	J. G. Scott	
IC Large letters with serifs	I	O	Irish Halfpenny George II	J. G. Scott	
IC Large letters with serifs	I	R	Halfpenny 1773	C. Brunel	
IC (and 1783 reverse)	I	O	Halfpenny 1770–5	Batty 4303C	

For key to column headings and abbreviations, please refer to page 161.

COUNTERMARK	A	B	COIN TYPE	SOURCE REF.	C
IC Large letters with serifs in inverted serrated heart-shaped indent	R	R	Halfpenny 1770-5	J. G. Scott	
IC (deep) Large letters with serifs	I	O	Farthing 1772	A. G. Davies	
IC Small letters with serifs	I	R	Cronebane Halfpenny (D & H 59)	C. Brunel	
I.C Medium letters with serifs	I	IXO 2XR	Penny 1797	Baldwin	
I.C (and A19 reverse)	I	O	Halfpenny 1806	Batty 4303B	
ID	I	O	Irish Halfpenny 1774-83	Szauer 163	
ID Large letters with serifs	I	O	Irish Halfpenny 1781	Szauer 96	
ID	I	O	Halfpenny 1775	Szauer 236	
ID Very large letters with serifs	I	O	Halfpenny 1806	J. G. Scott	
ID Large letters with serifs in serrated rectangular indent	R	O&R	Penny 1797	Szauer 58	
I.D In notched square indent	R	†	Farthing 1825	SNC Apr. 1897	
I.D.	†	†	Farthing George IV	Duffield 1014	10
†E Large letters	I	O	Penny 1797	J. G. Scott	
IF Medium letters with serifs in rectangular indent	R	O	Isle of Man Halfpenny 1733	Seaby	
IF. in rectangle	†	†	Halfpenny George II	SNC Dec. 1908	
IF in rectangular indent	R	†	Halfpenny George III	Duffield 332	
IG	†	†	Farthing 1674	Duffield 1068	11
IG in a heart	I	O	Evasion Halfpenny (Atkins 60)	J. G. Scott	
I.G Large letters with serifs in serrated rectangular indent	R	O	Penny 1797	A.G. Davies	
IH	†	†	Halfpenny George II	SNC June 1906 9157/8	
IH	†	†	Penny George III	SNC June 1906 9157/8	
IH Large letters with serifs (and IP obv.)	I	R	Penny 1797	J. G. Scott	
IH (or H†) Very large crude letters with serifs	I	O	Penny 1797	A. G. Davies	
IH	I	O&R	'Long live the King' Halfpenny 1795	Batty 4399 Duffield 333 and SNC Dec. 1908	12
IH (and TH/S obv.)	†	R	English token Halfpenny, 18th century	Szauer 108	
IH Medium letters with serifs	I	O	Middlesex Halfpenny 1794 (D & H 1024)	J. G. Scott	
IH/(rose) in heart-shaped indent	R	†	Halfpenny token †	SNC June 1906 9157	
IH (or HI) Large letters with serifs	I	O&R	Penny 1806	C. Brunel	
IH (or HI) Large letters with serifs	I	O	Flint Penny 1813 (Davis 7-15)	City Museum, St. Albans	
IH (or HI) Very large letters with serifs (and ✠ on reverse)	I	O	Birmingham Threepence 1813 (Davis 34-35)	C. Brunel	
I.H Large letters with serifs	I	O	Halfpenny George II	Seaby	
I.H Large letters with serifs in serrated rectangular indent	R	R	Halfpenny 1737	Baldwin	
I.H. (or .H.I) Large letters with serifs in serrated rectangular indent	R	O	Halfpenny 1806/7	C. Brunel	

For key to column headings and abbreviations, please refer to page 161.

COUNTERMARK	A	B	COIN TYPE	SOURCE REF.	C
Ħ in heart-shaped notched indent	R	†	Halfpenny 1694	SNC Apr. 1897	
II Medium letters with serifs	I	O	Halfpenny 1719	J. G. Scott	
IK Medium plain letters	I	O	Halfpenny 1724	J. G. Scott	
IK Large letters with serifs in rectangular indent	R	O	Halfpenny George II	J. G. Scott	
IL Large letters with serifs	I	O	Halfpenny Charles II	Seaby	
IL Large letters with serifs in serrated rectangular indent (and I. LORD on reverse)	R	O	Halfpenny George II	J. G. Scott	
IL	†	†	Halfpenny †	SNC Nov./Dec. 1920 Col. 527 88102	
IL in heart-shaped indent	R	†	Penny †	Gibbs 147	
IL Large letters with serifs	I	O	Birmingham Penny 1811 (Davis 49–55)	Seaby	
IM Large letters with serifs	I	O	Penny 1797	J. G. Scott	
IM Large letters with serifs (and CANIF obv. & rev.)	I·	O	Penny 1797	J. G. Scott	
IM Small letters with serifs in rectangular indent	R	R	Leith Halfpenny 1797 (D & H 58 etc.)	Seaby	
I.M (twice) Large letters with serifs in serrated rectangular indent	R	O	Penny 1797	Baldwin	
IM/H Large letters with serifs	I	R	Halfpenny George II	C. Brunel	
IP	†	†	Halfpenny George II	Duffield 335	
IP Large letters with serifs (and IH rev.)	I	O	Penny 1797	J. G. Scott	
IP and four ornaments	†	†	Halfpenny 1799	Duffield 336 SNC Dec. 1908	13
I.P and four ornaments	I	O	Halfpenny 1799	Batty 4305C	13
IP	†	R	Kirk medalet cf Davis & Waters 652	Batty 4322N	
IP Large letters with serifs	I	R	Manchester Halfpenny 1793 (D & H 128–34)	Seaby	
IP Large letters with serifs	I	O	Irish Halfpenny 1805	J. G. Scott	
IP	†	†	Halfpenny George IV	SNC Dec. 1908	
I.P Large letters with serifs in notched oval indent	R	R	Halfpenny 1807	J. G. Scott	
IR Large letters with serifs in square indent	R	R	Halfpenny 1740	Szauer 97	
IR in heart-shaped indent	R	†	Anglesey Penny 1788	SNC Apr. 1897	
IR	†	†	Irish Penny 1822	SCMB Jan. 1971 TP364	
IR in 'radiant circle'	R	†	Farthing 1825	Gibbs 162	
I.R Large letters with serifs	I	O&R	Penny 1797	J. G. Scott	
I.R Large letters with serifs in serrated rectangular indent	R	O	Halfpenny 1799	Baldwin	
IS in heart-shaped indent	R	†	Irish Halfpenny 1741	SNC Apr. 1897	
IS Large letters with serifs	I	O	Halfpenny George II	J. G. Scott	
IS (twice) Large letters with serifs	I	O	Penny 1797	Nat. Museum of Wales	
I.T. in serrated oblong indent	R	†	Farthing George III (pierced)	SNC Jan./Feb. 1921 Col. 82 89467	

For key to column headings and abbreviations, please refer to page 161.

COUNTERMARK	A	B	COIN TYPE	SOURCE REF.	C
IW Medium letters with serifs in serrated rectangular indent (twice)	R	O	Penny 1797	J. G. Scott	
(large St Andrew's cross) surrounded by broad spiked border	I	R			
IW Medium letters with serifs	I	5XO 7XR	Penny 1797	J. G. Scott	
IW Large letters with serifs	I	O	Penny 1806/7	J. G. Scott	
IW Medium letters with serifs in serrated rectangular indent	R	O	Irish Halfpenny 1805	Baldwin	
I.W Large plain letters in serrated rectangular indent	R	R	Halfpenny 1806/7	Seaby	14
I.W.G	I	†	Penny 1797	Gibbs 165	
I.Y Medium letters with serifs	I	2XO 1XR	Halfpenny 1799	J. G. Scott	
J Large letter with serifs in serrated oval indent	R	O	Halfpenny 1799	Burns and Remick 'The Coinage of Jamaica' 1966, p. 34	
J Large letter with serifs	I	O	Penny 1860–94	J. G. Scott	
JA Medium letters with serifs	I	O	Irish Halfpenny 1782	Szauer 98	
J*B	†	†	Irish Farthing 1760	Duffield 1549	
J.B (three times) Medium letters with serifs	I	R	Halfpenny 1806	J. G. Scott	
JD Medium letters with serifs	I	R	Kent Halfpenny 1794 (D&H 35)	Seaby	
JF Very large letters with serifs	I	O	Halfpenny 1734	A. G. Davies	
JF Large letters with serifs in notched oval indent	R	O&R	Halfpenny George IV	Baldwin	
J.F (and R GAIR)	I	R	Halfpenny 1806	Batty 4095	
JG/T Large letters with serifs	I	R	Halfpenny 1807	A. G. Davies	
JGT Large crude letters with serifs, double struck	I	O	Penny 1892	C. Brunel	
J.G.	I	†	Halfpenny George III	Andrews 1091	
JH Large letters with serifs in crude shield-shaped indent	R	O&R	Halfpenny 1806/7	J. G. Scott	
JH.	I	†	Penny 1797	Chitty 108	
JH Large letters with serifs	I	O	Halfpenny 1806/7	C. Brunel	
J. HARRO . . . (N?) Medium letters with serifs	I	R			
JH Medium letters with serifs	I	R	Farthing 1845	J. D. Stott	
J.H.	I	†	Penny George III	Andrews 1102	
J·H Medium letters with serifs	I	5XO 10XR	Penny 1797	Baldwin	
JL	†	†	Halfpenny Charles II	SCMB Jan. 1971 TP318	
JL Large letters with serifs	I	O&R	Halfpenny 1799	J. G. Scott	
JM Large letters with serifs	I	O	Halfpenny 1799	Seaby	
JM	I	O	Halfpenny 1807	Batty 4318G	
J.M.P. in oblong indent	R	†	Irish Halfpenny 1781	Gibbs 280	
J.P.T Medium letters with serifs	I	O	Twopence 1797	Seaby	
JR Medium letters with serifs	I	R	Twopence 1797	Seaby	
JR Large crude letters with serifs	I	O	Penny 1797 (pierced 6 o'c)	Baldwin	

For key to column headings and abbreviations, please refer to page 161.

COUNTERMARK	A	B	COIN TYPE	SOURCE REF.	C
JR/No. 7	I	†	Penny George III	Andrews 1196	
JR (ligate) Very large letters with serifs(on obv. also large crude G or castle-like device [⌂])	I	O&R	Irish Penny 1805	J. G. Scott	
JS Large plain letters	I	O	Irish Halfpenny 1805	J. G. Scott	
J.S Large letters with serifs	I	O&R	Penny 1797	Baldwin	
JT.JB Very large letters with serifs	I	O	Penny 1797	J. G. Scott	
JW Large letters	I	O	(Irish) Halfpenny 1823	Batty 4318E	
JW Large letters with serifs	I	O	Farthing 1875H	J. G. Scott	
J*W Medium letters with serifs in serrated rectangular indent	R	O	Penny 1806/7 (pierced 8 o'c)	J. G. Scott	
J.W.M.	I	R	Halfpenny 1775	Batty 4318F	
K Large letter with serifs	I	R	Halfpenny 1733	Szauer 102	
K Large letter with serifs	I	R	Portsea Halfpenny 1794 (D & H 71)	J. G. Scott	
L in circular indent	R	†	Halfpenny †	Gibbs 156	
L	†	†	Clifton token 1735	Duffield 515	15
L Large crude letter with serifs	I	†	Halfpenny †	J. G. Scott	
L Medium plain letter	I	O	Halfpenny George II (pierced 3 o'c)	J. G. Scott	
LDR Large letters with serifs, line around, in lozenge-shaped indent, and B	R	O	Penny †	Gibbs 454	16
	I	R			
LT Large letters with serifs	I	O&R	Penny 1797	Seaby	
M in heart-shaped indent	R	O	Halfpenny George I	Batty 4426A	

COUNTERMARK	A	B	COIN TYPE	SOURCE REF.	C
M	†	†	Halfpenny †	Duffield 1122	17
M 'deep and large'	I	†	Isle of Man Penny 1786	Gibbs 174	
M in small diamond-shaped indent	R	O	Exeter Halfpenny 1792 (D & H 2)	Batty 143	
M	I	O	Kent Halfpenny 1794 (D & H 29)	Batty 439	18
M Very large letter with serifs	I	R	Penny 1797	Baldwin	
M Large plain letter	I	O	Penny 1797	A. G. Davies	
M Medium letter with serifs	I	22XO 21XR	Penny 1797	J. G. Scott	
M script	I	O	Halfpenny George III	SNC Sept. 1897 2377	
M Large letter with serifs	I	R	Penny 1806	J. G. Scott	
M (three times)	†	†	Halfpenny 1806	Duffield 1522	
M/(sun with rays)/B all within oval	†	†	Penny †	SNC Apr. 1897 2175	
M/1918 Large letters with serifs	I	O	Halfpenny 1911	J. G. Scott	
M25 Small plain letter	I	O	Penny 1927	J. G. Scott	
J. McC	I	†	Penny George III	Andrews 1039	
J. McC in rectangle	†	†	Penny George III	Andrews 1040	
J. McK	I	R	Irish Halfpenny 1805	Batty 4428E	
MA/R Large letters with serifs (and RW obverse)	I	R	Dublin Penny 1813 (Davis 17–21)	Dr.G.H.L. Bullmore	
MB	I	O	Halfpenny 1750	Batty 4456	
M.C Medium letters with serifs	I	O&R	Farthing 1872	C. Brunel	

For key to column headings and abbreviations, please refer to page 161.

COUNTERMARK	A	B	COIN TYPE	SOURCE REF.	C
M.D Large plain letters	I	O&R	Dublin Halfpenny 1792 (D & H 269 etc.)	Szauer 103	
MEL Medium plain letters	I	R	Penny 1861	J. G. Scott	
MG Large letters with serifs	I	O	Halfpenny 1917	J. G. Scott	
MH Large letters with serifs in serrated rectangular indent	R	R	Leeds Halfpenny 1791	Seaby	
MH Large letters with serifs	I	R	Penny 1918	J. G. Scott	
M.J.E Large letters with serifs	I	O	Penny 1797	Seaby	
MK Large letters with serifs	I	O	Irish Halfpenny 1781(?)	Seaby	
MM Large letters with serifs	I	†	Halfpenny †	Charles Dobie	
MN Very large letters with serifs	I	O	Penny 1806	C. Brunel	
MG (MQ monogram?)	I	R	Irish Halfpenny 1775–82	J. G. Scott	
MS	I	†	Halfpenny George II	Szauer 129	
MS and OIN in rectangular indents	R	R	Halfpenny George II	Batty 4471	
MS Large letters with serifs	I	O	Halfpenny 1861 (pierced 12 o'c)	J. G. Scott	
M.S.	I	†	Halfpenny George III	Duffield 1487	
MT Large letters	I	O	Halfpenny 1799	Batty 4428G	
+N(?) Large plain letter	R	O	Halfpenny George II	C. Brunel	
N (large, reversed) and ss	†	†	Irish Farthing 1760 George II	Szauer 144	
N Large letter with serifs (and s obv.)	I	R	Halfpenny 1860–94	J. G. Scott	
NC	I	O&R	Halfpenny 1807	Szauer 172	

COUNTERMARK	A	B	COIN TYPE	SOURCE REF.	C
N.H Medium letters with serifs	I	3XO 4XR	Penny 1806	J. G. Scott	
NK Medium letters with serifs (and EB rev.)	I	O	Penny 1853	Baldwin	
NO 66 Large letters with serifs	I	R	Irish Halfpenny 1742	Szauer 106	
N/SD	I	†	Halfpenny 1806	Duffield 1183	19
O Medium letter	I	O	Halfpenny George II	J. G. Scott	
O.B. Large letters in indented square	R	†	Irish Halfpenny George II	Duffield 1494	
O.B. Large letters	R	†	Irish Halfpenny George II	Duffield 1497	
oBo Large and very large letters	I	O	Irish Penny 1805	C. Brunel	
OF-FY and wheel	I	†	Penny 1797	Gibbs 165	
OIN and MS in rectangular indents	R	R	Halfpenny George II	Batty 4471	
OO Medium letters	I	O&R	Twopence 1797	Szauer 56	
P Medium letter with serifs (and T GOODMAN)	I	O	Halfpenny 1774	J. G. Scott	
P Large letter with serifs	I	O	Halfpenny 1773	J. G. Scott	
P Large letter with serifs/4	I	R	Guernsey 4 Doubles 1830	A. G. Davies	
P Large letter with serifs	I	O	Penny 1831	J. G. Scott	
P Medium letter with serifs	I	O	Penny 1882H	J. G. Scott	
P Large letter with serifs and small loop (four times)	I	O	Halfpenny 1770–5	C. Brunel	
PBH Large letters with serifs in serrated rectangular indent	R	†	Counterfeit Halfpenny (?)	Birmingham Museum	
PC Large letters with serifs	I	O	Penny 1797	J. G. Scott	

COUNTERMARK	A	B	COIN TYPE	SOURCE REF.	C
PD	I	†	Halfpenny George III	Szauer 130	
PF Medium letters with serifs	I	O	Irish Halfpenny 1781	Szauer 237	
PI/GT Large letters with serifs	I	†	Halfpenny †	C. Brunel	
PK Large plain letters	I	†	Irish Token Halfpenny 18th century	Szauer 107	
P*K↑ in notched square	R	†	Counterfeit Halfpenny 1750	Gibbs 153	
PL in notched square	R	†	Halfpenny †	Gibbs 156	
PM Large letters with serifs	I	R	Farthing token 1794	Szauer 149	
PMN Large crude plain letters in rectangular indent	R	R	Penny 1797	A. G. Davies	
PS Large letters with serifs	I	R	Irish Farthing 1744 (cast forgery)	J. G. Scott	
PS (twice) Small letters with serifs (and SK on reverse)	I	O	Penny 1797	Baldwin	
P+S Large letters with serifs in serrated rectangular indent	R	O	Halfpenny 1806/7	Seaby	
R (twice) Large letter with serifs	I	O	Halfpenny 1748	A. G. Davies	
R (twice) Large letter with serifs	I	R	Penny 1797	J. G. Scott	
R (five times)	I	†	Penny †	Andrews 1191	
R Very large crude letter with serifs	I	R	Penny 1806 (pierced 10 o'c)	A. G. Davies	
R Large letter with serifs	I	1XO 2XR	Farthing 1829	J. G. Scott	
R Large letter with serifs	I	O	Halfpenny 1858	J. G. Scott	
R (twice)	I	†	Penny 1797	Gibbs 165	

COUNTERMARK	A	B	COIN TYPE	SOURCE REF.	C
R.B in a square indent	R	†	Halfpenny †	SNC Nov./Dec. 1920 Col. 527 88104	
RD/2 Large letters	I	†	Halfpenny †	C. Brunel	
RE Medium letters in square indent (and WE, E obv.)	R	R	Penny 1797	J. G. Scott	
R.E Large letters with serifs	I	2XO 2XR	Penny 1797	J. G. Scott	
RG Large letters with serifs	I	R	Halfpenny George II	Seaby	
RG Small letters with serifs	I	R	Macclesfield Halfpenny 1789	Seaby	
RH in rectangular indent	R	O	Halfpenny William III	Batty 4605A	
R.H	I	†	Twopence 1797	Gibbs 166	
RHH (twice) Large letters with serifs	I	O	Robert Hopwood & Son Token Halfpenny 1852	A. G. Davies	
R.H.&S. and 446	†	†	Robert Hopwood & Son Token (Breton 898)	Duffield 343	
(sword)/RI three times	R	†	Irish Halfpenny †	Gibbs 282	
RxI	†	R	Warwickshire Halfpenny 1788 (D & H 336)	Batty 2684A	
R.K Large letters with serifs	I	O&R	Irish Halfpenny 1766	J. G. Scott	
R.K Very large letters with serifs in serrated rectangular indent	R	O	Penny 1806/7	Seaby	
R.M. in an oblong indent	R	†	Halfpenny †	SNC Jan./Feb. 1921 Col. 82 89461	

For key to column headings and abbreviations, please refer to page 161.

COUNTERMARK	A	B	COIN TYPE	SOURCE REF.	C
RP Medium letters with serifs	I	R	Farthing 1873	C. Brunel	
RP/W Medium letters with serifs	I	O			
TH Large letters with serifs			Penny 1797	P. R. Davies	20
HP Large letters with serifs	I	R			
R.R Very large crude letters with serifs in roughly oblong indent	R	R	Penny 1797	C. Brunel	
RR/D Small and medium letters with serifs	I	R	Penny 1797	C. Brunel	
RS Medium plain letters in notched square indent	R	†	Halfpenny † (pierced 12 o'c)	Baldwin	
RS	I	R	Hull Halfpenny 1794 (D & H 23)	Batty 2829	
RS (twice) Large letters with serifs	I	O&R	Penny 1797	J. G. Scott	
RS Large letters with serifs	I	R	Penny 1806	Baldwin	
R^{d}S Large letters with serifs in rectangular indent	R	R	Glasgow Halfpenny 1795 (D & H 6)	J. G. Scott	
RT Medium letters with serifs in notched rectangular indent	R	O	Penny 1797	J. G. Scott	
RU Large letters with serifs	I	O&R	Farthing 1773	C. Brunel	
RW Large letters with serifs (and MA/R rev.)	I	O	Dublin Penny 1813 (Davis 17–21)	Dr.G.H.L. Bullmore	
RW Large letters with serifs	I	O&R	Halfpenny Token 19th century(?)	C. Brunel	
RY/HW	I	R	Halfpenny †	Gibbs 173	
HW	R	O			
S	I	†	Halfpenny †	Duffield 1191	21
S Large letter with serifs (double struck)	I	O	Farthing 1737(?)	J. G. Scott	

COUNTERMARK	A	B	COIN TYPE	SOURCE REF.	C
S	†	†	Dublin Farthing (D & H 396)	Duffield 513 Szauer 42 (SNC Aug. 1912)	
S (twice) Large plain letter	I	R	Counterfeit Dublin Halfpenny 1792	Szauer 111	
S in circular indent	R	†	Halfpenny 1806	Duffield 1521	
S	†	O&R	Halfpenny George III	SNC Sept. 1897 2377	
S Large letter with serifs	I	R	Irish Farthing 1806	Szauer 147, 241	
FS Large letters with serifs	I	O			
S 'in five places' Small letter	†	O&R	Birmingham Threepence 1813	Duffield 316	
S Large letter with serifs	I	O	Penny 1874H	J. G. Scott	
S Medium letter with serifs (8 times)	I	O	Penny 1868	J. G. Scott	
S Large letter with serifs (and N rev.)	I	O	Halfpenny 1860–94	J. G. Scott	
SA	I	O	Coventry Halfpenny	Batty 2527B	
S	I	R	1793 (D & H 238–245)		
SB in square indent (FAT BAIRNS incuse rev.)	R	O	Halfpenny 1775	Batty 5117	
SB	†	†	Halfpenny †	Duffield 1143	22
SB within large P	R	†	Counterfeit Halfpenny †	Duffield 1141 SNC Apr. 1897	22
SB/W Large letters with serifs	I	O	Penny 1797	C. Brunel	
SB Large letters with serifs (and IB or JB obv.)	I	R	Penny 1797	J. G. Scott	
S.C. (twice) Medium letters with serifs	I	O	Halfpenny 1772(?)	Seaby	

For key to column headings and abbreviations, please refer to page 161.

COUNTERMARK	A	B	COIN TYPE	SOURCE REF.	C
S.E.M Large letters with serifs 1872	I	O	Penny 1797	J. G. Scott	
Large figures with serifs	I	R			
S.H. (twice)	†	†	Penny 1797	Duffield 338	23
SJ/T retrograde for sealing —die?	R	R	Cast brass forgery Farthing 1847	J. G. Scott	
S.K Large letters with serifs	I	O	Penny 1797	A. G. Davies	
S.K Large letters with serifs (and PS twice obv.)	I	R	Penny 1797	Baldwin	
SL in notched square indent	R	†	Halfpenny 1806	SNC Apr. 1897	
SL	†	†	Halfpenny 1806, 1807	Duffield 1162	24
SM Medium letters in rectangular indent	R	O	Halfpenny George II	C. Brunel	
SM Large letters with serifs	I	†	Irish token Halfpenny 18th century	Szauer 110	
SM Large letters with serifs	I	R	Penny 1863	J. G. Scott	
SS under BEASLEY Large plain letters	I	†	Farthing †	Szauer 44A, cf. Szauer 111	
SS (and large reversed N)	†	†	Irish Farthing 1760 George II	Szauer 144	
SS (reversed) over WH	†	†	Irish Farthing George III	Szauer 157	
SS (and C rev.)	I	O	Irish Farthing 1760 George II	Szauer 161	
SS (reversed) Large plain letters	I	O	Irish Halfpenny 1694	Szauer 238	
SSS Medium letters	I	R	Tunstead (Norfolk) Penny 1812 (Davis 29)	C. Brunel	
S/S S/W	I	O	Halfpenny George II	J. G. Scott	
S Large letters with serifs	I	R			
ST Large letters with serifs	I	O&R	Halfpenny 1770–5	Baldwin	
ST Very large letters with serifs	I	†	Halfpenny †	Szauer 239	
S.T Large letters with serifs	I	O	Halfpenny 1799	Seaby	
T̶ Large letters with serifs	I	O	Halfpenny George I	J. G. Scott	
T Large letter with serifs in circular indent	R	R	Halfpenny 1799	J. G. Scott	
T Large letter	†	O	Halfpenny George III	SNC Sept. 1897 2377	
T Small letter with serifs	I	R	Halfpenny 1799	J. G. Scott	
T Large plain letter	I	O	Irish Halfpenny 1805	J. G. Scott	
T Medium letter with serifs	I	O&R	Halfpenny 1806/7	J. G. Scott	
T Very large letter with serifs (and E obv.)	I	R	Penny 1936	J. G. Scott	
TA Large crude letters with serifs in four-sided indent	R	R	Penny 1806	C. Brunel	
TB (FAT BAIRNS on rev.)	I	O	Halfpenny 1775	Batty 5116	
TB	†	†	Halfpenny Token †	Duffield 1196	25
TB in a square frame or ornamental punch	†	†	Penny 1797	Duffield 1195	25
TḂ Large letters with serifs	I	O	Halfpenny 1770–5	Baldwin	
TB Small letters with serifs	I	O	Anglesey Penny 1788	Seaby	
TB Very large letters with serifs	I	R	Halfpenny 1806	A. G. Davies	
TB Medium letters with serifs	I	O	Irish Farthing 1806	Szauer 242	
TB Small letters with serifs	I	O	Dublin Penny 1813 (Davis 13)	C. Brunel	

For key to column headings and abbreviations, please refer to page 161.

COUNTERMARK	A	B	COIN TYPE	SOURCE REF.	C
T*B Large letters with serifs in serrated rectangular indent	R	R	Suffolk Halfpenny 1795 (D & H 16)	Charles Dobie	
TBC Large letters with serifs (and S.COT rev.)	I	O	Penny 1797	J. G. Scott	
TC Medium letters with serifs	I	O	France: Sol 1785B	J. G. Scott	25
TC (twice) Large letters with serifs	I	R	Halfpenny 1806	J. G. Scott	25
T.C. in rectangular indent	R	R	Halfpenny William III	Batty 4880A	
T.C Medium letters with serifs	I	O&R	Warwickshire Halfpenny 1790 (D & H 387)	J. G. Scott	
TCC Large letters with serifs	I	R	Irish Halfpenny 1805	J. G. Scott	
TCH Medium plain letters	I	O	Halfpenny 1775	C. Brunel	
Td Medium letters in square indent (five times)	R	R	Irish Halfpenny George II	Ashmolean Museum	
TD Large letters with serifs in serrated rectangular indent	R	O	Halfpenny 1752(?)	J. G. Scott	
TD Medium letters with serifs	I	O	Penny 1797	J. G. Scott	
T.D	I	†	Penny 1797	Gibbs 165	
TF Large letters with serifs	I	O	Penny 1797	J. G. Scott	
T.F Medium letters with serifs	I	O	Birmingham Halfpenny 1794 (D & H 73 etc.)	Szauer 114	
T.F monogram in a square	†	†	Irish Halfpenny Token (19th century?)	SNC Nov. 1905 2159	
T.G.	I	†	Halfpenny 1807	Duffield 1491	
TH/S (retrograde) in shaped oval indent (and IH reverse)	R	O	English Token Halfpenny 18th century	Szauer 108	
T over H (monogram) twice Large letters with serifs	I	R	Penny 1797	J. G. Scott	
TJ Very large letters with serifs	I	R	Penny 1861	J. G. Scott	
T (crude) M Large letters with serifs	I	R	Halfpenny 1774	J. G. Scott	
T:P Large letters with serifs in shaped indent	R	R	Middlesex Halfpenny (D & H 295)	Dr.G.H.L. Bullmore	
TR	†	†	Irish Halfpenny George II	Caldecott Sale Lot 439	
TR/(heart) Small letters with serifs in heart-shaped indent	R	4XO 4XR	Halfpenny 1806/7	J. G. Scott	
TR Very large letters with serifs	I	2XO 1XR	Penny 1797	C. Brunel	
TR Large letters with serifs	I	R	Dublin Halfpenny 1802 (D & H 349-50)	Szauer 115	
TS	I	O&R	Halfpenny 1720	Batty 4887A	
TS Large letters with serifs in rectangular indent	R	O	Irish Halfpenny 1742	J. G. Scott	
TS	I	R	(Irish) Penny 1805	Szauer 171	
TS Large letters with serifs	I	R	Penny 1806/7	J. G. Scott	
T.S Large letters with serifs	I	O	Penny 1873	Seaby	
TT Very large (13mm) letters with serifs	I	O	Halfpenny 1799	C. Brunel	
T.T Medium letters with serifs	I	R	Penny 1797	Baldwin	

For key to column headings and abbreviations, please refer to page 161.

For key to column headings and abbreviations, please refer to page 161.

COUNTERMARK	A	B	COIN TYPE	SOURCE REF.	C
T.T.	I	O	Dublin Halfpenny 1793 (D & H 235 etc.)	Batty 3552A	
TW Medium letters with serifs in notched triangular indent	R	O	Irish Halfpenny George II 1760	J. G. Scott	
T.W Large letters with serifs in serrated rectangular indent	R	O	Penny 1797	A. G. Davies	
T.W Large letters with serifs	I	O&R	Penny 1797	J. G. Scott	
T.W 408	I	R	Halfpenny 1853	Batty 4906B	
U Large letter with serifs	I	O	Halfpenny 1799	J. G. Scott	
v in circle within a rayed circle	R	†	Penny 1797	Gibbs 149	
w in a shaped indent	R	†	Halfpenny George II	Szauer 118	
w (twice)	†	†	Irish Halfpenny George II	Szauer 153	
w in square indent	R	†	18th century token	Duffield 1538	
w Medium letter with serifs		O	Portsea Halfpenny 1794 (D & H 68 etc.)	J. G. Scott	
w Large plain letter (and D rev.)	I	O	Penny 1797	J. G. Scott	
w Medium plain letter 16 times, forming a cross, surrounded by a circle of 22 w's	I	R	Penny 1797	J. G. Scott	
w Small plain letter	R	O&R	Penny 1797	A. G. Davies	
w	I	O&R	Birmingham Workhouse Token 1788	Duffield 317 (Davis 43)	27
w Medium letter with serifs	I	1XO 2XR	Penny George IV	J. G. Scott	
WA Large letters with serifs	I	O	Penny 1797	J. G. Scott	
WB Large letters with serifs	I	O	Halfpenny 1773	Baldwin	
WB* (four times) round D in centre Large plain letters	I	O	Halfpenny 1799	Seaby	
WB Large plain letters in rectangular indent	R	R	Penny 1797	J. G. Scott	
WB Large plain and serif'd letters respectively	I	R	Halfpenny 1806/7	J. G. Scott	
W.B.K Very large letters with serifs	I	O	Penny 1862 (pierced 12 o'c)	C. Brunel	
WC Large letters with serifs	I	O	Halfpenny 1770-5	J. G. Scott	
WC Large serif'd and plain letters respectively	I	R	Halfpenny 1799	J. G. Scott	
WC Very small letters with serifs in rectangular indent	R	R	Irish Halfpenny 1805	A. G. Davies	
WC Medium plain letters n oval indent	R	O&R	Halfpenny 1806	C. Brunel	
WC in rectangular indent	R	R	Halfpenny 1806	Batty 4964D	
W.C Medium letters with serifs in a rectangle	I	O	Halfpenny 1806	J. G. Scott	
W+C/M Large letters with serifs in serrated heart-shaped indent	R	O	Halfpenny 1806	V.G. 1144	
WC/P w (inverted M) C Large letters with serifs	I I	O R	Penny 1797	J. G. Scott	
WD Large letters with serifs	I	O&R	Penny 1797	A. G. Davies	
WD Large letters with serifs	I	R	Penny 1797	Seaby	
WD	I	†	Irish Penny †	Andrews 1071	

COUNTERMARK	A	B	COIN TYPE	SOURCE REF.	C
WE Large crude letters in rectangular indent, E below in similar indent (and RE on rev.)	R	O	Penny 1797	J. G. Scott	
W.E Large letters with serifs	I	2xO 3xR	Halfpenny 1743	J. G. Scott	
W.F Medium letters with serifs in serrated rectangular indent	R	O	Halfpenny 1773	A. G. Davies	
W.F Very large letters with serifs	I	R	Penny 1797	Seaby	
WFH Large letters with serifs (and 1843 obv.)	I	O&R	Penny 1797	A. G. Davies	
W.G Very large letters with serifs	I	O	Penny 1797	J. G. Scott	
WG Small letters with serifs in serrated rectangular indent	R	R	Halfpenny 1806/7	C. Brunel	
W.G and WG Very large/large letters with serifs	I	O&R	Penny 1797	J. G. Scott	
(a heart) with W+G+M	†	†	Penny 1806	Duffield 1109	28
WH Large crude plain letters	I	†	Irish Halfpenny George III	Szauer 117	
WH under SS (reversed)	†	†	Irish Farthing George III	Szauer 157	
W.H. and D MAHON	I	†	Halfpenny 1770–5	Batty 4428B	
W.H.	I	†	Penny George III	Andrews 1239	
W.H.	I	O	Irish Halfpenny 1783	Szauer 162	
W.H Large letters with serifs	I	R	Halfpenny 1770–5	Szauer 116	
W.H I FLANAG(AN)	I / I	R / O	Irish Halfpenny 1781	Batty 4090A	
WI Medium letters with serifs	I	†	Halfpenny †	J. G. Scott	
WI Piece from centre of Halfpenny George III	I	†		Duffield 1243	29
WI Large letters with serifs	I	O	Penny token 1812 (Davis 40 – not local)	J. G. Scott	
W.I Medium letters with serifs in serrated rectangular indent	R	O	Halfpenny 1774	Seaby	
WKFH Large letters with serifs (crude work)	I	O&R	Penny 1797	C. Brunel	
WL Large letters with serifs	I	O	Penny 1797	Bell 'Copper Commercial Coins' p. 112	
WM Large letters with serifs/1832 (smaller)	I	O	Halfpenny 1806/7	A. G. Davies	
WMJ	†	†	Irish Token Halfpenny 18th century	Szauer 158	
W.M.T. Medium letters	I	O&R	Penny 1797	Ashmolean Museum	
WP Large letters with serifs (and H. PEEBLES obv.)	I	R	Penny 1797	J. G. Scott	
WP Large letters with serifs in serrated rectangular indent	R	O&R	Penny 1807	Szauer 57	
W.P Large letters with serifs	I	O	Twopence 1797	Seaby	
W.P Small letters with serifs (and T.ARNOLD/ E.HARRIS)	I	O	Irish Halfpenny 1805	J. G. Scott	
W.R	†	†	Halfpenny †	SNC Jan./ Feb. 1921 Col. 82 89465	
WR	I	O	Evasion Halfpenny 1731 (Atkins 207 var.)	Batty 4868	

For key to column headings and abbreviations, please refer to page 161.

COUNTERMARK	A	B	COIN TYPE	SOURCE REF.	C
WR monogram (reversed) Large letters with serifs	I	O	Irish Halfpenny 1782	J. G. Scott	
WR monogram Very large letters with serifs	I	O	Penny 1825	J. G. Scott	
WR Large letters with serifs	I	O	Twopence 1797	Baldwin	
WR Large letters with serifs	I	O	Penny 1831	C. Brunel	
W.R Large plain letters in serrated rectangular indent	R	R	Penny 1797	Gibbs 455	30
W.R Large letters with serifs in serrated rectangular indent (and I. MONDAY)	R	O	Penny 1797	Parsons p. 22 fig. 10	
WS Small letters with serifs	I	2XO 1XR	Halfpenny 1694	J. G. Scott	
WS Large letters with serifs in rectangular indent	R	O	Penny 1797	J. G. Scott	
WS Large letters with serifs	I	R	Halfpenny 1799	J. G. Scott	
W.S Large letters with serifs in serrated rectangular indent, rosette (?) (8 segments) incuse below	R	R	Penny 1797	London Stamp Exchange May 1973	
W:S (twice) Very large letters with serifs	I	O	Penny 1797	Seaby	

COUNTERMARK	A	B	COIN TYPE	SOURCE REF.	C
W:S Medium letters with serifs	I	4XO 4XR	Penny 1841	J. G. Scott	
WW Large plain letters	I	O	Halfpenny 1770-5	J. G. Scott	
WW	I	†	Penny 1797	Bell 'Copper Commercial Coins' p. 112	
WW (twice)	I	†	Penny George III	Andrews 1240	
WW Large letters with serifs (and J. ROSE obv. and rev.)	I	R	Irish Penny 1805	C. Brunel	
W.W Large plain letters in serrated rectangular indent	R	R	Birmingham & Neath Penny 1811 (Davis 49–55)	Seaby	
X in circle within rayed circle (also script N or ID)	R	†	Twopence 1797	Gibbs 148	31
Y Large letter with serifs	I	O	Penny 1797	A. G. Davies	
Y Small letter with serifs	I	O	Irish Farthing 1806	C. Brunel	
ZFX Large letters with serifs	I	O	Penny 1797	J. G. Scott	
ZZ	I	R	Penny George III	Andrews 1005	
J. ABEY	I	O			

For key to column headings and abbreviations, please refer to page 161.

NOTES ON THE INITIALS LISTED IN APPENDIX 2

1 £B – could be ₴B, an old form of IB.

2 DM – see also 123.57 in Table 1 above.

3 F. This piece was excluded from Table 1, as it was evidently countermarked by the issuer of the token rather than by another trader. It is only included here for the sake of completeness.

4 FD – see also Pridmore's 'Notes on Colonial Coins – Trinidad' in Spink's Numismatic Circular 1961, p. 141–2, 168–9, and 'The Coins of the British Commonwealth of Nations', Part 3, p. 221–2, 225–6.

5 G – this is listed by Duffield under Guadeloupe. As he says 'some of them are at least uncertain'. This is so of most countermarks on copper coins attributed to the West Indies – see note 8 below.

6 GS – see also Pridmore's 'The Coins of the British Commonwealth of Nations', Part 2, p. 107, 'Ceylon no. 94, 95: – GS & Co. (George Steuart & Co.). The Ceylon countermarks are in this form *GS & Cº*. The pieces listed here are of a different type GS, and of varying sizes: letters 6 mm high (Davies, penny), 4 mm (Davies, farthing), and 7 mm (Brunel, penny). See also 98.1B in Table 1 above.

7 (broad arrow) H18 and H47 – these may be government marks, possibly countermarked by workers in a munitions factory.

8 IA etc.: E. Zay assumed (Spink's Numismatic Circular, June 1906, cols. 9157/8) that the large number of countermarks of I followed by another letter were

colonial pieces from the same source: 'Pour ma part, j'ai recueilli un grand nombre de vieux sous anglais, en majorité, français et autres et de simples flans contremarqués en creux ou en relief d'un I (parfois d'un J afin qu'on ne prît pas la lettre pour un chiffre), suivi d'une autre lettre, ainsi: IA, IB, IC, ID, . . . IF, IG, IH, IJ . . . IM, IN . . . IP, IQ IR, IS, IT, IV, IVW, IW. Peut-être arriverai-je à compléter l'alphabet. . . .

Les contremarques d'une apposition relativement récente figurent sur des pièces de 10 centimes de Napoléon III, 1853 avec JB; 1854, IS et 1855, IR qui se retrouvent encore sur d'anciens sous. Comme il est interdit d'oblitérer les monnaies nationales, elles n'ont pas dû être appliqués en France. En résumé, ces pièces me paraissent avoir été employées comme jetons dans un établissement colonial inconnu jusqu'ici. Mais quel est le nom dont la lettre I est certainement l'initiale, et pourquoi cette variété de poinçons pour une même contremarque?'

The reason for the profusion of these pieces is more likely that I used to be interchangeable with J, and John was, and still is, among the most common of English Christian names. The variety of different forms of countermark indicates, of course, the great number of different issuers. Some of these pieces may well have served as shop tickets, or tokens, in areas of local currency shortage. Others may be brand marks, vandalised pieces, or 'love tokens'.

It was common, if unscientific, practice about 1900–20 to attribute these countermarked pieces to the West Indies – I(sle of) B(arbadoes), I(sle of) D(ominica), I(sle of) G(uadeloupe) etc. However, Pridmore has shown conclusively that there is no evidence at all for this, and this is confirmed by common sense, since copper coins were not popular in the West Indies.

9 I.B – Duffield says 'possibly for "Island Barbadoes"' – see note 8 above.
10 I.D – Duffield says 'this was presumed to be for Island of Dominica' – see note 8 above.
11 IG – see notes 5 and 8 above.
12 IH – the three sources listed probably describe the same piece. Duffield, at any rate, probably quotes Spink's Numismatic Circular.
13 IP, I.P – the three sources probably describe the same piece. The ornaments described in Spink's Numismatic Circular are ♈/▣ to left of I.P, ⑊⑊ / ⊛ to right.
14 I.W – Monica Bussell of Seaby's attributed to an issuer of colliery truck tickets in North East England, but this has not been confirmed.
15 L – Duffield says 'attributed to Wales'. The piece is listed under Ireland. See also Duffield 514: 'eighteenth century token of Clifton, 1735, cm. on obverse 'L. Walton', and on reverse '1735'.' (Listed in Appendix 1.)

The latter piece could be a copperas-gatherer's token from Walton on the Naze, Essex – see D. L. F. Sealy's article in 'Bulletin of the Token Corresponding Society', Vol. 2, No. 3, March/April 1974 p. 47–8.
16 LDR – the text of the Gibbs catalogue shows LD.R. The plate shows no stop. The piece was attributed by

Gibbs to Sierra Leone, though the authority for this is not known.
17 M – this is listed by Duffield under Montserrat, although he says that incomplete descriptions prevent a positive attribution. See note 8 above.
18 M – see note 3 above.
19 N SD incuse – Duffield lists this under San Domingo and says 'the above stamps are believed to be intended for "Napoleon" and "San Domingo", and to have been so stamped about 1808 or 1809'. See also VG 1016 and 123.230 in Table 1 above.
20 Mr. P. R. Davies suggests that these initials could refer to 'Royal Prince of Wales Theatre, Half Price'. The Prince of Wales' Royal Theatre, Tottenham Street, London, was opened by the Bancrofts in 1865 and closed by Edgar Bruce in 1882. This is a possible explanation, although the workmanship of the piece is crude, and the legend is far from explicit – hardly indicating that significant numbers of these tickets were produced. Equally, the piece could be a 'love token' or vandalised coin.
21 S – this is listed by Duffield under The Saints. See note 8 above.
22 SB within a large P, SB – these are listed by Duffield under St. Bartholomew. See note 8 above.
23 S.H. – Duffield says 'these initials are for "Samuel Hamer", an uncle of Mr. S. H. Hamer, of Halifax, Yorks., England, the prominent collector of English tokens . . .'.
24 SL – listed by Duffield under St. Lucia. See also note 8 above.
25 TB – listed by Duffield under Tobago. See also note 8 above.
26 TC – see also Pridmore's 'A curious (Ceylon?) countermark' and 'The TC Countermark' in Spink's Numismatic Circular November 1959, p. 203, and June 1960, p. 131–2 respectively.

The pieces listed here have letters 6 mm and 3.5 mm tall respectively, compared with Pridmore's 6.5 mm (countermark 13 mm wide).
27 W – see Davis (countermarks) 43. This is excluded from Table 1 as these pieces were countermarked by the Workhouse rather than by another trader. It is included here for the sake of completeness.
28 W+G+M and heart – listed by Duffield under Martinique. See also note 8 above.
29 WI – listed by Duffield under West Indies in General. See also note 8 above.
30 W.R – this is attributed by Gibbs to Sierra Leone, but see Pridmore's 'The officially mutilated coinage of British West Africa' in Spink's Numismatic Circular, February 1954. This shows there is no evidence that copper coins were countermarked officially. In any case this countermark is totally different from the official one, having crude plain letters in relief, uncrowned rather than serif'd letters, incuse, crowned.
31 X – Gibbs' description is 'also cspd script "N".' Baldwin's marked copy has ID instead of N.

PLATE 1

1·1 A

3·1

3·3

5·2

6·1A

8·1A

9·1

10·1

11·1

13·2

13·3

15·1A

14·4

15·3

17·1

18·3 B

18·7

19·1

PLATE 2

21·1 21·2 21·3

22·1 22·5 A 22·6 22·10 22·11

22·12 A 22·14 B 22·14 A 22·24 A

22·27 22·28 A (Cmk.1) 22·28 B (Obv) (Cmk.2) 22·28 G (Cmk.3)

22·28 I (Cmk.4) 22·28 J (Rev.) (Cmk.5) 22·29 22·31

PLATE 3

22·35

22·36

22·40 A

22·44

22·50

22·53

22·56

22·57 B

22·57C

22·62B

22·64

22·72 B

24·1

24·4

26·1A

24·2

25·4

28·1A

28·1 B

PLATE 4

28·2

28·4 A

28·4 B

28·4 C

30·1

28·4 F

28·4 G

30·3

30·5 C

30·6

31·2 A

31·6

33·2

33·3

32·2

33·5

34·1 (rev.)

34·2

34·3

39·1

35·1

35·5 A

36·3

39·2 (obv.)

PLATE 5

40·2 (ii) 40·3A 40·3C 40·4

40·8 40·17 40·23A 40·31

40·16 40·40 40·26

50·1

57·1 48·1 72·2 72·4

72·1

77·2 88·1 91·1A 77·3

PLATE 6

92·1

96·1A

96·1B

98·1A

98·1B

98·1C

98·4

98·6

98·7

98·8

108·1

116·2

122·25

122·32

122·55

122·105

122·185

122·200

123·200

PLATE 7

122·76 (Obv.)

122·80

122·85

122·175

122·180

122·125

122·237

123·30

123·37

123·40 B

123·40 G

123·55

123·57

123·80

123·112

123·130

123·144

123·210

123·160

123·170

123·215

123·175

123·180

PLATE 8

123·50

123·96

123·182

123·270 A

·123·135

123·155

123·270 D

123·275

123·290

123·270 E

123·270 G

123·280

123·326

123·293

123·315

123·320

14·201

123·332

123·334

123·336

123·415

123·338

22·201

PLATE 9

22·202

22·203

22·205

22·206

22·207

22·208 A

22·210 B (Obv.)

22·210 A

22·210 B (Rev.)

22·211

22·214

22·216

22·213

22·218 A

22·218 A (i)

22·218 B

22·218 C

34·201

22·219 A

22·220

22·219 B

22·221

34·202

35·202 A

35·202 B

35·204

PLATE 10

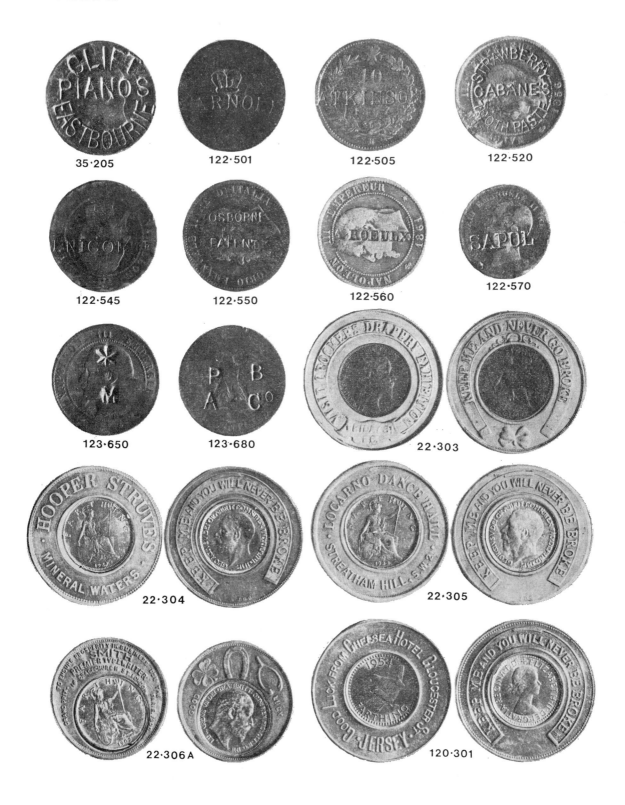

35·205   122·501   122·505   122·520

122·545   122·550   122·560   122·570

123·650   123·680   22·303

22·304   22·305

22·306A   120·301